Relational Wealth

Relational Wealth

The Advantages of Stability
in a Changing Economy

Edited by

Carrie R. Leana and
Denise M. Rousseau

OXFORD
UNIVERSITY PRESS

2000

OXFORD

Oxford   New York
Athens   Auckland   Bangkok   Bogotá   Buenos Aires   Calcutta
Cape Town   Chennai   Dar es Salaam   Delhi   Florence   Hong Kong   Istanbul
Karachi   Kuala Lumpur   Madrid   Melbourne   Mexico City   Mumbai
Nairobi   Paris   São Paulo   Singapore   Taipei   Tokyo   Toronto   Warsaw

and associated companies in
Berlin   Ibadan

Published by Oxford University Press, Inc.
198 Madison Avenue, New York, New York 10016

Oxford is a registered trademark of Oxford University Press

Library of Congress Cataloging-in-Publication Data

Relational wealth : the advantages of stability in a changing economy /
[edited by] Carrie R. Leana, Denise M. Rousseau.
        p.   cm.
    Includes bibliographical references.
    ISBN 0-19-513447-8
        1. Organizational effectiveness.   2. Industrial relations.
        3. Organizational commitment.   4. Business networks.   5. Competition.
    I. Leana, Carrie R.   II. Rousseau, Denise M.
    HD58.9.R45 2001
    658.4—dc21   00-044101

1 2 3 4 5 6 7 8 9

Printed in the United States of America
on acid-free paper

Acknowledgments

This project began with the idea that relationships among people have value in the realm of business, just as they do in other parts of life. Although simple and perhaps even obvious to the layman, this idea represents a significant departure from standard economic orthodoxy. Traditional valuation of business firms counts assets like money, equipment, and technology. Our intent was to refocus the lens through which business firms are viewed so that the value created by human interactions could be clearly seen. We realized that in order to do this we would have to devise a different way of talking about organizations and the wealth they create.

Hence, this book originated with a conversation. The conversation was a lengthy one among the group of organizational scholars who have summarized their thoughts in this book. These scholars are diverse in focus, but share the belief that it is necessary to change the dialogue regarding what constitutes value in business firms. Our collective efforts in this book are an attempt to begin that change.

As a vehicle for organizing this book, our authors participated in a conference, *Employment in the 21st Century: Organizational Behavior, Public Policy, and New Employment Relations*, in Pittsburgh, on 24–25 October 1997. Robert Reich, former U.S. Secretary of Labor, delivered the keynote address and gave our efforts a marvelous start. Other featured speakers also catalyzed our discussions, including George Becker, International President of the United Steelworkers of America; Jiro Kamimura, Chairman and CEO of Aristech Chemical Corporation; Jeffrey Pfeffer of Stanford University; Robert Tobias, President of the National Treasury Employees Union; and Joyce Westerfall, Vice President of Human Resources at Oracle. Carnegie Mellon University and the University of Pittsburgh generously provided support for this conference, as did the Society for the Psychological Study of Social Issues and the Institute for Industrial Competitiveness. We are particularly grateful to Mark Kamlet, Dean of the Heinz School of Public Policy and Management at Carnegie Mellon, for his support and encouragement. The Learning Research and Development Center at the University of Pittsburgh provided the first editor with the time and the intellectual environment in which our ideas could develop. An H.J. Heinz II chair provided support to the second editor during the production of the conference and subsequent book.

Several other people were central to the completion of this book. Our assistants, Pat Koroly and Carol McCoy, did much to lend organization to the project. Cathy Sanderling did her usual superb job editing the manuscript. The dedication of Jessica Ryan at Oxford University Press ensured that the book came out on schedule and in good shape. We will also miss the solid presence of Herb Addison who recently retired from Oxford University Press. He was an early enthusiast for this project, as was Dan Fogel at the University of Pittsburgh. Janet Sarbaugh and Joni Schwager provided weekly doses of humor and cheer.

Finally, we would like to thank our families. Our spouses, David Goldman and Paul Goodman, gave us their ever-reliable encouragement and understanding. At the same time, we could count on them both for sharp insights and interesting perspectives as we grappled with the concepts we were trying to develop. And our children, Joe, Leanna, Jonathon, Jennifer, Daniel, Heather and Jessica, could always be counted on to provide us with the diversion and perspective we needed. Truly we are both blessed to have in our families such abundant sources of relational wealth.

Carrie Leana and Denise Rousseau
Pittsburgh, PA

Contents

Contributors

Maura A. Belliveau, *Duke University*

Judith R. Blau, *University of North Carolina*

Joseph P. Broschak, *University of Illinois*

Alison Davis-Blake, *University of Texas at Austin*

Russell W. Coff, *Emory University*

Daniel C. Feldman, *University of South Carolina*

Darlene Y. Gambill, *University of Pittsburgh*

Olenda E. Johnson, *North Carolina Agricultural and Technical State University*

Ellen Ernst Kossek, *Michigan State University*

Carrie R. Leana, *University of Pittsburgh*

Jone L. Pearce, *University of California, Irvine*

Jeffrey Pfeffer, *Stanford University*

Frits K. Pil, *University of Pittsburgh*

Gil A. Preuss, *Case Western Reserve University*

Joseph A. Ritter, *Federal Reserve Bank of St. Louis*

Denise M. Rousseau, *Carnegie Mellon University*

Maureen A. Scully, *Simmons Graduate School of Management*

Melvin L. Smith, *University of Pittsburgh*

Lowell J. Taylor, *Carnegie Mellon University*

Harry J. Van Buren, *University of Pittsburgh*

Relational Wealth

Relational Wealth

The Advantages of Stability in a Changing Economy

CARRIE R. LEANA AND DENISE M. ROUSSEAU

wealth n. 1. a great quantity of money or property value; 2.
a plentiful amount: a wealth of details. 3. all goods that have a
a monetary or exchange value. 4. Valuable contents or produce.
The Random House Dictionary

Work—and how it is carried out in organizations—is fundamentally about relationships: relationships between a firm and its employees; relationships of employees with one another; relationships between a firm and its investors, suppliers, partners, regulators, and customers. The nature of these relationships changes over time, and their value changes as well. When Westinghouse merged with CBS, the relationship between these two formerly independent entities became a—perhaps the—crucial element of the future success of both. When a professor is awarded tenure at a university, her relationship with members of her department changes from that of a transient outsider to a stable member of a community. The difference between accessing health care through an HMO rather than an individual physician, or investing one's money over the telephone through a Charles Schwab representative rather than through one's personal broker, is fundamentally about the nature and value of the relationship between provider and consumer.

Employment has traditionally also been described in terms of relationships. Employees had careers, which were carried out largely within the confines of one or a few organizations, and employers had the advantage—and obligation—of human capital that was developed internally to meet their needs. Contemporary employment practices, however, are increasingly discussed in terms that are more descriptive of economic transactions than

3

long-term relationships. Flexibility has become the new watchword in industry worldwide. The means of achieving employment flexibility, while still subject to much experimentation, follow an increasingly predictable path: reducing employment from a relationship to a short-term transaction via practices such as outsourcing, downsizing, and contingent work. The pursuit of flexibility began as a push for greater opportunities for firms to choose between different employees and forms of employment. But it has become synonymous with insecurity and the violation of many longstanding assumptions about the nature of work, workers, and firms.

From Oracle to TimeWarner to British Petroleum, firms proclaim the advantages of becoming "assetless." The pervasive seeking of flexibility has resulted in widespread efforts toward minimizing fixed costs by making employees a variable expense. This focus on reducing fixed costs, however, can only provide competitive advantage when it increases the wealth of the firm,[1] and cost-cutting, particularly through practices like downsizing, may be a double-edge sword that does not produce sustainable wealth.[2]

The market value of a firm, evident during acquisitions, is a widely used measure of firm wealth. But when a firm is bought, its fixed assets are only a small part of its market price. The value of its human capital, the quality of its labor force, including skills and marginal product, are factored in. But do fixed assets plus human capital sum to be the firm's total value? Not usually. Other factors that contribute to the firm's worth are also considered: the quality of the employment relationship based on a history of retention or turnover; the stability of the firm's market position historically and in future projections; and its reputation in the market for both customers and labor. This surplus value over fixed assets and human capital is an estimate of what we call the firm's relational wealth.

In this book we develop and discuss the concept of relational wealth—the value created by and for a firm through its internal relations among and with employees, as well as its external alliances and reputation. Relationships, we will argue, represent a form of wealth—albeit an underrecognized and thus underutilized and undervalued one in most firms—just as do money, land, equipment, and human capital. Unlike these other forms, relational wealth is noticed more readily in its absence than its presence, and it is what A. O. Hirschman called a moral resource—one whose value increases rather than decreases with use. This form of wealth has received a great deal of attention in other social science domains ranging from anthropology to criminal justice, but it is a concept that remains largely underdeveloped within an economic framework and within economic organizations that create material wealth. The phenomenon of relationships as wealth—that is, relationships as a distinct competitive advantage for a firm rather than just a byproduct of its activities—is the subject of this book. Our focus here is largely on employment relationships although we discuss other relationships such as those with suppliers, customers, and strategic partners as well.

The Nature of Firm Wealth

The meaning of firm wealth has changed over time. Twenty years ago, for example, inventory constituted a large chunk of the value of many firms; today, just-in-time practices have driven inventory value in many firms to near zero. Creditors have had to look to other indicators to appraise a firm. As firms seek to shed their fixed assets, such as equipment and real estate, in the pursuit of "assetless" flexibility, their relational wealth plays an increasing role in gauging the value of a firm. And, we argue, it is an asset few firms can afford to do without.

From a strategic standpoint, human assets have generally been recognized as likely sources of long-term sustainable competitive advantages.[3] Aspects like the competence of top management or, more recently, the "intellectual capital" of the firm's members, have long been valued by investors and are often figured into the firm's "worth." However, the measurement of human asset value is not an exact science and is thus subject to dispute. This results commonly in a fascination with what is measurable rather than what is most meaningful. For example, most discussions—and public policy initiatives—focus on formal schooling as the primary indicator of human asset value, despite the fact that for many occupational groups qualifying training occurs primarily on the job. This aspect of human capital derived specifically from on-the-job experience—or the firm-specific knowledge in which both employee and employer invest—is particularly important to our discussion.

One way of knowing whether an asset is seen as having long-term value is to observe whether firms capitalize their financial outlays in acquiring these assets, as opposed to treating them as an expense. This presents problems, particularly in valuing human assets, since conventional approaches, rooted largely in the industrial structure of the early twentieth century, shape accounting practices and tax laws. For example, capitalizing research and development expenditures underscores their investment nature and highlights the long-term assumptions about benefits to be realized. However, since a good deal of R & D expenses are people related, R & D investments, as well as other acquired intangible assets, such as activities aimed at enhancing employee skills or relationships, are treated as expenses and not investments.[4] The danger of letting accounting assumptions shape our strategic thinking are evident: if R & D are seen as expenses rather than long-term investments, short-term cost-cutting can undermine a firm's future innovations.[5] What we measure and how we measure it affects what we do with that measure.

To counter the misleading aspects of current managerial accounting practices, scholars have proposed that a firm's assets be conceptualized as "hybrid capital." A firm's value is a summation of its physical assets (such as real estate and equipment), financial capital (cash and investments), human capital (knowledge and skills its workforce possesses), and some even more intangible factors (meaning more difficult to measure than the money in the bank) that contribute to a firm's competitive positioning.

Proponents of a hybrid capital perspective speak of these diffuse intangible assets in various terms, sometimes placing them under such general rubrics as "social capital" or "comparative flexibility." But these intangible contributions to competitive positioning include a firm's reputation, its culture, and its capacity to implement change. The essence of such intangible assets is relational wealth.

The Nature of Relational Wealth

Relational wealth refers to resources created for a firm through its internal relations among and with employees, as well as its external alliances and reputation. Relational wealth is an intangible asset that successful firms optimize and leverage. By optimization we do not mean that successful firms all attempt to maximize their relational wealth; neither do they all attempt to keep it at a minimum level. Rather, successful firms calculate the extent to which relationships can add value and enhance wealth, then manage those relationships accordingly. By leveraging, we mean that successful firms implement business strategies that distinguish them from their weaker competitors based on the competencies and flexibility relational wealth provides.

There are several important aspects of relational wealth that are potential sources of value to firms. These are also the levers for managing the level of relational wealth for the firm.

Trust

Some level of trust is fundamental to creating or sustaining relational wealth. Trust refers to the positive expectations firms and workers have of each other's intentions and behavior. It is valuable to firms because it reduces the need for monitoring and increases individuals' willingness to be flexible. Trust can arise for different reasons among firms and between firms and workers. Firms may trust one another because of previous experience or reputation. Managers tend to trust workers on the basis of their competence, while workers trust managers and their firms generally on the basis of their levels of perceived integrity.[6] As illustrated by the following comments of a manager describing his arrangements with a supplier, trust can be fundamental to accessing relational wealth in both employee and supplier/customer relations.

> One of our fellow plants is our major supplier of metal—our only supplier of metal, basically. They're helping train our guys in synchronous manufacturing and we are helping to train theirs. We're sending out people to each other's plants. I've got a great commitment

from this organization. We're talking about saving money. We're looking at tooling fixtures. Why do we have to have duplicate fixtures? I
mean it's phenomenal how much redundancy we have in our systems
because we don't trust one another. Because we don't have a relationship.[7]

Trust, based on a history of goodwill, also makes it possible to re-create
relationships with the same people or firms even under changing circumstances. The classic example of changing the deal while keeping the people
based on a history of goodwill is the transformation of Motorola from a
functionally structured, "stovepipe" corporation into a decentralized, adaptive, self-organizing network of functions, products, and diverse markets.
Inspired by a popular management book he read on a long airplane flight,
Bob Galvin, Motorola's CEO in 1982, realized the need to transform his firm
to be more flexible in the face of impending competition. Working through
the transformation meant pushing the responsibility for greater flexibility
down to the lowest levels of the firm, and cultivating more local respon-
siveness. Trust in the leader amplified by Galvin's trust in his employees
reformulated Motorola from top to bottom in three years without a layoff.
A workforce that thought of itself as "Galvanized" shifted its view of the
term, which had meant durability in the past and now meant stimulation
and innovation. As Galvin's experience at Motorola indicates, where there
is a history of trust, change in performance demands and accountabilities
are more readily accepted on the basis of sustained good faith and fair dealing over time.

Firms frequently face the need to restructure work and performance demands in response to competitive pressures. In the new organizational era
of hypercompetition and divergent global and local labor markets, trust can
take many forms. Day laborers and firms that hire them manifest what can
be termed fragile trust, where each is willing to rely on the other in a limited
way based on a consideration of what is in their short-term self-interest.
The high-involvement workforce and the firm employing it operate from a
broader base of "resilient trust," where each partner is expected to contribute a high degree of mutual concern and shared interests.

Regardless of the type or duration of the relationship, trust operates in a
bandwidth where the amount of trust that parties (e.g., employee-employer;
customer-supplier) are willing to give each other depends on the specific
risks and the circumstances. The concept of trust's bandwidth can be illustrated by considering the roles that different actors play in an individual's
life. We may trust our spouses with everything from child care to finances
and tell them our innermost secrets, but usually we don't trust them to do
surgery if we have an appendicitis. In contrast, the surgeon to whom we
entrust our lives is often a relative stranger in whom we place our trust
under a very specific, narrow, albeit crucial condition. Fragile trust has as
its basis economic calculations and typically is limited to a specific set of
activities for which we have transacted. Thus its bandwidth is typically

narrow. Resilient trust has a wider bandwidth where shared interests and mutual concern create a confidence in the competence and intentions that others bring to a broad array of activities.

An important issue concerns whether there is an optimum range of trust to permit firms and workers to access the full potential of relational wealth. Contemporary workforce changes have severely limited willingness to trust, certainly at the broadest range of the bandwidth, particularly where work has an impact on nonwork life (e.g., time and investment in family). As we will describe, trust's lower bandwidth can be costly to firms and workers.[8]

Knowing Who Knows What

The knowledge that resides in ongoing interactions among people provides a significant form of relational wealth. Rather than knowledge being viewed as an asset possessed by a single person, knowledge can also take the form of knowing how to access important information from others (including coworkers). The most common—and often most useful—form of "memory" in organizations resides with the people who recall "who knows what" in the organization. A good example of the utility of this "knowing who knows what" knowledge is the story of a flood in a plant along the Allegheny River in Pittsburgh. As the flood waters rose, workers attempted to find the heavy metal doors that previously had been put in place to stop water from rushing into underground corridors. They found the doors where they had been moved for storage—in a basement from which they could no longer be removed because the elevator had been replaced by a one too narrow to accommodate them. The manager who placed the doors in the basement had retired two years before the elevator was refurbished, and the current management, with no flood experience, had no idea how large the doors actually were. In this case, the organization "remembered" what the doors were for but not how big they were. (Years later, the doors are still stuck in storage.) As this example illustrates, "knowing who knows what" is a key aspect of memory and learning.

Organizational memory is more than recall of facts. Knowing how to work together is a form of knowledge not easily replicated when a work group disbands or when a new member is added. In a work group assembling a radio, for example, a team composed entirely of people who have worked together before will perform better than a group of individuals each of whom has assembled radios but who have never worked together before. The concept of "transactive memory" accounts for the performance difference.[9] Experience working together enhances performance—so much so that a few days' absence on the part of a single member can reduce performance and increase accidents.[10] The high rate of accidents among contract workers compared to regular employees is at least in part attributable to lack of familiarity. The value of knowledge individuals possess depends for its function on the effective interaction and cooperation of people working together. Its maximum performance is critically dependent not just on what they think and how they think as individuals but on how and what they think as a team.[11]

Reputation

Reputation is the regard with which one is held in a broader community. Reputation has been found to have a direct effect on firm performance: firms convicted of illegal acts (such as price fixing or violating child labor laws) experience lower sales growth and earn lower returns.[12] One advantage of reputation is that it creates the capacity to form new relationships with different people. The advantages of trust, described earlier, may accrue through a transference process, where a third party's view of another as trustworthy warrants one's trustworthiness to others with whom the trustor has little or no experience. A buyer who trusts a supplier's salesperson may transfer such feelings of trust to others in the firm. Employees who trust a company can motivate a friend to seek employment there.[13]

Reputation affects both the employability of persons as well as the capacity of firms to access highly qualified employees. Employers of choice are those firms with reputations for human resource practices that workers value (including reasonable pay and benefits, career opportunities, and family support) often characterizing firms targeting a particularly desirable and difficult-to-access segment of the labor market, such as the highly skilled or committed.[14] Employers of choice attract more qualified workers in tight labor markets and retain their people during slack markets. Reputation affects worker opportunities, too. In dynamic labor markets such as in Silicon Valley, the ability of people to find employment is often through word of mouth and personal contacts.

The ability of people to work together once hired may itself be affected by reputation. "Swift trust" is a concept coined to explain how it is that individuals with distinctly different skills can come together to work in a temporary organization like a political campaign or a film shoot or a temporary task force within a firm. In film making, some people may be local; others might have flown overnight to get there. But a team of technical specialists with different backgrounds can come together to work effectively, to make a video in a day, because they have confidence in one another's ability to do their own jobs, based on the reputations that got them that job in the first place.[15] Note that swift trust differs from deep abiding trust but is a form of relational wealth in highly mobile labor markets.

Infrastructure

Institutions promote relational wealth when they reinforce the capacity of persons and groups to form new relations and to plan for the future by making commitments that are likely to be kept. In the broadest sense, institutions are the formal and informal mechanisms that enable cooperative relations in a society. Often referred to as the civil society, institutions promoting relational wealth include: (1) a legal system providing a stable and enforceable set of codes and statutes; (2) cultural norms supporting generalized trust in the society; (3) within the economic sphere, social structures promoting network ties between workers, workers and firms, and between firms; and (4) the social supports outside firms that enhance worker quality of life and resilience in the face of change (e.g., educational opportunities).

Institutions promote relational wealth when they reinforce the capacity of persons and groups to form new relations and to plan for the future by making commitments that can later be kept (e.g., laws, reputation networks). Relational wealth in firms is explicitly multilevel because of the collective nature of firms, comprising individual, dyadic, group, firm, and interfirm relations.

Legal Environment

The environments workers and firms are located in can foster or obstruct their ability to sustain relations over time, build trust, or maintain a reputation. Institutions foster shared expectations that make interdependence possible. We can drive safely in traffic because we believe that all traffic participants will abide by "rules of the road." In post-Communist eastern Europe, laws, particularly regarding firms and property, were poorly developed, and in many cases there were few legal deterrents to theft of either physical or intellectual property. Reputational sanctions were made inefficient by weak social structure and high levels of societal mistrust coupled with low information sharing. In contrast, infrastructures in Japan foster a high degree of cooperation and mutual support through social networks and the power of reputation, even in the absence of written contracts.[16]

Cultural Norms

Societal norms, such as generalized trust, supplemented by a legal system supporting individual rights, are a powerful source of relational wealth, while a litigious culture and overloaded legal system can undermine relational wealth. In the United States, interfirm relations sustained over time often involve limited reliance on legal contracts, stressing instead degrees of mutual interdependence. In Japan, the arrangements of networks of local firms that exchange goods, services, and often workers, with little formal documentation, have been referred to as contracting without contracts.[17]

Societal institutions and culture significantly contribute to the formation of relational wealth. One major source of relational wealth comes from the willingness of people to contribute not only to the benefit of themselves and their immediate family and friends but to the larger society as well. Relational wealth is characteristic of *le sens civique* in France, such that civil servants are respected for contributing to society and government is esteemed. It is also a characteristic of societies where volunteerism and donations to public charities are high.

Consider what it is like in countries where a broader interest in the welfare of society is lacking. In Poland, for example, young Samaritans such as Bozena Kubuszok routinely bump up against a "volunteerism stigma." Her friends and family were incredulous of her plans to work with Habitat for Humanity in Poland, alongside former U.S. president Jimmy Carter. "They said, 'Are you stupid? Going to work without being paid. You should rest on your vacation.'" As global charitable organizations such as Habitat for Humanity try to foster a culture of volunteerism in the former Soviet bloc, there is a problem of learning to trust institutions as well as people. "If a friend of a friend asks you to do work for them, you do it. If an institution writes you a letter to do the same, you figure how much money is your time worth," says Marianna Torok, head of the Budapest-based non-profit Information and Training Center.[18]

Social Structure

Just as trust can be focused on a specific individual or organization, it can also be generalized so that one may trust individuals or institutions without having direct personal contact or experience with them. Absence of generalized trust gives rise to an "intuitive accounting," where people engage in a calculus to determine whether to contribute and when to trust.[19] Generalized trust is found in a community (firm or region) characterized by a network of people, firms, and governmental organizations where optimism and positive attributions exist regarding the formation of new relations. The sociologist Francis Fukuyama has described the advantages of relational wealth characterizing one part of Italy that has been the most economically dynamic over the past generation. In central Italy this area has been referred to by Italian sociologists as Terza Italia (the third Italy). Its growth exceeds the larger firms of northern Italy and that of the small family enterprises characteristic of the South. While peasant familism remains dominant in the impoverished South, the family businesses of the Terza Italia are innovative, export oriented, and in many cases develop and use high technology. These small family businesses tend to cluster together into industrial districts, Italy's version of Silicon Valley or Boston's Route 128. In certain cases these industrial districts have been deliberately fostered by local governments, which have provided training, financing and other services. In other cases, family businesses have formed spontaneous networks with other like-minded companies and subcontract with other small firms for supplies and marketing services. In the rest of Italy, where social structure—and trust patterns—differ, industrial districts have not been successful.[20]

What Relational Wealth Is Not

In defining relational wealth, it is important to distinguish it from other concepts and thus define what it is not. Relational wealth is not human capital, the knowledge, skills, and ability that individuals possess, although clearly by having individual members strong in skills such as communication and networking the relational wealth of the firm can be enhanced. Relational wealth derives not from the store of knowledge that individual members possess but from the ability of the firm and its employees to access that knowledge, including how well they work together as a team.

Relational wealth is not individual social capital or the value created for individuals by their personal networks.[21] Individual social capital and the networking strategies pursued by employees in and outside organizations can contribute to relational wealth, particularly if these strategies are grounded in the previously described attributes such as trust and reputation. However, relational wealth as we are discussing it here is an attribute of the organization whose value accrues to the organization directly and its individual members only indirectly. In this regard it is closer to what has been termed organizational social capital (as discussed by Van Buren and Leana in chapter 13) or the value of the shared commitment and stability engendered by a workforce strong in trust and collective goal orientation.[22]

Relational wealth is not croneyism, or the ties of individuals banding together against a hostile social setting where laws are not enforced and where particularism dominates. For example, in China, guanxi—the phenomenon of social connections which give rise to dyadic relationships based on mutual interest and benefit—is an important component of local organizational effectiveness. Guanxi is established by cultivating personal connections based on instrumental behaviors, including bribery, gifts, and favoritism (e.g., hiring the son of an important government minister to strengthen ties to that official). Such connections have fewer benefits, and may even be criminal, in societies governed by the rule of law and where firms compete in a market economy.

The Erosion of Relational Wealth

Our life is not a mutual helpfulness; but rather, cloaked under the laws-of-war, named "fair compensation" and so forth, it is a mutual hostility. We have profoundly forgotten that cash payment is not the sole relation of human beings; we think, nothing doubting, that it absolves and liquidates all engagements of man.
                          —Thomas Carlyle, *Past and Present* (1843)

Although Carlyle was describing a society of a century and a half ago, the erosion of relational wealth, particularly in the United States, within and outside firms, is a topic that has received much attention and has been the subject of hand-wringing by writers and public policy makers across the political spectrum.[23] The erosion of relational wealth is manifested in complex and multifaceted ways: the lack of civility in public discourse; the private consumption of recreation, schooling, and transportation that used to be consumed by individuals as members of a larger community; the lack of loyalty and commitment between employee and employer. Within the economic sphere, several factors have contributed to the erosion of relational wealth, including the following:

- Inequity in risk and gain
- Institutionalized conflict between labor and management
- Poorly managed organizational change, coupled with appropriation of worker investments by shareholders
- Lags between changes in organizational environment and development of legal and other societal infrastructures
- Employees working more and getting less

Inequity in Risk and Gain

A trend that has intensified in recent years is the enormous returns to private capital accruing disproportionately to select individuals within a firm and in society as a whole. Just as sports franchises try to put together winning teams by acquiring a star player, many firms will pay large sums to add or keep a few key members who are believed to be able to bring the organization to new heights of efficiency and/or profitability. This tendency to seek out and reward a few key individuals possessing supposedly superior levels of human capital has been called the winner-take-all phenomenon[24]—one that is expected to continue to be pronounced in an economy centered on individual knowledge and skills.

Perhaps the most readily cited example of the winner-take-all phenomenon in American businesses over the past decade is the pay gap between CEOs and the remainder of the workforce. The rationale for high executive compensation (coupled in many instances with stagnant or declining earnings for other employees) is that the CEO and others at the top of the firm (in contrast to those at lower levels) are thought be critical to the effective functioning of the business, possess a rare set of traits and talents that cannot be easily duplicated, and thus disproportionately encapsulate much of the human value of the enterprise. Thus, the lucky few at the top are richly rewarded, sometimes at the expense of those in lower levels and, at best, without regard for them. Manifestations of the resentment caused by such disparate rewards—and the accompanying erosion of relational wealth— are plentiful. The AFL-CIO, for example, maintains a website so employees can monitor the compensation packages their executives receive. Cowherd and Levine report on a study of manufacturers that found that interclass pay inequity (i.e., between those at the top and bottom of a firm) had a significant negative impact not only on perceptions of fairness but also on objective measures of product quality.[25]

Institutionalized Labor Conflict

The history of unionism in the twentieth century is an indicator that relational wealth can be lost as well as created. There was a spiral of distrust in key American manufacturing firms in the first three-quarters of the twentieth century. From the 1920s to the 1950s, unionized plants were more productive than nonunionized ones, while the reverse held subsequently. By the 1970s there was an adversarial pattern of labor management relations characterized by legal formalism. The 1982 national agreement between the United Auto Workers and Ford consisted of four volumes, each two hundred pages in length, supplemented at the plant level by another thick collective bargaining agreement specifying work rules, terms and conditions of employment, and the like. Wages were tied not to the worker but to the job classification, and bumping rights, seniority privileges, and the like were all set forth in explicit detail. Disputes arising in the workplace tended to be referred to the legal system for resolution rather than being worked out informally. In labor management relationships, trust was low, communication limited, and reputations uniformly negative.[26]

In contrast, unionism in many U.S. industries since the 1970s has drawn more heavily on mutual interests and the strength of relationships. In the steel industry, for example, the United Steelworkers Union now has contracts with nearly all of the major U.S. steel producers that stress partnership, mutual gain, and the reliance on informal dispute resolution rather than litigation as a first step in resolving differences. These partnerships were initiated by the Union—once a paragon of formal, contractual labor relations—and have resulted in successful changes not just in work processes and employment practices but in the use of new technology and capital investment decisions as well.

Poorly Managed Organizational Change

Change is not synonymous with instability. From the transformations of Motorola in the 1980s into a global competitor (without a layoff) to plant closings that have left the communities where they were located whole and their former workers newly employed, change can promote new forms of stability and adaptation. However, the costs of poorly managed change are high. Cascio and his colleagues observed that stock price declines three years after downsizing in typical firms. Follow-up studies of outplaced managers and other professionals indicate that the aftermath of job loss is reluctance to commit to new employers.[27]

In a highly instructive contrast, two plant closings, a year and a few miles apart, indicate the radically different consequences that follow from differently managed organizational change. In 1982, GM announced on short notice a "temporary shutdown" of its Fremont, California, plant. Little planning was done, and within three weeks, thousands of workers were thrown out of work. A year later, in Milipitas, California, Ford also closed a plant, giving six months' notice and setting up employee task forces to help manage the closing, develop appropriate supports for workers soon to be terminated, and promote outplacement. Following the GM plant closing (and subsequent announcement that it was permanent), spousal abuse and suicide rates were high among its former workers, with few finding new jobs even after two years. In contrast, the majority of former Ford workers were reemployed elsewhere, and no indicators of heightened abuse or suicide were observed.

While change may be inevitable, how it is managed is a choice. Choosing to manage change without regard to the effects on employees, their families, and their communities erodes a firm's relational wealth. While managers may argue that financial circumstances force such "slash and burn" approaches to change, there are long-term social costs that may eventually offset the short-term financial savings of approaches such as GM's in this instance. These social costs are first and primarily borne by the affected individuals and communities, but the firm also suffers losses in the form of damaged trust, knowledge, teamwork, and reputation.

Lags in Development of Supporting Infrastructure

Relational wealth links a distribution of risk balanced by commensurate sharing of gain. When not just wages, but health care benefits and retirement security operate like winner-take-all markets, relational wealth is further eroded as the difference between "haves" and "have nots" further widens. Many European and Asian countries guard against such disparities by providing universal health care to all citizens, regardless of job or income status, and a standard pension for retirement. Thus, an economic infrastructure is created that also affects the relational infrastructure of the society.

In the United States, health care and retirement benefits have largely been governed by market forces rather than through government mandates.[28] Recent efforts in the United States to widen the availability and security of health care and pensions through measures that tie these benefits to individuals rather than to specific jobs or organizations are attempts to provide a floor, if not a ceiling, to reduce gross disparities between the different players in the labor market. The labor market "winners" might still be richly rewarded, but at least the "losers" might fulfill their basic health care and security needs. Such measures not only provide economic benefits but also serve to stave off some of the erosion of relational wealth as they protect against some market inequities. These measures are modest, however, and the general lack of such economic infrastructure in the United States contributes to the general decline of relational wealth in our society.

Working More and Getting Less

Even in growth economies, prolonged unemployment and underemployment are evident in certain regions. Forecasts for unemployment in the early 2000s suggest that many industrial nations, including France, Germany, Finland, Norway, and Sweden, will experience an increase in the percentage of the labor force unemployed in comparison to their experience in the 1980s. In the United States and the United Kingdom, the forecast is brighter, though it varies significantly by region[29] Part-time employment has risen substantially in many industrialized nations (France, Germany, U.K., U.S.), and the so-called transitional workforce has become a topic of interest to academics, public policy makers, and managers.

Expanded employment, however, is not necessarily an unmitigated good. Even with a thriving economy, households in the United States have barely kept up their living standards by using two incomes to pay for what one wage was once able to buy.[30] In those families where both parents work, parents spent 40 percent less time with their children in 1990 than in 1965, a drop from thirty to seventeen hours per week.[31] The latter is in part attributable to the increase in work hours for Americans despite declining work hours in other industrialized countries. Not surprisingly, while both full- and part-time employment rates are higher in the United States than in most of Europe, the relative income equality in the United States is lowest among industrialized nations.[32] This pattern continues to edge its way into the next generation, with more American teenagers working than their European and Japanese counterparts.[33]

Building and Sustaining Relational Wealth in an Economy of Continuous Change

Our discussion so far has centered on the importance of relational wealth and the factors contributing to its erosion in many firms and in whole societies. If one accepts its importance, the vital question, of course, becomes how to build and maintain relational wealth, particularly in an economy that at first glance appears indifferent to its presence and seemingly hostile to its nurturance and stability over time. Balancing the mandates and benefits of both flexibility and stability are key elements. While these two are often seen as opposite ends of a single continua (i.e, a firm can either be flexible or stable), particularly with regard to employment practices, we argue here that flexibility and stability can be complimentary and that both are necessary for long-term success.

The Much-Touted Mandate of Flexibility

Much is made of the dynamism of the global economy and the restrictions it places on the ability of organizations and individual employees to stand in place. Instead, the ability to not just react to but anticipate and shape change is key to success. With regard to employment, flexibility refers to the capability of workers and firms to form new employment arrangements. Conventionally we often think that flexibility varies from the very high flexibility of winner-take-all performers who are recognized as stars, to the low flexibility characteristic of individuals whose skills have little value on the external or internal market. However, high levels of flexibility can also mean the capacity to create new employment arrangements within the same relationship. This more complex view is apparent when we consider the different meanings flexibility has for individuals and for firms.

For individuals, flexibility is largely a function of mobility within and outside a given firm. Flexibility for individuals places a premium on the ability to move from one firm to another, to learn new jobs in the same firm, to do several different types of tasks in the same day, and to adjust quickly to different kinds of cultures and group settings. Such flexibility has been consistently associated with higher levels of human capital in the form of general education and job training.[34]

For firms, flexibility is the capacity to attract and manage individuals with needed competencies, while terminating or retraining them when demand for those competencies declines. For firms flexibility requires the ability to shift the use of labor as market demands change. Flexibility can mean cross-trained workers able to broadly contribute to the firm. It can also take the form of accessing at least some segment of the firm's labor through outsourcing or the use of temporary employment. Such arrangements have the advantage of adjusting to short-term fluctuations in labor demand, while making it possible to retain the core of the workforce, which provides the firm with a competitive advantage. These arrangements also have their limitation. The primary danger of outsourcing—shifting labor usage to contractors—is in the degree to which what is outsourced reflects capabilities best retained within the firm (i.e., skills and competencies directly related to the core business) or in the migration of risky activities requiring careful monitoring to contract labor, without appropriate safeguards. A case in point is the recent Valuejet crash, where an airline's failure to monitor the procedures used by its contractors in disposing of hazardous materials resulted in the loss of over a hundred lives.[35] These limitations point to the need for stability as well as flexibility within firms.

The Unsung Benefits of Stability

As dynamic as markets can be, there are numerous individual, organizational, and societal forces promoting stability. Organizations and their managers manifest a distinct preference for predictability and uncertainty reduction. Firms seek markets where their resources give them a competitive advantage, where there is considerable present and anticipated value to the knowledge, skills, and abilities workers and firms have developed. Without stability, there is little potential to convert present knowledge, skills, and ability into future value. Forces for stability for individuals are rooted in the real constraints people face regarding cognitive, physical, and emotional limits and the difficulties in planning for and coping with increasing levels of uncertainty. People are tied to places via family, friends, and mortgages. Moreover, there is ample evidence that while change can be stimulating and challenging, an inverted U–shaped curve exists where too much change creates distress that cannot be readily handled by individuals or firms.

These inclinations toward stability by both organizations and individuals can be dismissed as weaknesses by proponents of continuous change. An implicit assumption in modern organizational culture is that structure and formality are bad. Structure equals bureaucracy which equals "red tape" and inefficiency. However, most research on the dysfunctional consequences of bureaucracy focuses on extreme degrees of structuration and neglects what Max Weber realized over a hundred years ago: that bureaucracy can also promote fairness and consistency. Expanding our organizational experiences to include developing countries, it becomes apparent that some aspects of "bureaucracy" can be beneficial. Pearce, Branyiczki, and Bigley observe in a comparison of Hungarian and U.S. firms that the presence of procedures and rules promotes a sense of consistency and fair play regarding organizational policies, and its absence accounts for the substantial levels of mistrust and sense of inequity characteristic of Hungarian firms. In developed countries, the ambient infrastructure provided by procedures, rules, and contracts is taken for granted and therefore discounted.

Consistent procedures and well-understood rules are not ends in themselves but means to an end, particularly with regard to creating trust and mutual predictability in relationships. A core feature of stability is the ability of firms and employees to make commitments to each other, that each can trust the other to keep promises. Stability encompasses the sustained (or even increasing) value of capacities developed over time by workers or firms to achieve their goals. Stability brings repositories of knowledge that can be leveraged in the future; contrary to contemporary biases, its absence rather than its presence may indicate outmoded or nonadaptable capabilities.

Our traditional notions of stability (and the negative connotation it has taken on for many firms and employees) are bound up in the concept of the traditional corporate job. Long-term employment within a single firm, having an internal labor market, constitutes a reliable source of personal wealth for workers and stability for firms. However, such a job may reflect a circumstance that was more of an anomaly during the past thirty years rather than a common experience for American workers. Martin Carnoy describes the traditional corporate job as one that was distinctly male and restricted to certain elites. More common in history and in general was the "female job" (nonlinear career path, sporadic participation in labor market, etc.). Indeed it is significant that women in their forties in the U.S. labor market are generally more employable than men in professional jobs precisely because employers take it for granted that women might be (re)entering the workforce after raising children while men at that age need to have succeeded already or be dismissed as "has-beens." The culture of work could change to accept that men also go back to school or start new careers later in life—a phenomenon that Nanette Fondas has referred to as the feminization of work.[36] Thus, the "model" job may not be the "modal" job as economies change. Stability may be valuable in terms of predictability, but when it becomes rigid and intransigent it has lost its long-term value. The unsung benefits of stability derive from recognizing that it means the capacity to pattern work relationships on trust and cooperation—and that such a pattern need not be static.

A Winning Combination

Recognition of the potential competitive advantage that relational wealth provides is evident when flexibility and stability are considered together. This approach can emphasize one or the other attribute, but the important factor is their combination. Pursuing a strategy of maximal flexibility in employment without regard to stability results in organizations focused solely on the short-term "slash and burn" approaches to change and in an alienated workforce. In turn, stability that is not flexible leads to rigidity, lack of adaptiveness, and the fulfillment of bureaucracy's negative stereotypes. Each is undesirable alone and, when pursued singularly, sows the seeds of its own destruction over the long term. When combined, stability and flexibility make possible the choice of appropriate business strategies coupled with the alignment of sustainable human resources practices.

The Strategy of Stable Flexibility

A strategy of stable flexibility places the emphasis on change and dynamism while acknowledging and accommodating needs for stability. For example, reputation can provide stability even in a very dynamic labor market, simultaneously promoting the relational wealth of the firm and the mobility of individual workers. Investment banking is a highly competitive business characterized by high turnover of personnel who manifest very loose social ties to one another. A recent study observed friendship or advice relationships or ties of only around 2 percent among a sample of investment bankers. In contrast, individual ratings of investment banker trustworthiness display interrater agreement of .80, indicating a high level of knowledge about individuals even in very dispersed networks.[37] The previously mentioned capacity of ad hoc groups and temporary organizations to work cooperatively together on the basis of swift trust is directly linked to the availability of information about individual competencies derived from occupational networks for reputation. Credentialing mechanisms signaling worker competence accomplish the same purpose, as is the case in the German and Dutch school-to-work systems, where employers access reliable workers from trade schools themselves known for the quality of their graduates. In all these examples, reputation and infrastructure provide the needed stability in an otherwise constantly changing market. Thus, stability under conditions of flexibility means knowledge derived from experience regarding how to work interdependently (for the firm as a whole as well as for specific work groups) and/or the capacity to trust and to anticipate what others will do in the future.

The Strategy of Flexible Stability

Much recent work in the area of human resources management has focused on the so-called high-involvement, high performance work organization. Here the emphasis is on stability in employment but with flexibility in the kinds of work employees do and the ways in which they may be flexibly deployed. Thus, the workforce is stable, but there is flexibility concerning how the work is carried out. Such high-involvement, high-performance work strategies emphasize employment security, investments in training and development, incentive compensation, and high levels of employee participation in decision making. In studies over a wide range of industries, high-involvement, high-performance work has been associated not only with individual satisfaction and career development but also with improvements in organizational performance, product quality, and efficiency.[38]

As these experiences indicate, stability under conditions of flexibility means knowledge derived from experience regarding how to work interdependently and the capacity to anticipate what others will do in the future. It draws primarily on the trust and "knowing who knows what" aspects of relational wealth. The previously described "stable flexibility" strategy draws more heavily on the reputation and infrastructure aspects of relational wealth.

Regardless of whether the "stable flexibility" or the "flexible stability" strategy is chosen, relational wealth is a core component. Relational wealth enhances flexibility through the ability to form new relationships in times of change, providing access to new resources and opportunities. It enhances stability by reducing coordination costs and the need for monitoring, creating a basis of predictability and the efficient use of existing resources. In effect, we argue in favor of stability in the midst of change through the enhanced flexibility that trust, reputation, and other relational supports provide.

Structure of This Book

This book is designed to offer both a broad overview of the nature of relational wealth in the modern firm as well as to offer insights into a variety of wealth-creating and -eroding mechanisms. This introduction addresses relational wealth and firm competitiveness. It addresses how employee and organizational relationships have value that is economic as well as personal or social. Part I addresses the role that financial markets and work practices addresses play in shaping labor markets, creating or eroding long-term competitive advantage from relational wealth. Part II addresses how attachments between firms and workers, including labor market intermediaries (e.g., temporary agencies and employer consortia), investments in employee training, and employee external networks, can reduce their mutual vulnerabilities. Part III focuses on the effect of adverse consequences of transactional employment arrangements on work and workers. Government and societal institutions, and the role they play in shaping or eroding relational wealth are the focus in Part IV. Finally, we close by addressing the future of employment relations and the prospects for relational wealth enhancing that future. In it we call attention to the reemergence of the public scholar, an academic who addresses and attempts to rectify, rather than merely observe, critical problems in society. We outline how public scholarship by organizational researchers is critical to the successful creation and deployment of relational wealth in the face of the narrow market-mindset prevailing in business today.

Notes

1. There is no single agreed-upon indicator of either firm wealth or performance. Indeed, Marshall Meyer and Kenneth C. O. Shaunghesy (1993, "Organizational Design and the Performance Paradox." In R. Swedberg (ed.), *Explorations in Economic Sociology.* NY: Russell Sage) describe the phenomenon of the performance paradox, where organizational performance measures tend to be weakly correlated. Performance has been assessed variously, as market share (e.g., A. Fiegenbaum and H. Thomas, 1990, "Strategy Groups and Performance: The U.S. Insurance Industry." *Strategic Management Journal, 11,* 197–215) Strategic groups and performance: the U.S. insurance industry, average return on assets (e.g., E. J. Zajac, 1990 CEO selection, successions, competition and firm performance: A theoretical integration and empirical analysis. *Strategic Management Journal, 11,* 217–230.), and even as subjective measures completed by CEOs (B. Wooldridge and S. W. Flood, 1990. Middle Management Involvement and Organizational Performance. "*Strategic Management Journal, 11,* 232–241).

2. Wayne Cascio, C. Young, and J. Morris, "Financial Consequences of Employment-Change Decisions in Major U.S. Corporations," *Academy of Management Journal* 40 (1997): 1175–89.

3. Russell Coff and Eric Flamholtz, "Corporate Investments in Human Capital: How Financial Accounting Standards Undermine Public Policy," *Stanford Law and Policy Review* (Fall 1993): 31–40.

4. Eric Flamholtz developed a framework for human resources accounting in the 1970s that met with tremendous resistance from both accounting professionals and firms. However, interest has continued in Europe, where academics and firms have continued to develop both models and measurement tools to assess assets other than traditional fixed assets.

5. R. A. Bettis, S. Bradley, and C. Hamel, "Outsourcing and Industrial Decline," *Academy of Management Executive* 6 (1992): 558–70.

6. On interfirm trust, see G. Walker, B. Kogut, and W. Shan, "Social Capital, Structural Holes, and the Formation of an Industry Network," *Organizational Science* 8 (1997): 109–25; on top-down trust, see George Graen and Terry Scandura, "Toward a Psychology of Dyadic Organizing," in *Research and Organizational Behavior*, edited by L. Cummings and B. Staw (Greenwich, Conn.: JAI Press, 1987), pp. 175–208; on managerial integrity as a basis for trust, see E. Whitener, S. Brodt, and X. Werner, "Managers as Initiators of Trust: An Exchange Relationship Framework for Understanding Managerial Trustworthy Behavior, *Academy of Management Review 23* (1998) 513–531.

7. Anil Mishra, "Organizational Responses to Crisis: The Centrality of Trust," in *Trust in Organizations: Frontiers of Theory and Research*, edited by R. Kramer and T. Tyler (Thousand Oaks, Calif.: Sage, 1996), p. 277.

8. See Carrie Leana, "Why Downsizing Won't Work," *Chicago Tribune Magazine*, April 14, 1996, pp. 14–16, 18; and Jeffrey Pfeffer, *The Human Equation* (Boston: Harvard Business School Press, 1998).

9. Richard Moreland, Linda Argote, and Ranjani Krishnan, "Socially Shared Cognition at Work: Transactive Memory and Group Performance," in *What's Social about Social Cognition? Research on Socially Shared Cognition in Small Groups*, edited by J. Nye and A. Brower (Thousand Oaks, Calif.: Sage, 1996), pp. 57–84.

10. Paul Goodman and D. Leyden. "Familiarity and Group Productivity," *Journal of Applied Psychology* 76 (1991): 578–86; Denise Rousseau and Carolyn Libuser, "Contingent Workers in High Risk Environments," *California Management Review* (1997): 103–23.

11. M. Darling, "The Knowledge Organization: A Journey Worth Taking," *Vital Speeches of the Day*, September 1, 1996.

12. M. S. Baucus and D. A. Baucus, "Paying the Piper: An Empirical Examination of Longer-term Financial Consequences of Illegal Corporate Behavior," *Academy of Management Journal* 40 (1997): 129–31. Effects are particularly evident in the period of three to five years after a conviction.

13. P. M. Doney and J. P. Cannon, An examination of the nature of trust in buyer-seller relationships. *Journal of Marketing, 61* (1997): 35–52.

14. On employer-of-choice, see Barry Gerhart and George Milkovich, "Employee Compensation: Research and Practice," in *Handbook of Industrial and Organizational Psychology*, edited by M. Dunnette and L. Hough (Palo Alto, Calif: Consulting Psychologists Press, 1992), pp. 481–569; on human resources practices targeted to specific employee groups, see Paul Ingram and Tal Simon, "Disentangling Resource Dependence and Institutional Explanations of Organizational Practice: The Case of Organization's Adoption of Flextime and Work at Home," *Academy of Management Journal* 38 (1995): 1466–82.

15. Tom Peters, *Liberation Management* (New York: Knopf, 1992).

16. Jone Pearce, Imre Branyiczki, and Greg Bigley. "Insufficient Bureaucracy: Trust and Commitment in Particularistic Organizations," *Organizational Science*, in press; M. Smitka, "Contracting without Contracts: How the Japanese Manage Organizational Transactions," in *The Litigious Organization*, edited by S. Sitkin and R. Bies (Thousand Oaks, Calif.: Sage, 1994), pp. 91–108.

17. S. Macaulay, "An Empirical View of Contracts," *Wisconsin Law Review* (1985): 465–82; Walker, Kogut, and Shan (1997).

18. *USA Today*, August 14, 1996,

19. Bies, The predicament of injustice: the management of moral outrage. In B. M. Staw and L. L. Cummings (editors) *Research in Organizational Behavior* (vol 9, pp. 289–319). Greenwich, CT: JAI Press 1987.

20. Frances Fukuyama, *Trust: The Social Virtues and the Creation of Prosperity* (New York: Free Press, 1995), pp. 102–4.

21. Ronald Burt, "The Contingent Value of Social Capital," *Administrative Science Quarterly* 42 (1997): 339–65.

22. Carrie Leana and Harry Van Buren, "Organizational Social Capital: The Case for Stability," working paper no. 755, Katz School, University of Pittsburgh, 1998.

23. See Fukuyama (1995); Patrick Buchanan, *The Great Betrayal: How American Sovereignty and Social Justice and Sacrificed to the Gods of the Global Economy* (New York: Little, Brown, 1998); Stephen L. Carter, *Civility: Manners, Morals and the Etiquette of Democracy* (New York: Basic Books, 1998).

24. R. Frank and Philip Cook, *The Winner-Take-All Society* (New York: Free Press, 1995).

25. Douglas Cowherd and David Levine, "Product Quality and Pay Equity between Lower-level Employees and Top Management: An Investigation of Distributive Justice Theory," *Administrative Science Quarterly* 37 (1992): 302–20.

26. Thomas Kochan, Harry Katz, and Robert McKersie, *The Transformation of American Industrial Relations* (New York: Basic Books, 1986). See also Fukuyama (1995), p. 226.

27. See Cascio, Young, and Morris (1998); see also Gay Fogarty and Denise Rousseau, "Spillover: The Impact of Downsizing on Psychological Contracts with Subsequent Employers," technical report, Heinz School, Carnegie Mellon University, 1998.

28. Legislation enacted in the 1930s and the 1960s to protect the elderly against destitution is an exception to this general approach.

29. M. Carnoy and M. Castells, *Sustained Flexibility* (Paris: OECD, 1997).

30. See John Sweeney, *America Needs a Raise: Fighting for Economic Security and Social Justice* (New York: Houghton Mifflin, 1996).

31. See Arlie Russell Hochschild, *The Time Bind: When Work Becomes Home and Home Becomes Work* (New York: Metropolitan Books, 1997).

32. James Lardner, "Deadly Disparities: Americans' Widening Gap in Incomes May Be Narrowing Our Life Spans." *Washington Post*, August 16, 1998, p. C1.

33. B. Vobejda, "Too Much Time on the Job Imperils Teens' Future, Panel Says," *Washington Post*, November 6, 1998, p. A3. A. Krueger, "Unemployment Chimera," *Washington Post*, March 6, 1998, p. A25.

34. T. W. Schultze, "The Value of the Ability to Deal with Disequilibria," *Journal of Economic Literature* 13 (1975): 827–46.

35. Rousseau and Libuser (1997).

36. Martin Carnoy and Manuel Castells (1997); Nanette Fondas, "Feminization at Work: Career Implications," in *The Boundaryless Career*, edited

by Michael B. Arthur and Denise M. Rousseau (New York: Oxford University Press, 1996), pp. 282–94.

37. Ronald Burt, personal communication, 1998.

38. See, for example, Frits Pil and John Paul MacDuffie, "The Adoption of High-Involvement Work Practices," *Industrial Relations* 35 (1996): 423–55; and, for a review, Casey Iochniowski, Thomas Kochan, David Levine, C. Olson, and George Strauss, "What Works at Work: Overview and Assessment," *Industrial Relations* 35 (1996): 299–333.

I.

RELATIONAL WEALTH AS COMPETITIVE ADVANTAGE

Traditional models of competitive advantage have stressed the importance, indeed the omnipotence, of market forces in determining firm performance. This perspective has extended to the realm of employment and is evident in how most firms view labor as a variable cost—one that is to be minimized through such practices as using contingent work and poaching workers trained by someone else rather than making the investment oneself. Conventional thinking regarding competitive advantage and market forces is dominated by the pursuit of short-term value and idealizes flexibility through being "asset-less." An alternative approach relies on relational wealth, which accesses a diverse portfolio of human, social, intellectual, and financial assets. The benefits of relational wealth are evident in high-performance workplaces and collaborative customer/supplier networks. Here, strategic thinking regarding competitive advantage stresses long-term value creation by cultivating assets that competitors cannot readily acquire. The chapters in this section discuss these competing models and how they are enacted in firms. All three chapters warn of the dangers for both employees and firms of overreliance on a short-term market focus in employment.

Russell Coff and Denise Rousseau describe how linkages between workers, their coworkers, work settings, and employers create strategic capabilities that are both valuable and difficult to imitate. Traditional notions about economic value focus on discrete assets such as real estate, equipment, or skilled workers. Relational wealth comprises the tacit connections among the more tangible assets of a firms. Readiness of firm members to collaborate with each other or with customers and suppliers is a function not only of individual talent but also of employees' collective experience and mutual familiarity. Employers trusting workers and workers their employers is a necessary condition for collective action of all kinds, from problem solving and the implementation of new technology to adaptation to changing economic conditions. Vital information regarding how to perform in a particular work setting, use specific equipment, or execute a course of action is often idiosyncratic to the context in which knowledge is deployed. Coff and Rousseau describe ways in which the powerful but often unacknowledged economic value embedded in relationships can be developed, deployed, and assessed.

Joseph Ritter and Lowell Taylor help us conceptualize more accurately who the stakeholders are in contemporary firms. They raise questions regarding how current securities and employment laws differently view the claims of various stakeholders to a firm's financial assets. Current laws in the United States favor the investments made by bondholders over those of stockholders, and those of stockholders over those of workers—although all three make some investment in the firm in anticipation of future gains. Through two fables, Ritter and Taylor show how the same logic that led to the rise of junk bonds in the 1980s is applied to employment practices in the 1990s and beyond. A key point in their analysis is that financial markets are human-made, a product of a country's laws, and can be changed as a better understanding of financial obligations and the functioning of incentives emerges.

Gil Preuss discusses market-focused and relational approaches to employment as applied in the health care industry. Knowledge in this setting, as in most others, is distributed across persons and work settings. Successful problem solving requires willing and skilled collaboration among people with different specialties, divergent skills, and often unique information regarding patient condition and care history. Complicating the deployment of collective knowledge in health care is the need for rapid development of communities of practice, able to collaborate in an ongoing fashion while adapting to changing technology, tighter regulation of costs, and increasing patient acuity. He concludes that a relational approach to employment, particularly in the case of nurses, offers opportunities to develop unique competitive advantage with demonstrable benefits for performance.

1

Sustainable Competitive Advantage from Relational Wealth

RUSSELL W. COFF AND DENISE M. ROUSSEAU

You think because you understand one and one equals two
that you understand one. But you must also understand
"and."

—Sufi

Relational wealth can be construed as "soft" in comparison to more concrete "hard" assets such as technology, capital, or even human skills. In
contemporary management thinking and economic decision making, "hard"
assets are valued while other resources are often discounted. We attempt
here to make the nature of seemingly intangible relational wealth more palpable and understandable to scholars and practitioners. We specify forms
that relational wealth can take as well as the contextual factors that give
rise to it. We address how relational wealth, in the form of linkages workers
have with their work settings and firms, constitutes sustainable competitive
advantage. Through theory building, we address specific ways in which
relational wealth is formed within firms and how this wealth helps firms
capitalize on tangible assets such as technology and skills. Our analysis also
raises the question whether relational wealth is as beneficial for employees
as for firms.

Sustainable competitive advantage is increasingly founded on human- or
knowledge-based assets.[1] Strategy research finds competitive advantage embedded in the capabilities of teams and social networks, in part because
these group dynamics are especially difficult to imitate.[2] Even if competitors
know that a firm's strategic capability is built on the linkages among its
people, such ties are so complex and idiosyncratic that they cannot be readily copied. To date strategy research has not examined the specific features
characterizing the competitive advantage inherent in such complex inter-
relationships. Nonetheless, it is clear that the firm benefits greatly from em-

27

ployees' knowledge and skills. Is a sustainable competitive advantage also good for employees? We know that many employees willingly invest their time and effort to build personal networks. One reason for this is that individuals often attain personal advantages such as promotions and pay raises within the firm through such networks.[3] In addition, external networks can help individuals fare better in labor markets that are plagued by poor information regarding either worker competence or job availability. However, we know little about the portability of "soft" assets residing in linkages between people and settings within a firm and how these assets impact worker employability.

This chapter presents a model of how relational wealth is developed and how it may, in turn, generate outcomes for the firm and its members. It highlights the mediating processes that link people to each other and to the firm, leading to the development of relational wealth. We use these mechanisms to detail how relational wealth leads to a sustainable competitive advantage for the firm and how it might also create opportunities for the firm's employees as well as employees outside the firm.

A Model of Relational Wealth

The business strategy literature has left relational wealth largely as a black box. Research to date has not addressed how relational wealth is formed or how it attains the properties that grant it strategic value. Drawing on diverse literatures at the firm, group, and individual levels, we present a model (figure 1.1) of how relational wealth is formed, how it takes on strategic properties, and its ultimate impact on worker employability.

Consider the array of unconnected resources or inputs available to a firm. Inputs that consist of human, physical, and other resources that firms can directly acquire are the independent variables in our framework. These resources might include the firm's inventory of skills (human capital), technology and physical resources (physical capital), and the organizational climate (an aspect of social capital). Although these components might be valuable in and of themselves, they cannot form the basis of a sustainable advantage because rival firms could also acquire these inputs. The firm's strategic capability is built on the interaction of these resources. As Barney notes, "physical technology, whether it takes the form of machine tools or robotics in factories or complex information management systems, is by itself typically imitable."[4] So it is with human assets, which can be hired away, though specialization and tacit knowledge can make newly hired human assets difficult to utilize.[5] These resources can be valuable in and of themselves but their true strategic capability is embedded in their joint interaction.

Conventional thinking may cause firms to attempt to improve their performance by merely increasing one form of asset, such as hiring experienced individuals from another firm. Attempts to attain competitive advantage

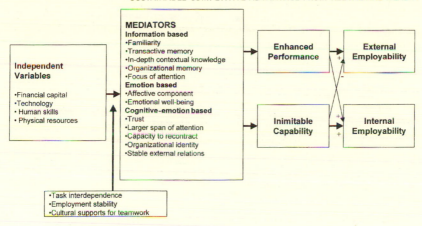

Fig. 1.1. A model of relational wealth, firm performance, and employability

through human capital make sense where jobs are self-contained, short-term, and common across firms. However, such efforts to capture competitive advantage by recruiting "talent" will be insufficient where tasks are interdependent, relatively specific to a firm, and take some time to complete. Task interdependence and firm-specific knowledge give rise to conditions under which relational wealth can emerge through complimentary combinations of human skill, motivation, and organizing, aligned with other physical assets, to create work contexts that only time and experience can produce.

Relational wealth resides in the connections workers have with each other, their work settings and its technology, and the larger work group and firm, where certain linkages facilitate task performance and goal achievement. By its very nature, relational wealth *mediates* among the attributes and capacities of people, groups, and firms (including firms' human and financial capital) and affects successful work coordination, task performance, and goal achievement. For inimitable benefits to accrue from inputs, they must be bound together in an inimitable way. Thus, although hiring talented individuals will not automatically yield relational wealth, acquiring an intact work group or business unit might, if the ways in which group members relate to themselves and others are preserved through the acquisition. The head of Coopers and Lybrand's Madrid office took his entire ninety-person team—one-third of the firm's Spanish operation—with him when he moved to Ernst and Young. Such an acquisition is more than the capture of talent; it brings existing work relations, shared knowledge, and established routines for collaboration beyond anything individuals can provide to a firm in isolation. In effect, such mass movements of personnel suggest that relational wealth is in fact being recognized as a source of competitive advantage.

Because relational wealth comprises connections among organizational components (people and groups), as opposed to the components themselves, it is not always easily observed or measured. Conventional accounting practices typically disaggregate the firm through an economic meat grinder, ignoring relational values in the process of costing out the firm's components. In contrast, relational wealth is embodied in the old saying, "The whole is greater than the sum of its parts." This creates dilemmas when managers and stakeholders cannot understand the nature of the firm's strategic advantage. Because relational wealth resides among internal connections, it may be invisible not only to those outside of the firm but also to internal stakeholders who may not have direct contact with those deploying relational wealth to meet business goals. Shareholders, board members, and even senior executives may have difficulty recognizing the competitive advantage realized by the firm via processes that to them are intangible.

Consider the case of Boeing in the 1990s. Despite the largest surge in aircraft orders in the past half century, Boeing—the airline manufacturer that essentially invented the jet age—posted its first red ink in fifty years ($176 million) in 1997. This loss, coupled with a nearly 30 percent decline in its stock value, occurred despite Boeing's powerful position in the $65 billion world jetliner market. Huge layoffs in the preceding mid-1990s had cost the firm nearly 25 percent of its experienced workers. These layoffs were driven by the desire to cut costs, although Boeing was already the world's lowest cost aircraft producer. The cutbacks drove many of the company's long-time suppliers out of business as well, leading to serious parts shortages when orders eventually increased.[6] After half a century as the world's leading aircraft manufacturer, Boeing is recently unable to fill growing numbers of aircraft orders because of operational problems among its surviving workforce and limited supply networks. What exactly did Boeing give up through mass layoffs and the erosion of its supplier network? We argue that Boeing gave up not only people and suppliers but also the economic value embedded in connections among its people, work groups, and suppliers.

Relational Wealth as a Mediator

Relational wealth is inherent in the connections among individuals, technology, and other tangible resources available to a firm. The firm's basic inputs can become organized into inimitable combinations via three forms of connection: information, emotional, and cognitive-emotional.

Information-based Relational Wealth

The information people possess about equipment, work processes, and each other shapes how a firm's resources are deployed. The time one spends in a particular setting leads to specific knowledge about how *those* persons, *that* equipment, *this* set of procedures, and *these* facilities function together. In particular, work setting–specific knowledge regarding relations can promote easier coordination, eliminate impediments to performance, and reduce errors and instances of unsafe acts. When a firm targets senior employees through layoffs, for example, it can effectively lose a generation of workers who understand how and why certain procedures came about and when they are being applied inappropriately. Laying off large segments of the workforce effectively dissipates setting-specific knowledge regarding interdependence.[7]

Four important cognitions shared by participants in a work setting can give rise to relational wealth: familiarity with the work group, in-depth contextual knowledge of interactions among components of the setting, memory (both transactive and organizational), and focus of attention.

Familiarity

Performance at the individual, group, and organizational level is affected by familiarity, which consists of the information people possess about how to work with a particular group of others. Regularly bringing employees together to perform interdependently affects several organizational outcomes. At the simplest level, people who work together on a regular basis, be it in systems design, production work, or construction, can communicate more efficiently, often in an oral shorthand, making it easier to anticipate what each needs from the other. In coal mining, for example, Goodman and Leyden found that accidents increased on the day when miners who had been absent returned to their work group, as they needed to familiarize themselves with what the group had been doing in their absence and the group needed to readjust to working with them.[8] Likewise, in a highly visible example of concern for familiarity, the American space shuttle program has engaged in a widely publicized debate regarding the wisdom of cutting the number of annual flights from six to three. The focus of this debate is the potential consequences associated with shuttle personnel's loss of familiarity, as well as the difficulty of retaining a critical mass of experienced personnel on the project for only three launches.

One reason that familiarity affects performance is a generic characteristic of newcomers—their dependence on greater information exchanges and more direction to perform effectively, particularly when they work interdependently with others. The presence of newcomers also increases the cognitive burden on their coworkers and supervisors. Moreover, existing mechanisms for performance management (such as performance appraisal processes) may work less well or be inapplicable to newcomers whose managers are unfamiliar with their performance. Yitzhak Fried and his colleagues have found that supervisors are less likely to provide performance reviews and task-related feedback when they are unfamiliar with their subordinates.[9] Familiarity may thus be required for basic organizational mechanisms to function.

In-depth Contextual Knowledge

Both in-depth contextual knowledge and familiarity deal with information regarding a particular work setting, but the depth of knowledge one possesses is an important distinguishing feature. In-depth contextual knowledge refers to specific information about the functions of persons, facilities, and procedures in a particular setting. If a member's absence from work for a few days can create hazards and coordination costs within a work group, as in the case of familiarity, the consequences are more adverse when numerous newcomers are introduced in settings where deep knowledge is required for safe operation and ease of coordination. Consider the frequent experience that office equipment used by only the same few people behaves more reliably than equipment used by many. This commonplace feature of everyday life is taken to a more complex level in dynamic work settings where in-depth knowledge exists regarding not only equipment but also group relations, organizational routines, interactions between technology, and social systems embedded in certain physical settings.

A more complex set of cognitions than familiarity, in-depth contextual knowledge represents deep and often uncodifiable knowledge regarding variability in equipment, the effects of one's behavior on others, and the nuances that must be understood to communicate effectively. Pil and Leana point out in chapter 6 that even general problem-solving or interpersonal skills are more valuable to a firm when learned *in situ*, because training that taps deep knowledge of context is more sustainable and translates more readily into behavior.

Two examples illustrate the effects of the presence and absence of in-depth contextual knowledge.

Loading docks: same facilities, different results. A trucking firm serves the largest chain of supermarkets in Holland (more than 150 stores), deploying almost four hundred truck runs a day based on just-in-time logistics supported by onboard computers. Of the chain's several distribution centers (DCs) stocking trucks for delivery, one stood out: trucks regularly left that DC late, despite having arrived on time. All others met the supermarket chain's standard of 95 percent on-time departure and arrival. Despite comparable technology and facilities, several factors differentiated the low-performing DC from those that met the standards. Although workers at typical DCs averaged more than five years of tenure and turnover was negligible, the average tenure at the low-performing DC was less than one year and turnover was high. Moreover, although managers at other DCs had provided warm, colorful uniforms with their logo and insulated gloves, the low-performing unit had not; its workers wore a variety of street clothing, some with gloves and others without.

The low-performing DC was a source of frustration to the drivers: orders were slow to arrive by cart from storage to the truck, containers were damaged, and not all items listed on the bill of lading were brought to the loading dock. Workers had difficulty loading trucks in a timely fashion, and truckers often had difficulty determining who actually worked on the dock. These delays were met with frustration on the part of the truckers and denial of responsibility by DC personnel. In contrast, workers in high-performing DCs developed relationships with the truck drivers—whom they often knew by name—and were very likely to cooperate with them to solve problems in a friendly way. These DCs had established routines for loading based on preparations made prior to a truck's scheduled arrival, creating a standardized loading process with which both the dock crew and truckers were familiar. Loading dock workers at high-performing DCs were recognizable by the uniforms they wore, replete with the supermarket's logo. The uniforms provided by these DCs were highly insulated, which kept employees warm when working in the refrigerated loading zone and reduced injuries, particularly because of the insulated gloves the DC had provided to the loading crew. Wide disparities in interactions between drivers and loading crews, in degrees of knowledge and experience among loaders regarding the task and work setting, in whether routines for coordinating work existed, and in the capacity and willingness of people to solve problems add up to a considerable difference at the low-performing DC, in contrast to others, in the quality of connections between the firm and workers. In effect, disparities in relational wealth separate the low-performing DC from the rest.[10]

Contract labor: the problem of "strangers on site." The absence of in-depth contextual knowledge has been implicated in the increased accident rates associated with use of contract workers.[11] Workers unfamiliar with a specific setting are more likely to abuse or misuse equipment, leave equipment in inappropriate (and unsafe) places, and fail to advise others of conditions that may create barriers to successful and safe work performance. In construction and production settings where equipment can be moved, site-specific knowledge has been shown to reduce hazards and delays caused when equipment is placed in inappropriate locations. This has been referred to as the "strangers on site" phenomenon: in high-risk workplaces, the presence of people who are strangers to one another can pose a significant danger because of the absence of linkages between those persons and the limited communication and coordination systems that typically characterize work environments with a high influx of strangers: "On the day of the explosion . . . we have five contractors on the worksite in the general area of the explosion, plus the production operators . . . you can't have 15 people being independently responsible" (manager of mining facility).[12] In such cases the whole may indeed be less than the sum of the parts. Firms that create ongoing relations with only a few contractors tend to perform better because of these contractors' greater site-specific knowledge and familiarity with local practices and personnel (consistent with the levels of client involvement among labor intermediaries that Davis-Blake and Broschak describe in chapter 5).

Even when people have in-depth knowledge about their own work setting and work group processes, failure to recognize that contextual knowledge differs from one group to another can have severe consequences for interdependent groups who work together sporadically or on a short-term basis. Following the collapse of a beam that killed a construction worker during the building of a new airport in Pittsburgh, designers and manufacturers realized that they had read the shop drawings differently from the fabricators and inspectors. As an Occupational Safety and Health Administration official noted, all of the engineering plans lacked clarity. What was clear to one group was unclear to another, which had its own methods for representing the work to be done.[13] Together, the examples of the distribution center and the perils associated with using contract labor suggest that in-depth knowledge of setting and personnel comes with frequent contact and interaction, easing coordination and reducing risk of dysfunctional behaviors and averse performance consequences.

Memory

The term "memory" refers to the retention of information and the capacity to access that information when needed. From the perspective of relational wealth, two forms of collective memory can provide competitive advantage: transactive memory and organizational memory. Transactive memory is information retained and accessed by group members regarding the task information coworkers possess ("knowing who knows what") and shared knowledge regarding effective means of organizing work. Moreland and his colleagues find that groups with a history of working together tacitly understand how to coordinate, which improves their collective performance.[14] As people work together, they not only acquire more information about specific tasks but also discover relevant information other group members possess. Moreover, over time, groups appear to learn to make better use of the knowledge individual members possess. Transactive memory constitutes socially shared cognitions that enable members to encode, interpret, and access information together that team members could not individually recall.

Transactive memory reduces coordination costs, shortens the time required to do work, and improves the quality of that work. It has been observed in work groups assembling everything from radios to origami in laboratory studies, producing fast food in pizza franchises, and manufacturing industrial products in factory shift work. Replacing workers due to turnover, absenteeism, leaves of absence, and transfers can disrupt transactive memory, because newcomers generally know less than old-timers about the group's task and because newcomers and old-timers are unfamiliar with one another's abilities and interests. Even when turnover or personnel leaves do not introduce new members, transactive memory may be disrupted. Evidence indicates that each group member may specialize in recalling a different aspect of the task. Task coordination practices based on a group with one complement of members may work less well when one or more of those members are not present.[15]

Another form of collectively retained and accessed information is organizational memory, where organizations store knowledge about their prior experiences for future use. Recent advances in information technologies have enabled the creation of electronic networks that can store large amounts of information. However, to a great extent people appear to underutilize electronic systems and instead rely on two traditional sources for information—established routines and procedures and, of course, other people.[16] Organizational memory depends on there being some degree of continuity in personnel and stability in coordination mechanisms over time. There are many ways to store collective information for future use, from paper files to technology to team member memories. Their joint effect is to facilitate coordination, reduce transaction costs, and preserve knowledge for future use (as in the case of the thirty-year flood described in chapter 1).

One particularly important application of collective memory is in crisis management. Peter Senge has argued that people are more likely to respond appropriately to rare events when they are able to draw on past experience.[17] The importance of collective memory is often more evident when it is absent, and failure to remember historical responses to infrequent events can lead to costly errors. Responses to hazardous situations or crises are more appropriate where members share memory regarding previous occurrence of such low-frequency events.

Focus of Attention

When members of a collective share an understanding of common goals, a focus of attention emerges that can create synergistic behaviors among persons and groups. This shared focus is enhanced by dense networks, in which people have close ongoing relations with those around them. The impact of dense networks on focus of attention is manifest in a common feature of many intensive socialization experiences: the isolation of newcomers from outside influences, as in the case of monasteries and boot camps. Indeed, developmental psychologists have argued that dense networks and the focus of attention they offer at the expense of other influences are what intact families and community supports provide to children. When these close networks are present, children are less likely to engage in dysfunctional behavior, such as drug use or truancy. In the workplace, focus of attention reduces costly distractions, lowering transaction costs and easing coordination. If carried to the extreme, however, dense networks can inhibit adaptability.

Cap Gemini, an information technology (IT) consulting firm based in Europe, regularly brings new recruits and experienced consultants together for group activities that build their social relations with each other. Articulating a common value system emphasizing innovation, development, and community, which supports a project management process followed world wide by its consultants, increases the likelihood that Cap Gemini employees will agree on priorities and be able to work cooperatively with each other as well as with clients.

An individual's capacity to focus attention on numerous goals simultaneously is constrained. (Variations of short-term memory's "7-plus-or-minus-2" rule have been offered as one explanation of limited focus of attention.) For effective collective action, the firm that captures the focus of individuals and groups via a shared set of specific goals is likely to be more successful than a firm whose members have no collective goals.

Implications

Relational wealth derives from the existence of a relatively stable collective, with continuity of membership and repeated interactions over time. Some level of attrition and recruitment may aid group learning and refresh communication and socialization among team members. However, radical changes in the collective's composition in a short period of time may erode its relational wealth.

Emotion-based Relational Wealth

Shared experiences of personal connectedness and psychological security reflect linkages among persons, groups, and the organization that are emotional or affective in nature. Affective attachments have the advantage of being resistant to many forms of instability. People and groups with emotional attachments are more likely to stay together through economic setbacks and other tough times. Similarly, when conflicts occur, people with high attachment are more likely to remain with the firm if good faith efforts are made to resolve conflicts.[18] In contrast, those with less attachment are more likely to quit without seeking to resolve disputes. Two forms of emotion-based relational wealth are affective commitment and emotional well-being.

Affective Commitment

This type of commitment occurs when individuals and groups accept and adhere to common organizational values. When affective commitment is part of the tie that binds persons and groups to the firm, we observe higher rates of discretionary behaviors that are aligned with the firm's interests, including citizenship behavior, higher quality of service and innovation.[19] These voluntary contributions to the firm—essentially performance beyond expectations—are made without the explicit promise of rewards (such as pay increases) or the strict requirements of formal control mechanisms (such as managerial directives). In effect, the firm receives the benefit of a workforce that "goes the extra mile" without having to be forced or incented to do it.

Emotional Well-being

This frequently overlooked dimension of relational wealth refers to the psychological comfort people derive from connectedness and psychological security. A sense of emotional well-being, particularly when shared by a group, reduces adverse reactions to external stressors such as job demands or competitive pressures.[20] The widespread presumption that people have an infinite capacity for change, manifested in the works of popular writers such as Kanter and Handy, flies in the face of evidence that nearly all transitions, from job loss to role change, can be experienced as stressful.[21] High levels of stress have been found to impair performance, memory, problem solving, and behavioral flexibility.[22] Firms that manage change in ways that protect their employees' emotional well-being are in effect protecting both their relationship and their investment.

Implications

Emotion-based linkages among people and firms are robust in the face of many forms of instability from internal organizational conflicts to economic downturns. However, these linkages are impaired by high rates of job insecurity and turnover. Cultivating an attachment to one's firm and coworkers can make an employee resilient in the face of turbulence as well as promote greater and voluntary contributions to the firm.

Cognitive-Emotional-based Relational Wealth

Emotional factors are closely intertwined with beliefs and perceptions. At the heart of the intersection of cognitive and emotional processes is trust.

Trust

Individuals exhibit trust when they are willing to be vulnerable to the intentions and actions of another.[23] Trust has many bases and forms; when it links people and groups to firms, it generally makes it possible for workers to willingly contribute their efforts to the firm without expecting an immediate payout and increases the extent to which the firm's managers can rely on their workers to have the firm's interests at heart (and vice versa). Not surprisingly, employee trust in the organization's manager has been found to be directly related to sales and profitability and inversely related to employee turnover.[24] Trust has the added advantage of increasing the workers' capacity for change by reducing the uncertainty and psychic discomfort from change that otherwise impair individual and group adaptability.[25]

Capacity to Recontract

This concept refers to the potential to change an existing relationship (i.e., "changing the deal while keeping the people"[26]). Recontracting is particularly crucial in firms that need new or greater performance contributions from their workforce. It is a form of relational wealth because recontracting is only possible where there is collective belief that the firm and its managers are trustworthy. Such beliefs enhance change recipients' perceptions that managers have provided appropriate information regarding the reasons for change and have taken employee interests into account.

Larger Focus of Attention

Focus of attention in this context refers to the number of goals pursued at one time. When employees have greater psychological comfort and shared understandings with coworkers, they are better able to pursue several performance goals simultaneously. It is widely observed that little work gets done in organizations during turbulent times, where abrupt changes in top management have occurred or in the midst of layoffs. When workers feel secure and able to trust, their focus of attention widens, enhancing firm flexibility and performance. High stress levels, in contrast, result in narrower attention spans.[27]

One central quality of high-performing firms is their capacity to achieve multiple, simultaneous goals instead of only a single goal. Thus, firms such as Xerox or General Electric tend to pursue several goals (e.g., market share, return on assets, customer satisfaction, and employee satisfaction) in contrast with firms that have a more limited capacity to focus their members' attention. Firms that pursue more discrete short-term cost-cutting measures or concentrate on enhancing shareholder value at the expense of innovation or long-term growth may develop a highly distressed workforce with a relatively narrow focus of attention.

Identity

When a member's sense of self incorporates his or her relationship with the firm, this expanded self creates a psychological state, at once cognitive and affective, where one believes oneself to be part of a larger whole. Member identification with the firm can be a driving force behind its performance, worker well-being, and resilience (of both firm and workers) in times of change.[28] Identification generates greater willingness to cooperate, makes people responsive to nonpecuniary rewards such as praise and reputation, and generally enhances willingness to pursue collective interests over personal ones.[29] Recall the distribution center example earlier, in which something that seemed simple—the wearing of company uniforms—conveyed to the drivers which people worked for the firm and were there to help them, while reinforcing in the workers' minds their membership in the firm. Mechanisms signaling a sense of "we" as opposed to "I" enhance identification with a group or firm, and such beliefs are likely to be shared among members of a social unit.

Stable Relations

Firms benefit when they build ongoing relationships over time with external constituents (such as customers and suppliers). The trust reflected in these relationships is linked to greater market knowledge and specific information on customer/supplier needs, which can lead to financial benefit.[30] Firms building stable customer/supplier relations obtain the benefits of collaboration, including joint participation in design and cost-containment activities.[31] In a study of upscale dress firms within the New York apparel industry, firms with close ties to their subcontractors had higher survival rates than firms that maintained arm's-length relations with subcontractors.[32] Subcontractors, who might perform discrete tasks from making patterns to cutting fabric to sewing dresses, benefited the firm (and themselves) by maintaining close ties such that information is exchanged in a proprietary, detailed, and tacit way. Constant communication was the norm in such close relations among apparel firms, entailing anything from exchanging information on costs or profit margins to sharing knowhow regarding technical activities. The ability to solve problems "on the fly" was also more common in close relations. Not surprisingly, the closest relationships observed typically were between individuals who had long relationships with their respective firms as well as with each other.

Implications

Cognitive-emotional linkages, like those stemming from information and emotion separately, are sensitive to member mobility and attrition, may enhance resilience in times of change, and can create competitive advantage for a firm.

From an organizational perspective, all three types of mediators directly affect the capacity to enhance firm performance and achieve a greater number of goals. They also increase the chance of meeting existing goals and doing so reliably, without unintended dysfunctional consequences such as operational errors or accidents.

All of these mechanisms provide competitive advantage when certain boundary conditions are met. First, task interdependence must exist, creating the need to coordinate among persons and groups. Second, competitive advantage is enhanced when variable task conditions (equipment, work processes, setting characteristics) make coordination more difficult. When task interdependence and variability exist, linking the firm's tangible assets through the mechanisms constituting relational wealth increases worker and work group effectiveness, as well as the capacity of the firm to implement change with the workforce it has.

The Role of Relational Wealth in Creating a Sustainable Competitive Advantage

Sustainable competitive advantage, a critical dependent variable in our model of relational wealth, is increasingly attributable to a firm's unique resources.[33] This attribution marks a significant shift from past theories that have focused on market positioning and industry structure to explain competitive advantage.[34] For relational wealth to lead to sustainable competitive advantage, two criteria must be met. First, the relational wealth must lead to some capability that improves the firm's economic performance. Second, that capability must not be available to other firms, or the advantage would not be sustainable. Improvements to a firm's competitive performance enhance its market position by either differentiating the firm in the eyes of customers or making it a low-cost producer. Examples of capabilities that help differentiate a firm might include superior customer service, unique product design, or excellent quality. Examples of capabilities that lower costs might include engineering for low-cost manufacturing or Internet-based customer service that minimizes labor costs.

Barney identifies three factors that hinder imitation: firm specificity, causal ambiguity, and social complexity (which we define as an essential aspect of relational wealth).[35] Firm-specific resources often arise from unique historical conditions, which mean that rivals cannot obtain the resources in competitive markets.[36] Causal ambiguity refers to situations in which the causal link between the resource and performance is unknown or not well understood.[37] Here, competitors cannot even identify what they should try to imitate. Finally, socially complex resources consist of social networks and broader linkages between persons and the firm that underlie a firm's strategic capability. The complexity of these resources makes them very hard to duplicate even if a competitor knows that they are the source of a firm's success. Social complexity can be the essence of relational wealth.

The Performance Implications of Relational Wealth

To some extent we outlined the performance implications of relational wealth in the previous section. Information-based relational wealth enhances performance by assuring that task-relevant knowledge is stored and later recalled when and where it is needed. Emotion-based relational wealth enhances performance because those who are emotionally bound to the firm are more likely to go above and beyond the requirements of their jobs and to remain with the firm through turbulence. This level of commitment, when broadly shared by employees, allows the firm to accomplish more with the resources it has. Finally, cognitive-emotional relational wealth also helps enhance firm performance. The existence of trust, organizational identification, and the capacity to recontract help the firm respond to a dynamic environment. That is, the relational wealth may help employees tolerate the changes that are required to periodically reconfigure the organization. This also should yield performance advantages for the firm by enabling it to retain competent people and redeploy existing resources toward new strategic goals.

Keeping Capability from Rivals

The second property of a strategic capability, keeping it from rivals, has not been studied with respect to relational wealth. There are three ways that rivals can obtain a capability: (1) acquire it in competitive markets; (2) imitate it, or (3) acquire a substitute that is strategically equivalent. Relational wealth has properties that prevent all of these mechanisms, as follows.

Relational Wealth Cannot Be Easily Acquired

Although some firms may attempt to acquire relational wealth by poaching talented individuals from competing firms, hiring people and acquiring the relational wealth they helped create elsewhere are not quite the same thing. Suppose a firm has an advantage arising from the relationships and communication channels developed within its integrated product design and manufacturing team. Even if a rival were to hire away a talented team member, that firm would find it difficult to duplicate the original success because the relationships that play a crucial role were embedded in the idiosyncratic nature of the original firm and its employees—and there they remain. In other words, a new network of relationships must be formed, which will be specific to the rival's organization and employees.

Networked employees: "stars" need not apply. A production process is socially complex when the product is greater than the sum of separable resources that are not owned by a single person.[38] Competitors will find it hard to duplicate an advantage if it results from a collection of valuable firm-specific complementary resources embedded in personal relationships.[39] A competitive advantage is more sustainable when it does not depend heavily on one person, because if one "star" individual understands and can recreate the network of relationships in another firm, there is an incentive to hire that person away. The capability must be embedded in linkages among persons and the firm in a way that makes it difficult to move or recreate those networks in another firm.

This implication is counterintuitive in some sense because its suggests that a firm that wants to create sustainable competitive advantage should not try to acquire the very best talent in a given technical area. However, we are not suggesting that firms hire mediocre employees—instead, they should develop, acquire, and maintain highly skilled individuals willing to fit into a complex social network rather than cultivating superstars who may prefer to work alone.

Acquiring teams and firms. Although it is not generally possible to duplicate a capability by hiring individuals, it may be possible to acquire relational wealth by acquiring teams, divisions, or even entire firms. Nevertheless, there remains a question of whether the acquired relational wealth can be integrated with the rest of the firm. As described earlier, relational wealth is context-specific and requires supporting systems and values that may not be present in the acquiring firm. One example of a successful transfer of such wealth is the case of Ernst and Whinney and Arthur Young, two accounting firms that merged to form Ernst and Young in 1989. Similar values and professional standards, coupled with a relatively high retention of people, led to rapid integration of the firms and a net gain in which the whole was greater than the sum of its parts. Similarly, the merger of Carnegie Institute of Technology with Mellon College of Science in 1968 enabled two independent academic organizations to successfully form Carnegie Mellon University. This unified whole was achieved by levering the disciplinary differences and comparable academic values and norms comprising the formerly independent colleges. In contrast, the difficulty—and ultimate failure—of other mergers or acquisitions, such as Dart Kraft or IBM Rolm, may be due to failure to integrate each firm's distinct forms of social complexity.

There are two caveats regarding the difficulty in acquiring relational wealth. First, poaching firms can in fact cause real damage to a competitor. When significant numbers of employees are hired away from a firm, it can erode the cognitive and emotional ties linking members to the firm, its external stakeholders (customers and suppliers), and one another. Second, where external networks play a larger role than internal factors in generating the firm's capability, a rival luring key employees away might gain access to their external ties in the process. Unlike internal connections among people and the firm, these external contacts might yield valuable industry information that applies to the rival as well as the original firm (e.g., client lists). If the contacts are with customers, the employee might even be able to coax customers to follow him or her to the rival firm.

Relational Wealth Cannot Be Imitated

Imitation requires a deep understanding of the underlying dynamics of the capability. This deep understanding of a given firm's relational wealth may be difficult to come by. Critical information embedded within a firm typically includes skills and routines that are specific to particular people and the setting in which they work. The emotional and cognitive-emotional aspects are tied to specific interpersonal relationships and broader worker attachments to the firm. Relational wealth is based on socially complex resources that permeate the organization and are not easy to identify without directly contacting organization members. The subtleties of these complex networks are all but invisible to observers who do not participate in the process. Put another way, relational wealth is both tacit and firm-specific and so rivals cannot duplicate it in another context.

Relational Wealth May Have
No Strategic Substitutes

A capability cannot yield a sustained advantage if rivals have access to a comparable strategic substitute. For example, a specialized information system is only an advantage if it surpasses all options available to competitors. It is generally not worthwhile for most firms to develop specialized word processing software, given the quality of alternatives available.

In the case of relational wealth, the linkages among members and the firm—along with the context within which they are embedded—are unique. The resulting capability should surpass generic alternatives available to the firm and its rivals.[40] This is especially true of the generic resources (physical technology, general human skills, capital) available in external markets. In order to achieve an acceptable substitute, rivals would actually have to develop their own form of relational wealth internally. Given that relational wealth must be developed over time, a competitor cannot create it quickly, if at all. Therefore, firms that achieve an advantage based on relational wealth are likely to sustain that advantage over time.

Internal and External Employability

As the preceding discussion illustrates, relational wealth holds great promise as a source of sustainable competitive advantage. Yet the question remains whether relational wealth is as advantageous to workers as it is to firms. A major concern is its impact on worker employability. To address this issue we must distinguish between internal and external mobility. As we will show, the form of relational wealth that leads to a sustainable advantage has a distinct impact on the two types of mobility.

Internal Employability

Internal employability includes both job retention and internal mobility. Other things being equal relational wealth is derived from stable employment, which in turn enhances internal mobility. Internal mobility refers to both lateral and vertical movements within the organization, as reflected in opportunities for promotions and lateral job changes. The types of network ties that lead to a strategic capability may provide employees with some very significant internal opportunities. First, a rapidly growing firm with a sustainable competitive advantage should create more opportunities for employees as it expands. The fact that the relational wealth grants the firm a unique strategic capability also creates new internal opportunities and challenges for employees.

Second, employees benefit from the fact that an advantage is hard to imitate because it relies on relational wealth. This means that the firm cannot easily go to external labor markets to fill important positions. Outside hires would face a steep learning curve as they tried to develop the internal networks required by the job. Because existing employees already have a series of personal networks, they may have a better chance to assume internal positions that open up.[41] As such, the very relational wealth that creates a strategic capability helps employees take an active role in finding new opportunities within the firm. Firms leveraging relational wealth in the marketplace offer stable employment and greater development opportunities, often positioning themselves as employers of choice.

External Employability

External employability is a more complex problem, and it is hard to predict what the net effect of relational wealth will be on employability outside of a firm. First, the fact that a capability is hard to imitate means that an individual's knowledge and skills may have limited applicability in another firm. This is especially true of relational wealth because many interpersonal relationships cannot transfer to the new firm. In this case, many of an employee's skills cannot be applied in another firm and in themselves do not generate external employment opportunities.

We normally think that the types of networks that enhance outside job offers include contacts at other companies. However, most forms of relational wealth entail internal contacts and embed workers more tightly into their current employer. Thus employees who participate in generating high relational wealth for a firm may themselves possess fewer external contacts than those in firms where relational wealth is lower.

In contrast, the enhanced performance caused by the successful cultivation of relational wealth can send potential employers a positive signal regarding worker capabilities. For example, Microsoft programmers probably have little difficulty finding jobs after having been associated with a "winner." This might be the case even though much of an employee's programming knowledge and relational wealth is specific to Microsoft Corporation and cannot be readily applied in another firm. Nonetheless workers with firm-specific skills may have less external mobility through skill transference, but individuals who possess skills in building relational wealth, such as managers of high-performing units, may be more likely to reap employment opportunities elsewhere.

On balance, the positive signal of being associated with a winner probably outweighs concerns that one's knowledge and skills cannot be applied in a new context. Even if an individual's tacit knowledge cannot transfer to a new employer, the ability to function in and perhaps to build a socially complex setting may be sufficiently rare and valuable that other employers are willing and anxious to take a risk.

Not All Turnover Is Bad

As we conclude this discussion of the value of relational wealth to firms and to workers, it is important to reaffirm the boundaries of our argument. First, we must reiterate that the benefits of relational wealth accrue in firms with highly interdependent work. Thus, firms with highly interdependent teams of production workers have greater prospect for relational wealth—and more adverse consequences from attrition—than do firms where individuals may work on separate projects (indeed, universities with research professors working independently of each other are prime examples of low relational wealth environments, despite the existence of tenure). Second, when firms depend on repeated business with the same customers or suppliers, relational wealth resides in those external relationships. Firms that sell uniform commodities or have few dedicated suppliers reap little external advantage from relational wealth. Finally, under truly turbulent market conditions where virtually no advantage can be sustained in the face of economic uncertainty, relational wealth and other firm-specific assets may offer little economic value. In the rest of the world market, where people work interdependently and firms can accumulate distinct knowledge to position themselves in a dynamic but not totally chaotic marketplace, tremendous competitive advantage resides in the intangible, often invisible, connections that constitute relational wealth.

Conclusion

Our purpose in this essay was to link the concept of relational wealth to the competitive strategy literature, specify the mechanisms that comprise relational wealth, and to explore the resulting implications for employee mobility. We have demonstrated how relational wealth can lead to strategic capabilities that are both valuable and hard to imitate. We have also addressed the question of employability, examining whether the types of networks that form the basis of a sustainable advantage can also help employees enhance their own opportunities. Internal opportunities are clearly enhanced, because the strategic capability that relational wealth provides increases the odds that such opportunities will emerge. Nonetheless, external employability is more difficult to predict. The types of resources based on relational wealth are not easily transported to other firms, unless a critical mass of employees are acquired by another firm. However, being associated with a labor-market "winner" can help individual employees find alternative employment. We conclude that the forms of relational wealth that lead to a sustainable advantage also enhance overall employability while promoting employment stability. Relational wealth, then, creates truly win-win conditions for firms and employees.

Notes

1. J. B. Barney, "Firm Resources and Sustained Competitive Advantage." *Journal of Management* 17 (1991): 99–120.

2. Actually, the term used in the strategy literature is "social complexity." Its meaning bears a striking similarity to "relational wealth" as used in this book; however, relational wealth is conceptualized more systematically in light of behavioral research. Thus, we use the more richly articulated concept of relational wealth here.

3. R. S. Burt, "The Contingent Value of Social Capital," *Administrative Science Quarterly* 42, 2 (1997): 339–65. F. Luthans, S. A. Rosenkrantz, and H. W. Hennessey, "What Do Successful Managers Really Do? An Observation Study of Managerial Activities," *Journal of Applied Behavioral Science* 21, 3 (1985): 255–70.

4. Barney (1991), p. 110.

5. S. A. Lippman and R. P. Rumelt, "Uncertainty in Inimitability: An Analysis of Interfirm Differences in Efficiency under Competition," *Bell Journal of Economics* 13 (1982): 418–38. M. Polanyi, *The Tacit Dimension* (Garden City, NY: Doubleday, 1966). D. Teece, "Toward an Economic Theory of the Multiproduct Firm," *Journal of Economic Behavior and Organization* 3, 1 (1982): 38–63.

6. J. Greenwald, "Is Boeing Out of Its Spin?" *Time*, July 13, 1998, pp. 67–69; H. W. Jenkins, "Boeing's Trouble: Not Enough Monopolistic Arrogance?" *Wall Street Journal*, December 16, 1998, p. A23. *International Directory of Company Histories*, vol. 10, edited by Paula Kepos (Detroit: St. James Press, 1995).

7. A. K. Mishra and G. M. Spreitzer, "Explaining How Survivors Respond to Downsizing: The Role of Trust, Empowerment, Justice and Work Redesign," *Academy of Management Review* 23 (1998): 567–88.

8. P. S. Goodman and D. Leyden, "Familiarity and Group Performance," *Journal of Applied Psychology* 76 (1991): 578–86.

9. Y. Fried, R. B. Tieg, and A. R. Bellamy, "Personal and Interpersonal Predictors of Supervisor Avoidance of Evaluating Subordinates," *Journal of Applied Psychology* 77 (1992): 462–68.

10. D. Gobits, "Performance Management in Distribution Centers," class project, Heinz School of Public Policy and Management, Carnegie Mellon University, 1998.

11. J. C. Wells, T. A. Kochan, and M. Smith, "Managing Workforce Safety and Health: The Case of Contract Labor in the U.S. Petrochemical Industry," Beaumont TX: John Gray Institute, 1991; L. L. Rethi and E. A. Barrett, "A Summary of Injury Data for Independent Contractor Employees in the

Mining Industry from 1983 through 1990," U.S. Department of the Interior, Bureau of Mines, Informational Circular 9344, 1993.

12. D. Conaway, "Panel Discussion on Independent Contractors," in *Proceedings from the Twenty-fifth Annual Institute on Mining Health, Safety, and Research*, edited by G. Tinney, A. Bacho, and M. Karmis, 1995, p. 160.

13. "Eight Firms Fined in Two Fatal Midfield Terminal Accidents," *Pittsburgh Press*, January 30, 1994; For more discussion see D. M. Rousseau and C. Libuser, "Contingent Workers in High-risk Environments," *California Management Review* 39, 2 (1997): 103–23.

14. R. L. Moreland, L. Argote, and R. Krishnan, "Socially Shared Cognition at Work: Transactive Memory and Group Performance," in *What's Social about Social Cognition? Research on Socially Shared Cognition in Small Groups*, edited by J. L. Nye and A. M. Brower (Thousand Oaks, Calif.: Sage, 1996), pp. 57–84.

15. Ibid.

16. P. S. Goodman and E. Darr, "Exchanging Best Practices through Computer-aided Systems," *Academy of Management Executive* 10 (1996): 7–19.

17. P. M. Senge, *The Fifth Discipline: The Art and Practice of the Learning Organization* (New York: Doubleday, 1990).

18. S. L. Robinson and D. M. Rousseau, "Violating the Psychological Contract: Not the Exception but the Norm," *Journal of Organizational Behavior* 15 (1994): 245–59.

19. L. Van Dyne and J. A. LePine, "Helping and Voice Extra-role Behaviors: Evidence of Construct and Predictive Validity," *Academy of Management Journal* 41 (1998): 108–19.

20. C. A. Heaney, J. S. House, B. A. Israel, and R. P. Mero, The Relationship of Organizational and Social Coping Resources to Employee Coping Behavior: A Longitudinal Analysis. *Work and Stress* (1995), 9, 416–431.

21. R. M. Kanter, *When Giants Learn to Dance* (New York: Simon and Schuster, 1989). C. B. Handy, *Age of Unreason* (London: Hutchinson, 1989). R. H. Price and R. Hooijberg, "Organizational Exit Pressures and Role Stress: Impact on Mental Health," *Journal of Organizational Behavior* 13 (1992): 641–51.

22. B. M. Staw, L. Sandelands, and J. Dutton, "Threat-rigidity Effects in Organizational Behavior: A Multilevel Analysis," *Administrative Science Quarterly* 26 (1981): 501–24.

23. R. Mayer, D. Schoorman, and J. Davis, "An Integrative Model of Organizational Trust," *Academy of Management Review* 20 (1995): 709–34.

24. Ibid.

25. D. M. Rousseau and S. A. Tijoriwala, "What's a Good Reason to Change? Motivated Reasoning and Social Accounts in Organizational Change," *Journal of Applied Psychology 84* (1999): 514–528.

26. D. M. Rousseau, "Changing the Deal while Keeping the People," *Academy of Management Executive* 10, 1 (1996): 50–61.

27. Staw, Sandelands, and Dutton (1981).

28. R. P. Castanias and C. E. Helfat, "Managerial Resources and Rents," *Journal of Management* 17, 1 (1991):155–71. R. S. Weiss, *Staying the Course: The Emotional and Social Lives of Men Who Do Well at Work* (NY: Free Press, 1990).

28. J. Pfeffer, *Competitive Advantage Through People: Problems and Prospects for Change* (Boston: Harvard Business School Press, 1994).

29. J. S. Coleman, *Foundations of Social Theory* (Cambridge: Harvard University Press, 1990).

30. M. Fichman and P. S. Goodman, "Customer-Supplier Ties in Interorganizational Relations," in *Research on Organizational Behavior* 18 (Greenwich, Conn.: JAI Press, 1996), pp. 285–331.

31. A. K. Mishra, "Organizational Responses to Crisis: The Centrality of Trust," in *Trust in Organizations: Frontiers of Theory and Research*, edited by R. M. Kramer and T. R. Tyler (Thousand Oaks, Calif.: Sage, 1966), pp. 261–87; B. A. Gutek, *The Dynamics of Service: Reflections on the Changing Nature of Customer Provider Interactions* (San Francisco: Jossey-Bass, 1995).

32. B. Uzzi, "The Sources and Consequences of Embeddedness for the Economic Performance of Organizations: The Network Effect," *American Sociological Review* 61 (1996): 674–98.

33. B. Wernerfelt, "A Resource-Based View of the Firm," *Strategic Management Journal* 5 (1984): 171–80.

34. M. E. Porter, *Competitive Strategy* (New York: Free Press, 1980).

35. Barney (1991).

36. R. Amit and P. J. H. Schoemaker, "Strategic Assets and Organizational Rent," *Strategic Management Journal* 14, 1 (1993): 33–46.

37. Lippman and Rumelt (1982).

38. A. A. Alchian and H. Demsetz, "Production, Information Costs, and Economic Organization," *American Economic Review* 62 (1972): 777–95. P. Milgrom and J. Roberts, *Economics, Organization, and Management* (Englewood Cliffs, N.J.: Prentice-Hall, 1992).

39. D. Teece, G. Pisano, and T. Shuen, "Dynamic Capabilities and Strategic Management," *Strategic Management Journal* 18, 7 (1997): 509–33.

40. I. Nonaka, "A Dynamic Theory of Knowledge Creation," *Organization Science* 5, 1 (1994): 14–37.

41. Burt (1997).

2

Are Employees Stakeholders?

Corporate Finance Meets the Agency Problem

JOSEPH A. RITTER AND LOWELL J. TAYLOR

This chapter tells two economic tales that appear at first glance to be unrelated to one another and, more generally, unrelated to the theme of this book. The first of these stories focuses on how the fortunes of one firm's owners and creditors can be radically and unexpectedly affected—for better or worse—by the actions of an outside investor with deep pockets. The second is about agency theory, the musings of neoclassical economists about how a firm's manager might motivate workers to pursue the best interest of the firm. These two stories share a striking similarity of logic, and we juxtapose them to highlight aspects of the first tale that usually escape attention in discussions of the second. In particular, workers can be subject to the same vagaries of opportunistic corporate finance trends and management fashion that bedeviled debt-holders during the wave of leveraged buyouts in the 1980s.

Both stories have interesting and important lessons that may not necessarily be well known beyond the tribe of scholars who pass them on to students in their finance and economics courses. Presentation of these stories side by side clarifies the nature of relational wealth within firms, specifically the role of workers as potential stakeholders in their organizations.

A Fable of Corporate Finance: How to Make a Fortune without Creating Value

Our tale begins with a business venture that holds considerable promise for generating cash flow one year hence, although the firm operates in a risky environment and could just as easily go bankrupt. As one might imagine, the investors and creditors have a wide range of concerns, including the changing cost structure of the firm's production, the unforeseeable responses of competitors, the vagaries of management decisions, and many other factors that are difficult to assess. However, the story is easier to tell if we imagine that the circumstances of this firm are extraordinarily (and unrealistically) simple.

The situation is this: the firm holds a patent that gives it production rights to a product in perpetuity. The firm also has all of the physical assets—the buildings, machinery, and so forth—that are necessary to carry out a projected flow of production. These assets can be sold for a fair market value of $55 million should the firm go bankrupt. At present it is unknown whether the product will be successful; this will become apparent in a year's time. If it is successful, the firm will generate $12 million profit per year indefinitely. If the product is unsuccessful, the firm will fold. Everyone involved, including participants in financial markets, agrees with this assessment. They also agree that the prospects of success or failure are exactly fifty-fifty.

We might ask a class to calculate how much this firm is worth to risk-neutral investors who can find elsewhere a perfectly safe investment that promises a return of 10 percent. If the firm is found to be successful in the coming year, it will generate $12 million profit annually and will thus be worth $132 million next year.[1] Since the risk-free rate is 10 percent, the present value of this outcome is $120 million. If the firm is unsuccessful, the firm will be worth $55 million; the present value of this outcome is $50 million. Because the probability of each outcome is 0.5, the firm is valued at $85 million.[2]

In answering our question about the value of the firm, we did not need to know *anything* about how the firm financed its venture. To tell our story, though, it helps if we specify how the value of the firm might be allocated among creditors and shareholders. Here's one possibility. The firm has issued 400,000 one-year bonds that will each pay $110 next year. In addition, the firm has 1 million shares of common stock, or equity. The important distinction between debt and equity, from an investor's point of view, is the order in which creditors will be paid in the event the firm is dissolved. If the firm goes bankrupt, it has a legal obligation to repay debt first. It does this by distributing any available funds to bondholders, up to the full $110 face value, if possible. Equity holders are residual claimants who must wait in line behind the bondholders and may end up with nothing when a firm goes under.

Notice that in our example the firm's bonds are a perfectly safe investment. Even if the firm goes bankrupt, it will be worth $55 million, which is greater than the $44 million face value of all the bonds. Since the bonds are risk free, the market rate of return on them will be 10 percent, and their current market value is $100. Thus, the 400,000 bonds raised $40 million for the firm.

Having settled this, it is easy to see that the firm's common stock must sell for $45 a share. How can we be sure? There are two ways to check. First, from a shareholder's perspective, there are two equally likely possibilities. If the firm goes bankrupt next year, $11 million gets allocated to the 1 million outstanding shares. ($11 million is what is left of the $55 million scrap value after bondholders are paid the $44 million that is owed to them.) This is $11 per share next year, or a present value of $10. On the other hand, if the firm is successful and shareholders want to maintain the same financial structure, they will continue to roll over the debt, paying $4 million per year in interest. Thus, shareholders collectively own two-thirds of the flow of net revenue, a total of $8 million, or $8 per share, indefinitely. The present value per share of this circumstance is $80. The value of a share is the average of these two potential outcomes ($10 and $80) so the price must be $45. Second, more directly, recall that our financial markets are comprised of well-informed risk-neutral investors, all of whom agree on the fundamental prospects of the firm—that is, they agree that the value of the firm is $85 million. The bonds are worth $40 million, so the value of the stock must be $45 million, or $45 per share.

Now comes the interesting part of the story—the part in which someone makes a lot of money without creating any value. Suppose a financier with deep pockets targets this firm for a leveraged buyout. The financier offers to pay stockholders $50 per share, a healthy premium over the agreed-on fair-market value of $45. The clever part of this scheme is the way in which money is raised to cover the purchase. The financier issues 600,000 bonds on exactly the same terms as the bonds the firm already issued.[3] If the firm is successful, both the old and new bonds will pay their face value of $110 next year. The present value of this outcome is $100 per bond. But if the firm fails, the bondholders will get a return of only $55 per bond: the $55 million scrap value of the firm divided by the total number of bonds, which is now 1,000,000. The present value of this latter outcome is $50. These high-risk "junk bonds" will sell for $75, equal to the average of the two outcomes. Note that the investor's $75 is buying a risky promise of $110, a return of nearly 47 percent. The higher potential return compensates investors for the risk of a capital loss should the firm fail. After the financier tenders this offer, the firm has become very highly leveraged. Still, the firm's overall value has not changed, because its "fundamentals"—including its likelihood of success and ability to generate a steady cash flow with its product—are not affected by transactions made in the financial markets. However, there are winners and losers as a consequence of the leveraged buyout.

Let's think about the winners. First, there are the owners of the firm's equity. Out of the blue, they are presented with the opportunity to sell their stock for a premium over market value. One million shares change hands, and each trade returns a $5 windfall to the owner. The net gains here are $5 million. Second, there is the financier herself. She sells 600,000 bonds at a market value of $75 each, for a total of $45 million, which covers all but $5 million of the $50 million required to purchase the firm's outstanding shares. But these shares are still worth $10 million: next year the firm will either be worth nothing or $22 million ($132 million minus $110 million owed to bond holders); the present value of $22 million is $20 million. Multiplying that by the probability of success (0.5) and subtracting the $5 million cost leaves a tidy profit of $5 million. Of course, if the financier is smart she will have bought a significant amount of the equity at $45 *before* announcing the $50 per share tender. In that case she also reaps some of the gains realized by shareholders. (United States law does limit how much she can buy before formally announcing her takeover bid, so she can't get the entire $10 million.)

The losers in this scenario are the owners of the original debt. Before the leveraged buyout, their 400,000 bonds were worth $40 million. After the buyout they are worth only $30 million because, with the announcement of the buyout, the market value of their bonds has dropped by 25 percent overnight (from $100 to $75). The gains and losses are perfectly symmetrical: The equity holders and the financier gain $10 million, while debt holders lose $10 million. Nothing else changes.

To sum up this story line, we started with a firm that generates value in the usual way. The firm has technological expertise that is protected by a patent, physical assets, and a production plan that holds promise for creating goods that are valued by consumers. Competitive financial markets correctly assess the value of the firm at $85 million. The firm becomes 'he subject of a leveraged buyout, but the reshuffling of assets in the acquisition creates no value. Although the transaction creates a fortune for one group of investors, their entire gain takes place at the expense of the initial creditors, who find that the value of their claim on the firm is now diluted. Nobel laureate Merton Miller wryly describes this type of transaction: "The benefits of this dilution accrue, of course, to the stockholders, which is why it has often been labeled theft, particularly by the adversely affected bondholders. Finance specialists prefer the less emotionally charged term uncompensated wealth transfer."[4]

Two details merit attention. First, a curious reader might wonder why refinancing the firm does not change its value. In telling the story this way we are invoking the beautiful work of Miller and Modigliani, who show that when financial markets function properly, a firm's financial structure does not affect its value.[5] In the forty years since the "Miller-Modigliani theorem" was first formulated, scholars have spent a great deal of time trying to understand the circumstances in which its logic is not precisely correct—that is, seeking to understand how financial structure *can* matter. One possibility revolves around the differential tax treatment of returns to equity and debt. Another is that the behavior of the firm's management might depend on the financial structure of the firm (perhaps, for example, a higher debt load gives executives' an incentive to increase efficiency). In our example, however, the financial restructuring would have to reduce the firm's value substantially before the leveraged buyout we outline would become unprofitable.[6]

Second, it is worth mulling over the forward-looking behavior of investors in our model. In calculating the firm's market value, we relied on investors' ability to value assets accurately by judging future contingencies. The opportunity for an outsider to grab an uncompensated wealth transfer indicates that some investors did not correctly foresee *all* possibilities. In particular, bondholders did not include in their calculus the possibility that the firm might become a target for a leveraged buyout. Had they done so, the original 40,000 bonds would have had a lower market value and higher rate of return, or the terms of the bonds would have contained a restrictive covenant prohibiting further issue of senior debt. This lapse provided an innovator—the financier—with her shot at a free lunch. We will discuss this subject further after we present our second fable.

The Fable of the Worker and the Boss:
Agency Problems and the Value of the Job

Our second tale is often told under a title that includes the phrase "principal-agent problem." As in the first story, one of the key players is a firm, but this firm is not a black box that generates an uncertain stream of revenue. Instead, our firm is now a flesh-and-blood enterprise, consisting of two people—a manager and an employee. The situation is interesting because the manager is always inclined to pursue the interest of the firm (perhaps because the manager owns it), while the employee is not.[7] The story doesn't hinge on the worker and manager being at complete odds over every aspect of their work environment. We only require that the manager's objectives differ, at least to some degree, from those of the worker's. For example, the worker's internal motivation might prevent her from openly shirking her duties, but the manager may expect an even higher level of performance.

This setup is a classic principal-agent problem. The tale has a happy ending if the principal (in this case the manager) can structure incentives so that the employee (the agent) finds it in her own interest to pursue the principal's objectives. Many resolutions of this story have been proposed. One rendition goes this way: the manager motivates the employee to pursue the firm's interest by paying a piece rate. For example, a salesperson can be compensated by commission, a machine operative paid according to the number of gun barrels she mills, or an agricultural worker paid by the number of bushels of peaches picked or grape vines pruned. Sometimes a piece-rate scheme is a good solution to the principal-agent problem, but in other cases it is not. The problem with piece rates is that the principal is likely to get exactly what he pays for. When pay is based on an observable measure of output, the agent has an incentive to manipulate the output measure without truly increasing the value to the firm—to pursue quantity at the expense of quality, for example. Furthermore, a daily objective measure of output may not exist, especially for a work setting in which it is difficult to distinguish a particular worker's performance from the overall performance of a group.[8]

Our main interest here is a particularly clever alternative to resolving the principal-agent conflict, originating in the work of Edward Lazear.[9] The basic agency problem at issue is simple: a worker can put forth either high or low effort, and workers prefer to work at a lower level of effort. (We use the terms "high" and "low" in the relative sense; this fable is not necessarily about "shirking," despite the prevalence of the term in the economics literature.) In particular, the worker is indifferent between working at a high-effort level for a wage of $10,000, working at a lower effort level for a lower wage of, say, $8,000, or not working for a particular firm at all. In economics terms, $10,000 and $8,000 are the worker's "reservation wages" for the high- and low-effort levels. This form of the agency problem is obviously simple; it is intended merely to capture the essential idea that the worker's and manager's objectives differ. The manager's problem is to induce the worker to provide the higher effort level. This may not be as simple as it sounds. The manager can offer the high wage and ask the worker to respond by working harder, but the worker may find it in her best interest to provide a lower effort. After all, if the manager does not observe that she is working at the low-effort level, the worker may be able to work at her preferred effort level and still receive the high wage. Even a threat of termination will not suffice here, because the worker is indifferent between working hard at the higher wage and simply accepting a position at another firm. The problem is this: from the perspective of the employee, as long as she works at the higher effort level, *the job itself has no value*; she is just as happy to lose the job as to keep it. (Note that we define value relative to the worker's market opportunities.)

Lazear's solution to the agency problem relies on the fact that if the worker and the manager have access to credit markets and can borrow or lend (save) as they desire, they will be indifferent about the timing of wage payments from the manager to the worker. This gives the firm the opportunity to use "work–life incentives." Suppose that the worker and manager both believe that the value of the worker's contribution to the firm will be constant over the course of her tenure, as will her reservation wages for high and low effort levels. In the absence of the principal-agent problem we have just described, she would just be paid higher wage, $10,000 in each period of employment, as illustrated by the flat wage profile in figure 2.1. However, Lazear offers an alternate plan. Early in her career, the worker is offered a wage that is *less* than the value of her contribution to the firm, while it is understood that later in her career she will be paid a wage that exceeds $10,000. That is, the worker is given an upward-sloping wage, as shown in figure 2.1. This wage path will be constructed so that the total present value of compensation provided over the worker's career is the same for this upward-sloping wage path as for the flat wage path paying a constant $10,000 throughout her career. This is where credit markets enter the picture: If the worker can save and or borrow freely she is indifferent about the timing of wage payments and will care only about the present value of compensation. She is therefore willing to take this job.

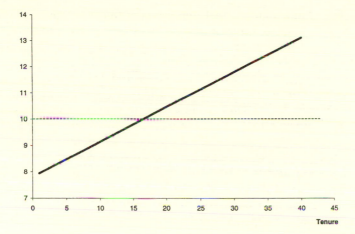

This scheme helps with the principal-agent problem in the following way. Early in her career, the worker earns a relatively low wage but in doing so earns the promise of higher compensation as she gains seniority. She is essentially posting a "performance bond" that is repaid over time if she remains with the firm. The important consequence of this scheme is that *it makes the job valuable.* Having made this investment in her job, our worker is no longer indifferent between continuing her present job and accepting a job elsewhere.[10]

Because the job has value, the worker has an incentive to avoid termination. This gives the manager the leverage he needs to implement an implicit "carrot-and-stick" personnel policy. The stick is the threat of dismissal for workers who are not providing the mutually understood level of effort. The carrot is the promise of continued employment at a job that has value—a job that is worth more to the worker than her outside opportunities. Lazear summarizes his view of this theory as follows:

> I believe that this view of life-cycle earnings corresponds quite closely to that that held by personnel managers. Senior workers are paid high salaries in the firm not so much for their current productivity but as a reward for their past productivity and as a motivator for the current productivity of their junior counterparts.[11]

The economics literature features many variations on Lazear's resolution to the principal-agent problem, models that use intertemporal tradeoffs as a means of providing work incentives.[12] Other examples include promotion tournaments and above-market wages ("efficiency wages"). The hallmark of these approaches is that they give the job value, and this in turn has salutary effects on worker behavior—increased effort, for example, or reduced turnover. Further, this value can only be fully captured by continued employment.

Two final points remain. First, the use of upward-sloping wage profiles (or other implicit contracts) requires that workers trust the firm to honor its implicit arrangements. If a firm's management can establish a reputation as a reliable and honorable employer, it will be able to offer efficient implicit contracts that will mutually benefit the worker and the firm. A reputation for following through on implicit contracts is thus a valuable asset. Relational assets that do not show up in corporate financial reports can nonetheless represent an important part of a firm's value. Firms that are seen as unreliable will not be able to use work–life incentives and must search for other—often more expensive—means of motivating workers.

Second, our story describes workplace incentives in purely monetary terms, which may strike some readers as odd. A successful work environment depends to a large degree on worker morale, which is engendered by a sense of fairness, reciprocal trust, and unity of purpose. It is reasonable to wonder about the effectiveness of current and expected financial rewards as a means of building morale. Economists' standard response is that adequate financial rewards are a necessary, though generally not sufficient, condition for good workplace morale. In any event, we emphasize that the *conclusion* of the story may ring true, even if the plot line does not. The conclusion, after all, is this: workers are more likely to pursue the interests of management (to be hard-working, cooperative, loyal, etc.) when they value their jobs—that is, when they prefer working in their current job to other available opportunities.[13]

Firm Finance Meets the Agency Problem: Workers as Stakeholders

The final step in this chapter is to combine the two stories. We start by considering a firm similar to the one in our second story, whose workers are paid according the work–life incentive scheme outlined by Lazear. In essence these workers post performance bonds with the firm by accepting upward-sloping wage profiles—working at a wage lower than the value of their marginal product early in their careers in exchange for the expectation of higher wages and greater job security as they gain seniority. Under this arrangement—as workers literally become creditors of the firm—our two stories begin to merge. By offering upward-sloping wage profiles, the firm implicitly obligates itself to its current workforce; workers are investing in their jobs with the firm, and the firm owes these workers the promised seniority. The firm accepts such obligations, indeed insists on them, because this personnel practice is an efficient way of resolving the firm's agency problem; it is a mutually advantageous means for establishing a productive working relationship.[14]

The debt held by workers is almost certainly the least subordinate of the firm's obligations. If the firm goes bankrupt, for example, workers who are approaching the high-wage portion of their careers will never be paid back for the investments they made early in their careers. Similarly, if a firm that uses promotion tournaments violates its implicit promise by shrinking its middle management ranks, workers typically have no legal recourse for reclaiming their lost investment.

This idea of workers as creditors is not intended to be allegorical or illustrative; is it meant to be taken literally. If firms use work–life incentives as an effective personnel tool, then workers are creditors of the firm, just the same as bondholders. This leads us back to the idea of "uncompensated wealth transfer" described earlier. Consider a firm whose obligations include debt to workers along with other debt and equity. We have already seen that a financial "innovator" can reap fortunes, not by creating value but by creating a transfer from one group of the firm's stakeholders, the bondholders. Precisely the same point can be made with respect to the other creditors, the workforce.

Many, perhaps most, managerial innovations create wealth by increasing the value of the firm through the reallocation of workers to positions in which they will be more productive, eliminating unprofitable ventures, or closing inefficient plants. Other innovations, however, may reduce the overall value of the firm to stakeholders (including worker-creditors, bondholders, and shareholders) but still may be advantageous to the party making the changes. A subset of this latter category may be the abrogation of implicit contracts with employees. As an example, Shleifer and Summers cite the stripping of retirement benefits that are not explicitly protected by the Employee Retirement Income Security Act (for example, certain medical and insurance benefits).[15] These benefits are a form of deferred compensation that is intended to have a positive effect on employee performance; they generally are an important part of a firm's work–life incentives. Removal of assets from a pension fund may increase shareholder value, but this increase in shareholder value may be a not-too-subtle version of "uncompensated wealth transfer." Moreover, such an action could reduce the total value of the firm if failure to honor an implicit contract with older workers makes it more costly in the future for the firm to resolve the agency problem with younger workers. Nonetheless, an organization might find it profitable to strip its pension fund and cut retirement benefits if the size of the uncompensated wealth transfer exceeds the losses that might accrue as the firm squanders its reputation as an honorable employer.

Shleifer and Summers note that a hostile takeover presents a particularly opportune time for a firm to violate implicit contracts with its workers (and possibly its suppliers and the communities in which the firm has plants). One case they examine in detail is Carl Icahn's 1985 takeover of Trans World Airlines. Icahn, they show, paid a $300 million to $400 million premium over market value for TWA shares. This should not be viewed as an indication of the effect on the total value of the firm, though. The increase in the value of the shares took place in large measure as a consequence of reduced labor costs. Indeed, the net present value of the concessions extracted from the company's main unions (those representing pilots, flight attendants, and machinists) was an estimated $600 million. The wealth transfer from workers easily exceeded the increase in the market price of shares.

Most instances of uncompensated wealth transfer will be subtler than this case, and they need not occur only, or even primarily, when a hostile takeover takes place. Any change in management or managerial philosophy that increases shareholder value by violating implicit contracts is a potential example of the phenomenon.

Concluding Remarks

The idea that management or outside investors can create profit for themselves or for stockholders by breaking implicit contracts with labor sounds like a violation of the "no free lunch maxim." If workers are truly rational, they will generally be disinclined to enter into arrangements in which future managerial decisions are likely to result in large losses to themselves. In particular, workers will only accept a firm's commitment when they believe that the firm will find it in its *own* best interest to honor the commitment. (This is why the contract can remain implicit.) If forward-looking workers can always spot firms that are not trustworthy, it will limit the opportunity for firms to transfer wealth by violating implicit contracts with labor.

This brings us back to a point raised earlier in this essay. In the conclusion to our first fable, we discussed the issue of whether the initial bondholders foresaw the possibility of a takeover. In our numerical example, they did not. But had they done so, they would have incorporated the possibility of a capital loss into the original price of the bonds or eliminated this possibility altogether by altering the structure of the legal contract between the firm and its creditors. While implicit work contracts have no formal legal contract to alter, there are three other ways in which the firm and workers might take into account the risk that the firm will violate its implicit contract. First, the worker and manager may correctly envision all of the possibilities but may not know in advance which of them will transpire. In this case, the terms of the implicit contract might be set in a way that makes the worker willing, *ex ante,* to accept the terms, even knowing that if events unfold in certain ways she will be laid off before the end of her career. This scenario is analogous to bondholders who correctly evaluate the possibility of a leveraged buyout and consequent capital loss. They hate the buyout when it happens, but they also know that purchasing bonds is a gamble and that they have received an appropriate return on their investment. The wealth transfer is, in this instance, not uncompensated. The second possibility is that the sequence of events—changes in the competitive environment that spark a takeover, for instance—that leads to violation of the implicit contract move was not contemplated in advance (at least by workers). Management abrogates the contract opportunistically, knowing that the situation has evolved in an unforeseen way that makes the contract disadvantageous for the firm. Third, we should bear in mind the possibility that the firm's managers see only short-term gain without properly recognizing the central role of relational wealth. They fail, in short, to understand the long-run costs incurred by loss of reputation as a reliable employer. We suspect that this view may be what some have in mind when they complain about Wall Street's obsession with short-run gain.

Economists often focus their attention on equilibrium outcomes under rational behavior and expectations. That is, they study the first of the three possibilities outlined in the preceding paragraph, assuming in particular that individuals incorporate the likelihood of all future contingencies into their current decision making. In that instance, it is perhaps misleading to describe workers as stakeholders in their firms because the term "stakeholder" implies a claim or right to be consulted concerning the disposition of the firm.[16] It is true that when jobs are valuable, workers will lose out if they are laid off, but if workers are well aware of all the risks when they accept their jobs, such unlucky outcomes are simply the result of uncertainty inherent in the business environment. There is no more reason to pay attention to the plight of a dislocated worker in this case than to a speculator who has taken a loss on the international currency market.

On the other hand, we have considered here the possibility that workers will sometimes fail to foresee all possible outcomes in a rapidly evolving economy. Workers in this instance are in a very real sense stakeholders; they are literally creditors who are subject to the same sort of uncompensated wealth transfer as ordinary debt-holders.

We believe that the issues we raise in this chapter are a useful way to understand features of worker-firm relationships, especially in a swiftly changing economic environment. We resist the temptation to suggest any easy policy responses to the issues we raise. The problem is that contracts between workers and managers are implicit; policy makers will rarely, if ever, have the facts necessary to determine whether managerial decisions are reallocations of resources that add value or are inefficient, opportunistic wealth transfer. The same policy that protects workers from opportunistic layoff inhibits the flexibility needed for workers and firms to enter into an efficient implicit contract.[17]

More generally, this essay does not challenge the general proposition that the extraordinary vitality and productivity of a competitive economy hinges in large measure on the ability of entrepreneurs and managers to rapidly reallocate capital assets and labor to their most productive uses. Our intention is rather to emphasize that in even in the simplest stories that economists tell about firms and workers, workers emerge as stakeholders who are deeply affected, for better or for worse, by decisions made in the interest of their firm. Workers are creditors subject to the same opportunistic corporate finance and management "innovations" that created large losses for bondholders in companies targeted for leveraged buyouts.

Notes

Views stated here are those of the authors and not necessarily those of the Federal Reserve Bank of St. Louis.

1. When the safe rate of return is r, the present value of an ongoing stream $1 per year payments, starting in the current year, is $(1 + r)/r$. Thus, the value next year of a stream of $12 million payments, when the safe interest rate is 0.10 (10 percent) is $(1.1/0.1)*$12,000,000 = $132,000,000$. Also, when the safe return is 0.10, $120,000,000 today will return $1.1*$120,000,000 = $132,000,000$ next year. So the value *now* of a stream of $12 million payments starting *next year* is $120 million. These calculations are exact if the payments go on forever. If they stop at some time far in the future, the numerical error is small.

2. The answer is a bit trickier if investors are not risk neutral. (Risk neutrality just means that the investor is willing to accept a fair gamble.) In this latter instance, calculating the firm's value requires attention to how the firm's outcomes are correlated with other risky investment vehicles available in the marketplace. None of this is important to the rest of our story, though.

3. Some bridge financing is required until the financier gains control of the firm and is able to obligate it to future payments.

4. Merton H. Miller, "The Modigliani-Miller Propositions after Thirty Years," *Journal of Economic Perspectives* (Fall 1988): 114.

5. Franco Modigliani and Merton H. Miller, "The Cost of Capital, Corporation Finance and the Theory of Investment," *American Economic Review* (June 1958): 261–97.

6. Of course, if the firm was not initially optimally leveraged, or if for some reason the manager is failing to maximize value, the outside investor might be able to *increase* the value of the firm by refinancing. Indeed there is considerable evidence that this happens in some takeovers. The lesson of the story nonetheless pertains; increases in efficiency need not always be a precondition for a profitable buyout.

7. It is interesting to imagine how the plot changes if the manager also has objectives that differ from those of the firm's owner, but that is another story. See Michael C. Jensen and Kevin J. Murphy, "CEO Incentives—It's Not How Much You Pay, but How," *Harvard Business Review* (May/June 1990): 138–49.

8. For a nice discussion of the limits of piece rates see Robert Gibbons, "Incentives and Careers in Organizations," working paper no. 5705, National Bureau of Economic Research August 1996. Cambridge, Mass.

9. Edward P. Lazear, "Agency, Earnings Profiles, Productivity, and Hours Restrictions," *American Economic Review* (September 1981): 606–20.

10. There are some nagging loose ends about how work–life incentives motivate the worker at the beginning and end of her career, but they are not relevant here. We discuss them in our article, "Economic Models of Employee Motivation," *Federal Reserve Bank of St. Louis Review* (September/October 1997): 3–21. (Available at www.stls.frb.org/docs/publications/review/97/09/9709jr.pdf.)

11. Edward P. Lazear, *Personnel Economics* (Cambridge, Mass.: MIT Press, 1995), p. 42. Lazear has also observed that work–life incentives form the basis of a persuasive explanation of mandatory retirement policies,

which were common in the United States before they were outlawed. The firm needs some way to truncate the stream of high wage payments at the end of the worker's career. The simplest way to do this is a rule that cuts off employment at a fixed date.

12. See Ritter and Taylor (1997), where we summarize the various economic approaches to employee motivation.

13. Moreover, the key role of expectations concerning long-term agreements between management and workers is common across scholars who study management-worker relations. "Psychological contracts," discussed by Denise M. Rousseau (*Psychological Contracts in Organizations: Understanding Written and Unwritten Aagreements* [Newbury Park, CA.: Sage 1995]), for example, have a somewhat different behavioral foundation from the "implicit contracts" that appear in Lazear's work–life incentives but play a similarly central role in workplace organization.

14. We develop the idea that workers are creditors of a firm formally in our "Workers as Creditors: Performance Bonds and Efficiency Wages," *American Economic Review* (June 1994): 694–704. In that article we show that consideration of the role of workers as creditors can substantially change the nature of labor market equilibria.

15. Andrei Shleifer and Lawrence H. Summers, "Breach of Trust in Hostile Takeovers," in *Corporate Takeovers: Causes and Consequences*, edited by Alan Auerbach (Chicago: University of Chicago Press, 1988).

16. Indeed, many economists dislike the use of the term "stakeholders" as a way of characterizing a firm's employees for just this reason.

17. Similarly, laws restricting corporate takeover activity might limit some wasteful activity but also cause massive inefficiency in the market for corporate control. See Michael C. Jensen, "Takeovers: Their Causes and Consequences," *Journal of Economic Perspectives* (winter 1988): 21–48.

3

Relational Wealth and Skill Development within Evolving, Competitive Markets

GIL A. PREUSS

Over the past fifteen years, competitive and technological developments have increased the demand for high-quality, customized, and rapidly developed products and services. These developments have spurred organizations to adopt new business strategies and human resource practices. Some firms have adopted high-involvement or high-commitment approaches as a way to increase flexibility and improve performance.[1] These practices strive to strengthen the relationship between employers and employees by ensuring job security, while at the same time placing greater demands on employees to be flexible and actively involved in process improvement. As addressed in chapter 1, these high-involvement strategies strive to ensure long-term competitive growth by building both organizational flexibility and stability.

In contrast, other firms have increasingly viewed long-term relations with their employees as a constraint on organizational flexibility.[2] These firms attempt to build flexibility by integrating market mechanisms into the firm's employment relationships, replacing long-term commitment with a focus on short-term value, contingent pay, and uncertain employment duration.[3] The core employee group, which has relative job security and long-term organizational commitment, shrinks as an ever-increasing proportion of employees are engaged through contingent relationships.[4] Moreover, even within the core group, employee expectations regarding future relationships with the firm shift toward short-term exchanges and an assessment of the immediate value of continuing employment. The result is a looser connection between employees and employers, with each focusing on ways to maximize personal returns rather than building mutual success over time. These employers feel little responsibility to maintain long-term employment stability or security, while their employees will readily leave an employer for a new position at a competing firm. The historical exchange of short-term organizational flexibility for implicit long-term employment security—once considered a source of advantage for large firms—is thus replaced with an exchange based on simple market mechanisms.[5]

Whether firms are adopting high-involvement work systems or market mechanisms, a key component of the resulting organizational flexibility is the need to ensure the availability of necessary skills within the organization. As technologies or markets shift, employees need new skills to meet organizational demands. Firms in high-involvement work systems carefully select and continuously train employees to meet skill demands. On the other hand, firms that adopt market mechanisms meet these shifting skill demands by replacing one skill group with another, typically through downsizing or outsourcing. Because this willingness to replace workers with "outdated" or traditional skills reflects newer organizational realities, downsizing and skill shifts will become common occurrences as firms respond to evolving technological and competitive demands.

However, this strategy lowers relational wealth and decreases an organization's capability to compete successfully, particularly where knowledge is situated in specific contexts or where strong relations among employees are necessary for successful task accomplishment. While organizations hire employees with specific skills to meet current demand, the incorporation of market mechanisms into employment relations breaks relationships that have developed over time among employees and leads to the loss of organization-specific knowledge that employees have accumulated through years of experience. In addition, merely incorporating market mechanisms into an organization does not create systems for employee skill development but rather shifts responsibility and risk from managers to employees. Finally, high-involvement work systems frequently require skills beyond those developed through initial and continuous training initiatives.[6]

To develop organizational capacity for flexible stability, all organizations must establish processes through which employees can continuously learn new skills as demanded by work systems, the firm, and the environment. Overall, organizations and employees face three important challenges in developing and maintaining skill level within the workplace; the initial development of employee skills, their integration within a broader skill community, and the continuous development of skill as technology and organizational demands evolve. This chapter examines the capacity to achieve these objectives by analyzing organizational human resource practices and, in particular, the role of relational wealth in organizations as the basis for understanding the development and use of skills in the workplace.

As throughout this book, relational wealth is defined here as "the value of the shared commitment and stability engendered by a workforce strong in trust and collective goal orientation."[7] Relational wealth develops through organizational and human resource practices that promote the development of trust, relationships among employees, and long-term commitments between the firm and its employees. In addition, while relational wealth is distinct from human capital, its capacity to increase the human capital that is available within the organization is addressed in this chapter.

After broadly discussing the challenges organizations face, I examine the effect of specific practices through an analysis of acute care nursing work in hospitals, including specific examples and results that support the proposed practices. The chapter concludes with a broader discussion of these practices and their adoption within other firms and other industries.

The Changing Demands for Skill in Organizations

Technological shifts and production process innovations have changed the nature of skills demanded by firms.[8] This shift has occurred not only in the area of expertise demanded but also in the nature of the skills demanded—increasingly, organizations search for employees with broad, general skills that can be applied across diverse settings and situations. For example, instead of selecting new employees on the basis of industry experience, Honda USA focuses on their ability to work well in groups, solve problems, and think creatively. Similarly, when Chaparral Steel hires new employees, it specifically searches for those without previous steel production experience, instead hiring people who enjoy hands-on experimentation. When Microsoft hires new employees, it wants not simply people who know specific programming languages but those who think on their feet.[9] For all of these firms, the rationale is that general skills are more difficult to develop than specific production and programming skills. Moreover, skills such as creativity, a willingness to experiment, and the ability to solve problems, can transfer easily across specific settings and work processes.[10]

Overall, organizations are increasingly demanding "general" human capital, or capabilities that are deployable across settings and organizations. In contrast, "firm-specific" human capital includes capabilities that are deployable only within a specific organizational setting. More important, firm-specific skills frequently cannot be used in other settings even within the same firm because they are distinct to a particular system or work process.

The increasing demand for general human capital reflects two converging trends. First, as indicated earlier, firms are increasingly adopting high-involvement work systems in response to increasing competitive pressures and the demand for high-quality, flexible production.[11] The success of these work systems depends on decentralized responsibility and increased employee involvement in decision making.[12] As front-line workers take on responsibility, they must be able to understand and evaluate available information. The second trend arises from the need for organizational flexibility. As managers recognize that firms must quickly respond to evolving technological and competitive dynamics, they search for employees whose skills can evolve over time. Employees who hold only specific production knowledge are less attractive to employers who seek to move them fluidly across traditional boundaries or introduce new technologies into the production system.

While the description of firm-specific and general skills suggests that they are distinct, their relationship in organizations is actually tightly linked. Firm-specific and general skills depend on each other in the conduct of work within an organization. To successfully accomplish a task, verbal or written understanding is insufficient. Rather, a person must have the capacity to "get things done" in numerous contexts.[13] For example, designing a specific machine for use in a production line requires the integration of information regarding other equipment, employees, and the materials to be used—much more than just an understanding of mechanical engineering.

The capacity to bring together general and firm-specific skills requires moving into a "community of practice" as well as an organizational community, which involves the development of specific knowledge that enables one to apply general skills to particular tasks. As people develop greater skills, they move from the periphery into the core of the community of practice.[14] For example, new employees in an automobile plant might have the general ability to solve problems creatively and work well in groups, but they must also learn how to build cars while working within specific routines for collecting information and addressing workplace problems. As a result, employees entering an occupational community learn to couple specific knowledge with existing general skills.

The movement into an organizational community also requires employees to develop specific knowledge that enables them to apply general skills to situations within a particular firm. First, because organizations differ in the routines and processes through which work is conducted, the capacity to succeed in a particular organization depends not only on existing skills but also on specific knowledge regarding the organization and its processes. Second, employees moving into an organizational community must develop relationships with other people in the organization and gain specific knowledge about the skills other employees hold. Many problems require collaborative efforts among people holding diverse skills and distinct information. Rarely does one person hold all necessary skills and information required to address a complex problem. Relational wealth developed through the movement into an organizational community ensures that employees know who holds this knowledge and enables them to access this distributed knowledge for use on the job. As a result, the skills available to a worker are greater than just the skills he or she personally holds. The capacity to access distributed knowledge as part of the regular work process is an integral part of successful work and is one clear benefit of relational wealth.[15]

Ultimately, though, organizations must continue building their employees' skills over time. Research suggests that relational wealth plays a critical role in ensuring long-term skill development and knowledge diffusion, as learning is frequently a communal process.[16] When people tell stories about their experiences as a way to convey specific information,[17] others may build on this information through additional stories that support initial observations or expand on a particular point. In addition, the ways in which people understand problems are shaped by their experiences or roles within the organization. By supporting communal consideration of problems, relational wealth promotes the incorporation of multiple views and increases the learning of each party. In its absence, people rarely will share important information, ideas, and skills that may benefit others and the organization.

Within evolving competitive environments, firms must also strive to build skills across traditional organizational boundaries. Even employees with deep skills in a particular area may be unable to adapt to shifting technological or environmental demands. Instead, both employers and employees must constantly grow and evolve to meet the new demands they face. This learning process depends on the relationships, trust, and long-term commitment that grows from the relational wealth that develops across organizational boundaries.

To meet the needs of planners, evaluators, and accountants, managers try to separate jobs and people through clear, rational boundaries and distinctions. They adopt specific areas of responsibility, task assignments, and employee skills as the basis for hiring, evaluating, and organizing. This focus on formal structures and clear distinctions has been at the core of organizational theory since its inception.[18] Historically, organizations that have clearly differentiated skills and tasks they assign to individuals have had broad market success.[19] Moreover, clear structures promote skill development within narrow jobs, enabling organizations to improve performance within each position.

However, traditional organizational structures limit an organization's capacity to develop relational wealth across boundaries.[20] Structural divisions develop distinct ways of understanding the environment and varied interests among groups and individuals. These divisions create distinct knowledge bases among groups in the organization. For example, an electrical engineer working on a particular product or set of products will develop expertise in that domain. Though the expertise deepens over time, it may also become increasingly narrow. One way organizations currently seek to address this separation in expertise is through the use of cross functional teams to address complex problems. This enables organizations to integrate diverse skills and perspectives into a decision. This also promotes individual learning when people work together to confront diverse pieces of information and strive to use diverse tools to address a problem.[21] People are pushed to expand beyond the knowledge traditionally held within a single function. Alternatively, organizations can incorporate work organization and human resource practices that promote the continuous development of relationships, exchange of information, and evolution of jobs over time.

Overall, firms within evolving competitive markets face several challenges in their pursuit to continuously build employee skills. As suggested, relational wealth plays an important role in enabling skill development as new employees enter organizations, as they move toward the core of a community of practice and an organizational community, and as their skills evolve to meet demands placed on the organization. In the next section, I analyze the health care industry, focusing on specific organizational practices that promote the development of relational wealth and showing how these practices enable skill development and organizational success.

Health Care and the Development of Skill

Health care delivery in the United States is in the midst of dramatic restructuring, spurred by increased economic pressure, new technological developments, and the aging American population. As a result, health care providers are searching for new ways to provide high-quality and cost-effective patient care. Moreover, the average acuity of patients in hospitals has increased over the past decade, as insurers intensify their efforts to lower patient care delivery costs. Hospitals are, therefore, challenged to elevate employee skills, ensure their continuous evolution in response to technological and structural demands, and build low-cost care processes. Organizations throughout the economy are facing the same challenges. (The data used for the following section come from a broad examination of hospital restructuring.)[22]

Overall, this analysis focuses on two central questions facing hospitals in the current evolving competitive environment. First, what enables hospitals to flexibly respond to changing competitive demands? Second, how do alternative ways of organizing the provision of care in hospitals shape critical patient and organizational outcomes? (The data used for this study include observations of care providers and work processes in several hospitals, interviews conducted with over one hundred employees at all levels of the organizations, and surveys distributed to more than three thousand nursing unit employees in sixteen hospitals. The specific analyses and conclusions described in this section arise from these data.)

Relational Wealth and Skill Development within Acute Patient Care

As in other settings, the demand for flexibility within hospitals rests on employees who hold general skills that can adapt across different situations. Over the past thirty years, hospitals have increasingly hired nursing staff who hold general skills, such as knowledge of abstract principles, including an understanding of basic science.[23] These abstract principles serve a critical function as nurses confront new issues, learn about new medicines, or work in new environments. Employment decisions based on abstract principles, however, are insufficient for meeting the demands of high-quality patient care and ensuring the continuous development of skills. For example, a general knowledge of physiology is insufficient for a nurse to work successfully on an orthopedics unit. The nurse must also learn how this abstract knowledge relates to particular procedures, the typical paths to recovery, and potential adverse developments. According to nurse managers, it takes a new nurse at least one year to gain the necessary skills to operate effectively on his or her own. As nurses move into the nursing community of practice, they attach specific skills to the abstract principles learned in school. The importance of both abstract knowledge and firm-specific skills is evidenced by observations that both formal education and time spent on the job improve the quality of information available for decision making and decrease the frequency of medication errors on the unit.[24] To ensure the delivery of high quality care hospitals seek to increase the speed of a nurse's movement into the community of practice. Several important organizational practices employed by the hospitals in this study appear to ease and speed this process. First, hospitals promoted employee learning through extensive formal training, both on initial entry into an organization and regularly thereafter. Continuous skill development—through advanced education as well as on-site training programs—helps nurses gain critical knowledge as technologies evolve, patient acuity increases, and new systems are integrated into the work process.

A second key practice adopted by hospitals is the use of mentoring as a new employee transitions into a community of practice. Senior nurses act as mentors to new staff by working closely with them as they begin to attach specific skills to existing general skills. Over time, as an employee develops skills and moves into the core of a community of practice, the mentor's role shifts toward developing relationships with other care providers and learning a broader set of routines necessary for successful work.

Third, several hospitals have adopted broad nursing jobs to promote learning as part of the job. Responsibility under these broad jobs ranges from bathing and feeding a patient to the coordination of patient care across shifts and functions. Broad nursing jobs can speed the movement of new staff into a community of practice by promoting their attachment of specific skills to abstract principles and by easing the capacity of care providers to learn from experience. As a nurse treats a patient along a broad dimension of care, she observes the patient's response to specific care paths and understands how one behavior is linked with others in complex care processes. By maintaining responsibility for the same patients over several shifts, a nurse will better understand changes in their condition. The result is that a closer link is made between decisions and patient responses, and that link can be used to determine future care both for this patient as well as others.

Finally, to ensure the rapid movement of people into a community of practice and the continuous development of skills within this community, several hospitals maintain key skills in the front-line production process and create an environment where nurses work with one another to address complex problems. While organizations typically promote top performing employees out of front-line work, several of the hospitals I observed maintain nursing skill in direct patient care even after nurses can advanced degrees. These hospitals maintain advanced skills on the front line by expanding skilled nurses' roles within the care process rather than shifting them to management. For example, nurses with master's or doctoral degrees take on tasks previously conducted by physicians or managers, such as developing systems of care and educating other care providers, while maintaining their direct patient care responsibilities as well.

When skilled employees provide direct patient care, their skills are immediately available to others who seek assistance with workplace developments. In addition, experienced nurses often develop expertise in specific areas of patient care, such as the treatment of postsurgical pain or the prevention and treatment of pressure sores. When these people are kept within direct patient care, a nurse with only limited knowledge of postsurgical pain treatment can still use the knowledge held by others in treating a patient if the available relationships enable her to access this skill. The expertise developed by one person is then available to others. By keeping skilled nurses in the direct care provision process, both new and experienced nurses can learn from others with specific areas of expertise.

The capacity to use this distributed knowledge, though, also requires an environment where employees regularly seek and receive assistance from each other. In my observation of nurses conducting patient care, employees regularly consulted with each other to integrate their experiences into patient care decisions. In fact, over 50 percent of the registered nurses surveyed first sought out the advice of another nurse when confronted with a problem they could not address on their own. During visits to nursing units, I observed one nurse approach another to clarify specific medications, while several coworkers sought out another to learn a new technique in treating a specific disease. When particularly complex problems arose, the nurse manager on one unit organized informal gatherings to discuss the problem. This joint problem solving improved the learning among nurses and further built relational wealth within the unit.

The adoption of market mechanisms within organizations, the breakdown of trust among coworkers, and the absence of strong relationships tends to reduce the capacity of care providers to access this key knowledge and use it fully within their own work. This was directly observed in hospitals where more extensive use of external contingent employees is correlated with diminished mutual learning among care providers. As relationships are framed within short-term market transactions, the capacity to build relationships and skills decreases.

In contrast, several benefits were observed when mutual consultation and learning were encouraged and where complex problems were seen as opportunities for broad learning. When nurses sought each other out for assistance as part of the care process, more extensive mutual skill development occurred on the unit. In addition, more extensive mutual learning on the unit was correlated with higher quality patient information available for decision making[25] and increased willingness among nurses to disagree with a physician over specific medical decisions regarding patient care. This capacity to build employee skills, promote mutual learning, and develop high-quality patient information is central to the delivery of high-quality patient care.

The final demand on skill development is the capacity to fluidly adapt the skills of employees across traditional boundaries. Traditional models of organizations generally suggest that clear and narrow job definitions enable people to develop expertise within the job. In contrast, the demand for skill adaptation necessitates a reevaluation of job structures in organizations. While clear job boundaries may promote deep knowledge within a narrow domain, "fuzzy" job boundaries and overlapping responsibilities across employees may provide critical opportunities for improving skills and organizational outcomes.

The value of fuzzy organizational boundaries was first noticed at one of the hospitals studied. Over time, several nurses gained in-depth knowledge about the properties of specific medicines used on their unit, by interacting for years with physicians and other nurses on the unit. As a result, these nurses began to assume joint responsibility for the type of medications being prescribed to patients. While this responsibility was not originally a core component of their job, the skills they developed over time reshaped and broadened their responsibilities. During the conduct of her work, one nurse observed that two medicines with similar underlying properties were prescribed to a patient. Before giving both medicines to the patient, the nurse asked for confirmation from the overseeing physician, who subsequently changed one of the prescriptions. In a more traditional setting, the nurse would not have had the necessary skill to observe the potential problem, nor would she have taken the responsibility to question a physician's work. In this setting, however, fuzzy organizational boundaries helped develop the nurse's ability to evaluate the medications prescribed and address a potential problem before it arose. Similarly, fuzzy boundaries among registered nurses, licensed practical nurses, and nursing assistants provide important opportunities for developing skills and building organizational capacity.

In a more formal examination of fuzzy job boundaries, I examined the division of labor among care providers on acute care nursing units, including licensed practical nurses, nursing assistants, and registered nurses. Typically, each occupational group holds distinct skills and fulfills a distinct function within the unit. In fact, among hospitals undergoing workplace restructuring, part of the change initiative is to clearly define responsibilities and minimize overlap across occupational groups. In contrast to the current restructuring initiatives, I find that hospital units with greater overlap in the responsibility of care providers develop better patient information, and exhibit lower rates of medication errors.[26]

The challenge for hospitals is how to develop fuzzy job boundaries that promote skill development among care providers. One possible way is to assign joint responsibility for certain tasks across multiple occupational groups. A second practice in developing fuzzy job and skill boundaries is demanding that nurses assume direct responsibility for coordinating care with physicians, nutritionists, physical therapists, home health aides, and nursing homes. This responsibility enables them to learn directly from other parties. For example, nurses may participate in the residents' morning rounds to provide physicians with patient information and learn about changes in patient care and status. During these conversations, the nurses learn about recent research and practice changes while the physicians grow to understand the nature of nursing. Similarly, nursing assistants improve their skills over time through direct coordination with registered nurses. Skill distinctions become more ambiguous as knowledge crosses traditional boundaries. Moreover, the demands on each party increase to clearly articulate positions within a framework understood by the other.

Organizational Practices for Relational Wealth and Skill Development

Organizations face unique pressures as they respond to increasing competition, new technologies, and evolving demands from external constituencies. In the current environment, organizations commonly respond to this pressure by integrating market mechanisms into their employment relationships. The result, however, is the disintegration of key relationships among employees that enable the development and use of employee skills on the job. Through an analysis of work organization and human resource practices in acute care hospitals, I highlight specific practices that develop relational wealth and show how relational wealth improves organizational capacity to build skills and performance over time.

Organizations are pressured to develop systems that speed the movement of employees into a community of practice while building strong relations among community members. Several specific work organization and human resource practices observed in the field appear to support this process. The adoption of broad jobs with extensive feedback, the wide-scale use of mentoring, and the maintenance of skilled workers in front-line work ease the integration of new employees into an organization and the help them develop the skills necessary for the successful accomplishment of work. These three practices enable the rapid development of firm-specific knowledge and relational wealth within a community of practice, in an organizational community, and across traditional organizational boundaries.

First, organizations must create broad jobs that enable employees to learn through the work process. Enabling workers to observe the outcomes of the decisions that they make develops this learning. Similar to models proposed more than twenty years ago by Hackman and Oldham, broad jobs build feedback directly into the conduct of work, thus improving an understanding of work processes.

But beyond simply attaching routines and firm-specific skills to general knowledge, research shows that situated learning enables people to adapt routines to address the problems within particular circumstances.[28] In contrast to apprenticeship-based skill development, general skills enable people to question and improve work processes as they apply their broader knowledge base to existing routines.[29] Broad jobs promote this learning process by supporting deeper employee skills and new organizational routines.

The second practice supporting the rapid integration of employees into a community of practice is active mentoring. As stated, new employees enter an organization with general skills but with limited ability to apply these within particular settings or to particular problems. The mentoring process is a formal tool to build this capacity and move people rapidly into a community of practice within a specific organization. In addition, mentoring promotes the development of relationships and an understanding of the knowledge distributed throughout the organization.

A third important practice for the development of employee skills in the work process is maintaining skilled employees in front-line work. Typically, organizations promote skilled employees out of front-line work and into management. In nursing, this occurs as highly qualified nurses are promoted to nurse managers or other hospital administrators. In high-technology firms, the best engineers are frequently made managers in order to supervise the work of others. This contrasts with the practice observed in several hospitals where they actively seek to keep highly skilled nurses in direct patient care. Similarly, managers at Microsoft created career paths within functional areas to reward top performers appropriately while maintaining their skills within the program development arena. This not only supports the development of better software programs through the continued direct work of these skilled employees but also allows new employees to interact and learn from leading programmers.[30]

Fuzzy Occupational Boundaries and Skill Development

While the use of teams is one mechanism to build contact across boundaries, improve decision making, and promote learning, organizations can achieve similar outcomes by establishing fuzzy boundaries across jobs and skill areas. Fuzzy set theory focuses on the nature of boundaries across categories.[31] In contrast to traditional assumptions about categories—clear boundaries and membership in a group—"fuzzy sets" are based on the concept of varied group membership that changes depending on the context. A benefit of evolving categories is that they can more easily respond to shifting demands; a clearly defined category cannot easily evolve over time. Organizations that establish fluid job borders promote the movement of skills and people from one group to another. In addition, fuzzy boundaries ease the evolution of a community of practice by enabling workers to integrate new skills and tasks into their jobs over time.

As described, traditional firms hire a person with a specific set of abilities and place him or her in a job with distinct characteristics defining the necessary skills to accomplish desired tasks. If the job requires additional, firm-specific skills, the organization may provide training. Fuzzy boundaries suggest a different interaction among the organization, an individual, and skills. A person is hired into a position, but her skills change over time on the basis of individual motivation and ability. The position is loosely defined and is often shaped by the person's interests and skills as well as changing demands on the organization. While core responsibilities exist, other areas of responsibility and associated skills evolve. Just as employees move from the periphery to the core in a community of practice, so too can they develop skills and responsibilities that overlap with separate groups.

In many ways, this model is similar to a professional firm or research environment. As a formal mechanism to achieve this end, some companies allow employees to spend a percentage (e.g., 15 percent) of their time on individually selected projects, enabling the development of new ideas as well as promoting the growth of the person and the organization.

The presence of fuzzy boundaries suggests not that distinctions among groups disappear but rather that borders that once clearly differentiated engineer from production employee or nurse from doctor become blurred over time as people pursue interests and seek new skills. Fuzzy task and skill boundaries break down traditional organizational divisions and build up the flow of knowledge and skill in an organization.

To support the process of building fuzzy boundaries, organizational practices must promote the fluid movement of information, ideas, and skills. Employees must directly coordinate their work across traditional boundaries, enabling them to understand the broader demands of the work process. Coordination responsibilities also pressure employees to improve their understanding of the work process and build new skills. With direct responsibility for coordinating decisions' employees must clarify their views and improve their understanding of the situation acting as an incentive to promote skill development.

Over time, fuzzy boundaries across jobs and skills enable organizations to evolve more fluidly. Individuals develop skills according to their particular interests and interactions. Job categories and responsibilities shift as technological and organizational demands suggest new ways of organizing work. Most important, occupational groups are not constrained by organizationally defined structures. Employees develop broader skills that they can then apply more fully within the organization as it too evolves.

Conclusion

Overall, this chapter suggests that specific work organization and human resource practices can increase the capacity of new organizational members to quickly enter their jobs, work successfully, and continue to develop skills over time. Moreover, these job characteristics shape firms' ability to compete successfully while responding to technological and competitive developments.

The form of flexibility adopted recently by managers based on the integration of market mechanisms into work relations will poorly serve an organization as it seeks to compete within continuously evolving environments. The limited commitment expressed by each party will result in short-term perspectives rather than efforts to maintain and develop necessary skills. This tendency to lose firm-specific skill, and the breakdown of relational wealth, will significantly hurt the organization's capacity to address complex problems and improve its performance over time. While several researchers and practitioners have suggested that the new employment contract is based on the joint effort by firms and employees to build skill, the capacity to achieve this result demands the growth of organizational relational wealth and specific work organization practices.[32]

Relational wealth in organizations is critical not only for the individuals who seek to build skills and accomplish their work but also for organizations whose employees must integrate widely dispersed knowledge to address specific problems. In contrast, the dominance of market mechanisms in shaping employment relationships reduces employees' incentive to build relational wealth in organizations and results in employee focus on building skills necessary for career advancement in other firms. In other words, rather than focusing on building organizational capacity, employees search for their next job.

Examining the role of relational wealth in organizations highlights its centrality in building both individual human capital and organizational production systems. Practices that create linkages across employee, deepen existing knowledge and skills and enable workers to develop new skills as they build connections and conduct work across traditional boundaries. The absence of relational wealth greatly diminishes organizations' capacity to build needed skills over time.

Notes

1. Several authors have examined the diffusion and benefits of high-involvement work systems, including Tom Kochan and Paul Osterman in *The Mutual Gain Enterprise* (Boston: Mass. Harvard Business School Press, 1994); John Paul MacDuffie in "Human Resource Bundles and Manufacturing Performance: Organizational Logic and Flexible Production systems in the Auto Industry," *Industrial and Labor Relations Review* vol. 48, no. 2 (1995), pp. 197–221; and Jeffrey Pfeffer in *The Human Equation* (Boston: Harvard Business School Press, 1998).

2. Peter Cappelli, *The New Deal at Work: Managing the Market-Driven Workforce* (Boston: Harvard Business School Press, 1998).

3. Brenda Lautsch, "Contingent Employment: Employer Strategic Choice and High Performance Work Organizations," manuscript, 1994. Vancouver, Canada, Simon Frasier University.

4. Many firms, in fact, appear to adopt both high-performance practices together with efforts to reduce long-term employee commitment. At times this may occur in different parts of the organization or even for the same

employee group, where a core group is placed within a high-commitment environment and others are employed on a contingent basis (Lautsch, 1998).

5. Paul Osterman, "Choice of Employment Systems in Internal Labor Markets," *Industrial Relations* (1987) vol. 26, no. 1: 46–67.

6. Gil Preuss, *Sharing Care: The Changing Nature of Nursing in Hospitals* (Washington, D.C.: Economic Policy Institute, 1998).

7. Chapter 1.

8. Richard Murnane, John B. Willett, and Frank Levy, "The Growing Importance of Cognitive Skills in Wage Determination," National Bureau of Economic Research working paper no. 5076, Cambridge, Mass. 1995.

9. Michael Cusumano and Richard Selby, *Microsoft Secrets* (New York: Free Press, 1995), p. 93.

10. Murnane, Willett, and Levy (1995).

11. Paul Osterman, "How Common Is Workplace Transformation and Who Adopts It?" *Industrial and Labor Relations Review* (1994): 173–88.

12. Thomas Bailey, "Discretionary Effort and the Organization of Work: Employee Participation and Work Reform since Hawthorne," manuscript, 1992. Manuscript prepared by the Alfred P. Sloan Foundation, New York.

13. Jean Lave, *Cognition in Practice: Mind, Mathematics, and Culture in Everyday Life* (Cambridge, England: Cambridge University Press, 1988).

14. Lave and Wenger, *Situated Learning* (Cambridge, England: Cambridge University Press, 1991).

15. Stephen Barley, "Technicians in the Workplace: Ethnographic Evidence for Bringing Work into Organization Studies," *Administrative Science Quarterly* vol. 41, no. 3 (1996): 404–41; Marcy Tyre and Eric Von Hippel, "The Situated Nature of Adaptive Learning in Organizations," *Organization Science* vol. 8, no. 1 (1997): 71–83.

16. Karl Weick, *The Social Psychology of Organizing* (New York: Random House, 1979); Julian Orr, *Thinking about Machines: An Ethnography of a Modern Job* (Ithaca, NY, Cornell University Press 1996); J. Brown and P. Duguid, "Organizational Learning and Communities-of-Practices: Toward a Unified View of Working, Learning and Innovation," *Organization Science* vol. 2, no. 1 (1991), pp. 40–57; C. Argyris and D. Schon, *Organizational Learning* (Reading, Mass.: Addison Wesley, 1978).

17. Orr (1996).

18. Henry Fayol, *General and Industrial Management* (New York: Pitman, 1949); Max Weber, *Economy and Society*, vols. 1 and 2, editors Guenther Ross and Claus Wittich (Berkeley: University of California Press, 1978).

19. Alfred Chandler, *Strategy and Structure: Chapters in the History of the American Industrial Enterprise* (Cambridge, Mass.: MIT Press, 1962).

20. James March and Herbert Simon, *Organizations* (Cambridge, Mass.: Blackwell, 1958).

21. Tyre and Von Hippel (1997).

22. Gil Preuss, *Committing to Care: Labor–Management Cooperation and Hospital Restructuring* (Washington, D.C.: Economic Policy Institute, 1998a); Gil Preuss, *Sharing Care: The Changing Nature of Nursing in Hospitals* (Washington, D.C.: Economic Policy Institute, 1998).

23. Institute of Medicine, *Nursing Staff in Hospitals and Nursing Homes: Is It Adequate?* (Washington, D.C.: National Academy Press, 1996).

24. Preuss (1998).

25. Preuss (1998).

26. Preuss (1998).

27. J. Richard Harkman and Greg Oldham, *Work Redesign* (Reading, Mass.: Addison-Wesley, 1980).

28. Tyre and Von Hippel (1997).

29. Arthur Stinchcombe, *Information and Organizations* (Berkeley: University of California Press, 1990).

30. See Cusumano and Selby (1995) for greater detail.

31. Lotfi Zadeh, "Fuzzy Sets," *Information and Control* 8 (1965): 338–53.

32. Rosabeth Moss Kanter, *World Class: Thriving Locally in the Global Economy* (New York: Simon and Schuster, 1995).

II

HOW RELATIONAL WEALTH REDUCES VULNERABILITIES FOR FIRMS AND WORKERS

Relational wealth is founded on trust. Trust is central to realizing competitive advantage for the vast majority of firms. Under a market-focused view of employment, employers cannot be confident that workers will act in ways that contribute to their business interests over the long term. Workers are likely to be neither motivated nor sufficiently knowledgeable to act in the firm's interests. Unless the employer is willing and able to constantly scrutinize and supervise workers, it is difficult to function without trust. Yet without some degree of stability in employment, workers and their greater mobility become a source of vulnerability to the firm.

In this section, chapters address how the attachment between firms and workers reduces their mutual vulnerability while enhancing their flexibility in the face of market changes and competitive pressures. Jone Pearce focuses on the trustworthiness of employees as a key concern of firms. She argues that employability derives not simply from worker skills and the demand for them in the marketplace, but also from how trustworthy workers seem to their potential employers. Pearce argues that overreliance on short-term market practices in employment has increased rather than decreased employers' vulnerability to workers. Firms traditionally coped with this vulnerability through long-term employment, creating reliable firsthand knowledge regarding worker skills, motivations, and readiness to work toward the common goal of firm success. Increasing worker mobility means that firms must rely on secondhand indicators such as credentials, personal attributes, and reputation as signs of trustworthiness. Moreover, firms whose trustworthiness has eroded in the eyes of employees are poorly positioned to recruit workers they themselves can trust. In effect, erosion of trustworthiness is a downward spiral.

The increasing vulnerability many firms face to workers has expanded the role of employment agencies, now more formally called labor intermediaries. Alison Davis-Blake and Joseph Broschak describe the various roles employment agencies can play in helping their clients access qualified labor. Based on their original research into the emerging functions of labor intermediaries, Davis-Blake and Broschak present a framework for understanding the interaction between the client firm and the intermediary. They develop four general types of interaction, ranging from a "people source" approach that treats temporary workers as disposable commodities to a "client extension" approach, where the employment agency works closely with the client firm, in effect becoming an extension of its human resources function. As Davis-Blake and Broschak cogently argue, the former approach depletes relational wealth, whereas the latter can enhance it. They note that a growing segment of the contingent workforce is recreating with its new employers some of the attachment and loyalty that characterized the more traditional core workforce.

Employee vulnerability is closely tied to the extent of training and development investments available to workers. Frits Pil and Carrie Leana differentiate between training and development initiatives that treat workers as free agents in a highly mobile job market versus those that target skills, knowledge, and in-context learning to promote high performance within a firm. The essential contrast they make is between employers that "buy" skills in the market as opposed to "making" them in-house. Pil and Leana argue that the former tactic increases employer vulnerability to other firms, which can easily poach their employees. Moreover, it exacerbates problems of "fit" caused by lack of compatibility between worker skills and firm-specific needs. The alternative relies on relational wealth and is a cornerstone of high-performance work models, shown to enhance firm performance. Skills programs centering on the firm, by using in-context training and development, can decrease the vulnerability of workers to job loss due to enhanced skill matching. At the same time, this relational approach to training limits the firm's vulnerability to untrustworthy employees and poaching by competitors.

Another perspective is offered by Maura Belliveau, who discusses the limitations of secondhand indicators of trustworthiness and ability, particularly credentials. Credentialing in the form of schooling is a means for potential employees to signal their capabilities, including skill set and social connections. It also provides employers with a means of reducing their risks in selecting employees by allowing them to access individuals already screened by others (e.g., schools). Based on original research conducted in sample elite universities and MBA graduates, Belliveau indicates that neither firms nor workers may be effective in their use of credentialing as a basis for establishing employment relations based on trust. Her findings further support relational rather than market-focused employment practices, including selection.

4

Employability as Trustworthiness

JONE L. PEARCE

Whenever employers hire someone they put themselves at risk. They depend on employees to act in ways that help rather than hinder the organization and to refrain from using the information they gain to harm their employers. This is because employees are hired to act *for* their employers, making decisions and carrying out responsibilities on their behalf. Although all employers have ways to monitor their employees, such monitoring is expensive and narrow in scope except in the simplest and most physical of jobs. In addition, as the number of employees grows, employers must trust some employees to monitor the actions of others, which leads to the question of who watches the watchers. In other words, every employee makes an employer vulnerable.

This chapter develops this argument and then applies it to the concept of employability. As noted in chapter 1, societal changes have eroded organizations' relational wealth. Those changes have also made employability more problematic for individuals. Because employees cannot assume stable, lifetime employment, they must find ways to enhance their employability without becoming dependent on one employer. Here it is proposed that enhancing one's employability is a matter of understanding employers' vulnerability and the ways they manage it when making hiring decisions.

Employers are vulnerable to the depredations and inattention of every one of their employees, and they cope with this vulnerability by employing workers whom they trust.[1] Because of this, workers' employability must depend on their ability to convince employers that they are trustworthy. Fortunately, how trust is cultivated and sustained within organizations is a subject of extensive scholarship, allowing us to draw on the literature on trust to gain insights into the problem of employability in a work world based on flexibility.

For many reasons, it is unusual to frame employability in terms of the trustworthiness of potential employees. First, more of us have been applicants than have been employers, so we naturally focus on how those who need a job are needy and anxious. Because employers usually have more power and are less dependent than an individual employee, it is easy to overlook their vulnerability when hiring. However, recent social, economic, and legal changes have made employers' trust in potential employees a central concern. As suggested in chapter 1, we know that one of the best ways for people to build trust in one another is for the parties to have interacted in the past and to expect continuous and future on interaction. People learn who they can trust on the basis of their experiences and are more interested in cultivating another's trust if they expect to continue working with them.[2] Yet today we see that work is increasingly contingent and fewer employees expect long-term relationships. This means that the trust employers and employees develop when they maintain long-term relationships can no longer be assumed. When fates were tied together, cheaters in employment relationships could expect to get caught eventually. In short-term relationships, such trust cannot be assumed by either party.

Further impediments to the building of trust between employers and employees come from increased hiring as organizations cope with demands for flexibility. More new hires mean more frequent risks taken on strangers. Present employment trends have made the trustworthiness of potential and current employees increasingly problematic. This means that employers must actively select for and build that which they could assume in more stable environments.

The increased use of long-term partnerships, contracting, and other network organizational forms has raised the visibility of this kind of vulnerability. Formal contracts make vulnerability to others more explicit than has been the case in the tradition-bound informality of employment relations. When depending on another autonomous person or organization, this vulnerability is more explicit, with the limitations of contracts and the importance of trust now explicitly acknowledged.[3]

Similarly, the recent explosion in employee litigation against former and current employers, as well as customer and shareholder lawsuits based on the actions of employees, has heightened employers' awareness of their vulnerability to employees. Employees increasingly sue their employers for sexual harassment, age discrimination, and wrongful termination. Thus, each new hire subjects an employer to vulnerability, the possibility that he or she will act incompetently or maliciously in the employer's name, may disrupt the workplace by not working effectively with others, and may file a costly lawsuit against the employer. Every act of hiring is a potentially large risk to the employer. Thus, one way that the changes that are eroding relational wealth adversely impact employers is by increasing their vulnerability to employees.

Although the framing of employability as employees' ability to signal their trustworthiness to vulnerable employers has not been explicitly formulated as such, there is indirect evidence that it is of increasing concern to those who hire. One reflection of this is an examination of the articles published in *Personnel Psychology,* the preeminent scholarly journal for human resources management professionals and researchers, which over the past three decades has given increasing attention to the issue of employee trustworthiness. The 1997 volume featured twelve articles regarding employee selection (the way these management representatives frame employability), five of which at least indirectly touched on assessment of a potential employee's trustworthiness. In contrast, only one of the eight employee selection articles in the 1987 volume was concerned with assessing trustworthiness, and none of the eight such articles in the 1977 volume mentioned the issue. This indicates that the trustworthiness of potential employees has become increasingly important for those who develop selection policies and procedures.

This is in contrast to the conventional view of employability as a problem of the workforce not possessing "marketable skills." This is only one component of employability.[4] Obtaining rare, valuable skills is not simply a matter of taking trade school courses or brushing up on computer skills, because easily acquired skills typically are not rare (or valuable) for long. All too often, popular writers assume that workers are not obtaining the skills they need in order to be employable because they are lazy or ignorant. This argument, however, appears to be pernicious—it may foster anxiety and cause people to needlessly waste time and money. Of course, job-relevant knowledge, skills, and abilities are critical to potential workers' employability. Yet trustworthiness is a necessary—and underappreciated— condition of employability. Certainly, a large component of employees' trustworthiness is a confidence in their ability to apply their knowledge and skills effectively to situations as they present themselves. Without trustworthiness, job-relevant knowledge, skills, and abilities do not create employability—employers are too vulnerable to take that risk. In summary, for all but the most technical and easily monitored tasks, a person's employability comes down to a matter of another's trust in them. Someone else must be willing to depend on the person and to put themselves at risk when they employ them.

If we reframe employment as vulnerability, with employability indicated by the extent to which employees are judged trustworthy, several provocative implications follow. First, gaining employability can be rearticulated as the need book to establish one's trustworthiness. Second, this book is premised on the idea that people who traditionally did not have to worry about their employability after becoming established in their jobs must increasingly worry about it throughout their working lives. Consequently, employability has become a practical problem of cultivating and sustaining one's trustworthiness. We can gain insight into how potential employees demonstrate their trustworthiness by studying those whose occupations have required them to continuously sustain it. Finally, although the primary focus of this chapter is on how employees can enhance their employability through a better understanding of their employer's concern for trustworthiness, this analysis also has implications for employers.

Establishing Trustworthiness

Fortunately, we know a great deal about how to cope with vulnerability, and we can draw on that knowledge to enrich our understanding of employability. The study of how the vulnerable cope is a centerpiece of the social sciences. Economists approach the problem by seeking to align incentives, sociologists look to the institutions that maintain social order in the face of vulnerability, and psychologists study why certain individuals are more willing to risk vulnerability than others.[5] Most of these disciplines view vulnerability as raising the question of trust. In order to take action in almost any social setting, one must find a way to act *despite* vulnerability—in other words, one must trust. We can draw on the research of these disciplines to understand how potential employees may establish their trustworthiness to employers.

The fact that so many scholars representing all of the social sciences and humanistic specialties have written about trust means that sorting through these works becomes a monumental task in itself.[6] In applying that literature to the problem of establishing one's trustworthiness to potential employers, Zucker's categorization is useful.[7] She grouped the different trust creation strategies used in societies into three (process-based, characteristic-based, and institutional-based) categories based on the primary mechanisms used.

Process-based Trust

This form of trust is based on exchanges that have occurred in the past and are expected to occur in the future. Trust grows from a chain of reciprocal relations and mutual obligations.[8] Like the resilient trust described in chapter 1, participants have clear expectations of what they owe and are owned because they know or are known to one another. Process-based trust can be established in two ways. In small, stable societies, normative expectations can become firmly established because relationships change little over time. Alternatively, in more complex systems, people learn to restrict their exchanges to those they have worked with in the past and personally know.

The first way process-based trust creates employability can be seen in the implicit normative expectations of stable societies, which are similar to large, stable organizations. When promotions are internal and all employees expect lifetime tenure, they have time to get to know one another and "learn the ropes."[9] They also "know who knows what." When employment could be assumed in these stable organizations, both employees and employers knew what was expected of them and that if they met those expectations, they would be trusted. This trust in employees' knowledge, job familiarity, and common relationships enhances workers' employability in that organization, as others in the organization learn to trust them. This type of trustworthiness is gained implicitly and informally, without design or craft. As Hall has noted, this implicitness means that what makes one employable is only tacitly, inarticulately known.[10]

As we observe the rise of more complex, temporary organizational forms and shifting network arrangements among organizations, we also see a shift away from process-based trust, based on implicit knowledge, to trust based on repeated interactions with the same specific partners. Both Jones and Bryman and colleagues have reported that those working in industries characterized by temporary project groups rely on the same partners whenever possible.[11] Jones described this phenomenon when observing the film industry; Bryman and colleagues studied teams at construction sites. They note that the employees in these temporary workplaces needed time to get to know their partners before they could trust each other to perform well and be reliable. Thus, while employability in large, stable organizations is largely a matter of avoiding a serious breach of known expectations, employability in a work world characterized by shifting network arrangements consists of being personally known to those who can give you work. Your employability is only as strong as your personal network. So it seems that the increased uncertainty of employment and more complex and ad hoc working relationships have increased the burden of establishing one's process-based trustworthiness as an employee.

Characteristic-based Trust

People's trustworthiness can also be signaled by their ascribed characteristics, such as family background or national origin. These serve as indicators for common cultures, shared background expectations, or expected patterns of behavior. Much premodern business was based on this form of trust; for example, early bank loans were made within kin and ethnic networks.[12] Where governments are weak or unreliable, it continues to dominate as the basis for business relationships.[13]

The use of ascribed characteristics as a basis for inferring the trustworthiness of potential employees has long been a dominant method of assessing employability.[14] Employers tend to assume that younger people will learn new skills quickly, older people are assumed to be more reliable, married people are assumed to be less likely to quit, and so on. This method of assessing the trustworthiness of potential employees dominates because it is inexpensive (neither employer nor employee is required to invest in the relationship) and simple (no formal legal or governmental systems are needed to support it). Yet in the past few decades this method has also been heavily denounced, and for good reason. Using ascribed characteristics as the basis for determining trustworthiness is not only error prone, it excludes those with characteristics not represented among decision makers (who are inherently biased toward people who are like themselves). It is interesting that 1977, the year with the lowest proportion of articles on the assessment of trustworthiness in *Personnel Psychology*, came at the height of concerns for integrating those previously excluded based on their race or gender into desirable jobs. Unfortunately, this laudable goal (fairness for those historically excluded based on ascribed characteristics) has, ironically, forced underground the consideration of trustworthiness among potential hirees.

This is reflected in the discipline of professional human resources management which has been built on the development of techniques that constrain the ability of those making hiring decisions to consider an applicant's trustworthiness. It does so by denying employers their conventional characteristic-based method without offering any useable replacement. Jacoby describes the development of professional human resources management as a long process of wresting control of hiring from shop-floor bosses, practices that have become increasingly institutionalized through formal tests of technical skills that prevent immediate supervisors from falling back on race, ethnic, or gender biases for which the corporation would be legally liable.[15] Yet such centralized selection systems invite sabotage by ignoring supervisors' need to trust potential subordinates.

As a result—despite the decades-long campaign to discredit ascribed characteristics as surrogates for trustworthiness—those making hiring decisions continue to use them.[16] Those concerned with both employability and fairness can change this reliance on biased assumptions by recognizing that many who use ascriptive characteristics in hiring (however implicitly) are really seeking a cheap, relatively easy (albeit flawed) way to determine a potential employee's trustworthiness. Armed with knowledge of employers' perception of their own vulnerability, potential employees can search for other ways to signal their trustworthiness. For example, they could cultivate process-based trust by developing personal relationships within an organization or emphasize their trustworthiness in previous settings rather than just their technical skills. A negative example can illustrate how potential employees sometimes inadvertently signal untrustworthiness. When employees try to carefully control which references a potential employer contacts, they appear to be hiding something. Applicants look much more trustworthy when they invite the potential employer to contact anyone who knows their work.

Institution-based Trust

Zucker's final basis for trust is centered on generalized expectations that extend beyond a particular exchange or person and is taken for granted by the participants. This form of trust can be in the form of expectations for a particular role, organization, or intermediary mechanism. For example, the trust that patients place in physicians independent of their experiences with individual doctors or any of their ascribed characteristics. Institution-based trust is used when the complexity of a situation or the need for impersonal exchanges overwhelms the process- and characteristic-based forms of trust—which rely to a greater extent on knowing the people and settings involved. Not surprisingly, as employment has become more unstable and both employees and employers have been forced to work more often with strangers, reliance on the institutional bases of trust has grown.

An example of reliance on institutional trust as it relates to employability is reflected in workers' cultivation of trust in themselves by lobbying for occupational licensing requirements and forming professional associations that require specific credentials for membership. This creates a trustworthy identity for members of a particular occupation, allowing the possession of credentials to substitute for personal knowledge of the applicant. Prospective employees may prominently display credentials, certificates, licensures, and association memberships on their resumes to signal that they can be trusted to adhere to professional standards. The "professionalization" of occupations that previously required no specialized training is one response of employees who find that employability has become problematic for them. One of the most visible examples of this process is the MBA degree. While it is true that managerial work has gotten more technical, a case can be made that the demand for professional certification to enhance employability is at least as responsible for the growth in the number of MBA degrees awarded worldwide as is any desire to obtain greater technical knowledge.

The other form of institution-based trust, the use of intermediaries, is based on the idea that some vulnerabilities do not depend solely on intentional betrayal. Events beyond the control of either party can prove costly. To mitigate this risk, individuals and organizations employ intermediaries to produce trust. Examples include insurance companies insuring equipment that is shipped, public accounting firms auditing organizational records, and the signing of formal contracts (not because the parties expect to seek their enforcement in court but as a signal that both are committed to the relationship). All of these uses of intermediaries signal that the parties have done everything reasonable and acted in good faith to guarantee the relationship—creating greater trust in what would otherwise be an intolerably risky exchange.

Traditionally, such formal intermediaries were rarely needed to guarantee employability. Instead, informal intermediaries were the norm, reflected in the fact that most employees obtain their jobs from family members or friends.[17] For example, research has consistently shown that the vast majority of blue-collar workers continue to find their jobs through friends and relations.[18] While such informal intermediation may rely on reputation to build trust, it has several advantages for both potential employees and employers. Employees can learn a great deal about the work and their potential coworkers before starting a job, more than someone hired through a formal advertisement and interviewed by human resources staff. More important for this discussion, employers can be more confident in new hires who are recommended by current employees. Employees have an incentive to be honest about their recommendations because they are placing their own reputations on the line for someone else.[19] This partly accounts for the continued higher success rate of employee referrals compared to other sources of new hires.[20] Thus, despite its adverse impact on those without connections through their friends and family, referral-based hiring remains popular. Despite the advantages of informal intermediation and the complexity of needed job skills, rapid workplace changes have impelled organizations to rely more on referrals from formal intermediaries. Examples include search firms, temporary agencies, and campus placement offices. These formal intermediaries are expected to evaluate the workers they recommend, and the agents are aware that they will not receive future fees from an employer if they provide untrustworthy employees.

In summary, employers determine the trustworthiness of potential employees by selecting someone they already do trust, relying on easily measured signals of trustworthiness (whether those are personal characteristics or professional credentials) and on intermediaries to vouch for a potential employee's trustworthiness. As worklife has become unstable, employers must rely more often on more explicit (and more expensive) means to assess employability.

Enhancing Employability: Implications for Potential Employees

If employment is becoming more unstable, establishing one's trustworthiness as a potential employee is becoming both more difficult and more important. Increasing employment instability has disrupted the established patterns of trust cultivation and maintenance in some industries. Trust that could formerly be assumed has become problematic and must be actively managed. Employers have not had the opportunity to develop trust in potential employees during the natural course of working. As a consequence, one's trustworthiness is more often based on personal knowledge, credentialing, and formal intermediation.

Unstable employment requires workers to cultivate personal trust relationships with broader and perhaps different sets of individuals. Thus, the familiar admonishment to get out there and "network." However, once employees understand that they must establish trust, not mere face recognition, more effective approaches to networking can be developed. Process-based trust, for example, is based on actually working with the potential employee (or with someone who knows him or her well). Simply making someone's acquaintance does not establish a relationship of mutual trust. In the project-based industries of filmmaking and construction, trust is based on past working relationships, not acquaintanceship.[21] Thus, networking needs to consist of more than just attending social functions; it needs to include some knowledge of a potential employee's performance.

Furthermore, the development of personal networks can be burdensome and time-consuming. As noted earlier, process-based trust builds one relationship at a time and is inherently limited—we can only know so many people. While such networking can be targeted, increased instability makes it more difficult to know which relationships will be important over time. It seems clear that those seeking to improve their employability would benefit from a greater reliance on institution-based approaches to establishing their trustworthiness.

Like networking, heightened credentialing is proliferating in these more unstable times, as discussed in chapter 6 by Pils and Leana. Yet efforts to credential and professionalize occupations are more often mocked than analyzed. Much of this effort is probably intended to restrict the number of competitors in a particular field. However, this chapter suggests that credentialing efforts also create a more efficient basis for determining the trustworthiness of potential employees. Those who scoff at the professional aspirations of members of "lower order" occupations need to understand this as a reaction to the increased vulnerability of everyone in this more complex and uncertain environment.

Finally, a reliance on formal intermediaries also seems to be increasing. Yet potential employees seem to have difficulty establishing and controlling intermediaries. This is largely because successfully establishing the trustworthiness of their members requires intermediaries to police and expel members who are not trustworthy. The difficulty and associations have had in enforcing their codes of professional conduct has been well documented. Such acts undermine the solidarity these associations need, and the cost of retention of untrustworthy members has only an indirect effect on those who have the burden of voting to expel. This implies that there will be an increase in independent, honest brokers such as placement officers or search firms whose own success depends on accurately distinguishing between trustworthy and untrustworthy prospective employees.

In short, while evidence from the film and construction industries suggests that increased investment in cultivating personal networks of those who can vouch for your trustworthiness is probably unavoidable, care should be taken to recognize that job-performance trustworthiness is what needs to be established, and that can take a great deal of time. In addition, the expansion of credentialing, occupational professionalization, and reliance on professional intermediaries are practices that should be encouraged. Such entities produce trust in a working environment where trust is becoming ever more problematic.

Enhancing Relational Wealth: Implications for Employers

This framing of employability as trustworthiness also has implications for employers. One of these implications, the theme of this volume, is to recognize that relational wealth has value. Trust is valuable to organizations, and the loss of implicit trust-building, along with increasing organizational instability, requires more expensive methods of assessing trustworthiness. Clearly, employers could benefit from being explicit and systematic in analyzing their need to hire trustworthy employees. Rather than overemphasizing technical skills, employers need to explicitly assess trustworthiness. While more difficult than assessing technical skills, the increased interest in this question (as reflected in the 1997 volume of *Personnel Psychology*) indicates that assessment professionals are working to make it easier.

In addition, employers should recognize that the need for supervisors and coworkers to trust one another requires some decentralization of selection decisions. In the past, centralized top-down human resources systems largely ignored the role of trust in the workplace—often quashing the informal systems supervisors and coworkers used to ensure a smoothly functioning workplace based on mutual trust. While there are potential problems (i.e., nepotism and homophilic bias) in relying on a subjective feeling such as trust in another, vulnerability has made the need for trust in the workplace so great that centralized objective selection systems that ignore the importance of trust push the assessment of trustworthiness underground. A more successful strategy is to recognize the importance of trustworthiness and to develop ways to assess it in an unbiased way. Through guidelines and training, personnel selection decisions can be delegated more confidently.

Finally, in these dynamic times employers might benefit from evaluating potential and current employees on the extent of their networks of personal trust relationships. Employees with networks that provide access to social groupings with the skills employers might otherwise have difficulty accessing are particularly valuable. Employers can enhance their relational wealth by recognizing that social knowledge is now as important in the cubicle as in the boardroom. While evaluating who someone "knows" has always been relevant to filling boards of directors and other elite posts, today's employment instability has made extensive personal contacts a valuable asset for employees throughout the organization.

Employability is a matter of trustworthiness, something that employment instability has made more problematic for employee and employer alike. What could be implicitly assumed in stable employment settings now requires more explicit planning and investment by both. Greater flexibility has created greater vulnerability, and vulnerability is managed most economically by trust. Those who most successfully cultivate and sustain such trustworthiness will have a substantial advantage in the workplace.

Notes

1. Most writers on trust have identified vulnerability in social exchanges as the reason for the need for trust. Prominent discussions of this includ C. F. Sabel, "Studied Trust: Building New Forms of Cooperation in a Volatile Economy," *Human Relations* 46 (1993): 1133–70; Gregory Bigley and Jone Pearce, "Straining for Shared Meaning in Organizational Science: Problems of Trust and Distrust," *Academy of Management Review* 23 (1998): 405–21.

2. The importance of past and expected future interaction in building and sustaining trust is well established; a recent empirical paper reporting empirical results is P. Hart and C. Saunders, "Power and Trust: Critical Factors in the Adoption and Use of Electronic Data Interchange," *Organization Science* 8 (1997): 23–42.

3. Interestingly, while the importance of trust in employability is largely ignored, its importance is a prominent feature of virtually all discussions of network organizational arrangements. See Jay R. Galbraith, *Designing Organizations* (San Francisco: Jossey-Bass, 1995); and Candace Jones, "Careers

in Project Networks: The case of the Film Industry," pp. 58–75, in (*Boundaryless Career: Work, Mobility, and Learning in the New Organization Era.* Edited by Michael B. Arthur and Denise M. Rousseau (New York: Oxford University Press, 1996).

4. Jeffrey Pfeffer, *The Human Equation* (Boston: Harvard Business School Press, 1998), has an excellent discussion of the folly of selecting employees solely on technical skills and the bankruptcy of many employers' claims to offer "employability" (skills kept current) instead of employment security.

5. Bigley and Pearce (1998) provide a review of many of the approaches to trust taken in the differing disciplines.

6. Ibid.

7. Lynne G. Zucker, "Production of Trust: Institutional Sources of Economic Structure, 1840–1920," *Research in Organizational Behavior* 8 (1986): 53–111.

8. Ibid.

9. This expression is taken from John Van Maanen, "People Processing: Strategies of Organizational Socialization," *Organizational Dynamics* 7 (summer 1978): 18–36.

10. Edward T. Hall, *The Silent Language*, 2nd ed. (New York: Doubleday, 1981).

11. Jones (1996); A. Bryman, M. Brensen, A. D. Beardswoth, J. Ford, and E. T. Keil, "The Concept of the Temporary System: The Case of the Construction Project," *Research in the Sociology of Organizations* 5 (1987): 253–83.

12. The ways in which those working in traditional societies without institutional protections of modern societies rely on personal networks in their business arrangements has been described by C. Geertz, "The Bazaar Economy: Information and Search in Peasant Marketing," *American Economic Review* 68 (1979): 28–32; S. Gordon Redding, *The Spirit of Chinese Capitalism* (New York: de Gruyter, 1990); and Jone L. Pearce, *Organization and Management in the Embrace of Government* (Manwah, NJ: Erlbaum, forthcoming).

13. Katherine R. Xin and Jone L. Pearce, "Guanxi: Connections as Substitutes for Formal Institutional Support," *Academy of Management Journal* 39 (1996): 1641–58; Pearce (forthcoming).

14. A. M. Spence, *Market Signaling: Informational Transfer in Hiring and Related Screening Processes* (Cambridge: Harvard University Press, 1974).

15. Sanford M. Jacoby, *Employing Bureaucracy: Managers, Unions and the Transformation of Work in American Industry, 1900–1945* (New York: Columbia University Press, 1985).

16. The continuing presence of racism in employment is discussed by Arthur P. Brief, Robert T. Buttram, Robin M. Reizenstein, S. Douglas Pugh, Judi D. Callahan, Richard L. McAllen, and Joel B. Vaslow, "Beyond Good Intentions: The Next Steps toward Racial Equality in the American Workplace," *Academy of Management Executive* 11 (1997): 59–72.

17. Descriptions of pre-twentieth century hiring practices are available in Alfred D. Chandler, *The Visible Hand: The Managerial Revolution in American Business* (Cambridge: Harvard University Press, 1977); and Jacoby (1985).

18. See Mark Granovetter, *Getting A Job: A Study of Contacts and Careers*, 2nd ed. (Chicago: University of Chicago Press, 1995) for a review and discussion.

19. Hiring the relatives and friends of current employees also provides an additional layer of management control, as was explained to me in 1974 by the personnel director of Mobil Oil corporation's Torrance Refinery, who practiced employee-referral hiring assiduously for nonprofessional white-collar and blue-collar jobs. Current employees would be conscientious so they would be "rewarded" by having their connection hired, and the new hire had an extra incentive to behave well, since his or her parent/sibling/best friend would be penalized if he or she didn't.

20. Alison E. Barber, *Recruiting Employees: Individual and Organizational Perspectives* (Thousands Oaks, Calif.: Sage, 1998).

21. See Annalee Saxenian, "Beyond Boundaries: Open Labor Markets and Learning in Silicon Valley," in *The Boundaryless Career,* Arthur and Rousseau (1996), pp. 23–39.

5

Speed Bumps or Stepping Stones

The Effects of Labor Market Intermediaries on
Relational Wealth

ALISON DAVIS-BLAKE AND JOSEPH P. BROSCHAK

Over the past decade, use of contingent work arrangements, such as part-time, temporary, and contract work has grown dramatically. In the United States, 20 percent of the jobs created from 1991 to 1993 were either part-time or temporary, and by 1995, nearly 30 percent of all American jobs involved some type of contingent work arrangement.[1] During the 1990s, contingent work spread from its traditional location in clerical, sales, and some service occupations (e.g., nursing, teaching) to include managerial, professional, and technical occupations. Individuals employed by temporary agencies represent one of the fastest growing segments of the contingent workforce. The number of temporary agencies operating in the United States has grown from one hundred in the mid-1980s to more than fifteen hundred in 1998, and the number of people working for temporary employment agencies has more than tripled.[2]

The rise of the temporary help industry is not restricted to the United States. The use of agencies as a source of temporary workers has also become relatively commonplace in Europe and Asia. Britain, France, and the Netherlands have long had a temporary help industry. Recently, Germany, Spain, and Italy have legalized temporary agencies and loosened restrictions against the employment of temporary workers.[3] In Japan, where twenty new white-collar occupations were opened to temporary workers in 1996 (previously, only six occupations were open to temporary workers), the Ministry of Labor estimates that temporary workers constitute as much as 12 percent of the paid labor force.[4] The Korean government legalized temporary employment agencies in 1998, and more than 140 temporary labor agencies were founded in the first four months after the law took effect.[5]

Despite the proliferation of temporary agencies, very little has been written about the effects on firms that use agencies to meet employment needs. A small but growing literature has examined the impact of temporary employees on their full-time, "permanent" coworkers.[6] However, this literature focuses on effects on individuals and does not address the organization-level consequences of using temporary agencies.

In this chapter, we attempt to fill this gap by examining the consequences for firms of using temporary agencies to meet some of their employment needs. We develop four models of the relationship between temporary agencies and client firms, arguing that each model creates distinct difficulties for managing the agency-client boundary. We argue that in nearly every model, the formation and maintenance of the boundary does not receive adequate attention from managers in the client firm. The models also differ in their impact on relational wealth, with only one offering the possibility of enhanced relational wealth. The remainder of this chapter is divided into four sections. First, we describe the research settings in which we gathered the data used to stimulate our conceptual thinking. Second, we develop our models of the roles played by temporary employment agencies. Third, we explore the boundary management issues that are associated with each of these models and link those issues to the existing literature on the consequences of using temporary employees. Finally, we discuss the impact each of these models has on relational wealth. We argue that one of the four models clearly enhances the relational wealth of the client by developing a strong client-agency relationship, providing access to new networks of employees and to other agencies, and enhancing the client's reputation in the labor market. A second model may create modest gains in relational wealth through access to new networks of employees and agencies. The remaining two models decrease relational wealth, either moderately or substantially.

Research Settings

This chapter brings together observations we made while studying temporary employment agencies and their clients in a variety of settings. Between 1995 and 1998, we interviewed approximately forty managers employed by temporary agencies or their clients. In client firms, we interviewed line managers who used temporary workers in their work groups, division general managers who set divisional policies about temporary employment, and human resource managers involved in hiring temporary employees at the divisional level or setting policies about temporary employment at the corporate level. Our interviews in temporary agencies included both managers who worked exclusively with a single client and served as the on-site manager of that client's temporary employees as well as managers who served multiple clients and were located in the offices of a temporary agency. These interviews were exploratory and covered a variety of issues about temporary employment.

We interviewed client managers employed by service and manufacturing firms that used temporary workers in lower skill positions, such as clerical and production jobs. The firms employed temporary workers as production line workers, secretaries, administrative assistants, and customer service workers—in jobs typical of those held by agency temporaries. The agencies we visited tended to specialize in the location and placement of lower skill temporaries.[7] Thus we learned relatively little about higher skill temporaries such as nurses, accountants, and engineers. As a result, the ideas we develop here may not apply to higher skill occupations.

Common Models of the Client-Agency Relationship

During our interviews, managers described many types of relationships between clients and agencies. However, one common theme was that the client, not the agency, determined the nature of the relationship. In nearly every case, requests for temporary workers originated with client line managers. When they identified the need for a temporary worker, client managers typically contacted agency managers, either by phone or via electronic requisitions, depending on the level of integration between client and agency. Clients described the position to be filled, the desired skill requirements of temporary workers, and the start date of the placement (most often the next day). Agency managers used this information to identify potential workers for the client from their existing pool of temporaries or to conduct interviews to fill the specified position.

Clients varied in the extent to which they used the same agencies repeatedly, provided well-specified job descriptions, and rehired the same individual temporaries. There was also considerable variance in the extent to which temporary workers were prescreened for and converted to permanent status, interviewed for person-organization fit, and oriented to the work site by a manager of the client or the agency. Clients sometimes asked agencies to provide detailed skills and work sample testing, a weekly orientation, and basic training for all new temporary workers. In other instances, clients requested only minimal agency screening of temporary employees and tasks such as orientation and training were left to the coworkers of the temporary employee.

Although agencies had preferred modes of operation, they typically adjusted their operating procedures to fit the client's business needs. For example, all of the agency managers we interviewed stated that good person-organization fit between the temporary worker and the client enhanced worker performance and retention (i.e., ability to stay for the entire length of the assignment).[8] Thus, most agencies preferred that the client's line managers interview potential temporary workers identified by the agency to ensure a good fit. However, line managers frequently expressed reluctance to interview potential temporary workers, preferring to delegate the task of determining fit to the agency. Agencies would sometimes send temporaries to a job "cold," without prior contact with anyone inside the client organization or without more than a cursory orientation to the client (e.g., a description of the client's location and hours of work). This practice was commonplace even though it substantially increased the risk of having to replace the temporary worker before the assignment was finished.

There are at least two reasons why clients control the details of their relationships with temporary agencies. First, agencies typically market themselves as having the ability to customize their services to meet client needs. In most transactions involving a customized service, the buyer controls the parameters of the transaction.[9] Second, when local economies are strong and unemployment is low, the labor market often is saturated with many temporary agencies pursuing few available temporary workers. This economic situation prevailed in nearly all of the locations we visited. With intense competition among agencies both for workers and for clients, flexibility becomes essential to getting and keeping clients.

When the client has control over the relationship, the client's culture and behaviors determine the role of the agency. We identified two client attributes that were central to determining the agency's role: the client's view of temporary employees and the client's level of involvement with the agency. Figure 5.1 illustrates four agency roles that result from the combination of these two client attributes.

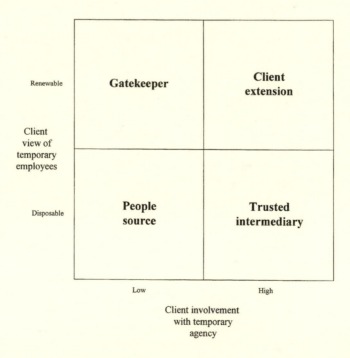

Fig. 5.1. Models of the client-agency relationship

Client View of Temporary Employees

Client firms could be clustered into two distinct groups: those who viewed temporary employees as a *disposable resource* and those who viewed them as a *renewable resource*. These differing views of temporary employees became evident when we asked clients to explain why they used temporary workers. Clients who viewed temporary workers as disposable tended to emphasize the fact that temporary workers could be fired at will, without explanation and without the involvement of the line manager. For example, it was quite common for the termination of temporary workers to be initiated by clients "off the clock": An agency manager would be notified after working hours that a particular temporary worker needed to be terminated. The agency manager would call the worker at home and tell him or her not to return to work the next day. These clients tended to view temporary workers as commodities that could be "ordered" (industry terminology for a client's request for a temporary employee) in much the same way that one orders spare parts for a piece of office equipment. These clients viewed temporary workers as a means to accomplish short-term objectives and did not view temporary employees as accumulating skills or knowledge that the client could use later. In one firm with this view, it was not unheard-of for temporary workers who had worked in a department for two or three years to be prevented by company policies from interviewing for a permanent position in the department. Although the logic of these policies was somewhat unclear, some key client managers believed that individuals employed as temporaries picked up "bad habits and bad attitudes" during their time as temporaries and thus were unsuitable candidates for permanent employment. These policies were enforced even if a temporary employee had been satisfactorily performing the exact job for which the department was hiring.

In contrast to the view of temporaries as disposable, some client managers viewed temporary workers as potential future employees and saw the time temporaries spent on the job as valuable learning time that would not need to be repeated if the temporaries were "converted" to permanent status. When we asked these managers why they used temporary employees, one of the most common answers was that they used temporary employment as a way to "test-drive" employees. In some ways, temporary employment replaced the organization's selection system. Managers used temporary employment as a way to identify the individuals they wanted to employ on a permanent basis. Some managers actually preferred to fill permanent positions with temporary employees instead of new hires because the risks associated with converting high-performing temporary workers to permanent status were relatively small. In this view, temporary employment offered credible information about a worker's future job performance and provided an alternative path for entering the organization that reduced many of the typical risks and uncertainties associated with hiring. Managers expected to benefit from the skills and information employees learned while in temporary assignments.

Client's Level of Involvement with the Agency

We observed two distinct styles of client-agency involvement, which were similar to the market and hybrid forms of governance described by Williamson.[10] Like Williamson's market style of governance, the low-involvement style entailed minimal cooperation between client and agency and no shared administrative infrastructure between the two firms. In contrast, the high-involvement style involved extensive cooperation and attempts to create shared information systems and administrative procedures.

In the low-involvement style, the client viewed the agency simply as a supplier of homogeneous workers who could not be differentiated from one another. Like a supplier of any commodity, the agency was expected to deliver its product with relatively little direction from the client. This was, by far, the most common mode of operation. When we asked agencies what difficulties they faced in dealing with their clients, the most common answer was lack of specificity about the job to be filled. It was not uncommon for clients to call agencies and place an "order" giving nothing more than a job title (e.g., production associate). Not surprisingly, this lack of specificity often resulted in mismatches between worker attributes and client needs. For example, one agency manager received a request for a production associate in an assembly plant. The client neglected to specify that, unlike typical production jobs at the plant, this particular job required heavy lifting. The client was dismayed when a pregnant woman arrived to fill the assignment and ultimately reassigned her to a less physically demanding temporary job in the same firm.

In this low-involvement mode of operation, clients sometimes actively resisted giving agencies even basic information that was necessary to make placements. One agency manager recounted a situation in which her agency had signed an exclusive contract to provide all temporary workers for a large manufacturing plant. Despite having placed nearly two hundred workers over a six-month period, the client still resisted the agency manager's attempts to visit the plant and see the facility in which workers were being placed. This behavior appeared to result from the client manager's view that it was the agency's job to deliver qualified employees with little client input rather than from a lack of trust in the agency. In some cases, a low-involvement style was part of a more general pattern of inattention to human resource issues. However, in other instances, low involvement was a purposeful client decision; the client felt that the "routine" task of securing temporary employees could be delegated to a trusted agency, thus allowing client personnel to concentrate on "more critical" strategic and operational issues.

Interestingly, the degree of involvement between client and agency did not depend on whether the client viewed temporary employees as disposable. We found low-involvement interaction patterns in situations where clients in tight labor markets actively recruited temporaries to convert to permanent status, even if the conversion meant paying additional agency fees.[11] The choice about involvement seemed more related to client expectations about agency roles rather than a client's view of temporary employees.

In contrast to the low-involvement model, we observed an alternate model of involvement in which clients and agencies shared a great deal of information and worked very closely together. This model had different manifestations depending on how the client used temporary agencies. In some clients, the firm's corporate human resources personnel negotiated national contracts with a limited number of agencies, and divisional human resource personnel actively worked to develop relationships with the local offices of those agencies. Relationship development activities included arranging facility tours for agency managers, sharing detailed information about the client's policies for authorizing and employing temporary workers, giving agencies in-depth job descriptions, and even sharing projections for the number of temporary employees the client would need. In this high-involvement mode of operating, client human resources personnel adopted a strategic role in recruiting and selecting temporary personnel but delegated the actual operations to agency managers.

An alternative manifestation of the high-involvement model occurred when client line managers had direct contact with temporary agencies. In this situation, a line manager would sometimes work exclusively with one agency (even when the manager was authorized to choose from several agencies) and would develop personal relationships with one or two of the agency's managers. Client managers attempted to work with the same agency managers repeatedly and tended to give them fairly specific feedback about why particular temporary employees were successful or unsuccessful. By working with particular client managers on specific placements over a period of time, agency managers developed substantial tacit knowledge about their needs.

Models of Client-Agency Relationships

The combination of the client's view of temporary employees and the client's level of involvement with the agency yields four distinct models of the roles temporary agencies play. We have labeled these models people source, gatekeeper, trusted intermediary, and client extension. We provide an example of each model and describe how a temporary agency working within that model functions in five critical areas:

- Selection (lead time, information provided by the client about the skill set required for the temporary assignment, attention to person-organization fit between the temporary employee and the client)
- Training
- Supervision (including providing performance feedback to the temporary employee)
- Discipline

- Retention (either for the length of the assignment or for conversion to permanent employment if desired by the client)

We chose these attributes because, as discussed earlier, temporary work can often be an alternative entry port into the organization. In fact, conversion of temporary employees to permanent status was commonplace even in some settings where temporary employees were not intended to become permanent hires. Given the frequency with which temporary employees become permanent workers, it is useful to know about how they are screened, trained, and evaluated prior to their change in status. These five attributes represent the key human resource management activities that occur between an individual's entry into and exit from an organization.[12] Table 5.1 provides a summary of the attributes of these four models of client-agency relationships.

People Source

In the people source model, client managers view agencies as vendors of a relatively undifferentiated commodity that can be produced almost instantly. We observed this type of relationship at a client that decided to experiment with direct shipping from the production line rather than from the warehouse. Because of uncertainty over whether the experiment would be successful, the client decided to hire temporary workers to perform the task, thinking that the temporary workers could simply be released from their assignments if the experiment failed, without any adverse effects on morale. At 5 p.m. on a Friday, a client manager telephoned the agency and ordered forty temporary production associates to begin at 8 a.m. on Monday. Ninety days after beginning direct shipping, the client decided that the experiment was unsuccessful and gave the agency only a few hours' notice before releasing all of the temporary workers.[13]

When a temporary agency acts as a people source, it operates with little or no lead time (8 a.m. phone calls ordering a worker immediately are not uncommon), minimal information about the skill set required for the job, and no attention to person-organization fit. In these situations, neither the temporary agency nor the client gives workers more than a minimal orientation (typically a few minutes) to the organization for which they will be working. Except for training required to operate specialized equipment, these temporary workers receive no formal training from the client. Any training that does occur tends to happen on the job from coworkers. In addition, poorly specified job requirements can result in a mismatch between a temporary worker's skills and the required tasks.

Because temporary workers are a commodity in which the client makes no investment, line managers typically give them no performance feedback. If a temporary employee commits sufficient errors that the supervisor considers his or her performance unacceptable, the worker is simply released, often without any explanation to the agency and nearly always without any

Table 5.1 Impact of Client-Agency Relationships on Human Resource Practices

Human Resource Practice	People Source	Models of Client-Agency Relationships		
		Gatekeeper	Trusted Intermediary	Client Extension
Selection				
—Lead time	Short	Short	Mixed—short from client but agency learns to anticipate	Moderate
—Information about job requirements	Little	Little from client; supplemented by agency tacit knowledge	Some—developed over time in conversations about specific placements	Large
—Attention to person-organization fit	None	Some—depends on level of agency tacit knowledge	Some—depends on level of agency tacit knowledge	Large
Training	On-the-job training from coworkers	Provided by agency plus on-the-job training from coworkers	On-the-job training from coworkers	Provided by client plus on-the-job training from coworkers
Supervision/Performance Feedback	Termination used as a substitute for feedback	By client manager—limited and targeted performance feedback	Supervision by coworkers and termination used as a substitute for feedback	By client manager
Discipline	Termination used as a substitute for discipline	Client-agency combination	Termination used as a substitute for discipline	Client-agency combination
Retention	Low	Moderate	Moderate	High
Friction between Coworkers	High	Moderate	High	Low
Friction between Employees and Managers	High	Moderate	Moderate	Low

explanation to the worker. Termination is typically used in lieu of discipline, with temporary workers being released for uttering a single word of profanity, for arriving a few minutes late to work, and for other minor misbehaviors that would typically result in a mild warning for permanent employees.

Given the lack of attention to person-organization fit and the use of termination as a substitute for feedback and discipline, it is not surprising that clients employing a people source model have low retention of temporary workers. Because of the lack of lead time, agencies are sometimes pressured into sending temporaries to clients before they have been thoroughly screened. In some cases, this caused agency managers to go to a client site and "walk a worker off the job" because the agency had unknowingly placed someone with a criminal record (in one case an individual who had been recently released from prison for capital murder) or someone who had failed a drug screen.

The low retention rates that occur in the people source model make the model self-perpetuating. High turnover among temporary workers gives agencies little lead time to replace workers who leave. Short lead times increase the probability that workers will not complete their assignments. Thus, agencies and clients can sometimes become trapped in a vicious cycle of rapid hiring and frequent termination, followed by more rapid hiring.

Gatekeeper

The gatekeeper model differs from the people source model only in the client's view of temporary workers. Although clients in the gatekeeper model still have little interaction with the agency, the client would like the agency to provide temporary workers who are a potential source of permanent employees. However, despite the client's wish for the temporary agency to be an entry port into the organization, client and agency spend little time discussing how the agency should recruit, screen, and select temporary employees.

We observed the gatekeeper model most clearly in a temporary agency that had an exclusive contract to provide all clerical and lower-level administrative temporary employees for a large manufacturing firm. The agency had a significant presence at the client site, including six of its own employees who wore client identification badges, worked exclusively at the client site, and were commonly mistaken for client employees.

The duties of these on-site agency employees illustrate some of the contradictions inherent in the gatekeeper role. This particular client was a highly desirable employer experiencing rapid growth in a very tight labor market, and one of the on-site agency's explicit mandates was to find people who would make good permanent employees. In fact, one of the agency manager's chief frustrations was that client line managers sometimes overstated the skills required for a temporary assignment in order to increase the probability of locating a high-quality, prospective permanent hire. As part of the contract between the client and agency, the agency performed a variety of preemployment skills tests, offered job-relevant training to temporaries, and supervised the enrollment of temporary workers in the client's in-house training programs.

However, the lack of interaction between client and agency often made it difficult for the agency to perform its role. It was not uncommon for recently appointed line managers to be unaware of the agency's existence and have no contact with agency personnel until they needed a temporary employee. Although last-minute, ill-specified employee orders were commonplace in this environment, the agency staff's on-site presence had allowed them to develop a great deal of tacit knowledge that assisted them in interpreting orders. Such tacit knowledge may be an essential element of the gatekeeper role. Paradoxically, the agency had become so good at finding and screening employees that the client had employed the agency to begin screening some of its "permanent" hires (including administering the agency's preemployment tests to potential "permanent" hires and doing targeted contract recruiting). The outsourcing of this task allowed the client's human resource personnel to focus on the recruitment and development of highly skilled professional and managerial employees. Thus the agency had assumed a position as an important gatekeeper for organizational entry. However, it was unclear that the agency was using any client-specified selection criteria in more than a minimal way.

In the gatekeeper model, a lack of interaction between client and agency creates short lead times and minimally specified job descriptions. The agency may pay some attention to person-organization fit, but only because it has gained the tacit knowledge to do so (by being on-site, for example). In the gatekeeper model, because the agency is preparing individuals for smooth organizational entry, the agency typically bears the responsibility for some worker training. As seen in the people source model, however, additional training tends to be ad hoc, consisting of whatever the individual learns from coworkers.

Responsibility for supervising temporary workers tends to shift from the agency manager to the client manager for whom the temporary is working, particularly given that the client managers are developing their own assessment of the employee's potential for permanent hire. Client managers give temporary workers limited, highly focused performance feedback. If the temporary employee appears to be a potential permanent hire, the client manager is likely to provide some feedback designed to shape the employee's performance.

Discipline is often a contentious area in the gatekeeper model. Because client managers are involved in supervision, they tend to provide warnings and other disciplinary measures for temporaries. However, agency temporaries are employees of the agency, not the client. Because of federal guidelines governing employment of temporary and contract workers, agency managers resist the idea of disciplinary conversations in which they are not involved. At times, discipline is provided solely by the agency manager (particularly in areas that client managers seem to be uncomfortable discussing, such as personal appearance and hygiene). However, unlike the people source model, termination is not the first resort when there is a problem with temporary worker performance. Counseling or discipline is attempted for all but the most egregious offenses. The area of discipline illustrates how, having passed through the portal of the temporary agency, a temporary employee has "quasi-permanent" status in terms of his or her relationship with the client line manager. Due to the use of discipline and more extensive screening, retention in the gatekeeper model is higher than in the people source model. However, limited lead times and sketchy job descriptions provided by the client still limit retention to moderate levels.

Trusted Intermediary

The trusted intermediary model features a relatively large amount of ongoing communication between agency and client but relatively little client investment in temporary employees. We observed this model in a financial services firm that commonly hired temporaries to perform tasks ranging from reconciling accounts to providing customer service over the telephone for traveler's check purchasers. The firm's product market was relatively stagnant, and the general manager had imposed an employee headcount restriction to which he granted very few exceptions. This restriction did not account for the fact that the firm had significant variation in its workload— for example, telephone calls peaked during the summer and holidays, when traveler's check use was high. Nor did it account for the fact that selected areas of the firm had grown so large that the permanent staff could no longer perform the work effectively. For example, reconciling accounts is a time-sensitive and time-intensive operation. Because of this, the firm was not allowed to accumulate a backlog of work.

Department managers employed temporary workers to circumvent the headcount restriction, but they had little expectation that these employees would become permanent. Differences between temporary and permanent workers were constantly reinforced, and unusually clear boundaries were maintained between the two types of employees. For example, although permanent employees could enter the human resources office to examine a list of internal vacancies created through attrition in order to apply for those jobs, temporary employees were required to learn about these vacancies in the newspaper or other public sources. If a temporary worker wanted to apply for a job, he or she had to go to the receptionist's desk outside the secure area of the building and fill out an application in a public cubicle. Permanent employees could fill out applications in the human resources office or at their desks. Temporary employees were forbidden from contributing to nonwork activities, such as blood drives, that were held on corporate premises and were not able to attend company functions, such as the employee-of-the-month awards. Department managers were also discouraged from including temporary employees in weekly potluck luncheons held in their departments.

Although the company had contracts with five temporary agencies, client managers tended to deal exclusively with one agency. These managers developed a close relationship with one particular agency manager, sometimes refusing to deal with anyone else at the agency. Client managers rarely provided written job descriptions or other formal documentation, but they contacted the agency manager to explain their decisions to retain or release a particular temporary worker. Thus, over time, the agency manager learned to understand and meet client needs, and in return line managers sometimes informally shared information about their upcoming needs for temporary employees. In addition, because the agency maintained a relationship with the client through several business cycles, the agency manager could anticipate regular fluctuations in the client's demand for temporary employees (such as the increased need for customer service personnel during the summer).

In the trusted intermediary model, lead times were mixed. Although short lead times still occurred, informal communication among agency and client managers, combined with the agencies' experience with the client, often gave agencies advance warning about needs for temporary employees. Over time, the agencies developed relatively clear information about the skill sets required for various jobs within the client firm as well as the culture of the firm and its various departments. Thus, although line managers did not formally request that the agencies consider person–organization fit, the agencies attempted to do so.

Because client managers did not expect temporary employees to become permanent, they were reluctant to invest time or money in them. Thus, temporary employees received virtually no training, and termination tended to replace negative performance feedback and discipline. From focus groups of permanent employees at this location, we learned that the lack of managerial training and supervision caused these responsibilities to fall entirely on the permanent coworkers of temporary employees. Given the relatively intricate nature of some of the accounting tasks, the permanent workers saw this as a burden. Despite the fact that managers used termination relatively frequently, reasonably good up-front fit led to moderate retention levels.

Client Extension

The client extension model is similar to the gatekeeper model in that a key task of the temporary agency is to find temporary workers who could become permanent client employees. However, unlike gatekeeper models in which agencies tend to operate without much client input, agencies involved in client extension models work more closely with their clients, becoming almost an extension of the clients' human resources function. As a result, this model can result in the creation of significant relational wealth.

We observed the client extension model at a payment processing center of a large financial services firm. This center not only provided services to the firm but also processed payments for a variety of other corporations outside the organization. At the time we visited this center, it had recently completed a transition from a people source model to a client extension model. Several years prior to our visit, the center had relied on large numbers of temporaries. However, the people source model led to extremely high turnover and low performance among the temporary workforce. A new human resources manager hired into the division was instrumental in eliminating the old model. As part of a strategic plan, the use of temporary workers was completely discontinued for several years. After they were reintroduced into the workplace, the center used far fewer temporary workers and focused on finding well-qualified people who not only could meet peak workloads but also could be available to fill permanent positions. This center operated in a labor market with very low unemployment and numerous employers of the low-skill clerical workers the center required. Thus, the focus on fewer, more highly qualified temporaries helped the center cope with difficult labor market conditions.

As part of the new human resources manager's strategy, the client firm conducted business with only one temporary agency. The client brought the agency manager in for site visits and provided details about the skill requirements of various jobs. Essential skills ranged from being able to operate extremely noisy and complex mail-opening equipment while being on one's feet for long periods of time to the rapid entry of information from checks and payment stubs into a computer. Where possible, the agency was informed in a systematic way about the client's future needs for temporary employees.

Compared to the other models we observed, the client extension model has numerous features that tend to increase relational wealth. Given the close connection between the agency and the client in the client extension model, the agency has moderate lead time to find people and a high level of information about the required skill set. Detailed attention is paid to person–organization fit, and the client typically provides required training. The performance feedback and discipline processes are two of the most distinctive features of this model. The center we observed used numerous metrics to track performance and provide feedback for both temporary and permanent employees. Client managers sought to improve the performance of all employees regardless of their work status. Client managers tended to use discipline before termination, although both agency and client managers were usually present at disciplinary conversations. Not surprisingly, at this facility, most temporaries completed their assignments and many were converted to permanent status.

Managing the Client-Agency Boundary

Academic research on temporary workers has consistently documented a number of dysfunctional effects that can occur when organizations use temporary and permanent employees in the same jobs.[14] The clients we observed commonly used both temporary and permanent employees to perform the same work, which is not unusual in the type of high-turnover, low-skill clerical and production jobs we studied. Even when temporary employees do not have permanent coworkers in the same job, they may still interact a great deal with other permanent employees in the workplace. (For example, a temporary employee occupying a support position such as departmental administrative assistant is likely to interact with all members of the department.) Research has begun to document that formal and informal interaction among temporary and permanent employees can have negative effects on the organization's permanent employees. Here, we briefly review the literature on the effects of using temporary employees and then discuss how inadequate boundary management between agencies and clients contributes to the well-documented dysfunctional effects of using temporaries.

Several types of friction occur between permanent employees and temporary workers who perform similar tasks. The use of temporary workers can increase conflict and tension in the workplace among coworkers and between workers and their supervisors. Full-time, permanent workers often perceive temporary workers as low performers because they lack experience in a job or with a particular organization. Temporary workers gain this experience from watching and talking to their permanent coworkers. Thus, the presence of temporary employees gives permanent workers the added responsibility of training, monitoring, and sometimes supervising the work of their temporary coworkers. These uncompensated extra duties increase resentment and friction between permanent employees and their managers. In some instances, full-time workers actually discourage the hiring of temporary workers because it makes their own jobs more difficult. The presence of temporary workers who can convert to permanent status can also hinder the promotion opportunities of low-skill permanent workers, further degrading the relationship between permanent workers and their supervisors.[15] It is not surprising, then, that across a variety of occupations and organizations, the presence of temporary workers in the same jobs as full-time, permanent employees has been shown to increase turnover intentions among permanent workers and to erode relations between permanent employees and their managers.

We argue that these dysfunctional interactions between permanent employees, temporary employees, and managers are due at least in part to the way in which the boundary between the temporary agency and the client firm is managed. At a minimum, in order for temporary employees to effectively contribute to the client, their skills must match job requirements and they must receive basic feedback about whether their performance meets expectations. However, we observed few situations where clients and agencies came together to systematically identify how the tasks of selection, training, supervision, and discipline should occur so that temporary workers could perform effectively. The failure to specify the allocation of these tasks between client and agency has two implications. First, these tasks are sometimes not performed at all, resulting in temporary workers who are mismatched or untrained for certain jobs. Inevitably, these employees must be replaced prior to completing the assignment. Second, coworkers perform these tasks out of necessity or frustration or both, yielding the dysfunctional workplace dynamics documented in the literature.

We see both of these effects in three of the four models of client-agency relationships. In the people source model, for example, little if any attention is paid to the allocation of tasks across the agency-client boundary. Agencies are expected to provide qualified workers despite receiving minimal information from the client. As noted in table 5.1, this model is associated with low retention rates and high levels of friction between coworkers and among employees and managers, due primarily to the introduction of poorly prepared temporary employees into the workplace. A similar scenario unfolds in the gatekeeper model—agency and client never decide who will perform the vital tasks of identifying required skill sets, training workers, and providing performance feedback. However, gatekeepers are able to partially overcome the lack of information about skill requirements through the development of tacit knowledge about their clients' needs and operations. In addition, the expanded role of the agency as a generalized organizational entry point allows gatekeepers to independently develop and administer training programs that are likely to enhance the job performance of temporaries. The combination of these two factors allows better person-organization fit and, subsequently, better retention in the gatekeeper model.

In the trusted intermediary model, communication between agency and client tends to focus solely on job requirements. This clearer communication of job requirements increases retention rates, but there is virtually no communication about training, performance feedback, or supervision, effectively relegating these tasks to coworkers. Finally, in the client extension model, clients and agencies actively communicate. Clients give agencies information on skill requirements and expected future needs for temporary workers and provide them with the time and opportunity to identify and train well-suited candidates. Under this model, not only is the retention of temporary workers expected to be high but the role of permanent workers in the supervision and training of their temporary coworkers should be minimal.

The preceding discussion suggests that the four models will have different effects on relationships between permanent and temporary employees and between permanent employees and their managers. We expect friction among coworkers to be highest in the people source and trusted intermediary models, where training, supervision, and performance feedback are left almost entirely to coworkers. We expect moderate levels of friction between coworkers in the gatekeeper model, where both the agency and the client managers make some investment in training and supervision. Coworker frictions should be lowest in the client extension model, in which information passes more readily across the agency-client boundary.

We expect that friction with coworkers will in turn create friction with managers, but research by George suggests that friction with managers can also occur independently. George reported that when permanent and temporary workers were employed in the same jobs, full-time workers tended to perceive the presence of temporary workers as evidence that their own jobs were insecure.[16] This suggests that client-agency models maximizing the extent to which temporary workers are seen as disposable are also likely to increase friction with management. In the people source and trusted intermediary models, clients tend to rely on termination instead of performance feedback and discipline. Frequent, visible termination of temporary workers may lead permanent workers to feel that their jobs are also insecure. However, in the trusted intermediary model, we observed that the distinction between permanent and temporary workers was carefully maintained so that permanent workers felt at least partially buffered from this insecurity. Thus, it seems likely that the people source model should generate the greatest friction with management, followed in order by the trusted intermediary, gatekeeper, and client extension models.

Labor Market Intermediaries and Relational Wealth

The role played by a temporary agency affects much more than interpersonal dynamics among coworkers and between employees and their managers. We argue that the role played by temporary agencies also affects the ability of clients to develop relational wealth. The client extension model ensures the development of relational wealth because clients have a high level of involvement with their temporary agencies and view temporary workers as a renewable resource. Likewise, the gatekeeper model leads to some relational wealth, but the low level of client involvement limits the potential for wealth creation. In the trusted intermediary model, some wealth is created through close interaction with a single agency, but these gains are offset by the substantial losses in relational wealth that occur due to low retention of temporary workers. Finally, the people source model reduces relational wealth because clients have little or no involvement with their temporary agencies and view temporary workers as a disposable resource.

Leana and Rousseau identify four sources of relational wealth: trust, knowing who knows what, reputation, and infrastructure.[17] The first three of these sources are directly relevant to the role of temporary agencies. Here we examine each of the four client-agency models and discuss their effects on the three sources of relational wealth. Table 5.2 summarizes our argu-

Table 5.2 Impact of Client-Agency Relationships on Relational Wealth

Sources of Relational Wealth	Models of Client-Agency Relationships			
	People Source	Gatekeeper	Trusted Intermediary	Client Extension
Trust				
—Inside client firm	Reduced	Somewhat reduced	Reduced	Not reduced
—Client-agency relationship	None created	Some created if agency on-site	Created between specific individuals	Created
Access to New Social Networks (employees and other agencies)	Limited by high turnover	Employees and agencies	Employees but not agencies	Employees and agencies
Client Reputation (in labor market)	Damaged	Unclear	Unclear	Enhanced

ments, and figure 5.2 displays the overall impact of these four models on relational wealth.

People Source

We argue that the people source role for agencies erodes relational wealth. As discussed in the previous section, the people source model can erode trust between permanent employees and their managers. In addition, the rapid cycling of people through the organization limits the ability of all employees (permanent or temporary) to develop stable networks of relationships that they can call on for advice and assistance. In the extreme, large-scale use of the people source model may actually damage a firm's reputation in the labor market. For example, the firm we observed using a people source model was, in many ways, a prestigious and desirable employer. The firm was highly profitable, had never had a layoff, had many opportunities for rapid advancement, provided above-average bonuses, and offered stock options to a wide range of employees. However, human resource managers in that firm reported that the most common cause of involuntary termination among permanent employees was "job abandonment" (leaving work permanently without giving prior notice). Turnover in the permanent manufacturing workforce was so high that the firm's human resources managers feared they had nearly exhausted the local pool of manufacturing employees.

This widespread job abandonment by permanent workers suggests that the firm had a poor reputation among at least one segment of the labor market, making recruitment and retention difficult despite its generous employee incentives. The loss of reputation among manufacturing employees was particularly problematic for this firm, given that low-cost manufacturing was a source of competitive advantage.

Client Extension

At the other end of spectrum, it seems clear that the client extension model, which is based on trust between client and agency, has the capability to enhance relational wealth. Without trust, sharing information such as projected employment needs would be impossible. Trust between workers and the firm may be eroded somewhat by the presence of temporary workers, but this erosion is limited by the client's philosophy of making temporary employees permanent. Relational wealth is also created because an agency that serves as an extension of the client has the capacity to enhance the client's reputation. Agencies are the first contact temporary workers have with the client, and how agencies describe the client's culture, human resource systems, and other features is likely to affect how potential temporary employees see the client.

Using temporary agencies gives clients the opportunity to expand their pool of potential employees by accessing worker populations that they

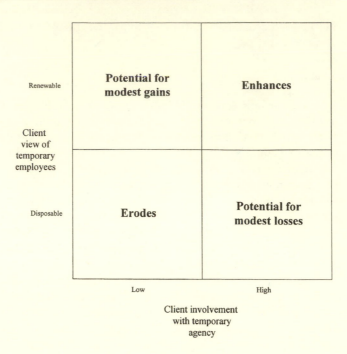

Fig. 5.2. Impact of client-agency relationships on relational wealth

might otherwise be unable to recruit. The client human resources personnel we interviewed saw agencies as specialists in reaching and screening individuals who desired temporary job assignments. Not all individuals seeking temporary employment are "discouraged" workers who use temporary employment as a last resort. Kalleberg and his colleagues report that between 29 percent and 57 percent (depending on gender, marital, and family status) of temporary employees seek such work voluntarily due to competing family demands, a desire or preference for temporary work, or other factors.[18] On the basis of our own observations, we agree. Many individuals enter and exit the labor force frequently and may decide whether to accept temporary work based on the desirability of assignments. The ability to locate and attract these workers requires the investment of enormous resources, which most clients are not prepared to undertake.

Although it was not evident in the specific example of the client extension model we observed, it is not uncommon for agencies with long-term client relationships to network with other temporary agencies in order to help meet client needs. It seems likely that accessing and interacting effectively with multiple temporary agencies would tax the capacity of most client firms. Agencies are able to take advantage of interlinked electronic communication systems, shared databases (such as the capacity for sharing candidate resumes) and other technologies, and common industry contacts that allow them to interact with one another.

Trusted Intermediary

For several reasons, the trusted intermediary model is likely to lead to modest losses in relational wealth. These modest losses in relational wealth are primarily due to the erosion of trust among coworkers and between permanent employees and their managers. The effects of the trusted intermediary model on firm reputation are unclear, probably depending on how successfully the agency matches temporary employees with the client. In the case we observed, the trusted intermediary role led to substantial retention of temporary workers in the client firm, including some individuals who returned to the client in multiple temporary assignments. These individuals had the potential to make valuable contributions to permanent workers' social networks because they had broader exposure to the client organization than many temporaries and even some of their permanent coworkers.

The agency's ability to create relational wealth by accessing the resources of other agencies may be limited by client resistance to accepting temporaries from other providers. In addition, the trusted intermediary model can erode trust in the workplace, as noted earlier. This loss of trust can be substantial and is likely to overshadow the modest positive effects that come from creating new networks between employees and enhancing the client's reputation in the labor market.

Gatekeeper

The gatekeeper model can create modest gains in relational wealth. As previously discussed, this model tends to evoke relatively less interpersonal friction and erosion of trust than either the people source or trusted intermediary models. Like agencies that function in the client extension role, those that act as gatekeepers generally have enough stability in their relationships with clients to invest in multiple agency networks and create relatively elaborate systems designed to locate qualified temporary workers. Because they serve as an entry portal for potential permanent employees, gatekeepers have the ability to enhance a client's reputation, although their incentives for doing so are mixed. On one hand, it is in the agency's interest to enhance the client's reputation so that temporaries will accept permanent positions as they become available. However, because temporary agencies have virtually no access to the client's permanent hiring plans, they are restrained from "selling" temporaries too strongly on any particular client in case it would cause the temporary workers to resist temporary assignments with other clients.

Conclusions and Future Trends

Temporary employment agencies clearly play an important role in matching workers with available jobs. It seems unlikely that the phenomenon of temporary work or of using agencies to locate, train, and supervise temporary workers will disappear. In many cases, temporary agencies appear to have become an integral component of their clients' human resources departments. Agencies can potentially provide clients with two critically important resources. First, agencies have expertise in locating, screening, and selecting available temporary workers. Clients may be unable or unwilling to develop this expertise on their own. Second, agencies can increase clients' flexibility by performing, on an "as needed" basis, many of the mundane recruitment, screening, orientation, and training tasks (for both temporary and permanent employees) that have traditionally been the responsibility of firms' human resources personnel. How a client develops and manages the client-agency relationship will affect the client's ability to create relational wealth when accessing the agency's resources.

When the client-agency relationship is well developed and properly managed, the use of temporary agencies can allow the client's human resources department to focus on recruiting and retaining high-skill technical and managerial personnel or to address issues associated with domestic and international expansion. In these cases, wealth-producing relationships can add value to client human resources departments. In other cases, clients rely on the temporary agency and its skills to replace rather than extend the client human resources department. Rather than deciding how the agency's unique strengths can complement its own human resources capacity, clients simply allow the agency to manage a segment of its workforce. The agency's ability to create relational wealth for the client in these circumstances depends on how well information about the client's needs flows to the agency through informal channels such as conversations with hiring mangers and observations by on-site agency personnel.

In part, the creation of relational wealth depends on the strength of the client human resources function. A weak human resources function precludes the creation of relational wealth. A human resources department that does not have a clearly articulated approach to people management and that exerts little influence over headcounts and hiring practices is unlikely to develop the level of involvement with a temporary agency that is necessary in order to create relational wealth. Similarly, a human resources department that operates on the premise that workers are disposable assets will not create relational wealth through employees anywhere in the firm. But while a strong human resources function is a necessary condition for the creation of relational wealth, it is not a sufficient condition. Relational wealth can only be created when client managers and human resources personnel recognize and utilize the potential synergies between agency and client. Human resources personnel must recognize the value of temporary agencies, have a clear purpose for the use of temporary workers, educate line managers about the strategic implications of using temporary workers, and actively manage the interface between the client and agency. Relational wealth is created not by chance but through the intentional and active participation of both client and agency.

As the use of temporary workers and temporary agencies continues to increase, we anticipate that two of the four models discussed in this chapter will emerge as most common. First, we expect to see a world in which the people source model will continue to exist. There will always be instances where workers are needed for short-term assignments, to perform peripheral or undesirable work, or to smooth out seasonal variations in demand. In these instances, clients may have little to lose by viewing temporary workers as a commodity and selecting agencies that can provide that commodity quickly and cheaply. However, we also expect the client extension model to gain acceptance as clients face increased competitive pressures, human resources departments become more strategically oriented, and temporary agencies become more sophisticated in the services they offer. The issue that many client firms must now face is how to use agencies in a way that creates and enhances the firm's relational wealth. The client extension model makes it clear that the client must invest in its relationships with temporary agencies before temporary workers can create relational wealth inside the firm. Both client and agency must share information about client needs, develop relationships and trust between individuals in the two firms, and articulate and understand the bases of the client's reputation. Such an approach requires conscious attention to the goals of the agency–client relationship as well as how they will be achieved. As demonstrated by the people source model, treating employees as commodities and agencies as commodity brokers may provide firms with short-term help in meeting human resource needs but will erode the firm's relational wealth in the long term.

The client extension model has much in common with Leana and Rousseau's idea of "flexible stability."[19] When we observed this model at work, it was clear that the client's workforce was generally stable and that temporary employees were seen as potential entrants to that workforce, not disposable commodities. One intriguing question is whether effective flexible stability requires the same relatively high level of employer commitment to all employees or whether a limited temporary workforce with a potential for future attachment to the firm can also provide flexible stability.

The client extension model is also reminiscent of the concept of "strong ties."[20] Strong ties require investments by both clients and temporary agencies, and as the cumulative amount of these investments increases over time, it is likely that the level of relational wealth will also increase. An important question to ponder is whether relational wealth creation is ultimately beneficial to both firms. While clients are well positioned to take advantage of the relational wealth created through their relationships with temporary agencies, agencies may not be so fortunate. Temporary agencies are generally small entities with relatively few long-term employees and a limited number of active clients. In order to create a large amount of relational wealth with a particular client, an agency must focus its limited resources on one (or a few) clients. This was evident in some agencies we observed, which had dedicated an entire office to one particular client or had located personnel on the client's premises. Strong ties between an agency and one client increase the agency's dependence on that client, but the dependence is asymmetric. In a market saturated with agencies, it is much easier for a client to replace an existing agency with one of the many other available agencies than for an agency to find new clients. Thus, it is unclear whether both client and agency can benefit from relational wealth creation or whether only the client ultimately benefits, while the less powerful agency risks losing all of the relational wealth it helped develop.

Notes

1. A. L. Kalleberg, E. Rasell, K. Hudson, D. Webster, B. F. Reskin, N. Cassirer, and E. Applebaum, *Nonstandard Work, Substandard Jobs* (Washington, D.C.: Economic Policy Institute, 1997); D. Feldman, H. I. Doerpinghaus, and W. H. Turley, "Managing Temporary Workers: A Permanent HRM Challenge," *Organizational Dynamics* 23 (1994): 49–63.

2. P. Capelli, "Rethinking Employment," *British Journal of Industrial Relations* 33 (1995): 563–602; J. Fierman, "The Contingency Workforce," *Fortune*, January 24, 1994, pp. 30–36; C. von Hippel, S. L. Mangum, D. B. Greenberger, R. L. Heneman, and J. D. Skoglind, "Temporary Employment: Can Organizations and Employees Both Win?" *Academy of Management Executive* 11 (1997): 93–104.

3. W. Echikson, "Rule-Heavy Europe Goes Temp," *Christian Science Monitor*, November 25, 1997, p. 1.

4. S. Houseman and M. Osawa, "Part-time and Temporary Employment in Japan," *Monthly Labor Review* 118, 10 (1995): 10–8.

5. "Korea—Temporary Employment Agency Market: An Overview," *International Market Insight Reports*, October 1, 1998.

6. See the following for examples of this research: A. Davis-Blake, E. George, and J. P. Broschak, "Mixed Blessings: How the Use of Contingent Workers Affects Full-time, Permanent Employees," working paper, University of Texas at Austin, 1998; E. George, "The Effects of External Workers on Internal Workers' Organizational Commitment," Ph.D. diss., University of Texas at Austin, 1996; J. F. Geary, "Employment Flexibility and Human Resource Management: The Case of Three American Electronics Plants," *Work, Employment, and Society* 6 (1992): 251–70; V. Smith, "Institutionalizing Flexibility in a Service Firm: Multiple Contingencies and Hidden Hierarchies," *Work and Occupations* 21 (1994): 284–307.

7. Kalleberg et al. (1997) reported that the three most common occupations among female agency temporaries were secretary, data-entry keyer, and assembler; among male agency temporaries, the three most common occupations were laborer, assembler, and truck/tractor operation.

8. J. A. Chatman, "Managing People and Organizations: Selection and Socialization in Public Accounting Firms," *Administrative Science Quarterly* 36 (1991): 459–84.

9. W. E. Baker, R. R. Faulkner, and G. A. Fisher, "Hazards of the Market: The Continuity and Dissolution of Interorganizational Market Relationships," *American Sociological Review* 63 (1998): 147–77.

10. O. E. Williamson, "Comparative Economic Organization: The Analysis of Discrete Structural Alternatives," *Administrative Science Quarterly* 36 (1991): 269–96.

11. Most contracts with temporary agencies require the client to pay the agency a fee if a temporary employee converts to permanent status within six months after the initial placement by the agency.

12. We do not include compensation in the list because, for nearly all of the jobs we observed, compensation was negotiated directly between the client firm and the agency. After deducting its fees, the agency paid the temporary employees. Compensation for the jobs we learned about tended to be at "market rates" for the type of work performed and did not vary much among the four models described in table 5.1.

13. For an in-depth description of this type of temporary work, see R. E. Parker, *Flesh Peddlers and Warm Bodies: The Temporary Help Industry and Its Workers* (New Brunswick, N.J.: Rutgers University Press, 1994). For a description of the psychological impact of performing this type of temporary work, see J. K. Rogers, "Just a Temp: Experience and Structure of Alienation in Temporary Clerical Employment," *Work and Occupations* 22 (1995): 137–166.

14. See Davis-Blake, George, and Broschak (1998); George (1996); Geary (1992); Smith (1994).

15. W. P. Barnett and A. S. Miner, "Standing on the Shoulders of Others: Career Interdependence in Job Mobility," *Administrative Science Quarterly*, 37 (1992): 262–81.

16. George (1996).

17. C. Leana and D. Rousseau, introduction to this volume.

18. Kalleberg et al. (1997).

19. Leana and Rousseau (1999).

20. R. S. Burt, *Structural Holes: The Social Structure of Competition* (Cambridge: Harvard University Press, 1992).

6

Free-Agency versus High-Involvement Approaches to Skill Development

Enhancing Relational Wealth

FRITS K. PIL AND CARRIE R. LEANA

As employees and the organizations they work for strive to balance short-term results with long-term performance goals, their efforts are complicated by demands for greater shareholder value, increased deregulation, and a trend toward focusing on core business elements. Furthermore, the global competitive advantage held by many U.S. companies is typically a result of more highly skilled, rather than less costly, workers. As a result, the United States faces significant challenges on the labor front, particularly in the area of training and skill development. This has spawned several private and public sector initiatives to encourage the development and utilization of skills within organizations. This chapter examines the logic behind these initiatives and evaluates their general effectiveness at promoting firm and individual investments in employee training. In particular, we focus on current government initiatives that support the "professionalization" of the workforce through the establishment of skill standards for occupational groups and individual jobs. These standards are intended to encourage personal responsibility for skill development, enabling individuals to act as mobile "free agents" rather than stable employees in a shifting job market. However, these efforts may be insufficient to achieve employee self-sufficiency and mobility, especially for low-skilled workers. In contrast, the policies that enhance worker-employer attachment and capitalize on the relational wealth of the firm and its employees may better serve the long-term interests of all parties.

In this chapter, we describe the skill standards approach to training and employee development and discuss the theory supporting this approach. We describe its weaknesses in practice and its potentially damaging and unintended consequences. Next, we propose an alternate approach, known

as high-involvement work systems and related training that together promote flexible stability in the workforce and thus build the firm's relational
wealth. We close with some suggestions for encouraging the development
of high-involvement workplaces and the employee training and development that accompany them.

Employee "Free Agents" and the Skill Standards Approach

Training and other forms of skill development play an important role in
wage and productivity growth. Indeed, research suggests that learning on
the job accounted for over half of the increase in America's production from
the 1920s to the 1980s.[1] Although data are sparse and not very current, most
estimates of organizations' formal training expenditures are between $30
billion and $40 billion per year.[2] Spending on informal training is believed
to be three to six times this amount. Based on this information, a conservative estimate of the amount that employers spend on training is on the
order of $120 billion per year.

The perceived benefits of training, along with the belief that the United
States underinvests in employee skill development compared with other
nations, has resulted in public policy initiatives to increase workforce skills.
These efforts typically focus on individual workers and are exemplified by
attempts to establish a national skill standards system for various occupations. We will focus on skill standards—a good example of the free-agent
approach to training—in order to contrast the free-agent approach with initiatives that capitalize on and build relational wealth.

Early efforts to establish national skills standards were undertaken at the
Department of Labor and by the National Education Standards and Improvement Council (NESIC) within the Department of Education. These efforts
are currently overseen by the National Skill Standards Board (NSSB), which
was created in 1994 to serve as a cornerstone of a national strategy to enhance workforce skills and facilitate the transition to high-performance
work organizations. The NSSB is intended to encourage the development
of a highly skilled, high-quality, high-performance workforce, with much of
the board's effort centering on the professionalization of workers. This takes
the form of increased codification and certification of the knowledge that
workers possess. Through this codification and certification it is hoped that
worker skills will improve and be more evident to employers, thus enhancing employee access to jobs and job mobility.

Efforts to introduce skill standards stem from major changes in the nature
of employment over the last two decades. Historically, employees worked
for one or just a few organizations throughout their careers, and their employers provided job security and opportunities for promotion and development through specified internal career ladders. More recently, employment practices—particularly those governing low-skill workers—have

undergone dramatic changes. One trend in particular is reflected in the desire of firms to maintain maximum flexibility in workforce deployment. This is evidenced by the trend toward downsizing and the growing use of contingent workers and "permanent temporary" employees.

The logic in such trends rests with the desire for flexibility. Firms with fewer core workers (workers possessing assurances of job security), and concomitantly more contingent workers, are presumed to be able to respond more rapidly to changes in market demand. One particular factor, the increasing importance of the service sector, has contributed to the popularity of the free-agent approach because it simplifies the difficulties associated with "stockpiling" output—in this case, extra workers—during periods of low demand. Firms implementing free agency minimize their commitments to workers, while individuals, in turn, are encouraged to shed the traditional role of an employee and instead behave like free agents in an ever-changing job market.[3]

The free-agent approach to employment is often coupled with a system that rewards a few key individuals who have supposedly superior levels of human capital, often at the expense of the collective workforce. Frank and Cook label this the winner-take-all phenomenon—one that is perhaps best reflected in the growing gap between the compensation of those at the top and those at the bottom of many firms.[4]

In combination, the trend toward free-agent employment coupled with winner-take-all compensation pose a particular threat to low-skill workers. These workers are generally not as mobile as their highly skilled counterparts and do not have a sufficient financial cushion to fund gaps or changes in employment. Such workers tend to have greater difficulty adjusting to changes in employment markets. Indeed, the rate of unemployment among the least educated is more than twice the national average.[5] The idea behind skill standards is that by offering these workers certification attesting to the skills they have attained beyond their minimal schooling, they will become more mobile and have an easier time finding new employment.

Evaluating Efforts to Promote Skill Standards

The free-agent model and associated public policy efforts to introduce skill standards can be evaluated from two perspectives—conceptually through the lens of neoclassical labor theory and empirically through the arguments used to promote skill standards to enable low-skill workers to gain mobility in the job market.

Theory and Evidence Regarding Skill Standards

Support for public policy efforts to promote the certification of skills is based on two characterizations of neoclassical labor theory: (1) the distinction between general and specific training and (2) the notion that firms can either "buy" skills in the market or "make" them in-house. General training can be used at more than one organization, while firm-specific training is of little use outside of the organization for which it was intended. Firms are believed to be more likely to "buy" general skills via selection systems that carefully screen for relevant education or work experience and to "make" firm-specific skills by training new hires who are relatively unskilled. In theory, skill standards that identify and define the general skills that workers possess increase the mobility of these workers in the labor market and make them less vulnerable to the shifting strategies and fortunes of any one organization. When an employee is seeking a new job, a potential employer can look at his or her documented skills and more easily identify a potential fit. At the same time, because particular skills are identifiable, employers can spend less on training and focus instead on selecting the right employees at the right time for their changing needs. In this model, selection systems serve as a proxy for in-house training programs.

The theory of how skill standards enhance the mobility of low-skill workers assumes benefits for both employees and employers. Unfortunately, in practice the theory does not always hold up. The proposition that selection and training systems are substitutes for one another is only partially supported. Research on jobs that generally require some education beyond high school (e.g., secretary, electric engineering technician, computer programmer) suggests that having these skills documented in the form of postsecondary education reduced employer expenditures only by 25 percent.

Defining the standard skills that should be certified for various occupations might be difficult. Many so-called general skills are really not so general. For example, we found that employees in high-involvement work settings receive a significant level of training in problem solving, technical, and interpersonal skills.[6] Firms provide training in these areas rather than relying on selection because such skills are believed to be more valuable to the firm when learned in the context of the job. The resulting skills tied to job settings cannot be purchased directly from the labor market. These skills are particularly important in high-involvement/high-performance work environments in which practices like teamwork and job rotation are the norm. They are also believed to be a significant characteristic of organizations using internal labor markets—not in settings where "free agents" come and go at will.[7] Consequently, the organizations that would be best served by skill standards (i.e., those seeking flexibility through short-term staffing arrangements) are precisely the organizations least interested in providing worker training and skill development.

If certification simplifies the hiring process by increasing the transparency of available skills, it should reduce the penalties to employers who use the market to handle fluctuations in labor requirements—the "hunter-gatherers" of skills. While the NSSB's goal of enhancing worker mobility would be achieved, this additional mobility can actually provide disincentives for firms to train employees because they fear that other employers will poach their well-trained workers.[8] Barron and his colleagues observed that firms may provide general training in situations where potential employers and recruiters do not know the extent or type of training workers receive[9] and thus can not easily identify the people they should target for poaching.[10]

There are numerous examples of what happens when skills employers pay for are signaled to the marketplace. In the United Kingdom, for example, efforts to introduce an apprenticeship system with standardized skills failed—despite the fact that apprentices were free—because employers did not want to lose workers they had trained.[11] In Denmark, which has a similar program, 35 to 45 percent of those trained through a formal apprenticelike program moved to other companies as soon as training was completed. The government in Denmark now has difficulty getting companies to participate, and the country has developed a bonus system to induce companies to sign on.[12]

Mobile employees do not always leave their jobs to work for other companies; problems can also arise when workers leave to further their formal education. Finegold and Mason, for example, describe the case of Cincinnati Technical College, a school that convinced a local corporation to sponsor twenty-one co-op spots in an effort to develop qualified manufacturing technician positions, with the idea that some of these students would work for the company after graduating. Of the twenty-one company-sponsored participants, twenty chose to continue their education and work toward four-year degrees rather than work for the employer. Understandably, the employer dropped out of the program after the first year.[13] As certification increases, the likelihood that workers will be hired away also increases, and employers have fewer incentives to provide training.

While skill standards are aimed at increasing employee mobility, it is not clear that lack of mobility is currently a problem for employees. In fact, just the opposite may be true. Some evidence suggests that employees in the United States are quite mobile. For example, Japanese workers have five jobs by the time they reach age sixty-five, versus ten jobs for U.S. workers.[14] The result is greater incentives on the part of employers to provide training in Japan. The real problem facing most workers in the United States may be not insufficient mobility but undesired mobility. The issue of low employer–worker attachment affects both low-skilled and high-skilled workers. Displaced workers have a difficult time finding new employment and often do so at significant pay cuts and with fewer benefits.[15]

While skill certification might enhance the portability of skills across industries, it is not clear what happens when people are credentialed to undertake tasks that are no longer needed, or what happens when the tasks are continually evolving[16] By some estimates, more than 40 percent of organizations that have downsized are replacing the eliminated workers with individuals provided by temporary agencies. At the same time, research suggests that organizations that make greater use of contract employees also provide less formal and informal training.[17] Under these conditions, skill certification is not likely to result in greater power in the job market for the worker.

Proponents of skill standards point to the success of such programs in other countries as a model for the United States. Although skill standards have indeed been successful in many countries, these programs are likely to be inapplicable to the United States. Germany and Denmark have very successful skill standards and certification mechanisms for their workforce and, in particular, front-line workers.[18] However, these countries also have strong traditions of cooperation among business, labor, and government in the management of their vocational education and training systems— traditions the United States lacks. These traditions grew out of apprenticeship systems dating back hundreds of years. In Germany, for example, wage determination by collective bargaining at the industry level limits the ability of companies to poach workers from one another. However, as in Denmark, the retention rate of apprentices in Germany is variable. Moreover, Germany's system may not be effective as sectoral shifts continue toward high-technology and service industries.[19] Alternate reference points are Australia and the United Kingdom, which have had only marginal success with their standards and certification efforts to date.

Finally, in considering the theoretical arguments for skill standards, it is interesting to look at (1) the empirical evidence regarding the types of organizations that provide the most training and (2) evidence on the returns to training. Training is most prevalent in firms that provide skills that are specific to those organizations and not useful to other firms in the local labor market. Creating standards for these low-demand skills would probably not increase the amount of training workers receive. In addition, large multi-site corporations provide the bulk of training. These firms enjoy economies of scale in their selection processes and training programs and typically have lower turnover rates. In contrast, smaller organizations and those with more contract ("free agent") employees provide less training. Skill certification would be unlikely to induce these firms to alter their training patterns.[20]

So far, much of our discussion has focused on the corporation's view of the advantages and disadvantages of skill standards. We believe the most productive efforts to enhance the skills and long-term viability of workers do focus on corporations. This is partly based on research that suggests individuals are not very good at deciding which skills will be most helpful to their careers. For example, a recent study found that more than 80 percent of workers with company-sponsored training experiences had careers in the field for which they were trained, compared with 50 to 60 percent of workers who undertook training on their own.[21] In an overview of a number of studies, Bishop observed that a large number of graduates from vocational and other non-employer-sponsored programs did not have jobs in their field of training. This is consistent with previous findings suggesting that employees who participate in formal, employer-sponsored training see their wages increase by almost 10 percent, but there is no significant effect on wages when employees pay for training that they select. This is but one more reason that the "free agent" model of formulating public policy toward employee development and training might not be serving the best interests of firms or individuals.[22]

Where "Free Agent" Skill Standards Make Sense

As noted, many of the skills necessary in the contemporary workplace are not easily certifiable. For example, when individuals join an organization, they do not understand its norms of communication, its policies and practices with regard to information sharing, or the distribution of knowledge among other members of the organization—all components of relational wealth. Some researchers (and more than a few managers) argue that an insufficient number of workers have the communication skills needed to operate in contemporary work environments. Thus, managers reconceptualize their workplaces as "learning organizations" and expend significant energy developing and enhancing these vital skills.[23]

Although communication strategies may best be learned in the workplaces where they will be used, more basic communication skills such as reading, writing, and the ability to understand and perform quantitative analyses are the domain of the educational system. Skill standards may make the most sense in this arena. For example, Japanese-owned automobile plants in North America now use college graduates for almost half their entry-level positions, although these positions require no more than a high school degree in Japan. The United States has little consistency across states and even within a state with respect to what it means to have a high school degree, let alone other types of certification of low-skill workers.[24] Thus, it could be helpful to corporations if a high school degree signaled competence in these and other basic skills.[25]

It can be useful to certify that an employee has skills that go beyond the basic knowledge learned in high school, especially in jobs that require certain minimum standards for safety reasons or consumer protection. This type of certification works well in fields such as health care, insurance sales, and law, as well as jobs in which standardized training is critical to ensuring that an organization's internal operations are consistent with external vendors or customers (e.g., certified public accounting). Certification can also be useful where the skills required are far removed from an organization's other activities and it would not be cost-effective to evaluate applicants or assure the availability of skills in-house (e.g., Novell Engineer training). In these instances, skill standards make sense; in most of the cases cited here, such standards already exist and thus require little in the way of additional government intervention.

Our discussion so far has focused on the limits of policy efforts that view individuals as the beneficiaries and decision makers regarding skill and knowledge development. We now turn to a different perspective that focuses on organizations as the primary actors in training initiatives. This perspective is based on a model that stresses high employee commitment and high-involvement workplaces rather than free agency and employee mobility. Through the promotion of the development of high-involvement work, the employment situation—particularly for low-skill workers—can be improved without running into the problems of the free-agent approach. This high-involvement approach requires firms to focus attention on building and sustaining relational wealth.

High-Involvement Training: An Alternative to the Free-Agent Approach

At the same time that free agency has become a dominant theme in contemporary employment practices, some writers have extolled the virtues of mutual dependence between employee and employer.[26] The traditional arguments against free-agent approaches to employment focus on the possibility that such methods deplete human capital. Writers across a broad spectrum of disciplines and ideologies have argued that fungibility in employment deprives workers of opportunities to build firm-specific human capital and have asserted that when human capital is developed, employees are less motivated to share their knowledge and skills with their employers.[27] When firms downsize, they reduce not just their labor costs but also the expertise and motivation of their workforce. Skill standards offer an alternative for rebuilding this human capital, but this approach appears to work better in theory than in practice.

As an alternative to the efforts to certify employees with skills as part of a free-agent model, some employers have chosen instead to develop high-involvement work environments. Studies of industries ranging from banking to steelmaking have found that organizations using the high-involvement employment model can realize significant increases in productivity, efficiency, and quality. High-involvement work offers employees enhanced opportunities to participate in workplace decisions, long-term investments in training, and frequently, job security.[28]

Employers following the high-involvement model strive for workers who are accountable, adaptable, and reliable. They want employees who have a sense of shared obligations and are willing to invest their time and energy to learn the norms, systems, and structures that make the organization effective. Through the high-involvement model, employers hope to develop a stable workforce capable of operating effectively and proactively in unstable, unpredictable global and local environments. These characteristics are hard to certify at the individual level, yet they are the outcome of systematic efforts to promote high-involvement work systems.

Through enhanced communication, trust, and the development of organizational social capital, high-involvement organizations leverage the human capital of the firm for the benefit of both the organization and its members.[29] The presence of trust between employees and managers is central to the adoption and implementation of high-involvement work practices, particularly in established ("brown field") facilities. Many high-involvement practices rely more on associability norms and trust relationships for their effective implementation than on hierarchy, rules and regulations, or formal control mechanisms. These high-involvement work environments require the establishment of collective identity and action, reliance on generalized trust, and a long-term orientation in relationships rather than formal monitoring and economic incentives.

Certifying High-Involvement Work Skills in Individuals

For several reasons, high-involvement work does not mesh well with the idea of worker skill certification. First, it is difficult to create a credentialing mechanism that certifies whether workers are amenable to and capable of performing in a high-involvement work environment. Employers in such environments need to know not just about a potential employee's skills and training but also about his or her aptitudes, attitudes, and dispositions— relatively subjective characteristics that are much harder to assess and to agree on. The Japanese-owned auto plants in North America provide an interesting illustration of this. In their recruitment processes, the plants select roughly one in twenty workers, and the selection processes are so involved and protracted that they can take as long as six months. The employees who are selected differ from the typical auto worker, with nearly 40 percent holding college degrees. The key factors in selection are not specific skills or learning but rather dispositions and attitudes—attributes that are not easy or necessarily desirable to certify. However, a very motivated company can also operate a high-involvement work environment with a much less selective work force. NUMMI, the Toyota/GM joint venture in California, has successfully operated a high-involvement work environment with an 80 percent selection ratio from a pool of workers accustomed to manufacturing jobs but with no previous experience with high-involvement work practices. These examples suggest that certification is less important than how motivated the employees and the company are, as well as how interested they are in working in a high-involvement fashion.[30]

Certification also contradicts the concept of high-involvement work, in that in many instances, certification encourages narrow specialization. In contrast, high-involvement work environments emphasize cross-specialization and broader learning, long-term skill development, and a willingness to redefine and reinvent jobs for workers whose skills do not match those immediately needed within the corporation. Skill requirements change rapidly. Unless companies are interested in updating worker skills and helping them adjust to shifts in skill needs, certification will only provide short-term benefits for employees.

Finally, individual skill certification focuses on labor supply rather than on labor demand. Even if organizations like the NSSB achieve their objective of training and certifying individuals who are capable of working in high-involvement environments, there will not necessarily be an automatic increase in demand for individuals with these skills. Giving companies an incentive to generate high-involvement workplaces, on the other hand, will by default motivate them to develop and train individuals.

For all of these reasons, high-involvement training may better serve the long-term interests of firms and individuals than will individual skill certification. We close with some suggestions about how public policy efforts that promote the use of high-involvement training may be enhanced.

Policy Efforts to Promote the Use of High-Involvement Training

We believe that the public sector can stimulate organizations to shift toward high-involvement work practices that emphasize long-term skill development and training, which have been shown to increase workers' attachment to the firm. One way to accomplish this is by establishing a set of standards at the organizational level and a concomitant certification process for high-involvement work sites. These standards would necessarily be flexible because there appears to be no single set of best practices that works well across all industries and organizations. Experiences with industry standards, also known as metastandards, can guide the creation of these organizational standards. To illustrate how a standard might be developed to stimulate the use of multiskilled workers in stable, long-term employment relationships, we can point to the International Organization for Standardization's ISO 9001, a standard that has received widespread acceptance as an indicator of management systems associated with superior quality. During the early 1990s, ISO 9001 expanded from one site in the United States to 8,400; over the past decade, this standard has been implemented in more than 120,000 certified organizations worldwide. Rather than focusing on outputs, the ISO 9001 standard focuses on management processes, acknowledging that these processes may differ from one company to the next. Companies must document the practices they have in place and keep records showing that these practices are followed. Customers might not know how a particular organization operationalizes its processes to meet the ISO 9001 objectives, but they can be assured that certified organizations have implemented practices that meet the ISO 9001 requirements and can document their continued adherence to those practices.

It is important for organizations to utilize practices that are believed to create desirable outcomes, are easily identifiable, and have outcomes that are easily tracked and monitored. Employers who have such standards will be able to attract the best job candidates, because individuals can view certification as an indicator of the most desirable employers. Because the standards only certify broad practices and outcomes, it is much harder for competitors to poach workers—unlike a model in which worker skills are certified. These standards would give employers a greater incentive to train and develop their workforce.

If properly developed, standards for high-involvement work sites could have an added benefit of reducing litigation risk for employers, who would have certified, audited employment practices that are nationally accepted. If high-involvement workplaces were viewed as desirable from a public policy standpoint, it would be relatively easy for the government to encourage their adoption, perhaps by giving priority in purchasing decisions to certified employers. As standards for corporations are developed and spread, the attention they receive will help managers, labor leaders, government officials, and academics focus on some of the key issues facing employers and employees alike.

Conclusion

Work-site standards are not the only tool that could be used to encourage employers to fully utilize the potential of their workforce and to increase the commitment between employer and employee. However, we believe that public policy efforts should focus on altering the incentives for employers rather than increasing the mobility of the work force. As discussed earlier, there has been a marked shift in recent years away from long-term employment relations and toward a transient, free-agent model. Because low-skill workers, in particular, are rarely viewed as "core" employees in this model, they are subject to the greatest employment variability and uncertainty in employment.

High-involvement employment and its development of relational wealth provides a powerful alternative. In this model, corporations develop their workers' abilities, embed these skills in an organizational communication and knowledge network, and turn them into a source of competitive advantage. High involvement workplaces develop high levels of relational wealth by integrating workers into the organizational knowledge structure, making them part of the information flows, and engendering trust and commitment to coworkers, management, and the organization. This benefits not just the organization but also individual workers, who receive higher wages, greater job security, and more interesting employment. Training and skill development are a lifelong process, and by providing companies with an incentive to actively participate in this process and reap its benefits, we can help ensure the competitiveness and viability of our industries for the long term.

Notes

1. P. Carnevale and L. Gainer, *The Learning Enterprise*, U.S. Department of Labor, Washington, D.C., 1988.

2. U.S. Congress, Office of Technology Assessment, *Worker Training: Competing in the New International Economy*, Washington, D.C., 1990.

3. M. Arthur and D. Rousseau. "The Boundaryless Career as a New Employment Principle," editor's introduction to *The Boundaryless Career: A New Employment Principle for a New Organizational Era* (New York: Oxford University Press, 1996), pp. 3–20.

4. R. Frank and P. Cook, *The Winner-Take-All Society* (New York: Free Press, 1995).

5. In 1994, the unemployment rates were as follows: below upper secondary education: = 12.6 percent; upper secondary education: = 6.2 percent; non-university-level tertiary education: = 4.3 percent; university-level education: = 2.9 percent; and average unemployment: = 5.8 percent (*Education at a Glance: OECD Indicators* [Paris: OECD, 1997]).

6. F. K. Pil and J. P. MacDuffie, "The Adoption of High-Involvement Work Practices," *Industrial Relations* 35, 3 (1996): 423–55; and F. K. Pil and J. P. MacDuffie, "What Makes Transplants Thrive: Managing the Transfer of 'Best Practices' at Japanese Auto Plants in North America," *Journal of World Business* (1999): 372–391; reprinted in extended form as: "Transferring Competitive Advantage across Borders: A Study of Japanese Transplants in North America," in *Remade in America: Transplanting and Transforming Japanese Production Systems*, edited by J. Liker, M. Fruin, and P. Adler (New York: Oxford University Press, 1999).

7. P. Doeringer and M. Piore, *Internal Labor Markets and Manpower Analysis* (Lexington, Mass.: Lexington Books, 1971).

8. While one could argue that employees should pay for training that leads to certification, the Fair Labor Standards Act does not permit employers to make employees take classes on unpaid time on subjects related to the jobs they perform at work.

9. Even with this uncertainty, Bishop found that formal training on the job at a previous employer increased initial productivity in a new job by 9.5 percent and reduced training requirements by 17 percent. J. Bishop, "The Impact of Previous Training in Schools and on Jobs on Productivity, Required OJT, and Turnover of New Hires," in *Private Sector and Skill Formation: International Comparisons*, edited by L. Lynch (Chicago: University of Chicago Press, 1994), pp. 161–200.

10. J. Baron, M. Berger, and D. Black, "General Training Made Specific: Reasons and Consequences," working paper, Cornell University, 1996. See also E. Katz and A. Ziderman, "Investment in General Training: The Role of Information and Labor Mobility," *Economic Journal* 7 (1990): 24–51.

11. P. Cappelli, "Observations on Apprenticeship Programs," presentation at the ILR Cornell Institute for Labor Management Policies conference, November 15–17, 1996.

12. N. Westgard-Nielsen and A. R. Rasmussen, "Apprenticeship Training in Denmark—the Impact of Subsidies," working paper, Centre for Labour Market and Social Research, Denmark, 1996.

13. D. Finegold and G. Mason, "National Training Systems and Industrial Performance: U.S.–European Matched-Plant Comparisons," *Research in Labor Economics* 18 (1999): 331–358.

14. M. Hashimoto and J. Raison, "Employment Tenure and Earnings Profiles in Japan and the United States," *American Economic Review* 75 (1985): 721–35.

15. C. Leana and D. Feldman, *Coping with Job Loss: How Individuals, Organizations, and Communities Respond to Layoffs* (Boston: Lexington Books, 1992).

16. If the focus of public policy was on making it harder for employers to eliminate employees, there would be a stronger incentive for employers to reduce the incidence of skill obsolescence (indeed, that is one reason that recent trends in union/management negotiations show efforts to reduce organizational flexibility in altering employment levels).

17. Frazis, H., M. Gittleman, M. Horrigan, M. Joyce, "Formal and Informal Training: Evidence from a Matched Employee-Employer Survey." Department of Labor Paper presented at the ILR Cornell Institute for Labor Management Policies Conference, November 15–17, Cornell University, 1996.

18. Despite all the attention focused on the German apprentice system, a survey that dates to the late 1970s found that German employees indicate that their most important source of training and place to acquire job skills was continuous training or on-the-job training—only 32 percent named their apprenticeship program or vocational school (J. S. Pischke, "Continuous training in Germany," working paper, Massachusetts Institute of Technology, 1996).

19. See P. Deissinger, "Germany's Vocational Training Act: Its Function as an Instrument of Quality Control within a Tradition-Based Vocational Training System," *Oxford Review of Education* 22, 3 (1996): 317–36; and Finegold and Mason (1999).

20. See J. Bishop, "On-the-Job Training of New Hires," in *Market Failures in Training*, edited by D. Stern and J. Ritzen (New York: Springer Verlag, 1991), pp. 61–96; and A. G. Holtmann and T. L. Idson, "Employer Size and On-the-Job Training Decisions, *Southern Economic Journal* 30, 3 (1991): 1333–81.

21. Mangum and Ball, 1992, cited in J. Bishop, 1996, "What We Know About Employer-Provided Training: A Review of the Literature." Working paper, Center for Human Resource Studies, Cornell University, 1996.

22. J. Bishop, 1996. "What We Know about Employer-Provided Training: A Review of the Literature," working paper, Center for Advanced Human Resources Studies, Cornell University, 1996; Mangum and Ball (1992); and P. Lengermann, "Training's Impact on Wages and Hours Worked: A Comparison of the Benefits and Costs of Training," *Economics and Education Review* (1996).

23. For a discussion of communication skills, see R. Marshall and M. Tucker, *Thinking for a Living: Education and the Wealth of Nations* (New York: Basic Books, 1992); and P. Cappelli et al., *Change at Work* (New York: Oxford University Press, 1997). References on learning organizations include T. Kochan and M. Useem, *Transforming Organizations* (New York: Oxford University Press, 1992); P. Adler and R. Cole, "Designed for Learn-

ing: A Tale of Two Auto Plants," *Sloan Management Review* (spring 1993): 85–94; and E. Schein, *Organizational Culture and Leadership* (San Francisco: Jossey-Bass, 1993).

24. While a greater focus on skills needed in the workplace may spur education reform, even here there is debate about whether skill standards created through interactions with business would help or hurt the education system. (See T. Bailey and D. Merritt, "Industry Skill Standards and Education Reform," *American Journal of Education* 105, 4 [1977]: 401–36.)

25. In addition, as Bishop (1996) points out, it would be particularly helpful if schools confirmed the graduation dates of alumni and provided transcripts when provided with signed release forms.

26. See, for example, J. Pfeffer, *The Human Equation* (Boston: Harvard Business School Press, 1998).

27. Contrast H. Braverman, *Labor and Monopoly Capital* (New York: Monthly Review Press, 1984); and O. Williamson, *Markets and Hierarchies* (Cambridge, Mass.: Free Press, 1975).

28. For a summary of this work, see C. Ichniowski, T. Kochan, D. Levine, C. Olson, and G. Strauss, "What Works at Work: Overview and Assessment," *Industrial Relations* 35, 3 (1996): 299–333.

29. Pil and MacDuffie (1996).

30. Pil and MacDuffie (1999).

7

The Institutional Context of Social Capital

The Influence of Assumed Social Resources on
Women's Employment Outcomes

MAURA A. BELLIVEAU

In 1995, Mark Granovetter's seminal work *Getting a Job* was republished.
One of Granovetter's significant findings was that mobility enhances social
networks, which in turn facilitate future mobility. Jobs demand that workers
cultivate and use specific social network structures, as well as providing
opportunities for workers to develop social capital.[1] These social resources
influence evaluations of potential employers, access to job interviews and
jobs, occupational status and compensation, promotions and ascendance to
top management, perceived influence within organizations, and speed of
reemployment after job loss.[2]

Although the vast majority of research has been devoted to *actual* social
ties and career outcomes, this chapter builds on Kilduff and Krackhardt's
cognitive approach by considering how perceptions and assumptions about
women's networks can lead to less desirable employment outcomes (i.e.,
discrimination among women as well as between men and women).[3] I argue
that there are employment situations in which the ties the job-seeker possesses are central to obtaining a good outcome via information about job
vacancies. In other cases, however, the job-seeker's actual social network is
less important than the assumptions an employer makes about his or her
network and concomitant access to information about job quality and
wages.[4] Just as empirical research demonstrates that individuals use their
social networks to decide what constitutes a "good job,"[5] I suggest that
employers consider job candidates' networks to determine what they will
perceive as a "good offer." This chapter focuses on perceived ties because
although employers would benefit from knowledge of a candidate's actual
social connections, they rarely have access to such information. I argue that
social capital is a more subjective form of economic value, and in the context of this book I suggest that relational wealth can be misestimated or

130

overlooked in predictable ways. This treatment is therefore somewhat differently focused from, though consistent in spirit with, recent empirical work by Fernandez and his colleagues which examines social networks from the employer's side of the labor market.[6]

To the degree that recruiters may assume that women have smaller, denser, more homophilous (i.e., same-sex) networks composed of more kin and low-status contacts, employers infer that women may have lower reservation wages than either men—whose networks are generally inferred to be larger, more diverse, and composed of more male and high-status contacts—or women who manage to signal social resources of greater value than the average woman's.[7] When an employer assumes that a woman possesses an inferior social network, it may induce the employer to offer her significantly lower pay than the employer would offer a man. This may occur for two reasons, which are discussed in this chapter. First, on the basis of assumptions about their network structures and therefore, access to information, employers may believe that women will be satisfied with lower offers.[8] Second, on the same basis, recruiters may believe that the biased (i.e., "gendered") nature of these offers cannot be discerned.[9]

In this chapter, I outline the research on the nature of women's networks, the gender wage gap, and how assumptions about women's social networks may influence the compensation they receive. In addition, I describe an empirical study that examines the simultaneous influence of institutional segregation (e.g., attendance at an all-female college, a signal of *likely* network composition) and *actual* social resources on women's pay entering the labor market. Finally, I discuss the implications of studying assumed social ties for research on employability.

Women and Social Networks

Although both women and men benefit from social networks, there is substantial evidence that women require different types of networks to succeed and may face constraints building networks that resemble those of their male peers.[10] Burt has analyzed the social networks and promotion rates of male and female managers, finding that similar network structures are associated with promotion for junior male managers and all female managers.[11] Burt concluded that junior male and all female managers lacked legitimacy. In his view, social capital is most valuable to managers, who must figure out how to best perform their job and then persuade others that their job performance is legitimate.[12] The inherent ambiguity and gender-coding of management as an activity suggests—and Burt's work reinforces—that female managers labor under a specter of illegitimacy and may depend more than managers in general on social indicators of their qualifications, organizational inclusion, and performance reputation.

Social capital is contingent in nature, as highlighted by the differential network structures required by women and minorities in organizations. Researchers have documented specific types of networks that are most useful to females and minorities in organizations.[13] For example, women who cultivate heterophilous networks (in this case, those including more male contacts) receive instrumental benefits such as information related to effective job performance and career advancement, because men tend to occupy both informal and formal positions of power in the organization. In contrast, homophilous networks provide psychosocial support.[14] Brass found that women with ties to men were more likely to gain influence and be promoted within an organization.[15] For female managers, Burt has described the importance of a hierarchical network constructed around a strategic partner who can function as a sponsor.[16] A woman benefits from her strong relationship to this partner, "borrowing" his network rich in "structural holes" to foster her career. Aldrich and his colleagues found that both male and female entrepreneurs possessed networks composed of more male than female professional ties.[17] In the area of compensation, Berger found that both men and women obtained higher pay when using male contacts to gain employment than when they used no social ties or only female contacts.[18]

Because men appear to be more likely than women to inquire about salary ranges for jobs, it seems logical that male contacts could provide richer information about wage dispersion for particular positions.[19] As Lin observed, dissimilar others (who are also likely to be weak ties) are more likely to provide better access to novel information.[20] He further asserted that weak ties are more likely to provide those in lower status positions with access to higher status contacts. For women, then, men can provide information regarding pay that differs from information available via homophilous ties and, in all likelihood, that information gives female job-seekers knowledge of the upper portion of the wage continuum.

It is more difficult for women to access male contacts than it is for men. McPherson, Popielarz, and Drobnic examined network homophily in the context of the availability of same-sex and opposite-sex contacts to determine how choice and access shape social networks. They concluded that observed homophily in networks is significantly influenced by social structure, in this case the availability of contacts of the same or of the opposite sex.[21] Brass's work within an organization similarly implicated structure as a determinant of women's networks, showing that workplace segregation made women less central to men's networks and led to the presence of fewer men in women's networks.[22] In addition to workplace obstacles to the creation of instrumental ties, women may face barriers in the form of the composition of the voluntary organizations to which they belong and socioeconomic determinants of contact.[23] Lin found that for women, family background was associated with access to weak ties and male ties, which then led to the higher status contacts instrumental to their job search. Given women's structural position in the workplace, household, and voluntary organizations, this would suggest a high degree of network homophily for women—a finding that has emerged when organizational rank, for example, is not controlled.[24]

Sex Segregation in the Workplace

Of course, the literature on sex segregation in the workplace highlights women's lack of access to male-dominated jobs and, consequently, male peers. Segregation generates network homophily for men too, but homophily has positive consequences for men in organizations. The gender segregation literature indicates that women receive significantly lower pay when they occupy jobs which are held predominantly by women.[25] Research on occupations indicates that the percentage of female workers in an occupation accounts for as much as 40 percent of the gender wage gap, while the percentage of female workers examined at the job level accounts for an even greater proportion of male-female earning disparities.[26] Although the gender wage gap appears to be shrinking,[27] recent studies indicate that jobs are still largely segregated.[28] Bielby and Baron found that women and men did not occupy the same job categories in 202 of the 393 California firms they studied.[29] Recent analyses of nonmanagerial positions suggest that segregation of jobs within establishments explains 83 percent of the gender wage gap.[30]

These studies demonstrate the deleterious effects on women's earnings when they work in different job and occupational categories from men. However, women tend to receive lower pay even when they work in jobs that appear highly comparable to those held by men. In explaining this effect, researchers suggest that jobs that become female-typed are valued less and job evaluation processes intended to provide objective assessments of job value are themselves affected by gender attitudes.[31] When men and women perform the same job, evaluators rate the "man's" job as more critical and view the man as having more responsibility.[32] Even when an occupation is accorded high prestige, men and women in that occupation do not benefit equally.[33]

In addition to lower pay, segregation tends to reduce women's access to information on "men's" job opportunities, advancement, and compensation.[34] This lack of information may obscure their awareness of gender discrimination, if it exists, because judgments of inequity rely on social comparisons, which themselves rely on the availability of referents.[35] Workplace segregation precludes these comparisons. Faye Crosby and others have observed the denial of personal discrimination among employed women—the paradox of the "contented female," in which an individual woman acknowledges that women as a group suffer but she personally does not. This paradox may be facilitated by the very segregation that is associated with lower pay.[36] Interestingly, subsequent analyses of Crosby's dataset of professional women revealed that women whose referents were either exclusively or predominantly male felt significantly more deprived and more dissatisfied with their jobs than women whose reference group was largely or solely composed of women. However, women who used men as referents also reported higher salaries than women whose reference group was either mixed or predominantly female.[37]

Despite considerable attention to similarity effects on referent preference,[38] it is important to note that, in many settings, women compare themselves to men as well as to women. For example, in a study of medical students, Felicio and Miller found that although men compared themselves primarily with other men, women compared their skills to those of both male and female colleagues.[39] Both men and women reported that convenience was a significant determinant of their targets of comparison. Major and Testa further demonstrated that when women can obtain information about men's outcomes, they make comparisons across gender lines and evaluate the fairness of their personal outcomes on the basis of the comparative information they obtain.[40]

The literature on sex segregation in the workplace highlights the importance of social structure in the psychology of entitlement, as well as actual occupational attainment. Social structure, then, is likely to influence women's compensation directly (by affecting the valuation of work and pay-setting), as well as indirectly, by influencing the composition—and/or perception of the composition—of women's social networks and the comparisons that they can make to learn about wage dispersion and evaluate their worth. Taken together, this research on social networks and gender segregation suggests that heterophilous ties have distinct importance to women's careers providing information about wage dispersion, signaling one's knowledge of appropriate wages, and signaling one's potential social resources by highlighting possible connections to men in general and high-status contacts in particular—even if such ties are not established in fact.[41]

Social Networks and Salary Offers: The Employer's Perspective

The fact that job candidates do use social comparisons to determine what is a "good" job offer suggests that it behooves recruiters and other firm representatives to try to determine a candidate's network and, concomitantly, the information the candidate is likely to use in evaluating the offer.[42] Baron and Pfeffer assert that wage inequality within organizations is curtailed where social comparisons operate more "vigorously," as when workers are in closer contact.[43] They discuss organizational contexts that decrease the likelihood that wage differences will be detected and increase the perceived legitimacy of wage differences between otherwise comparable employees (e.g., differentiation in job titles).

There are two fundamental assumptions underlying Baron and Pfeffer's discussion and the arguments in this chapter. First, employers have the latitude to set different wages for seemingly comparable employees occupying similar jobs. Although compensation experts suggest that firms create pay ranges for jobs (which may or may not be formally communicated to applicants or incumbents) on the basis of a variety of factors, including consistency with firm goals and compliance with legal requirements, even these ranges allow for recruiter discretion.[44] Second, when making salary offers to job candidates and existing employees, employers do consciously consider and recognize the constraint on wage differentiation presented by social structural influences on employee judgments regarding their compensation.[45] Although it is easier to predict the social comparisons that employees will make within an existing organization[46] than when hiring job candidates from the external labor market, data that are readily available on job candidates can be used to infer the social resources and concomitant wage information accessible to them.

Previous research has shown that perceived (or assumed) social resources affect important workplace outcomes such as performance reputation. In a study of the employees of a Silicon Valley firm, Martin Kilduff and David Krackhardt tested the idea that cognitive representations of networks may be as—or more—important than actual network ties.[47] Both in this study and my discussion here, a perceived, inferred, or assumed tie refers to a social connection that is believed to exist between actors, as reported by a third party.[48] (Perceived ties should not be confused with symmetric ties, where the actual parties agree regarding the existence of such a connection.) Kilduff and Krackhardt found that employee evaluations of peers' performance reputations were significantly related to the most prominent friend that the employees *thought* their peers had in their network rather than the most prominent friend their colleague *actually* had, establishing the importance of assumed social resources.

Assumptions about a person's social capital can be expected to substantively alter the person's actual network, as well. Research shows that individuals may actively seek to form ties with persons of high status.[49] Kilduff and Krackhardt's findings suggest that because perceived social ties can enhance an individual's status, they may lead to new actual ties, reducing one's dependence on existing ties and generating other positive outcomes such as more rapid mobility.

Contextual Effects on Social Resources: Institutional Affiliations and Assumed Ties

Empirical findings highlighting the benefits of third-party assumptions regarding another person's social resources leave open a critical question: how do observers infer social ties? Theorists such as Bourdieu and political scientists interested in civic involvement have focused on the role of institutions in creating and maintaining social capital.[50] Research on the social structuring of activities and relations suggests that institutional affiliations shape observer assumptions regarding the social resources a person possesses.[51]

Findings of "induced homophily" suggest that "there is merit in" the assumption that an individual's network composition (for example, with regard to gender) is highly correlated with the composition of groups to which they belong. As Smith-Lovin and McPherson point out, "[s]ocial networks are generated by organizations in that organizations provide the settings in which contacts develop. At the same time, networks modify the flow of people from one setting to another because they are the major source of information about, and recruitment to, organizations."[52]

With regard to weak ties, voluntary organizations have been described as an important source of potential contacts, but a less fruitful one for women whose affiliations are largely with organizations that offer more restricted opportunity to develop cross-gender and professionally relevant weak ties.[53] If features of a person's network, such as homophily/heterophily or contact status are of interest to a third party, these can be estimated by knowing what organizations or groups a person belongs to. Since social, educational, and professional organizations (e.g., current and previous employers, boards, government advisory groups, and voluntary organizations) often have membership criteria and mission statements that incorporate member characteristics, knowledge of organizational memberships provides information on the volume, social status, and homophily of the weak ties a person may possess.[54] Combining the easily accessed information regarding a job candidate's educational, organizational, and occupational memberships provides potential employers with cues as to the probable gender, racial, and class composition of a job candidate's social resources.

Inferring social resources from organizational affiliations is more straightforward than observing the presence or absence of actual ties between members of an organization. The reasons are two-fold. First, in some cases, people actively seek to conceal social ties because these relationships are most valuable when hidden (e.g., politicians who have particularly close ties to corporate executives in industries they regulate).[55] Second, even when secrecy is not a goal, interaction can be difficult to observe, particularly when it is infrequent. Third parties who rely on direct observation to ascertain social networks are likely to underestimate these ties.[56] In contrast, job seekers oftentimes freely provide information regarding their affiliations on their resumes, or note that an affiliation generated their employment inquiry (e.g., when firms advertise positions through professional associations).

Because employers seek to constrain spending on wages, they benefit from knowing particular candidate's social resources because the nature of these resources determines if the candidate "has" better or worse information about wages within their firm and their industry. Potential employers can make such a judgment with regard to female candidates by assessing the sex composition of the candidate's firm and organizational affiliations. To the degree that employers can discern women's ties to comparably experienced men, for example, they can estimate their access to wage information and decide to offer lower wages to those women who are assumed to possess fewer such ties. From this perspective, we expect female job-seekers who can signal higher levels of social capital to receive higher pay, even if their jobs do not draw on social capital as a criterion for job performance. In these cases, affiliations would serve to signal greater access to information about wages and job opportunities affecting pay even if the women possessing these affiliations lacked actual heterophilous ties.

Women's Institutional Affiliations, Social Resources, and Pay

Building on work that demonstrates the link between organizational characteristics and potential network ties, I suggest that firms recruiting college students may view the sex composition of their educational institutions as an indicator of their potential social networks and, in the case of female job candidates, the information they access about the distribution of salary offers for given job types. Specifically, women attending all-female colleges may be perceived as having more homophilous social networks and, therefore, limited access to information about men's offers, hence about wage dispersion. Therefore, recruiters would have greater latitude to discriminate in salary offers to these women, in contrast with their female peers attending a coeducational school of the same status, who would be perceived as having social networks fostering the detection of wage discrimination. I examine this subject in the context of a field study of salary offers made to female graduates of elite colleges on their entry into the full-time labor force.[57]

I will discuss findings showing that even after controlling for individual-level human capital variables, occupational category, and actual social ties, women graduating from two of the most elite women's colleges in the United States received significantly lower salary offers than their female counterparts at a coeducational school of the same prestige. These findings show a negative effect of institutional homophily on women's pay, even after accounting for actual network characteristics, in addition to human capital and job category controls, suggesting that salary offers are influenced by assumptions about women's networks and the gender-constrained salary information available to women through these networks.

As already noted, jobs generate social contacts that lead to future jobs. Research on employability and social capital can benefit from a focus on first jobs as well as actual job changes. Because my specific interest lies in women's careers, I have several important reasons for studying women's entry into the labor force directly from college. First, recent research indicates that much of the observed gender wage gap can be attributed to gender differences in initial salary.[58] Even among female MBAs, for example, Olson and her colleagues found that lower starting salaries were the major source of women's lower current salary levels when compared to their male peers.

Second, because detailed comparison data are typically available only for those candidates that are actually hired, discrimination in initial hiring can be more difficult to detect than discrimination in promotions, layoffs, or other forms of termination.[59]

I selected three geographically proximate schools of comparable status and selectivity: two from the "Seven Sisters," the most elite women's colleges in the United States, which developed historically as Ivy League counterparts, and one Ivy League school with the same ratings in student selectivity and quality, test scores, record of alumni achievement, and institutional history as the two women's schools.[60] Each of these schools is among the most rigorous and selective undergraduate institutions in America. According to the schools' recruiting offices, recruiters consider the schools to be a set, in that those recruiting at one typically recruit at all three. All three schools are located in the Northeast and place their graduates in the same industries, occupations, and geographic locations.

In spring 1992, the on-campus placement offices of each school distributed my questionnaire to students who had participated in on-campus interviewing that spring, whether they were known to have received a job or not. All students who had received at least one job offer—whether they had accepted, rejected, or were still evaluating the offer—were asked to complete the questionnaire. Students could return their survey to the placement office or directly to the researcher.

The survey instrument contained questions about students' academic background (grade point average, major); job offers (total number of offers received, job, firm name, initial salary offer, and final salary offer); and advice network. The network portion of the survey presented students with categories of people with whom they might have discussed their offer "to help you evaluate or negotiate an offer or offers." These categories were broken down by gender (e.g., "employed female family members," "employed male family members"). Students were asked to indicate the number of people in each category they conferred with in evaluating their offers. The job-offer portion of the survey enabled students to describe up to three offers.

I focused upon job offers emanating from on-campus recruiting activities for several reasons. First, on-campus recruiting it is an important vehicle for staffing at large firms, involving 16 percent of personnel budgets.[61] Second, at least two recent studies suggest that students recruited via college placement offices receive higher initial salaries.[62] Third, as already mentioned, the three schools in the sample attract the same firms from industries such as investment banking and consulting. Examining salary offers made via on-campus recruiting and controlling for characteristics of the individual job and candidate can highlight pay differences that result from recruiters' assumptions about network composition and access to information about male offers. Such assumptions regarding the institutional embeddedness of networks would be less salient in job searches conducted months after graduation. The dependent variable in this study was each student's maximum salary offer (or only offer, if she received only one).

Before examining the effects of actual and perceived network composition on compensation, it is important to determine whether women attending single-sex institutions truly had smaller and more homophilous advice networks. Analysis of the survey data revealed no significant differences in the total number of contacts, the number of men in the network, or men as a percentage of total network size between the women's schools and the coeducational college.

A "strong-form" argument regarding the significance of perceived social ties would hypothesize that the type of institution (here, a women's college versus a coeducational school)—as a proxy for likely network composition—would be predictive of salary offers but that actual ties would not. Although I expected a stronger effect for institution type than network ties, I expected significant effects for both. Therefore, I hypothesized that male contacts would be positively related to pay for women from institutions of both types, but women at single-sex colleges would receive significantly lower offers (using each student's maximum salary offer, if she received more than one) than their female counterparts at the coeducational college, even after controlling for individual-level human capital variables (e.g., grade point average, college major), the number of offers received by the student (a plausible human capital and informational control), the job category associated with the salary offer, average salaries and aggregate demand associated with job categories, and race/ethnic minority status.

I further hypothesized that male contacts would be most valuable for women at the coeducational school and for all women who were entering higher paying, male-dominated job categories. The opportunities coeducational school women had to confer with male contacts would yield highly interpretable wage information, since they would know more about these men's scholastic and extracurricular achievements. For women entering male-dominated fields, male contacts would be seen as more appropriate for these jobs and would therefore be conduits of valuable information about the true dispersion of salary levels for these jobs.

Separate from this issue of the quantity of contacts with men is the "return" associated with male ties. It was hypothesized that the number of male contacts would be related to higher levels of compensation for coeducational than single-sex college women. The rationale for this hypothesis is that the men in the coeducational women's network can provide richer information about wage dispersion than the men in the networks of single-sex college women. This hypothesis was tested and confirmed. The number of men in the network was significantly and negatively related to salary offers for the women's college students, indicating that the returns on male contacts in the form of higher compensation were evident for female students at the coeducational school but not for women from the single-sex colleges. I tested an additional hypothesis consistent with research showing the instrumental value of heterophilous ties. The interaction of the number of male contacts by the sex composition of the position associated with each woman's offer was found to be significantly and positively related to compensation offers. Thus, the number of men in one's advice network was more important for women who were entering male-dominated fields than for women entering job categories with a lower percentage of men.

These results provide some support for theories regarding the instrumentality of male contacts, as well as a more nuanced view of which women obtain the benefit of heterophilous contact. The two groups of women possessed highly comparable social resources but received different returns from those ties, consistent with the argument that the ties that are believed to exist may matter more than those that actually do.

A stronger test of the importance of assumed social resources involves the analysis of institutional effects. Analyses were conducted to determine the relationship between women's college graduation and pay, controlling for individual human capital characteristics, actual social resources, and occupational variables. As hypothesized, institution type—an indicator of the probable sex composition of women's social networks—had large and significant effects on women's offers. The single-sex college students received significantly lower offers than their coeducational counterparts, even accounting for all relevant controls. These findings are truly striking in that students sampled did not differ in their human capital and these schools have the same status and academic rigor and are perceived as comparable sources of talent by major recruiters. Specifically, they share the same selectivity and educational quality ratings and records of alumni achievement in male-dominated occupations.

Summary

Taken together, these findings illustrate the importance of having social ties and affiliating oneself with institutions that signal the attainment of those ties. The differential compensation described here is particularly significant in that it relates to salary offers made to highly similar, elite women exiting some of the highest quality institutions of higher learning in the United States, where the only major difference observed between the two groups was the probable sex composition of each group's social networks. These findings are of further significance in that the dependent variable of interest in this study—the salary offers associated with first jobs—has been shown to be significantly related to the gender wage gap later in a woman's career.[63]

Neither this study nor this chapter should be seen as advocating that women avoid single-sex institutions. There are important benefits to attending women's colleges, as demonstrated (albeit not unambiguously) by the research literature. Rather, it should be understood that third parties will consciously or unconsciously use affiliations as indicators of a job applicant's probable network composition. When women are perceived to have homophilous networks, they will also be construed as having more limited access to information than women at institutions that provide greater availability of heterophilous ties. Given the evidence that women do not receive the same returns from negotiations and external market strategies that men do,[64] it must be considered that women in the coeducational setting in this study were better off relative to their peers at all-female colleges because recruiters were aware that differential offers to men and women in this domain would be detectable. However, recruiters could assume that students at the same-sex colleges would not detect a differential if they compared their offers to those of their peers at their institution. From this point of view, the women in the coeducational setting may benefit from the "spillover" of wage-setting targeted at men.[65]

An important caveat to this formulation of wage discrimination is that firms' perceptions of candidates' social resources and assumptions about the wage information available via these resources must be separated from the effects of perceived ties on assumptions of a candidate's ability and fit. The empirical study described in this chapter distinguishes these effects in several ways. First, in all likelihood, the social contacts possessed by the women in this study were not connected to the recruiting firms (i.e., the students' applications for jobs were unlikely the result of employee referrals). These contacts therefore could provide no information to recruiters regarding a candidate's quality or fit. Second, traditional human capital measures for this population (e.g., grade point average and major), as well as a more telling measure of candidate quality, the number of job offers each woman in the sample received, are included as controls. Third, because the coeducational and women's colleges were carefully selected to be comparable on selectivity, academic rigor, and status, it is difficult to argue that recruiters believed the schools to be of differential quality. Women within the two institution types received the same number of offers and were recruited by many of the same firms, further attesting to their comparability. The annual return of these recruiters to these same campuses suggests that the firms see each school as a source of high-quality "matches."

The value of actual social ties rests in the information, status, and legitimacy that they confer. To the degree that some women's high levels of social capital are unknown to third parties who allocate valued career outcomes—jobs, project assignments, promotions, or compensation—they lose the benefits of social capital that have been well documented by social scientists. The very legitimacy problem that women in management face, for example, suggests that signaling actual social capital is all the more important for this group. To the degree that women are affiliated with organizations with largely female memberships (that are known as such) the more important this signaling process will be.

This chapter argues the importance of recent empirical examinations of the "demand side" of the social network equation. Because social resources can only be imperfectly assessed, it is important to understand the basis for estimates of social network size and composition, as well as the different ways in which actual versus assumed social resources are expected to affect career outcomes. Just as social network research indicates that different network concepts and measures are related to different career outcomes, more study is needed of the ways in which assumed versus actual social resources are responsible for certain aspects of career attainment. As suggested here, assumed resources will affect compensation more directly when wages are determined by an employer (e.g., when jobs are scarce) rather than when jointly determined by a candidate and firm via negotiation and where impressions such as perceived performance reputation are what matter.

Rather than arguing that actual social resources do not matter, this chapter provides some evidence that obtaining returns from social resources may be more contingent for women than men and among women, more dependent on their specific structural positions (i.e., institutional affiliations). Understanding the divergence between employer assumptions regarding women's networks and their actual resources is likely to provide valuable insight into why some women do not realize the returns to social resources that one might expect.

Notes

1. Ronald S. Burt, "The Contingent Value of Social Capital," *Administrative Science Quarterly* 42 (1997): 339–65; Joel Podolny and James N. Baron, "Resources and Relationships: Social Networks and Mobility in the Workplace," *American Sociological Review* 62 (1997): 673–93.

2. Mark S. Granovetter, *Getting a Job: A Study of Contacts and Careers* (Chicago: University of Chicago Press, 1995); Martin Kilduff, "The Interpersonal Structure of Decision-making: A Social Comparison Approach to Organizational Choice," *Organizational Behavior and Human Decision Processes* 47 (1990): 270–88; Roberto M. Fernandez and Nancy Weinberg, "Sifting and Sorting: Personal Contacts and Hiring in a Retail Bank," *American Sociological Review* 62 (1997): 883–902; Mark S. Granovetter, "The Strength of Weak Ties," *American Journal of Sociology* 78 (1973): 1360–80; Nan D. DeGraaf and Hendrik D. Flap, "With a Little Help from My Friends: Social Resources as an Explanation of Occupational Status and Income in West Germany, the Netherlands, and the United States," *Social Forces* 67 (1988): 452–72; Hendrik D. Flap and Nan DeGraaf, "Social Capital and Attained Occupational Status," *Netherlands Journal for Sociology* 22 (1986): 145–61; Nan Lin and Many Dumin, "Access to Occupations through Social Ties," *Social Networks* 8 (1986): 265–85; Nan Lin, John C. Vaughn, and Walter M. Ensel, "Social Resources and Occupational Status Attainment," *Social Forces* 59 (1981): 1163–81; Peter V. Marsden and Jeanne S. Hurlbert, "Social Resources and Mobility Outcomes: A Replication and Extension," *Social Forces* 67 (1988): 1038–59; Michael Useem and Jerome Karabel, "Pathways to Corporate Management," *American Sociological Review* 51 (1986): 184–200; Ronald S. Burt, *Structural Holes* (Cambridge: Harvard University Press,

1992); Daniel J. Brass, "Men's and Women's Networks: A Study of Interaction Patterns and Influence in an Organization," *Academy of Management Journal* 28 (1985): 327–43; Herminia Ibarra and Steven Andrews, "Power, Social Influence, and Sense Making: Effects of Network Centrality and Proximity on Employee Perceptions," *Administrative Science Quarterly* 38 (1993): 277–303; Maarten Sprengers, Frits Tazelaar, and Hendrik Flap, "Social Resources, Situational Constraints, and Re-employment," *Netherlands Journal of Sociology* 24 (1988): 98–116; Maura A. Belliveau, Charles A. O'Reilly, and James B. Wade, "Social Capital at the Top: The Effects of Social Similarity and Status on CEO Compensation," *Academy of Management Journal* 39 (1996): 1568–93; Jacqueline Berger, "Were You Referred by a Man or a Woman? Gender of Contacts and Labor Market Outcomes," working paper no. 353, Industrial Relations Section, Princeton University, 1995; Ed A. W. Boxman, Paul M. DeGraaf, and Hendrick Flap, "The Impact of Social and Human Capital on the Income Attainment of Dutch Managers," *Social Networks* 13 (1991): 51–73; Eva Meyerson, "Human Capital, Social Capital and Compensation: The Relative Contribution of Social Contacts on Managers' Incomes," *Acta Sociologica* 37 (1994): 383–99.

3. David Krackhardt. "Cognitive Social Structures." *Social Networks* 9 (1987): 109–34; David Krackhardt, "Assessing the Political Landscape: Structure, Cognition, and Power in Organizations," *Administrative Science Quarterly* 35 (1990): 342–69; Martin Kilduff and David Krackhardt, "Bringing the Individual Back In: A Structural Analysis of the Internal Market for Reputation in Organizations," *Academy of Management Journal* 37 (1994): 87–108.

4. I do not consider here an additional case, where social resources are directly job-relevant and, therefore, the employer must assess the social ties a candidate possesses in order to determine their ability to perform the job. See discussion in Jeffrey Pfeffer, "A Political Perspective on Careers: Interests, Networks, and Environments," in *Handbook of Career Theory*, edited by Michael B. Arthur, Douglas T. Hall, and Barbara S. Lawrence (Cambridge, England: Cambridge University Press, 1989), pp. 380–96.

5. Kilduff (1990).

6. Roberto M. Fernandez and Nancy Weinberg (1997); Roberto M. Fernandez, Emilio Castilla, and Paul Moore, "Social Capital at Work: Networks and Hiring at a Phone Center," *American Journal of Sociology* 105 (2000): 1288–1350.

7. It is important to note that research does not indicate that women have smaller networks than men (Claude Fischer, *To Dwell among Friends* [Chicago: University of Chicago Press, 1982]; Peter V. Marsden, "Core Discussion Networks of Americans," *American Sociological Review* 52 [1987]: 122–31), although their networks do differ from men's in the number of kin ties included. Claude Fischer and Stacey Oliker, "A Research Note on Friendship, Gender, and the Life Cycle," *Social Forces* 62 (1983): 124–32; Barry Wellman, "Domestic Work, Paid Work and Net Work," in *Understanding Personal Relationships*, edited by Steve Duck and Daniel Perlman (London: Sage, 1985), pp. 159–91. See Gwen Moore, "Structural Determinants of Men's and Women's Personal Networks," *American Sociological Review* 55 (1990): 726–35, for an analysis of gender differences in network composition after controlling for employment, age, and family variables.

8. It could be argued that employers do not consider the social comparisons that employees or candidates make regarding compensation. However, many firms' use of pay secrecy policies and wage surveys in setting salary levels suggests that, in fact, employers expect employees and job candidates to actively compare their pay to others to assess equity (and that in some cases employers seek to prevent this). See Brenda Major and Blythe Forcey, "Social Comparisons and Pay Evaluations: Preferences for Same-Sex and Same-Job Wage Comparisons," *Journal of Experimental Social Psychology* 21 (1985): 393–405; Brenda Major, Dean McFarlin, and Diana Gagnon, "Overworked and Underpaid: On the Nature of Gender Differences in Personal Entitlement," *Journal of Personality and Social Psychology* 47 (1984): 1399–1412; Brenda Major and Maria Testa, "Social Comparison Processes and Judgments of Entitlement and Satisfaction," *Journal of Experimental Social Psychology* 25 (1989): 101–20.

9. This analysis assumes that: (1) employers seek to constrain wage costs; and (2) employers, seeking to achieve this goal, consciously or unconsciously, view women as a group as more appropriate recipients of low wages than men and, therefore, make more unfavorable allocations of pay to women than men. It is not assumed that employers will universally offer lower pay to women than men, but that in contexts that allow for such allocations, they will take advantage of this opportunity.

10. Herminia Ibarra, "Homophily and Differential Returns: Sex Differences in Network Access in an Advertising Firm," *Administrative Science Quarterly* 37 (1992): 422–47; Herminia Ibarra, "Personal Networks of Women and Minorities in Management: A Conceptual Framework," *Academy of Management Review* 18 (1993): 56–87.

11. Burt (1992).

12. Burt (1997).

13. Brass (1985); Ibarra (1992, 1993); Herminia Ibarra and Lynn Smith-Lovin, "New Directions in Social Network Research on Gender and Organizational Careers," in *Creating Tomorrow's Organization: A Handbook for Future Research in Organizational Behavior*, edited by Cary L. Cooper and Susan E. Jackson (Sussex, England: Wiley, 1997), pp. 359–83.

14. Ibarra (1992, 1993); see Ibarra and Smith-Lovin (1997) for a review.

15. Brass (1985).

16. Burt (1992), pp. 156–7.

17. Howard Aldrich, Pat Ray Reese, and Paola Dubini, "Women on the Verge of a Breakthrough: Networking among Entrepreneurs in the United States and Italy," *Entrepreneurship and Regional Development* 1 (1989): 339–56.

18. Berger (1995).

19. Marian M. Extejt and Craig J. Russell, "The Role of Individual Bargaining Behavior in the Pay Setting Process: A Pilot Study," *Journal of Business and Psychology* 5 (1990): 113–26.

20. Nan Lin, "Social Resources and Instrumental Action," in *Social Structure and Network Analysis*, editors Peter V. Marsden and Nan Lin (Beverly Hills, Calif.: Sage, 1982), p. 134; see also James D. Montgomery, "Job Search and Network Composition: Implications of the Strength-of-Weak-Ties Hypothesis," *American Sociological Review* 57 (1992): 586–96.

21. J. Miller McPherson, Pamela A. Popielarz, and Sonia Drobnic, "Social Networks and Organizational Dynamics," *American Sociological Review* 57 (1992): 153–70.

22. Brass (1985).

23. For voluntary organizations, see J. Miller McPherson and Lynn Smith-Lovin, "Women and Weak Ties: Differences by Sex in the Size of Voluntary Organizations," *American Journal of Sociology* 87 (1982): 883–904, 1982. For women's socioeconomic background and networks, see Nan Lin, "Social Resources and Instrumental Action," in Marsden and Lin (1982).

24. Ibarra (1992).

25. Patricia A. Roos and Barbara F. Reskin, "Institutional Factors Contributing to Sex Segregation in the Workplace," in *Sex Segregation in the Workplace: Trends, Explanations, and Remedies*, edited by Barbara Reskin (Washington, D.C: National Academy Press, 1984), pp. 235–60.

26. Paula England and Dana Dunn, "Evaluating Work and Comparable Worth," *Annual Review of Sociology* 14 (1988): 227–48; Paula England, George Farkas, Barbara S. Kilbourne, and Thomas Dou, "Explaining Occupational Sex Segregation and Wages: Findings from a Model with Fixed Effects," *American Sociological Review* 53 (1988): 544–58; Jeffrey Pfeffer and Alison Davis-Blake, "The Effect of the Proportion of Women on Salaries: The Case of College Administrators," *Administrative Science Quarterly* 32 (1987): 1–24; Barbara F. Reskin and Patricia Roos, *Job Queues, Gender Queues: Explaining Women's Inroads into Male Occupations* (Philadelphia: Temple University Press, 1990); Elaine Sorensen, "Measuring the Effect of Occupational Sex and Race Composition on Earnings," in *Pay Equity: Empirical Inquiries*, edited by R. T. Michael, H. I. Hartmann, and B. O'Farrell (Washington, D.C.: National Academy Press, 1989), pp. 49–69; Donald J. Treiman and Heidi I. Hartmann, *Women, Work and Wages: Equal Pay for Jobs of Equal Value* (Washington, D.C.: National Academy Press, 1981).

27. On shrinking gap, see Francine D. Blau and Lawrence M. Kahn, "Swimming upstream: Trends in the gender wage differential in the 1980s," *Journal of Labor Economics* 15 (1997): 1–42; on persistence of segregation, see Donald Tomaskovic-Devey. *Gender and Racial Inequality at Work* (Ithaca, N.Y.: ILR Press, 1993). See Jerry Jacobs, *Revolving Doors: Sex Segregation and Women's Careers* (Stanford: Stanford University Press, 1989), for a discussion of changes across the twentieth century in nonfarm employment segregation.

28. Donald Tomaskovic-Devey, "Sex Composition and Gendered Earnings Inequality: A Comparison of Job and Occupational Models," in *Gender Inequality at Work*, edited by Jerry A. Jacobs (Thousand Oaks, Calif.: Sage, 1995), pp. 23–56.

29. William T. Bielby and James N. Baron, "Sex Segregation Within Organizations," in Reskin (1984), pp. 27–55.

30. Trond Petersen and Laurie Morgan, "Separate and Unequal: Occupation-Establishment Segregation and the Gender Wage Gap," *American Journal of Sociology* 101 (1995): 329–65.

31. Janet S. Chafetz, *Gender Equity: An Integrated Theory of Stability and Change* (Newbury Park, Calif.: Sage 1990); Reskin and Roos (1990);

John C. Touhey, "Effects of Additional Women Professionals on Ratings of Occupational Prestige and Desirability," *Journal of Personality and Social Psychology* 29 (1974): 86–9.

32. Leslie Z. McArthur and Sarah W. Obrant, "Sex Biases in Comparable Worth Analyses," *Journal of Applied Social Psychology* 16 (1986): 757–70.

33. Jacobs (1989).

34. Roos and Reskin (1984).

35. Faye J. Crosby, "A Model of Egoistical Relative Deprivation," *Psychological Review* 83 (1976): 85–113; Faye J. Crosby, *Relative Deprivation and Working Women* (New York: Oxford University Press, 1982); Crosby (1984); Joanne Martin, "The Tolerance of Injustice," in *Relative Deprivation and Social Comparison: The Ontario Symposium* 4, edited by James M. Olson, C. Peter Herman, and Mark P. Zanna (Hillsdale, N.J.: Erlbaum, 1986) pp. 217–42; Carol T. Kulik and Maureen L. Ambrose, "Personal and Situational Determinants of Referent Choice," *Academy of Management Review* 17 (1992): 212–37; Arie Kruglanski and Ofra Mayseless, "Classic and Current Social Comparison Research: Expanding the Perspective," *Psychological Bulletin* (1990): 108, 195–208.

36. Faye J. Crosby, "Relative Deprivation in Organizational Settings," in *Research in Organizational Behavior* 6, editors Larry L. Cummings and Barry M. Staw (Greenwich, Conn.: JAI Press, 1984), pp. 51–93.

37. Mark Zanna, Faye Crosby, and George Lowenstein, "Male Reference Groups and Discontent Among Female Professionals," in *Women's Career Development*, edited by Barbara A. Gutek and Laurie Larwood (Newbury Park, Calif.: Sage, 1987), pp. 28–41.

38. On referent similarity and choice, see Leon Festinger, "A Theory of Social Comparison," *Human Relations* 7 (1954): 117–40; George Goethals and John Darley, "Social Comparison Theory: An Attributional Approach," in *Social Comparison Processes: Theoretical and Empirical Perspectives*, edited by Jerry M. Suls and R. L. Miller (Washington, D.C.: Hemisphere, 1977), pp. 259–78; Major and Forcey (1985); Major and Testa (1989). On gender similarity not predicting referent choice, see Diane M. Felicio and Carol T. Miller, "Social Comparison in Medical School: What Students Say about Gender and Similarity," *Basic and Applied Social Psychology* 15 (1994): 277–96.

39. Felicio and Miller (1994).

40. Major and Testa (1989).

41. This assumes that men will share valuable job-related information with women as well as other men. Extant research does not clearly show the distinct effects of tie strength and homophily on the transmission of information regarding job openings and salary ranges for jobs. There is, however, some evidence that work-related information is transmitted in social situations that are single-sex; for example, see Susan Martin, "Sexual Politics in the Workplace: The Interactional World of Policemen," *Symbolic Interaction* 1 (1978): 44–60.

42. Kilduff (1990).

43. James N. Baron and Jeffrey Pfeffer, "The Social Psychology of Organizations and Inequality," *Social Psychology Quarterly* 57 (1994): 200.

44. For prescriptive guidance for compensation experts, see George T. Milkovich and Jerry M. Newman, *Compensation* (Homewood, Ill.: Irwin, 1993). For an examination of discretion in wage-setting, see Marta M. Elvira, "The Design and Outcomes of Reward Structures: Integrating Agency and Power Explanations of Incentives," Ph.D. diss., Hass School of Business University of California at Berkeley, 1995. See in particular chapter 4, "The Politics of Compensation Design," for evidence of poor oversight and central coordination of pay and concomitant managerial discretion with regard to pay. In this study, Elvira concluded that despite requirements for centralized approval of compensation schemes, managers at the business unit level typically implemented pay plans without submitting to such oversight.

45. Paul S. Goodman, "An Examination of Referents Used in the Evaluation of Pay," *Organizational Behavior and Human Decision Processes* 12 (1974): 170–95. Ivan Lansberg, "Social Categorization, Entitlement, and Justice in Organizations: Contextual Determinants and Cognitive Underpinnings," *Human Relations* 41 (1989): 871–99. Todd Zenger, "Why Do Employers Only Reward Extreme Performance? Examining the Relationships among Performance, Pay, and Turnover," *Administrative Science Quarterly* 37 (1992): 198–219. See Baron and Pfeffer (1994) for discussion.

46. See endnote 45.

47. Kilduff and Krackhardt (1994).

48. Krackhardt (1990).

49. Robert B. Cialdini (1989). "Indirect Tactics of Image Management: Beyond Basking," in *Impression Management in the Organization*, edited by Robert A. Giacalone and Paul Rosenfeld (Hillsdale, NJ: Erlbaum, 1989), pp. 45–56.

50. See Bourdieu (1989) for an extensive discussion of how social resources are assumed from educational affiliations; Dietlind Stolle and Thomas R. Rochon, "Are All Associations Alike? Member Diversity, Associational Type, and the Creation of Social Capital," *American Behavioral Scientist* 42 (1998): 47–65.

51. McPherson and Smith-Lovin (1982); Scott L. Feld, "Social Structural Determinants of Similarity Among Associates," *American Sociological Review* 47 (1982): 797–801.

52. Lynn Smith-Lovin and J. Miller McPherson, "You Are Who You Know: A Network Approach to Gender," in *Theory on Gender/Feminism on Theory*, edited by Paula England (New York: de Gruyter, 1993), p. 233.

53. J. Miller McPherson and Lynn Smith-Lovin, "Homophily in Voluntary Organizations: Status Distance and the Composition of Face-to-Face Groups," *American Sociological Review* 52 (1987): 370; J. Miller McPherson and Lynn Smith-Lovin, "Women and Weak Ties: Differences by Sex in the Size of Voluntary Organizations," *American Journal of Sociology* 87 (1982): 883–904.

54. McPherson and Smith-Lovin (1982); see also Belliveau, O'Reilly, and Wade (1996) for indices of affiliations as measures of social capital.

55. Bourdieu (1989).

56. Even when observation of all interaction is possible and practical, people demonstrate poor recall regarding specific interactions. For a discussion, see H. Russell Bernard, Peter Killworth, David Kronfeld, and Lee

Sailer, "The Problem of Informant Accuracy: The Validity of Retrospective Data," *Annual Review of Anthropology* 13 (1984): 495–517. For a discussion of methodological problems in measuring social resources—including weak ties—see Nan Lin, "The Position Generator: A Measurement of Social Capital," paper presented at "Social Capital and Social Networks" a conference at Duke University, Durham, N.C. October 1998.

57. Maura A. Belliveau, "Blind Ambition? The Effects of Social Networks and Institutional Segregation on the compensation of Elite Coeducational and Women's College Graduates," unpublished manuscript, Lowry Mays College of Business, Texas A&M University, 2000.

58. Barry Gerhart, "Gender Differences in Current and Starting Salaries: The Role of Performance, College Major, and Job Title," *Industrial and Labor Relations Review* 43 (1990): 418–33; Josephine E. Olson, Irene H. Frieze, and Deborah C. Good, "The Effects of Job Type and Industry on the Income of Male and Female MBAs," *Journal of Human Resources* 22 (1987): 532–41.

59. See Barbara Bergmann, *The Economic Emergence of Women* (New York: Basic Books, 1986), pp. 158–9.

60. Mariam K. Chamberlain, "Women's College," in *Women in Academe: Progress and Prospects*, edited by Mariam K. Chamberlain (New York: Russell Sage, 1988), pp. 107–32; Edward B. Fiske, *The Fiske Guide to Colleges*, 8th ed. (New York: Times Books, 1992); Helen L. Horowitz, *Alma Mater: Design and Experience in the Women's Colleges from their 19th Century Beginnings to the 1930s* (New York: Knopf, 1984); Paul W. Kingston and Lionel S. Lewis, "Studying Elite Schools in America," editors' introduction to *The High-Status Track: Studies of Elite Schools and Stratification* (Albany: State University of New York Press, 1990), pp. xi–xxxiv; *Lovejoy's College Guide*, 21st ed., edited by Charles T. Straughn II and Barbarasue Lovejoy Straughn (New York: Prentice Hall, 1992); *Peterson's Guide to Four-Year Colleges*, 22nd ed. (Princeton: Peterson's Guides, 1992). Although the schools in this sample cannot be identified, because research demonstrates distinct effects of attendance at Harvard, Yale and Princeton University on post-graduate career attainment, the Ivy League school in my sample is not one of these three schools.

61. George T. Milkovich and John W. Boudreau, *Human Resource Management* (Chicago: Irwin, 1997), 198.

62. Curtis J. Simon and John T. Warner, "Matchmaker, Matchmaker: The Effect of Old Boy Networks on Job Match Quality, Earnings, and Tenure," *Journal of Labor Economics* 10 (1992): 306–29; Herbert A. Chesler, "Proof of Worth: Career Services Help Leads to Better Jobs Faster," *Journal of Career Planning and Employment* 55, 2 (1995): 47–50.

63. Gerhart (1990).

64. Barry Gerhart and Sara Rynes, "Determinants and Consequences of Salary Negotiations by Male and Female MBA Graduates," *Journal of Applied Psychology* 76 (1991): 256–62; Jeanne M. Brett and Linda K. Stroh, "Jumping Ship: Who Benefits from an External Labor Market Career Strategy?" *Journal of Applied Psychology* 82 (1997): 331–41. But see the following for evidence that men's and women's negotiations behavior and outcomes may differ: Cynthia K. Stevens, Anna G. Bavetta, and Marilyn E. Gist, "Gender Differences in the Acquisition of Salary Negotiation Skills: The

Role of Goals, Self-efficacy, and Perceived Control," *Journal of Applied Psychology* 78 (1993): 723–35; Lisa A. Barron, "You Get What You Ask For: Differences in Men's and Women's Requests for Salary Increases in a Negotiation Setting," Unpublished manuscript, Graduate School of Management, University of California at Irvine 1998.

65. See Baron and Pfeffer (1994): 190–209, for a discussion of variation in inequality as a function of social contact and the presence or absence of social or organizational distinctions.

III

RELATIONAL WEALTH AND ORGANIZATIONAL ATTACHMENT

Organizational attachment—emotional, social, and economic—has been a central component of the traditional relationship between employer and employee in industrialized nations. In the United States, this attachment has been undermined to some extent by the rise in the use in contingent labor and the erosion of existing commitments and established relationships. Nonetheless, people and firms continue to make distinctive claims on each other and support a quality of attention to collective goals.

The first chapter in this section, authored by Olenda Johnson, Melvin Smith, and Darlene Gambill, cogently argues for a significant change in the nature of one dimension of attachment: worker identification with the organization. Organizational attachment, they maintain, is changing from a static, immutable condition to a process made fluid and malleable as firms adopt market-based employment practices. A more fluid identification challenges both firms and workers through its frequent manifestation of lower trust, commitment, and stability. Johnson and her colleagues point out that many erstwhile loyal employees now keep their resumes polished to provide some semblance of stability in their otherwise turbulent work lives. Identification in effect may be the height of the wealth embodied in worker-firm relationships. How contemporary firms address the advantages they accrue from even a modicum of identification is indicative of their potential for developing future repositories of relational wealth.

Daniel Feldman examines the motivations and attitudes of younger workers and new job entrants in his analysis of the problems with transactional employment. He points out that one of the most important questions facing organizations in the new employment model is how to balance the objective need for short-term results with longer-term needs for employee commitment and involvement. He argues that new entrants and recent arrivals into the workforce have grown highly skeptical about the motives and competence of management. Consequently, they are less likely to make the kinds of investments in their work and their employers that form the foundation of relational wealth and create competitive advantage.

Ellen Kossek's focus is on the working poor. For Americans, it is reasonable to argue that many workforce participants have traditionally had little exposure to the advantages that other workers with more marketable skills have derived from firms valuing their distinctive expertise and attachment. The working poor are a case in point of worker-firm experiences devoid of relational wealth. The two-tiered nature of the U.S. labor market after World War II differentiated between the stable careers of white males working as core members of organizations and the more volatile, unstable jobs associated with women and minorities, who both were valued less and generated only limited quotients of relational wealth as they moved from employer to employer with little evidence of advancement. Kossek confronts the two-tiered nature of the labor force head on, addressing what happens when the volatility that women and minorities traditional experience spills over into the "mainstream" of majority male employment. Kossek identifies a surprising convergence in the experiences of white-collar employees in U.S. corporations and the recipients of public welfare. She argues that both face a new policy of "tough love" conjoining the removal of income and employment guarantees under the rubric of self-sufficiency. Both professionals and welfare recipients are experiencing a sea-change in their relations with the dominant institutions in their economic lives: the firm and the government, respectively. Kossek argues that the move to market-based employment for both professionals and welfare recipients mandates a model of individually centered employability. In both circumstances, the lack of external relations and of credentials readily interpretable to an external market, and the investments each has made in the previous status quo, serve to erode relational wealth and undermine individual value on the external market. She further argues that individual employers have little incentive to invest in enhanced employability for the working poor. "Welfare to work" represents a classic commons problem, where individual firms will behave in self-serving way to gain cheap (and subsidized) former welfare recipients. The exploitation of welfare recipients on subsidy without replenishing their skills undermines the collective interest, with particularly egregious impacts on the families of these newly hired workers.

In the final chapter in this section, Maureen Scully offers a challenge to the critics of employment stability who claim that the new economy is a meritocracy rather than a bureaucracy. Scully reports on original data indicating that many workers are dubious about the existence of promotion and incentive systems predicated on the merit of individual workers. The market-focused view of employment maintains that the rational basis of worker advancement and earnings is a function of the individual's contribution to the economic interests of the firm. However, Scully demonstrates that firms' abilities to make personnel allocation decisions based on merit are extremely limited. Bias and political favoritism exists at all levels in firms—both traditional and modern. Social class adds to the distrust of the distribution rules apparently exercised by firms, with the most skeptical view of meritocracy evident among working-class participants, who themselves are frequently managed by less-skilled supervisors.

The success of organizational forms depends to some degree on their legitimacy in the eyes of the larger society of which they are a part. The very existence of meritocracies depends on the trustworthiness of the practices that differentiate work experiences on the basis of worker contributions. Scully suggests that those who are looking for fairness will rarely find it in modern organizations claiming meritocractic status. She suggests that the quality of the relationship between firm and worker may be as important to the functioning of meritocracy principles as are the market-focused tournaments and competitions supposedly intended to differentiate high and low firm contributors.

8

Reconstructing "We"

Organizational Identification in a Dynamic Environment

OLENDA E. JOHNSON, MELVIN L. SMITH,
DARLENE Y. GAMBILL

An organization's identity—the features of the organization
that are central, distinctive, and enduring—answers the question, "who are we as an organization?"
> —Stuart Albert and David Whetten (1985)

Organizational identification—the integration of one's organizational membership into one's self-concept—addresses the
question, "who am I?"
> —Blake Ashforth and Fred Mael (1989)

When individuals internalize the characteristics, norms, and
identity of the [organization], they shift their self-definition
from "I" to "we."
> —Marilynn Brewer and Wendi Gardner (1996)

In today's ever-changing organizational environments, "who are we" is not
easily defined.[1] Megamergers, acquisitions, spinoffs, reorganizations, and
bankruptcies alter the identity of organizations with increasing regularity.
Distinctive organizational attributes, such as core values and organizational
culture, are shifting as the dynamics of the macroenvironment fluctuate.[2]
Consequently, the way organization members identify with their organizations is also changing. The fluidity of organizational identities is affecting
the extent to which individuals incorporate their organizational relationships into their self-definitions and see themselves as part of a collective
"we." For example, within two and a half years of Westinghouse Electric

Corporation's acquisition of media giant CBS, Westinghouse sold all of its core industrial businesses, moved its Pittsburgh headquarters to New York, and changed its name formally to CBS, shedding one of the century's best known corporate names.[3] In that short span of time, Westinghouse completely discarded its identity, mutating into an entirely different organization. For Westinghouse employees, these transitions probably affected their organizationally based self-definitions. Those who remained with the organization were challenged not only to reassess the meaning and value of their identification with the company but also to redefine "who they were" in the context of a new organizational relationship. This chapter addresses the role of organizational identification as an indication of a firm's relational wealth. It argues that shifting member identification with a firm risks eroding the added value of the employment relationship. Identification, once lost, may be difficult to restore and workers may struggle to reconnect with the collective "we."

Challenges to organizational identification can affect the psychological and physiological well-being of organization members. Integrating an organization's identity with one's individual self-concept generally serves a number of favorable purposes, including enhanced feelings of self-worth, a sense of belonging, and a degree of psychological stability.[4] However, when the environment makes organizational identification difficult or threatens the stability of identification, workers may experience psychological discontinuity and physiological stress.[5] This can, in turn, affect their performance, ability to cope with change, and approach to managing their careers. Moreover, weakened identification impedes worker trust and commitment, affecting a firm's ability to generate and sustain relational wealth. Identification creates added value for the organization by increasing member-firm trust and commitment. As the psychological relationship between members and the organization is strengthened or weakened over time, trust and commitment are either fortified or diminished.

In this chapter, we explore identification from the workers' perspective, specifically their role as active participants in their own identification process.[6] We argue that certain transformations in the work environment—namely, industry consolidations, environmental uncertainty, boundaryless careers, and demographic diversity—are leading organization members to reconstruct the notion of "we" and adopt a fluid, adaptable approach to managing their identification with organizations. As the contexts supporting organizational identities change, workers must alter the way they create, maintain, and disengage from those identities. As career experiences become more flexible, workers may begin defining themselves more in terms of an occupation rather than a particular firm. At the same time, the increasing demographic diversity of the workforce may require workers to negotiate through a hierarchy of identities. Thus, organizational identification, once epitomized by the passive and assumed attachment of the "organization man," is evolving into a malleable process in which organization members decide how, whether, and to what degree they will psychologically identify with their organizations.[7]

The Challenge of Identification in Dynamic Contexts

Organizational identification is a context-driven process. The extent to which organizational membership shapes a person's self-definition is influenced by organizational cues that make membership psychologically salient. A sense of "oneness" with the organization is often created through a focus on traditions, rituals, myths, logos, and slogans, cultural components that represent "who we are as an organization."[8] More fundamentally, identification can be spurred by the core elements of an organization's identity— its products and services, business activities, strategic vision, and corporate image. Identification, therefore, can occur when organizational roles make distinctive organizational attributes more prominent.[9] Identification is also more likely when internal and external cues highlight the differences among competing organizations.[10] In other words, members achieve a greater sense of "we" when "us" is juxtaposed with "them."

Importantly, the strength and stability of members' identification with a firm is influenced by the durability of the contextual cues that make organizational membership psychologically salient. When cues shift, disappear, or become blurred, workers have more difficulty finding a base for their identification. In the Westinghouse/CBS merger, for example, the cues that evoked and sustained identification with Westinghouse (e.g., culture, symbols, mission) were eliminated. Workers who identified with the "old" organization were challenged to find other ways to support their psychological attachment to the "new" one. Along the same lines, obstacles for identification are created by the increasing number of strategic alliances between competing organizations. Partnerships and industry consolidations (e.g., Northwest Airlines and Continental Airlines; Travelers Group and Citicorp) reduce the contrast between the members' firm and its competition, weakening the relative clarity of any particular organizational identity.[11] Consequently, the lines between "us" and "them" become blurred, diluting the sense of "we" for members of the organization.

Organizational identification also is challenged by uncertainty in an organization's environment. An environment characterized by inconstancy affects both the organization's image and its members' ability to identify with it.[12] Because individual self-concept may be comprised of multiple identities (e.g., family, gender, religion), including many that are organizationally based (e.g., work teams, one's occupation, union membership), uncertainty may cause individuals to oscillate among various identities, possibly creating a sense of disequilibrium.[13] For instance, during the 1998 General Motors (GM) labor strike, workers likely experienced a number of identity swings, moving from "We, the GM workers," to "We, the United Auto Workers" (UAW), to "We, the victims of the GM strike," and finally back to "We, the GM workers." Such identity swings make identification unstable and may weaken a person's desire to identify with the organization. At the very least, oscillating between two or more identities is likely to lessen the strength of them all.

Environmental uncertainty also may create conflict among multiple identities, particularly if certain identities are derived from opposing forces (e.g., GM worker vs. UAW union member). The conflict is generated by the need to disidentify with the organization—that is, to specify what one is *not* while at the same time maintaining membership in the organization.[14] While some GM employees may have highly valued their identity as GM workers, they may have also felt forced to psychologically distance themselves from GM in order to identify with the UAW. Such context-driven dissonance can create identity "schizophrenia," in which pressure to adjust one's identity under tense circumstances creates stress for the person.[15] Organization members trying to balance the conflict among their multiple identities may struggle to maintain their identity with the organization.

Another way in which organizational identification is being challenged is through the trend toward the "boundaryless" career, an employment approach characterized by frequent job changes (including internal job rotations, lateral assignments, and external career opportunities) that emphasizes individual flexibility and mobility.[16] The net effect has been a reduction in the length of time a person remains with a firm. Data from a 1996 Employee Benefit Research Institute (EBRI) study show at least a 20 percent decrease in average job tenure for certain workers over a thirteen-year period. Median tenure ranged from 3 to 12 years in 1996, compared to 3.4 to 17 years in 1983, depending on the age of the employee.[17] These findings have several implications for organizational identification. The emphasis on mobility, for example, can require workers to decrease their identification in order to establish the flexibility needed to manage their careers in boundaryless environments. Individuals who identify too strongly may find it difficult to leave and to take advantage of opportunities elsewhere. At the same time, however, a strong identity may be needed to promote acceptance of lateral or internal reassignments as "career-building opportunities."[18] The more a worker identifies with the organization, the more he or she may be able to recognize and develop opportunities internally.

Finally, efforts to enhance diversity in the workplace, which tend to draw attention to demographic group memberships, present another challenge to organizational identification. Workplace diversity efforts increase the contextual salience of racial, gender, and ethnic identities, thereby attenuating cues that would facilitate organizational identification.[19] This is a particularly strong contextual force because of the value society typically attaches to demographic group membership, especially for members of historically underrepresented groups such as African Americans, women, and Hispanics.[20] For many of these organization members, their demographic group membership is perceived by them and others to influence all aspects of their organizational experiences.[21] Consequently, their racial, gender, and ethnic identities often supersede all other identities in terms of importance.[22] Members, therefore, are challenged to weigh their need to identify with their organization against the meaningfulness of their demographic group memberships.

Taken together, the contextual changes in the work environment pose numerous challenges for organizational identification. The forces described here suggest that workers will be compelled to adjust the way—and the degree to which—they define themselves in relation to their firms. The forces also show that dwindling member identification can jeopardize the strength of the employment relationship. Inevitably organizational identities will continue to shift, fade, become severed, or be replaced, requiring workers to employ different sets of psychological processes and social dynamics in order to adapt.[23] The challenge for workers is to develop an approach to reconstructing the notion of "we" that allows them to keep pace with a rapidly changing environment while also maintaining their psychological and physiological well-being.

The Importance of Identification for the Twenty-first Century Organization

Organizational identification is changing from a static, immutable process to one that is more fluid and malleable. The increasing fluidity of organizational identification requires members to adopt strategies that allow them to preserve and protect their psychological well-being and organizational success. Organizational identification may not be meaningful for all organization members. However, for those for whom organizational membership is central to self-definition, flexibility appears to be a key component for surviving and succeeding in a dynamic work environment.

The changing nature of identification is likely to affect other key aspects of the relationship between the organization and its members. Specifically, we expect changing identification processes to impact a firm's ability to maintain and build trust and commitment. Trust—specifically trust in the organization as an employer—refers to the members' belief that the organization will act in ways that are mutually beneficial or at the very least not harmful to members' individual interests.[24] Trust is considered an integral part of many organizational behaviors, including teamwork, leadership, and subordinate/supervisor relationships. The development of mutual trust benefits the firm because workers are more likely to act within the collective interests, while workers benefit from lessened concerns about job security.

Importantly, trust can increase when members possess a sense of shared organizational identity. Alternatively, trust can dissipate when identification is weakened or the organizational identity is abandoned.[25] As members adopt varying identification strategies, their choices are also likely to influence the nature of their trust relationship with the organization. Their mode of identification can require them to adopt new bases for establishing trust. On the one hand, members who choose to preserve their organizational identity may be willing to make the necessary adjustments to retain trust. On the other hand, as organizational identification becomes less stable, members may shift toward a type of trust that is based on "give and take" rather than shared identification.[26] In either situation, members may reevaluate their trust relationship as they reassess their organizational identity.

Similarly, organization members may also be forced to reassess their levels of organizational commitment. Organizational identification serves as a fundamental base for commitment, which can affect absenteeism, turnover, and citizenship behaviors. Identification influences the belief in and acceptance of organizational goals and values, as well as the desire to remain with the organization and exert considerable effort on its behalf.[27] As members alter their organizationally defined self-concepts, they are also likely to alter their levels of commitment. In addition, as the foundation of members' identification shifts from the organization to other sources (e.g., occupation or work team), they may become less committed to the organization and more committed to their new base of identification. For example, it is becoming increasingly common for the defection of one of an organization's top executives to result in the defection of several other key individuals within the organization. This may indicate their stronger commitment to (and perhaps identification with) the executive and work team than to the organization. Hence, as organizational identification continues to shift, organizational commitment is likely to be altered as well.

Ultimately, challenges to organizational identification—along with the consequences for trust and commitment—will influence the production of sustainable relational wealth. As organization members become increasingly tentative about their psychological attachment to organizations, value creation derived from the organizational relationship is likely to be impaired. Weakened identity contributes to diminished trust and lower levels of commitment. Conversely, strong identification builds these elements, resulting in stable human assets, a greater return on investments in human capital, and a solid base of organizational social capital. The end result is a distinct competitive advantage gained from the cumulative psychological relationships between the organization and its members. The greatest challenge for organizations and their members will be sustaining these relationships over time.

Identification as an Individual Choice

Workers can play a pivotal role in sustaining a firm's relational wealth by actively engaging in efforts to maintain their own organizational identification. Theory and research on social identity—the theoretical basis for organizational identification concepts—recognize identification as both a subconscious and conscious process. As a subconscious process, numerous experiments have shown that simply assigning a person to a group can be sufficient to engender group identification. Typically, these experiments involve arbitrarily classifying student subjects as members of a particular group and engaging them in some activity. Researchers then monitor their behaviors and cognitions, consistently observing that classification as a group member elicits cognitive responses (e.g., a shift from "I" to "we") and group behaviors (e.g., cooperation) that indicate that a group identity has been adopted.[28]

This effect has been shown to occur in organizations as well. An assessment of 2,535 new U. S. Army recruits, for example, found that the mere designation as army members generated a cognitive connection to the organization. Even as relative newcomers (three days after the induction and prior to the boot camp indoctrination), these new recruits exhibited strong levels of organizational identification, immediately using the term "we" rather than "they" when making reference to the army.[29] These findings suggest that simply labeling a person as an organization member can generate at least a minimal level of organizational identification, even when the person is unaware that identification is taking place.

In addition to subconscious identification, individuals may consciously select or disregard particular identities, choosing which group memberships (e.g., organization, profession, gender, family) they will incorporate into their self-definitions.[30] As people define and redefine who they are, they weigh the value and meaning of various group memberships. Most important are the extent to which a particular identity contributes to a positive self-concept and the emotional significance attached to the identity. If a valued identity is somehow threatened or group membership fails to enhance an individual's self-concept, he or she will attempt to reaffirm the valued identity and/or engage in efforts that protect his or her feelings of self-worth. In addition, the perceived benefits of group membership will further determine whether a person acts to sustain the identity or chooses to abandon it.[31] Individuals, therefore, are apt to adopt, discard, ignore, or switch an identity at any given time, unless the context supports its continuation. In fluid work settings, members can be expected to regularly reassess the meaningfulness of their various identities, revising their self-definitions as needed.

In sum, whether individuals believe they are a part of the organization involves both subconscious and conscious processes. The conscious act of choosing an identity suggests that workers can actively manage their identification process. In doing so, they are likely to consider the psychological and emotional significance of their organizational identities.

Managing Identification in Dynamic Contexts

There are a number of ways in which workers can manage the identification process. The methods they choose depend on the situation and its consequences for each person. If an organization member values an organizational identity, he or she may seek ways to preserve it. If the value of the identity has diminished or its order of importance has shifted, the member may adopt compromise strategies, enabling him or her to maintain some level of organizational identification while also protecting his or her self-concept.

Preserving Organizational Identities

Even in the face of organizational change, workers may desire to maintain their psychological identification with the organization. There are several reasons for choosing to preserve organizational identities. First, at a fundamental level, people have a need to maintain a degree of continuity and coherence in their self-concepts.[32] Discontinuity disrupts the way members conceive of themselves and the meaning they have attached to their organizational memberships. Second, because of the meaningfulness and emotional significance of membership, members may find it psychologically difficult to disengage from their identities, preferring instead to retain their organizationally based self-definitions. Third, organizational identification may continue to serve as a means of self-enhancement. Members may believe that the self-enhancing qualities of an organization (such its status) remain important to their overall sense of who they are, irrespective of other changes. Finally, members may see their organizational tenure and their level of organizational identity as being inherently interrelated. Therefore, identification may be perceived as a necessary condition in order to remain with the organization.

Maintaining an organizationally based self-concept is particularly challenging when the organization itself has changed. In such a situation, the contextual cues that make organizational membership psychologically salient might have shifted or even disappeared. The result is weakened member identification. One way for workers to maintain organizational identity is to detach their identity from the previous context and "remoor" the identity to elements in the new environment.[33] In other words, "we" is deconstructed by separating the organization's identity from the former elements and then reconstructed by linking the organization's identity to the culture, activities, and people that represent the new organization. Relocating the organization's identity yields new contextual cues for sustaining identification.

An example of identity remooring can be seen in the transformation of IBM. In the 1970s and 1980s, IBM was known for its strong corporate culture and, arguably, strong levels of organizational identification (recall the symbolism of the IBM "blue suit"). As market demands changed, IBM was forced to shed its old corporate image and alter the way it did business. For IBM employees, this transition likely elicited fundamental changes in the meaning and importance of their organizational membership and probably affected their ability to identify with the organization. For IBM employees to preserve their organizationally based self-concepts, it was necessary for them to let go of their psychological attachment to the old IBM and integrate the characteristics, norms, and identity of the new IBM into their self-definitions. Replacing old identification anchors with new supports likely allowed organization members to maintain some continuity.[34]

Another method for preserving organizational identity is to focus attention on the competition, thereby enhancing the psychological salience of the members' organization. Competitive salience is particularly relevant in the context of industry consolidations and strategic alliances. In these instances, blurred distinctions between "us" and "them" have diluted members' identification with the organization. Redefining the competition and redrawing the dividing line reconstitutes the sense of "we" for organization members. For example, the race to beat a competitor to the market with a new product, the intense competition for important human resources, and even interfirm rivalry for supporting social causes can raise the prominence of organizational membership. Workers can, therefore, sustain their organizational identity by recognizing competitive cues in their environment.

By remooring and redefining their sense of "we," organization members can maintain their identification in dynamic contexts. In remooring the organization's identity to the new context, members are able to sustain their identification by drawing on new cues in the organization's environment. At the same time, members can reconstitute weakened identification by redrawing and emphasizing competitive dividing lines. Both approaches reestablish the psychological salience of organizational membership.

Protecting Individual Self-Concept

People have an inherent desire to maintain a positive self-esteem derived from the psychological integration of their self-concept with group memberships. If the relationship between the individual and the group becomes unfavorable, theory argues that the individual will engage in efforts to restore his or her positive self-concept.[35] Threats to self-esteem can take many forms, including group uncertainty, a change in the group's status, and a belief that group membership is no longer self-enhancing. Thus, for workers who psychologically identify with the organization, their self-esteem appears likely to be affected by contextual changes (e.g., restructuring, uncertainty). When these changes negatively impact self-esteem, they will be motivated to protect their positive view of themselves.

Workers can take several approaches to protecting their self-concept, depending on the contextual drivers of the identity threat. First, if the organizational identity is no longer self-enhancing—and hence can no longer contribute to positive self-esteem—workers may choose to reduce their identification with the firm. Abandonment can mean leaving the organization, severing both physical and psychological attachments. This is likely to entail transferring one's identification to a new entity where positive self-esteem can be restored and reinforced. The worker might also extract the organization from his or her self-definition and begin to use the term "they" rather than "we" when referring to the firm. This dissociation creates psychological distance from the organization, thereby minimizing the organizational threat to self-esteem, especially when threats such as downsizing and restructuring occur.[36]

A worker can counter the consequences of reduced organizational identification by increasing his or her level of occupational identification. Occupational identification is the extent to which individuals incorporate their profession or work roles into their self-definitions. For some, occupation is a meaningful identity that influences self-concept.[37] Occupational identities are often incorporated into organizational identities. Brand managers at Procter and Gamble, for example, may define themselves as "P&G marketers," capturing their identification with both the organization and the occupation. Occupational identities are also multidimensional, encompassing various work roles. The Procter and Gamble managers may further define themselves as market researchers, advertisers, and promotion planners because of the multiple responsibilities of brand management. Thus, occupational identification offers a broad range of identities that can fill a void in self-concept or serve as a buffer to protect self-esteem when organizational identity is threatened.[38] Workers who shift their cognitive focus to occupational identities are less vulnerable to organizational changes. Furthermore, occupational identification may promote positive self-esteem by allowing workers to view themselves outside the boundaries of the organization, expanding their perceived self-worth.[39]

Finally, workers may protect their organizationally based self-concepts by cognitively adjusting how they and others view the organization. Organizational identification is influenced, in part, by how the organization is construed. A positive organizational image can be an important source of self-enhancement, while an unfavorable image can threaten members' self-esteem.[40] When corporate transitions and elements of the external environment influence workers' perception of the organization to which they are psychologically connected, they personally experience changes in the organization's image.[41] Workers can protect themselves from this threat by reconfiguring their view of the organization, perhaps by focusing on a favorable aspect of their organization or by comparing it to another that they perceive to have a lesser image.[42]

An example of cognitive reconfiguring can be seen in a study that examined members' responses to *Business Week* (*BW*) rankings of American business schools. This annual survey inevitably raises the ire of university members who perceive their *BW* ranking to be incongruent with their expected (usually higher) ranking and the image they maintain of their organization.[43] The researchers interviewed administrators, faculty, and graduate students—members they believed to have strong levels of identification—and recorded their reactions to their rankings. They focused on schools ranked in the "top 20," specifically selecting those that experienced some change in their ranking (either favorably or unfavorably) from the previous year. The researchers found that members who perceived the rankings to be a significant threat to their university's image often responded by highlighting positive aspects of their university that were not mentioned in the *BW* ranking or suggesting different comparison standards that may have resulted in a better ranking for their university. By adjusting their view of the organization, members also protected the parts of their self-esteem that were psychologically tied to the university, repositioning "we" in a more favorable light.[44]

Taken together, the self-protective strategies described here suggest ways in which organization members can minimize the psychological and physiological consequences of threats to their organizational identity. Dynamic environments lend themselves to a number of identity challenges that consequently threaten members' self-esteem. The protective strategies enable organization members to manage these transitions with limited impact on their positive self-concepts.

Hierarchically Valuing Identities

Inherent in the concept of organizational identification is the assumption that identities emerge in a sequential and orderly way. This assumption presumes that people are aware of a singular identity at a particular time. In actuality, people typically have multiple (often overlapping) identities that fluctuate as the context fluctuates.[45] People must, therefore, choose which identity they will attend to in a given context. The identities that are chosen depend on individual values and priorities, resulting in an identity hierarchy.[46] Hierarchically ordering multiple identities is especially important when certain identities are discordant or socially valued. Prioritizing allows members to negotiate complex multiple identities without eliminating any part of their self-definition.

Given the complexity of organizational identification, dilemmas among competing identities are likely to surface. Contextual influences may generate a number of potential identity conflicts—for example, union versus organization, organization versus family, division versus work team. When each identity is deemed important some form of balance is necessary for psychological well-being. Discarding either identity could be psychologically damaging.[47] Alternatively, members may adopt compromise strategies in which a discordant identity is placed lower on the identity hierarchy and the contextually relevant identity is moved to the top of the hierarchy. Rather than eliminating an identity from their self-definition, workers create a latent identity that is psychologically accessible when the context dictates.

For example, much has been written about the conflict between work commitment and family obligations.[48] Workers who view both their membership in an organization and their family roles as important are likely to experience identity conflict. Successful coping may require identification flexibility such that the identities become as fluid as the context.[49] Rather than completely forsaking either valued identity, fluid identification will enable workers to call forth a specific identity based on their priorities at the time. Hence, during the workday, identification as an organization member may be at the top of the hierarchy; whereas identity as a father or mother shifts to the top at the conclusion of the workday. This approach allows workers to create some degree of psychological balance among competing identities.

The placement of organizational identity within the hierarchy is influenced further by cultural and organizational socialization.[50] The meaningfulness of demographic group membership, for instance, and past experiences as an organization member may lead some workers to limit the hierarchical placement of their organizational identity. Society places great emphasis on race, gender, and ethnicity, frequently giving these identity groups priority in a person's individual self-concept. This is especially true for women and people of color.[51] In order to retain organizational identification within the confines of an always-present primary identity, a person can treat organizational identity as a perpetually latent component of his or her self-definition. Instead of attenuating the importance of the primary identity, a person might conceive of his or her organizational membership as a secondary identity that is accessed as needed. For instance, examinations of the organizational experiences of African Americans reveal that the most successful organization members are those who maintain strong levels of racial identity while also maintaining sufficient levels of organizational identification. African Americans who place their organizational identity above their racial identity or abandon their racial identity altogether often experience the greatest levels of psychological distress and threats to their positive self-esteem.[52]

In sum, identification is a complex, multifaceted process in which workers must navigate through multiple, multilayered identities.[53] Hierarchically ordering identities can assist in prioritizing identification in relevant contexts. At the same time, accommodating a secondary identity along with a primary identity can contribute to workers organizational success and psychological well-being.

Conclusion

All told, organizational identification remains an important issue for both the individual and the organization. The dynamics of the changing work environment have given a new meaning to the sense of "we." Members are not only reconstructing the definition of "we" but also redefining how, when, and to what degree they will integrate "we" into their self-concept. Whether members retain, abandon, or prioritize their organizational identities, their actions can influence the nature of their organizational relationships. Organizations seek members who are committed, and members value relationships based on mutual trust. Whether members identify with the organization is likely to influence the benefits each obtains from their relationship.

Notes

1. Sources of the epigraphs are as follows. S. Albert and D. A. Whetten, "Organizational Identity," in *Research in Organizational Behavior*, vol. 7, edited by L. L. Cummings and B. M. Staw (Greenwich, Conn.: JAI Press, 1985), pp. 263–95; B. E. Ashforth and F. Mael, "Social Identity Theory and the Organization," *Academy of Management Review* 14 (1989): 20–39; M. B. Brewer and W. Gardner, "Who Is This 'We'? Levels of Collective Identity and Self Representations," *Journal of Personality and Social Psychology* 71 (1996): 83–93.

2. See S. Tully "Mergers: Why the Historic Boom Will Keep Making Noise," *Fortune*, April 27, 1998, pp. 148–56; for a specific example on the effect of a merger on an organization's identity, see W. J. Holstein, "Chrysler's New Identity Crisis," *U.S. News and World Report*, October 26, 1998, pp. 50–2.

3. "Westinghouse Electric Corp.: CBS Purchase Completed in $5.4 Billion Agreement," *Wall Street Journal*, November 27, 1995, p. B3; K. Pope, "Westinghouse to Focus on Broadcasting—Manufacturer Plans to Sell Rest of Industrial Lines, Changes Its Name to CBS," *Wall Street Journal*, November 17, 1997, p. A3; J. P. Miller, "Emerson to Pay CBS $265 Million for Some Assets," *Wall Street Journal*, May 27, 1998, p. C18.

4. For a complete discussion on the potential benefits of organizational identification for organization members, see M. G. Pratt, "To Be or Not To Be? Central Questions in Organizational Identification," in *Identity in Organizations*, edited by D. A. Whetten and P. C. Godfrey (Thousand Oaks, Calif.: Sage, 1998), pp. 171–207.

5. J. M. Dukerich, R. Kramer, and J. M. Parks, "The Dark Side of Organizational Identification," in Whetten and Godfrey (1998), pp. 245–56. See also K. James, C. Lovato, and G. Khoo, "Social Identity Correlates of Minority Workers' Health," *Academy of Management* 97 (1994): 383–96, for psychological and physiological consequences related to other forms of identity.

6. For organization-level perspectives of managing identification, see J. R. Barker, "Managing Identification," in Whetten and Godfrey (1998), pp. 257–67; and D. M. Rousseau, "Why Workers Still Identify with Organizations," *Journal of Organizational Behavior* 19 (1998): 217–33.

7. Compare Whyte's original treatise on the "organization man" with recent discussions on identity in organizations: W. H. Whyte, *The Organization Man* (New York: Simon and Schuster, 1956); see also Whetten and Godfrey (1998).

8. Ashforth and Mael (1989).

9. Albert and Whetten, (1985); J. E. Dutton, J. M. Dukerich, and C. V. Harquail, "Organizational Images and Member Identification," *Administrative Science Quarterly* 39 (1994): 239–63.

10. Pratt (1998).

11. See, for example, K. T. Beddingfield and P. J. Longman, "Northwest's

Significant Other," *U.S. News and World Report*, February 2, 1998, p. 55; C. J. Loomis and J. Aley, "Citigroup: 'One helluva candy store!' " *Fortune*, May 11, 1998, pp. 72–80.

12. D. A. Gioia and J. B. Thomas, "Identity, Image, and Issue Interpretation: Sensemaking during Strategic Change in Academia," *Administrative Science Quarterly* 41 (1996): 370–403.

13. Dukerich, Kramer, and Parks (1998).

14. B. E. Ashforth, "Becoming: How Does the Process of Identification Unfold," in Whetten and Godfrey (1998), pp. 213–22; and Dukerich, Kramer, and Parks (1998). For an additional perspective on disidentification, see C. Steele, "A Threat in the Air: How Stereotypes Shape Intellectual Identity and Performance," *American Psychologist* 52 (1998): 613–29.

15. Dukerich, Kramer, and Parks (1998).

16. M. B. Arthur, "The Boundaryless Career: A New Perspective for Organizational Inquiry," *Journal of Organizational Behavior* 15 (1994): 295–306; D. M. Rousseau, "Organizational Behavior in the New Organizational Era," *Annual Review of Psychology* 48 (1997): 515–46.

17. These figures are for men in four different age groups: 25–34 (three years), 35–44 (six years), 45–54 (ten years), and 55–64 (twelve years). This compares to 1983 median tenure of 3.4, 7.7, 13.4, and 17 years, respectively. Average job tenure for women in 1996 showed less mobility, actually increasing compared to 1978 levels. However, this finding is consistent with the data on labor attachment for women and the surge of women in the workforce during this time period. See S. R. Schmidt and S. V. Svorny, "Recent Trends in Job Security and Stability," *Journal of Labor Research* 19 (1998): 647–68; and E. McShulskis, "Job Tenures Shift for Men and Women," *HRMagazine* (May, 1997): 20.

18. See Arthur (1994) for discussion on lateral career moves as a career enhancement strategy.

19. Pratt (1998); M. E. Elmes and D. L. Connelley, "Dreams of Diversity and the Realities of Intergroup Relations in Organizations," in *Managing the Organizational Melting Pot*, edited by P. Prasad, A. J. Mills, M. Elmes, and A. Prasad (Thousand Oaks, Calif.: Sage, 1997), pp. 148–67.

20. For discussion on the meaningfulness of gender, racial, and ethnic identities for certain demographic groups, see D. E. S. Frable, "Gender, Racial, Ethnic, Sexual, and Class Identities," *Annual Review of Psychology* 48 (1997): 139–62.

21. For discussions on the ways in which demographic group membership permeates the organizational experiences of racial and gender minorities, see D. A. Thomas and C. P. Alderfer, "The Influence of Race on Career Dynamics: Theory and Research on Minority Career Experiences," in *Handbook of Career Theory*, edited by M. B. Arthur, D. T. Hall, and B. S. Lawrence (Cambridge, England: Cambridge University Press, 1989), pp. 133–58; P. M. Elsass and L. M. Graves, "Demographic Diversity in Decision-making Groups: The Experiences of Women and People of Color," *Academy of Management Review* 22 (1997): 946–73; and B. R. Ragins, "Diversified Mentoring Relationships in Organizations: A Power Perspective," *Academy of Management Review* 22 (1997): 482–521.

22. M. Waters, *Ethnic Options: Choosing Identities in America* (Berkeley:

University of California Press, 1990); D. M. Messick and D. M. Mackie, "Intergroup Relations," *Annual Review of Psychology* 40 (1989): 84–93; B. E. Ashforth and R. H. Humphrey, "Labeling Processes in Organizations," in *Research in Organizational Behavior* vol. 17, edited by L. L. Cummings and B. M. Staw (Greenwich, Conn.: JAI Press, 1995), pp. 413–61.

23. Pratt (1998).

24. S. L. Robinson, "Trust and Breach of the Psychological Contract," *Administrative Science Quarterly* 41 (1996): 574–99.

25. R. J. Lewicki and B. B. Bunker, "Developing and Maintaining Trust in Work Relationships," in *Trust in Organizations*, edited by R. M. Kramer and T. R. Tyler (Thousand Oaks, Calif.: Sage, 1996), pp. 114–39; R. M. Kramer, M. B. Brewer, and B. A. Hanna, "Collective Trust and Collective Action: The Decision to Trust as a Social Decision," in Kramer and Tyler, (1996), pp. 357–89.

26. Lewicki and Bunker (1996) refer to this as calculus-based trust, where trust is determined by the assessment of relative outcomes and costs associated with the relationship between the member and the organization.

27. See Ashforth and Mael (1989); Pratt (1998).

28. For discussion and examples of the minimal group paradigm in arbitrary groups (i.e., identification derived from simple categorization), see D. A. Wilder, "Social Categorization: Implications for Creation and Reduction of Intergroup Bias," *Advances in Experimental Social Psychology* 19 (1986): 291–355; and S. L. Gaertner et al., "How Does Cooperation Reduce Intergroup Bias," *Journal of Personality and Social Psychology* 59 (1990): 692–704.

29. F. A. Mael and B. E. Ashforth, "Loyal from Day One: Biodata, Organizational Identification and Turnover among Newcomers," *Personnel Psychology* 48 (1995): 309–33.

30. B. E. Ashforth (1998), pp. 213–22; K. Deaux, "Reconstructing Social Identity," *Personality and Social Psychology Bulletin* 19 (1993): 4–12.

31. H. Tajfel and J. C. Turner, "The Social Identity Theory of Intergroup Behavior," in *Psychology of Intergroup Relations*, edited by S. Worchel and W. Austin (Chicago: Nelson-Hall 1986), pp. 7–24, K. D. Elsbach, "The Process of Social Identification: With What Do We Identify?" in Whetten and Godfrey (1998), pp. 232–37.

32. M. Breakwell, *Coping with Threatened Identities* (London: Methuen, 1986); M. A. Hogg and D. Abrams, "Social Motivation, Self-esteem and Social Identity," in *Social Identity Theory: Constructive and Critical Advances*, edited by D. Abrams and M. A. Hogg (New York: Springer Verlag, 1990), pp. 28–47.

33. K. A. Ethier and K. Deaux, "Negotiating Social Identity When Contexts Change: Maintaining Identification and Responding to Threat," *Journal of Personality and Social Psychology* 67 (1994): 243–51.

34. B. Morris and J. McGowan, "Big Blue." *Fortune*, April 14, 1997, pp. 68–79; W. J. Cook and W. Cohen, "Men in Blue," *U.S. News and World Report*, February 10, 1998, pp. 44–50.

35. Tajfel and Turner (1986).

36. Dukerich, Kramer, and Parks (1998).

37. G. A. Fine, "Justifying Work: Occupational Rhetorics as Resources

in Restaurant Kitchens," *Administrative Science Quarterly* 41 (1994): 90–115.

38. Ibid.

39. Ibid.

40. Dutton, Dukerich, and Harquail (1994).

41. Ibid.

42. See Tajfel and Turner (1986).

43. See, for example, the flood of responses in the "Readers Report" following *Business Week*'s October 19, 1998, announcement—November 9, 16, and 23 issues.

44. K. D. Elsbach and R. M. Kramer, "Members' Response to Organizational Identity Threats: Encountering and Countering the *Business Week* Rankings," *Administrative Science Quarterly* 41 (1996): 442–76.

45. Ashforth (1998).

46. Ethier and Deaux (1994).

47. P. A. Thoits, "Multiple Identities and Psychological Well-being: A Reformulation and Test of the Social Isolation Hypothesis," *American Sociological Review* 48 (1983): 174–87. See also Fine (1994); Dukerich, Kramer, and Parks (1998).

48. See, for example, K. H. Hammonds and A. T. Palmer, "The Daddy Trap," *Business Week*, September 21, 1998, pp. 56–66; S. A. Lobel and L. St. Clair, "Effects of Family Responsibilities, Gender, and Career Identity," *Academy of Management Journal* 35 (1992): 1057–69.

49. D. A. Gioia, "From Individual to Organizational Identity," in Whetten and Godfrey (1998), pp. 17–31.

50. Ashforth and Humphrey (1995).

51. Ibid.; M. Brewer, "A Dual Process Model of Impression Formation," in *Advances in Social Cognition*, vol. 1, edited by T. K. Srull and R. S. Wyer, Jr. (Hillsdale, N.J.: Erlbaum, 1998), pp. 1–36.

52. H. Ibarra, "Race, Opportunity, and Diversity of Social Circles in Managerial Networks," *Academy of Management Journal* 38 (1995): 673–703; D. A. Thomas, "The Dynamics of Managing Racial Diversity in Developmental Relationships," *Administrative Science Quarterly* 38 (1993): 169–94; E. Cose, *The Rage of a Privileged Class* (New York: HarperCollins, 1993).

53. See M. G. Pratt and A. Rafaeli, "Organizational Dress as a Symbol of Multilayered Social Identities," *Academy of Management Journal* 40 (1997): 862–98.

9

From the Me Decade to the Flee Decade

DANIEL C. FELDMAN

As the *New York Times* predicted at the beginning of the decade, the "Me Decade" of the 1980s was replaced by the "Flee Decade" of the 1990s.[1] The perceived need to always be ready to move is a key tenet of the "employability" model of employment relations—and this perception has profoundly changed the way we think about the nature of our careers today.

When William Whyte wrote *The Organization Man* forty years ago, he theorized that middle managers and top-level executives had to conform to rigid norms of behavior, both at work and in their personal lives, to have successful careers in corporate America. Two assumptions were implicit in Whyte's analysis: (1) that being a manager in a well-established corporation was a highly valued position in American society and (2) that the price of membership in this dominant elite was unflinching loyalty to the organization and strict adherence to its code of behavior.[2]

Based largely on the experiences of American managers in the post–World War II boom era, Whyte's analysis was strongly influenced by its era. Americans at this time were highly motivated to move up the ladder of financial security and well-being, while at the same time building deep roots in their corporations and communities. Even the geographical moves of employees were often to suburban neighborhoods populated by employees of similar corporations, who had similar personal values and lifestyles. In short, the level of trust among employees and between employees and management was high, and the intrafirm mobility of fast-track managers enhanced, rather than depleted, the relational wealth of the firm.

By the time Chris Argyris wrote *Integrating the Individual and the Organization* in 1964, there was greater optimism that the needs of individuals and the demands of organizations could be jointly met. Redesigning the nature of work, modifying management styles, and restructuring work teams could provide individuals with more challenging work and personal autonomy while still meeting the demands from organizations for high-quantity, high-quality output.[3]

It was also during this time that more attention was given to the "psychological contracts" between individuals and organizations. Rather than viewing the employment relationship as one in which employees needed to conform to organizational norms in order to keep their jobs, Argyris conceptualized organizational careers as exchange relationships in which individuals traded loyalty and hard work for long-term job security, advancement, and opportunities to grow and develop.

The period between 1973 and 1992 saw the genesis of the employability model of employment, in which individuals and organizations act as independent free agents pursuing their self-interests via short-term employment arrangements. From an macroeconomic perspective, the deindustrialization of major industries, the rapid increase in mergers and acquisitions, and the recessions that bracketed this period all led to widespread layoffs, increased job insecurity, and underemployment. Individuals became more interested in self-employment, subcontracting, and independent consulting—both as a means of becoming less dependent on the whims of large corporations and as a buffer against short-term unemployment and long-term underemployment.

In this model, flexibility replaced stability as the most salient component of the employment relationship. The principles of "just-in-time" inventory management were carried over to "just-in-time" human resource management. Developing trust among employees and employers was less critical, since employment contracts were shorter in duration and tended to be transactional rather than relational in nature.

Previous research on the consequences of the "employability model" has largely focused on individuals currently in the workforce, particularly veteran employees who have been displaced in some way by widespread changes in the psychological contract. For instance, there has been considerable investigation of the short-term reactions and coping behaviors of individuals who have lost their jobs through downsizing;[4] the negative spin off effects of downsizing on coworkers, family, and friends;[5] and the adverse consequences of underemployment for laid-off professionals and managers.[6] From an institutional perspective, this research has concentrated on the conditions under which organizations are most likely to downsize,[7] the groups of employees most likely to be vulnerable to job loss under conditions of organizational restructuring,[8] and the consequences of using contingent workers for both organizational productivity and strategic redirection of the firm.[9]

What have been infrequently studied and are the focus of this chapter are the consequences of the employability model for new entrants and recent arrivals into the workforce. While they were not victims of the downsizings and restructurings of the past decade, these young adults are acutely aware that the relationships they will have with their employers will be fundamentally different from those experienced by their parents. How can one "establish" a career when long-term relationships with organizations are almost impossible? How can one be "loyal" to an organization whose own long-term existence is in doubt? What good are training and guidance from a "one-minute mentor"? In short, how should one manage a career in an environment in which the establishment of relational wealth has been largely supplanted by the pursuit of shareholder wealth?

Because of personal experiences with friends and relatives who have lost jobs, as well as publicity in the media, new entrants and recent arrivals into the workforce have grown highly skeptical about the motives and competence of management[10] and the changing nature of the psychological contract.[11] "I'm not anti-boss, I'm anti-idiot" is not only the title of Scott Adams' recent "Dilbert" book but also the prevailing sentiment of recent college graduates. Moreover, despite finishing college, often with high grades, roughly 25 percent of recent graduates end up "underemployed" in jobs that do not use their education or in fields that hold little interest for them.[12] For many young adults, then, becoming a long-term manager in one organization is not a primary career goal. The desire to "get rich quick" is fueled not only by the desire for more material goods but also by the desire for enough income to be financially and psychologically independent of organizations altogether.

This chapter addresses two interrelated issues concerning the impact of the employability model on the careers of new entrants and recent arrivals into the workforce. First, I explore the "double binds" facing young adults in an employability labor market. In this type of labor market, for example, highly transportable skills and geographic mobility are important assets, but highly mobile lifestyles make it much more difficult to juggle dual-career marriages. Then, I explore some of the ways early career management strategies are changing in response to the new employment model, both from the perspective of recent arrivals managing their own careers and from the perspective of organizations that recruit, socialize, and train young adults.

The Paradoxes of the Employability Model for New Entrants into the Workforce

The emergence of the employability model has made the search for rewarding, achievable career goals—a challenging task for new entrants into the workforce even under the best of circumstances—much more complex. Young adults face five paradoxes in particular as they transition into the rapidly changing world of work.[13]

1. *Highly transportable skills and geographical mobility are critical to career success, but highly mobile lifestyles make the juggling of dual-career marriages much more difficult.* As the employability model became more salient to managers in the 1980s, the advice one heard most frequently was to "pack your own parachute."[14] That is, managers were urged to constantly seek out new opportunities for growth, to vigilantly monitor their present job situations for potential signs of downsizing or job loss, and to move on to new jobs at their own initiative and on their own timetable.

However, as more and more managers married or partnered with other professionals who had their own jobs and career investments, this advice became increasingly problematic. Finding alternative jobs for oneself is demanding enough; finding good jobs at the same time for both partners in a marriage (as well as a desirable location to raise children) is a daunting challenge. This problem is where the "free agent" model of managing careers breaks down. A "free agent" quarterback cannot automatically bring his receiver with him to a new team, nor can a professional always negotiate for a comparable job for a spouse.

Building a career in the employability model, where being a "free agent" is quite distinct from being a "solo agent," is a frustrating double bind. Thus, even if individual employees bought into the notion of building their own human capital at the expense of intrafirm relational wealth, external forces present a significant counterweight to that course of action.

2. *Many new entrants into the workforce want to be entrepreneurs, but they often have no capital or experience.* Particularly in contrast to the baby boomers, today's graduates view corporations with less regard and consider "the millionaires next door"—who have made lightning-strike fortunes—their new role models. However, most young adults have neither sufficient full-time work experience nor sufficient capital to launch successful entrepreneurial adventures. Furthermore, the failure rates of small businesses with relatively low startup costs (e.g., small restaurants) are still exceedingly high.

Thus, many new business school graduates face a vexing dilemma. On the one hand, the specter of working for large corporations is not an attractive future; on the other hand, they find that it is difficult to get financing for new ventures without previous work experience (preferably in large, established corporations). New entrants into the workforce, then, must choose between spending a few years "getting their tickets punched" in jobs and organizations in which they have little interest or plunging into new ventures without much business experience and a limited financial safety net.

3. *New graduates once turned to large organizations as their first employers to obtain good mentoring and formal training, but many large organizations are cutting back on these activities because they realize newcomers are likely to leave rapidly.* From the 1950s through the 1980s, new graduates (particularly from undergraduate and graduate business schools) sought employment with large, established organizations that promised stature and imprimatur upon completion of their formal management training programs. Successfully completing these programs sent the market a signal that these employees were desirable and came with a further warranty on their formal education. Moreover, even if one didn't find success (e.g., through a partnership or vice-presidency) at a major firm like Arthur Andersen, no stigma was attached to that failure; one could easily get a new job, often with a promotion and a pay raise, at another firm of equal or only marginally lower status.

The employability model, though, makes organizations question the wisdom of intensive training programs for new graduates. Now that the "ticket-punching" mentality has taken hold among many young adults,[15] it may be economically irrational for organizations to invest heavily in this type of training. In an environment in which many new graduates do not even bother trying to conceal their desire to move on,[16] senior managers have few incentives to invest in their junior colleagues.

Thus, just as young managers are deciding to bite the bullet and join large corporations to get the requisite training and experience, these firms are cutting back on the one enticement that made working for them palatable. For all the rhetoric about mentoring in corporations today, the lack of success of "assigned mentor" programs indicates the fragility and narrow bond of trust between mentors and proteges. A "one-minute mentor" is an all-too-frequent reality for many young managers and professionals today.

4. *Long-term employment in one corporation is a sign of durability and loyalty, but remaining at one organization for a long time can be deadly in the context of downsizing.* Still lingering from the postwar culture that William Whyte captured in *The Organization Man* is the notion that long-term employment in one corporation is a sign of personal and professional stability. Even though most managers know intellectually that planning a career around one firm is no longer rational, they still feel nagging fears that others will judge them as unable to stay with anything or assume that there is "something wrong" with them if they move around too much.

The employability model is distinctive in its notion of "anticipatory dissatisfaction."[17] That is, even if individuals are satisfied with their current pay, working conditions, and other conventional quality of work life indicators, they may still be negative about jobs that are not optimal for launching their *next* career moves.

This concern about "getting out before it's too late" has been heightened by the widespread layoffs of middle-aged middle managers. Consider two middle-aged managers who have both been laid off and are looking for new jobs. Manager A worked for twenty years for a single company in one industry. Manager B worked for four companies for five years apiece, in four different industries. Who will have a better chance of satisfactory reemployment? In all likelihood, it will be Manager B, whose wide diversity of experience is likely to be considered a plus. In contrast, in all likelihood, Manager A will be described as a "one-trick pony"—unfortunately, now with the wrong trick.

Job stability—so valued internally (until, of course, the downsizing)—is often interpreted externally as a lack of flexibility and desirability. New entrants into the workforce see the loyal, laid-off middle-aged manager as their future if they stay with any one firm too long. For them, building reputation across multiple firms seems like a much better bet than building reputation within a single firm.

5. *Even as young adults join the workforce as members of organizations, they desire to be as free of organizational constraints as possible.* Finally,

one of the greatest paradoxes facing new entrants into the workforce is try-ing to link up with organizations at the same time they are trying to keep their distance from them. Over the past few years, there has been consid-erable business writing about the growth of "virtual" or "loosely coupled" organizations in which groups of employees are brought together for specific purposes and then move on to other ventures with different coworkers or external partners. This literature has focused on the firm-level advantages of these virtual organizations in terms of optimal staffing levels, decreased labor costs, and flexibility to respond to changing environmental conditions. The individual-level benefits have received less attention in the literature; many individuals want to be as disconnected with specific organizations as they can possibly afford to be.

Why do so many young adults desire only loose ties to their employers? One major driver is the dramatic change at the interface of work and family. Research suggests that the number of hours American employees work in-creased 15 percent over the past twenty years and that women have been disproportionately negatively affected by the change.[18] As families with two working parents become the norm rather than the exception, careers such as consultant, subcontractor, entrepreneur, and telecommuter become even more desirable. It may be one of the few effective ways of decreasing the inequity between employee input and organizational benefit.

Above and beyond the threats of downsizing, the research evidence also suggests that employees have become disgruntled and cynical about the decline in the quality of organizational leadership.[19] Where business com-munication once meant unadorned simple language, today it entails eva-siveness and doublespeak. The stock market doesn't decline; it "retraces" or "consolidates at a new level." In many organizations today, one has the impression that communication is for the benefit of the sender, not the re-ceiver, and that the purpose is to obfuscate rather than clarify the infor-mation presented.[20] As the Dilbert books make painfully obvious, this often leads to a situation where employees see their managers as buffoons, blath-ering in higher and higher volume about fewer and fewer accomplishments.

Moreover, many young workforce entrants are not impressed with the daily quality of life within organizations. As noted earlier, employees are asked to work increasingly long hours, while organizations run "stress man-agement workshops" to help them cope. Organizations ask salespeople to increase sales each quarter, and at the same time travel, phone, and adver-tising budgets have been reduced. The problem is not just that the left hand doesn't know what the right hand is doing; it's that the left hand seems to have forgotten what it did five minutes ago. Furthermore, be it out of naivete or idealism, many young adults expect managers to make decisions and provide direction—only to discover that in many organizations today, ef-fective management is defined as the bland nondeliverance of decisions.

It is no surprise, then, that many new entrants into the workforce are anxious to telecommute from home, work flexible schedules, or become consultants. What all these work arrangements have in common is that they minimize the amount of time employees must physically spend in the office.

Career Management Strategies in the Context of the Employability Model

As the employee model of labor relations gives way to the employability model, the ways in which individuals manage their careers and the ways organizations develop their employees will change as well. Here I outline some of the ways that the career management strategies of young adults are likely to change as the employee model begins to wane; then I suggest some ways organizational tactics for managing employees' careers are likely to change in response to the rise of the employability model.

Individual Career Management Strategies

What these new career-management strategies have in common is the goal of bringing individuals' inputs *into equity* with their employers' rewards. These strategies achieve this goal by either increasing the potential gains employees can extract from corporations or decreasing the potential losses employees might suffer from overinvesting in corporations. From the individual's perspective, then, the emphasis seems to be on increasing one's own human capital and reputation *independent* of whatever impact that strategy may have on the organization's relational wealth.

Entrepreneurial Careers in One's 30s

As much as many young adults desire careers as entrepreneurs (as the growth of academic programs in entrepreneurship and small business administration suggest), the difficulties of launching entrepreneurial ventures right out of school are tremendous. Thus, although many new entrants into the workforce will be less than enthusiastic about working for bureaucracies, most will continue to seek initial employment with them for the quality training and the wide variety of experiences they provide. However, compared to the generation before them, young adults today are much more likely to seek out entrepreneurial opportunities in their thirties rather than later in life. Becoming an unemployed, or underemployed, middle manager is not a pleasant prospect, and waiting until the ax falls to make one's move is an appalling career vision for new entrants into the workforce.

Maintaining Technical Competence

Consistent with that viewpoint, young adults are also likely to work harder at maintaining and enhancing their basic functional and technical skills even after they reach the managerial ranks.[21] A generation ago, managers were urged to move away from technical positions into generalist positions to develop their managerial competencies.[22] The continuing downsizing in corporations today, however, reminds young adults that being a "jack of all trades and master of none" is a dangerous survival strategy (either within or outside the boundaries of formal organizations). Being able to demonstrate some tangible skill that yields measurable outcomes is a powerful career advantage.

The Search for Flexibility

Another likely change in the career strategies of the next generation is the explicit compromise made by dual-career couples who trade income for flexibility. The career-development books of the 1970s led young professionals to believe that they could successfully juggle two high-powered, upwardly mobile careers if they planned well enough and "worked smarter, not harder." Such cultural beliefs have given employees overly high expectations of the satisfaction they can derive from work. As a result, workers juggling work and family have become increasingly frustrated by the remarkable growth in the number of hours worked per week.[23]

Many of today's graduates look at the model their parents pursued with a mixture of envy and distaste: they envy their parents' energy and aspirations but wonder why sane people would voluntarily pursue such an arduous way of life. Many in this generation will trade a higher salary for more flexible, less demanding work schedules. While intellectually they know they can "have it all," many young professionals today are not quite so sure they want to pay the price to do so. The early signals of this "downscoping" trend—less luxurious homes, cars, and lifestyles—are already emerging among the baby boomers.

Changing Occupational Preferences

The desire for flexibility and the integration of work and family will also change individuals' preferences for different kinds of career paths in general. We are already beginning to see a growth in careers that can be readily pursued outside the context of large organizations and on a part-time or flexible scheduling basis (e.g., counselling, accounting, and nursing). Even within the professions, we see a redistribution of students entering specialties with more regular hours. An example is the net increase in medical students choosing family practice over emergency medicine. Although emergency medicine physicians may earn twice the salary of family practitioners, many more young adults are willing to make that tradeoff so they don't become part-time spouses or parents.

Cynicism about Teams

Young adults continue to be especially cynical about the rhetoric of teams. It is difficult to escape the continuous barrage of stories in both the academic and business press about the virtues of employee participation and the need for greater employee empowerment. Participation is credited for increasing acceptance and commitment to execute important management decisions,[24] while empowerment is touted as a way of facilitating constructive organizational change.[25]

However, new employees often have no idea how to successfully manage their individual careers in an increasingly team-oriented environment. For example, while management espouses the virtues of a group-based culture, young adults see that most important rewards are distributed according to individual achievement. Moreover, the shift to "people skills" as a criterion for promotion gives managers tremendous latitude to reward political allies and punish enemies. Consequently, while new employees understand the need for, and the benefits of, a team-based culture, they are cynical about supervisors' ability to accurately measure team contributions and set aside personal feelings when evaluating performance.

As a result, young managers and professionals are more likely to pursue a path of "antagonistic cooperation."[26] That is, young adults will learn the rhetoric and public behaviors consistent with a team-based culture but will continue to pursue their self-interests, albeit more covertly. Any trust that is built among team members, then, will be narrow and fragile.

Organizational Strategies for Managing Employees' Careers

Corporations are at a critical juncture in determining how employment relations will unfold in the next century. Now that firms have seen some of the downsides of increasing short-term shareholder wealth at the expense of long-term relational wealth, there is some hope that corporations will revert back to more trusting, long-lasting relationships with employees. However, much of the recent research on organizational career development suggests that many corporations are likely to continue pursuing a strategy of low-commitment rather than high-involvement human resource management. Recent volatility in world financial markets only heightens top management's view that less is definitely more as far as labor costs go.

Less Training

As noted earlier, organizations are likely to respond to the employability model by decreasing the amount of formal training they offer employees, particularly long-term, developmental training (e.g., management development training). If highly skilled workers are likely to leave within a two-year time frame, it may be more economically sound for firms to hire experienced, higher-paid personnel than less experienced employees who require training.

Moreover, organizations will try to tightly contain ancillary training costs as well. For instance, as in the military, private sector firms may make employees contractually bound to work for them an agreed-on length of time after the training is completed. A firm may also be less willing to pay for training that brings long-term human capital gains to employees rather than short-term productivity gains for the firm (e.g., subsidizing employees to earn MBAs when they are not yet managers). In addition, organizations may be more likely to outsource training to community colleges, universities, and professional associations to eliminate the cost of a permanent, professional in-house training staff.

Less Effective Mentoring

As an alternative to formal training, more and more organizations are turning to mentoring as a way of socializing and coaching new hires and young adults in the workforce. At this point, it is unclear that mentoring will be effective in an "employability" model of labor relations.

As traditionally conceptualized, mentoring is partially based on altruistic impulses on the part of mentors and partially based on exchange principles.[27] Over a period of several years, a mentor and protege work more and more closely with each other. The mentor serves as a role model, giving the protege career counseling, work-related coaching, and social support; in return, the protege provides the mentor with technical, political, and, to some extent, social support. The employability model makes it much less likely that junior colleagues will be around long enough for this type of slow, evolutionary relationship to form.

Instead, many organizations have turned to "assigned mentoring programs" as an alternative. In these programs, newcomers are assigned mentors to help socialize them. Unfortunately, these formally assigned mentors may not be particularly effective.[28] Assigning mentors often shortcuts the benefits of mentors and proteges mutually selecting one another on the basis of complementary needs and interests over a longer period of time. In addition, once mentoring becomes just another task to be done, the altruism and fun associated with that activity may also decline. Furthermore, in many organizations, these assigned mentors are only a few years older or more senior than the proteges, although research suggests that using mentors eight to fifteen years older than proteges enables mentors to impart more wisdom to and be less competitive with their proteges.[29]

Thus, while organizations may increasingly turn to assigned mentoring as an alternative to formal training, it is far from clear how well this strategy will work. From a purely calculative perspective, many senior professionals see the following scenario: new graduates and young adults are often paid only marginally less than the senior employees; these young adults are not especially appreciative of their seniors' mentoring efforts and do not always reciprocate; and they are typically anxious to pay their dues and move on as quickly as possible. It takes a great deal of altruism for senior colleagues to take on mentoring under these conditions. At its core, mentoring relies on trust between mentors and proteges, and at this time, it is unclear whether such trust exists.

Focusing on Loyalty to the Subgroup

Under an employability model of labor relations, organizations may begin to shift their focus from trying to build employees' loyalty to the organization as a whole to trying to build their commitment to their immediate work group.[30] Not surprisingly, employee loyalty to corporations undergoing successive restructurings and downsizings is low; it is difficult for employees to feel committed to an organization whose continued existence is in doubt. Moreover, as noted earlier, many new hires and young adults are not particularly impressed by either the rhetoric or the leadership abilities of top management. As a result, organizations may find it easier to create positive attachment to the immediate stimulus of the work group than to create organizational commitment to an amorphous, distant, and sometimes threatening corporate entity.[31] Indeed, perhaps the low magnitude results in the "organizational citizenship" literature[32] may be attributable to confusion over the beneficiaries of the citizenship behaviors. When faced with overworked and dedicated coworkers, professionals may be willing to go above and beyond the call of duty to defend their reputations to others outside the firm. When faced with similar requests from corporate management, young professionals may react less enthusiastically. In relational wealth terms, then, the focus may shift from relational wealth at the organizational level to relational wealth at the subgroup level.

Movement toward a Technological Version of "Family Friendliness"

Over the past ten years, organizations have engaged in more rhetoric about becoming "family friendly" through such efforts as child care and flexible hours. While the research evidence is mixed on the true extent of organizational efforts in these areas and the cost-effectiveness of such programs in attracting and retaining employees, at least some organizations have made significant strides toward accommodating two-career couples and single parents.

Whether organizations under pressure to downsize and control costs will increase their investments in traditional "family friendly" initiatives is open to question. Programs such as child care are expensive, create potential liabilities for the firm, and may not be cost-effective in certain geographical locations. However, one area in which organizations are likely to invest increased resources is the use of technology to help resolve work/family conflicts.[33]

Recent estimates suggest that more than 7 million U.S. workers telecommute every day, while an equal number are using telecommunications technology to complete work-related projects from home after hours.[34] Some preliminary research suggests that absenteeism and turnover decrease substantially as a result of telecommuting,[35] largely because it enables professionals to better balance work and family demands.[36] Recent innovations such as satellite locations that allow employees to share office space and computer technology enabling simultaneous transmission of information among coworkers help mitigate the expenses and inconveniences found in traditional telecommuting.[37] In the long run, this technological version of family friendliness may be less expensive for organizations to implement and may show even greater promise in the future.

A Concluding Note

As several researchers have noted, the shift to an employability model has also resulted in an increase of "careerist" behavior.[38] That is, in an environment that pressures employees to make a quick, positive impression, young professionals and managers are more likely to take a short-run orientation to business decisions, be excessively concerned with image management, and develop inauthentic, untrusting relationships with colleagues and supervisors.

The question facing organizations in this new employment model is how to balance the objective need for short-term results with longer-term needs for employee commitment and involvement. Can organizations devise methods to develop individual human capital and organizational relational wealth at the same time? Can young employees develop the type of human capital and personal reputation they need in an environment that features little long-term trust between labor and management? Integrating individual needs and organizational demands in some new configuration will be the major career-development challenge facing both young professionals and their employers in the years ahead.

Notes

1. S. W. Alpert. "Escaping the Career Culture," in *The New Paradigm in Business,* edited by M. Ray and A. Rinzler (New York: Putnam, 1993), pp. 43–9.

2. W. H. Whyte, Jr., *The Organization Man* (Garden City, N.Y.: Anchor Books, 1957).

3. C. Argyris, *Integrating the Individual and the Organization* (New York: Wiley, 1964).

4. C. R. Leana and D. C. Feldman, *Coping with Job Loss: How Individuals, Organizations, and Communities Respond to Layoffs* (New York: Macmillan, 1992).

5. See J. Brockner, "Scope of Justice in the Workplace: How Survivors React to Co-worker Layoffs," *Journal of Social Issues* 46 (1990): 95–106. See also B. Justice and R. Justice, *The Abusing Family* (New York: Human Services Press, 1976).

6. See D. C. Feldman, "The Nature and Consequences of Underemployment," *Journal of Management* 22 (1996): 385–409. See also H. G. Kaufman, *Professionals in Search of Work* (New York: Wiley, 1992).

7. See K. S. Cameron, R. I. Sutton, and D. A. Whetten, eds., *Readings in Organizational Decline* (Cambridge, Mass.: Ballinger, 1988).

8. See R. D'Aveni, "The Aftermath of Organizational Decline: A Longitudinal Study of the Strategic and Managerial Characteristics of Declining Firms," *Academy of Management Journal* 32 (1989): 577–605. See also D. C. Feldman, "The Impact of Downsizing on Organizational Career Development Activities and Employee Career Development Opportunities," *Human Resource Management Review* 5 (1995): 189–221.

9. See A. Davis-Blake and B. Uzzi, "Determinants of Employment Externalization: A Study of Temporary Workers and Independent Contractors," *Administrative Science Quarterly* 38 (1993): 195–223. See also J. Pearce, "Toward an Organizational Behavior of Contract Laborers: Their Psychological Involvement and Effects on Employee Coworkers," *Academy of Management Journal* 36 (1993): 1082–96.

10. T. S. Bateman, T. Sakano, and M. Fujita, "Roger, Me, and My Attitude: Film Propaganda and Cynicism toward Corporate Leadership," *Journal of Applied Psychology* 77 (1992): 768–71.

11. See S. L. Robinson and D. M. Rousseau, "Violating the Psychological Contract: Not the Exception but the Norm," *Journal of Organizational Behavior* 15 (1994): 245–59. See also W. H. Turnley and D. C. Feldman, "The Impact of Psychological Contract Violations on Exit, Voice, Loyalty, and Neglect," *Human Relations 52* (1999); 895–922.

12. D. C. Feldman and W. H. Turnley, "Underemployment among Recent College Graduates," *Journal of Organizational Behavior* 16 (1995): 691–706.

13. D. C. Feldman, "The Dilbert Syndrome: How Employee Cynicism about Ineffective Management Is Changing the Nature of Careers in Organizations," paper presented at the Academy of Management, Boston, Massachusetts, August 1997.

14. P. M. Hirsch, *Pack Your Own Parachute* (Reading, Mass.: Addison-Wesley, 1987).

15. M. R. Louis, "Managing Career Transitions: A Missing Link in Career Development," *Organizational Dynamics* 10 (1982): 68–77.

16. Robinson and Rousseau (1994).

17. See D. C. Feldman, *Managing Careers in Organizations* (Glenview, Ill.: Scott Foresman, 1988). See also B. M. Staw and D. C. Feldman, "Thinking about Jobs as Careers," working paper, Kellogg Graduate School of Management, Northwestern University, Evanston, Illinois, 1979.

18. See A. R. Hochschild, *The Second Shift: Working Parents and the Revolution at Home* (New York: Viking Press, 1989). See also A. R. Hochs-

child, *The Time Bind: When Work Becomes Home and Home Becomes Work* (New York: Metropolitan Books, 1997).

19. P. H. Mirvis and D. L. Kanter, "Beyond Demography: A Psychological Profile of the Workforce," *Human Resource Management* 30 (1992): 45–68.

20. Feldman (1997).

21. See Feldman (1996). See also Feldman (1997).

22. D. T. Hall, *Careers in Organizations* (Pacific Palisades, Calif.: Goodyear, 1976).

23. See Hochschild (1989, 1997).

24. V. H. Vroom and A. G. Jago, *The New Leadership: Managing Participation in Organizations* (Englewood Cliffs, N.J.: Prentice-Hall, 1988).

25. F. Shipper and C. C. Manz, "Employee Self-management without Formally Designated Teams: An Alternative Road to Empowerment," *Organizational Dynamics* 20 (1991): 48–61.

26. See A. Bloom, *The Closing of the American Mind* (New York: Simon and Schuster, 1987). See also P. Cohen, *The Gospel According to Harvard Business School* (New York: Penguin Books, 1973).

27. See K. E. Kram, *Mentoring at Work* (Glenview, Ill.: Scott Foresman, 1985). See also D. J. Levinson, *The Seasons of a Man's Life* (New York: Knopf, 1978).

28. G. Chao, P. M. Walz, and P. Gardner, "Formal and Informal Mentorships: A Comparison of Mentoring Functions and Contrast with Nonmentored Counterparts," *Personnel Psychology* 45 (1992): 619–36.

29. See Kram (1985). See also Levinson (1978).

30. Feldman (1997).

31. J. R. Hackman and G. R. Oldham, *Work Redesign* (Reading, Mass.: Addison-Wesley, 1980).

32. J. W. Graham, "An Essay on Organizational Citizenship Behavior," *Employee Rights and Responsibilities* 4 (1994): 249–70.

33. D. C. Feldman and T. W. Gainey, "Patterns of Telecommuting and Their Consequences: Framing the Research Agenda," *Human Resource Management Review* 7 (1998): 369–88.

34. See K. Barnes, "Tips for Managing Telecommuters," *HR Focus* 71 (1994): 9–10. See also J. C. Mason, "Workplace 2000: The Death of 9 to 5?" *Management Review* 82 (1993): 14–18.

35. J. M. Weiss, "Telecommuting Boosts Employee Output," *HR* 39 (1994): 51–3.

36. D. J. McNerney, "Telecommuting: An Idea Whose Time Has Come," *HR Focus* 72 (1995): 3–5.

37. See B. Geber, "Virtual Teams," *Training* 32 (1995): 36–40. See also S. Greengard, "Telecommuting Centers Provide an Alternative to the Corporate Office," *Personnel Journal* 73 (1994): 68.

38. See Feldman (1988). See also Robinson and Rousseau, (1994).

10

Learning from the Working Poor and Welfare Reform

Paradoxes in Promoting Employability

ELLEN ERNST KOSSEK

As we approach the millennium, it is ironic to note that managerial and professional employees working at leading U.S. corporations share at least one common reality with welfare recipients. They may not even be aware of each other and have vastly different financial circumstances. However, corporate employees and welfare recipients face newly adopted "tough love" policies and no long-term guarantee of an income. This chapter argues that investments in "employability"—that is, the capacity to access continued employment either with one's current firm or a new one—will *not* pay off under present social and economic conditions. Linking the experiences of the working poor to workers generally, I argue that investments in employability must be supported by parallel investments in relational wealth.

Over recent decades, a wave of corporate restructurings, mergers, acquisitions, and downsizings have resulted in workplaces characterized by job insecurity and a growing corporate view that workers are solely responsible for ensuring their own employability.[1] Over half of the largest U.S. employers, for example, have adopted career self-management training programs to meet this challenge.[2] This training is designed to help employees be resilient and take on new roles and responsibilities for career direction. Yet some experts doubt such strategies will be successful, arguing that employees will become paralyzed if previously paternalistic employers give them all of the responsibility for employability without providing a favorable context and tangible supports.[3]

Welfare reform also focuses on mandating employability. The recent reshaping of welfare policy assumes that welfare income will be replaced with labor-market income.[4] On August 22, 1996, federal legislation was enacted that terminated the Aid to Families with Dependent Children (AFDC) program, the main U.S. welfare program for more than six decades, and replaced it with a new and significantly different program: the Personal Responsibility and Work Opportunity Reconciliation Act of 1996.[5] Unlike AFDC, which essentially offered long-term financial assistance to single mothers and children, the new law sets lifetime limits on the number of years adults can be on welfare and places stricter work requirements on those receiving payments.[6] Many states have rushed to claim that mandated "workfare" has been a success because caseloads have decreased. Yet such claims contradict states' difficulties in meeting federal standards that require a percentage of families receiving welfare to have adults performing work activities as a condition of receiving welfare benefits.[7] Some public policy experts fear that the most impoverished recipients lack the job skills and social supports to become self-sufficient and that cutting off such recipients will lead to greater deprivation for the most needy families.[8]

Thus, critics of reshaped corporate employment agendas and the new "workfare" system are doubtful that the newly emphasized employability practices will work in light of existing institutions and limited social and workforce investment policies. The paradox of promoting employability as an isolated strategy is that it does not necessarily encourage the development of social and human capital, relational wealth, or common public goods such as low unemployment.

This Chapter's Relational Wealth Themes, Purpose, and Background

A main theme of this chapter is that the relational wealth of employed and unemployed individuals is generally eroding in U.S. society. Compared to several decades ago, these groups share the common fate of having their social standing and opportunities decline at the same time they are being urged to take greater personal responsibility to develop labor skills that can be deployed across many firms. A resounding message of the organizations with which employees and welfare-to-work individuals have had historical ties—employers and the government, respectively—is that all members need to constantly prove their individual credibility and trustworthiness in order to hope for an ongoing relationship. The goal of this chapter is to emphasize the social capital instability faced by both the lower and upper-middle economic social strata. The fundamental characteristic of the "new deal" between employees and employers or between welfare recipients and the government is that the relationship is no longer organization-bounded. Employment is not strongly based on firm- or government-sponsored training, compensation, or upward mobility practices. The longevity of opportunities is now predominately governed by market pressures, outside of the private or public organization's boundaries.[9] Yet these very market pressures generally lessen the development of individual social capital and relational wealth.

A second theme is that employers currently face many disincentives to invest in enhanced employability for either the working poor or employees in general. Unless individual firms recognize that investments in employability make sense for the collective (e.g., all employers, or employers and government acting together), corporate norms placing less value on contributions to public goods such as the reduction of unemployment and the development of societal human capital are unlikely to change.

This chapter examines several key lessons regarding employability that I learned while evaluating a very political and timely issue: state welfare-to-work reform efforts. Unlike social scientists who study the poor, I came to this research with the perspective of one who traditionally studies how general human resource policies and organizational behavior affect employees of large organizations. The managerial issues I typically focus on (human resource policy, work/family/life integration, and managing diversity) have become increasingly relevant to the working poor because of the mandated welfare-to-work programs being implemented nationwide. Based on my reflections from this experience, this essay discusses the general utility of implementing employability as an overarching human resource strategy.

Before discussing the lessons learned and the paradoxes of solely focusing on employability, it is useful to know the background against which they are derived. In 1994, an interdisciplinary research team began a three-year evaluation of the state of Michigan's welfare reform innovations. These reforms, known as the Social Contract program, were hailed as a national model. They were permitted under a federal waiver granted to the state prior to the 1996 national welfare reform act passed. Our goal was to assess the impact of the intervention—welfare reform stressing employability with negative consequences for noncompliance—on the economic and psychological well-being of welfare mothers and children. Michigan's caseloads are currently at their lowest level in sixteen years and are among the lowest in the nation, with a reduction of seventy thousand cases since pilot welfare reforms began in 1992.

Under the Social Contract program, new public assistance recipients at four state sites were randomly assigned to either the program or an exempt control group. In return for public assistance, the program clients were required to spend at least twenty hours a week in labor market activity. Acceptable activities included employment, job training, education, volunteer or community service, and certain self- or family-improvement activities (e.g., noncredit courses, substance abuse treatment). Policy makers hoped that the mandated participation in any kind of labor activity that utilized any level of human capital would enhance participants' job competence and self-confidence. A ground-breaking aspect of Michigan's Social Contract intervention is that it was the first state program in the nation to consider volunteer labor an appropriate welfare-to-work endeavor that fostered readiness for a career.[10]

We surveyed several hundred mothers and children (between the ages of nine and thirteen years) just prior to the initiation of the pilot program, then one year later. We matched survey responses with three years of archival data on earnings and client backgrounds kept by the Michigan Department of Social Services from 1994 to 1996. In general, our results mirrored those of another pilot workfare program in the state of Washington.[11] As in the Washington study, we found that mandated employment via welfare-to-work programs increased employment and training activity but had little impact on continuous employment and earnings over time.[12] In the Michigan study, earnings over time were significantly related to the hours of previous paid employment and worker education and employment assets, both measured prior to their participation in Social Contract. It appears that the human capital investments one develops before going on welfare may be the strongest predictors of one's postworkfare economic achievement. These results suggest that public policy interventions forcing individuals to enter the labor market in order to work themselves out of poverty do not necessarily ensure that they will. It also raises questions about the quality of human capital enhancements derived from government sponsored initiatives. These labor market experiences seem to be disconnected from what private employers desire.

Another interesting finding was that earlier ratings of mothers' psychological self-concept and involvement in unpaid activity (i.e., volunteering and self-improvement) had little or no relationship to being employed one year later. This was true for all study participants, not just mothers. We also found that some members of the control group were as active as those in the Social Contract program group, contradicting the stereotype that welfare clients will not work unless forced to do so. In summary, it was shown that publicizing a government expectation that welfare recipients should become employable through individual bootstrapping was not in and of itself an effective public policy.

Table 10.1 summarizes five main assumptions of an employability policy that help explain why it contributes to the perpetuation of inequality. These include a supply side public policy framing, a preoccupation with individual effort and the lore of bootstrapping, a bias against concerted employer action, an assumption of core workforce homogeneity, and social constructions of key management concepts that exclude those in the lower socio-economic levels. While we focus our discussion of these assumptions and their attendant paradoxes on employment policy for the working poor, the issues also are relevant to the general employer emphasis on employability practices, which affects a growing number of employees today. As the editors of this book argue, focusing on employability as an isolated human resource strategy may have a corrosive impact on individual businesses and society as a whole. The chapter concludes with a discussion

Table 10.1 Employment Policy and the Perpetuation of Inequality:
The Paradoxes of Promoting Employability

Prevailing Assumptions and Emphases:	What these Approaches Overlook:
Supply side focus: (e.g., "lousy" or poor-quality, workers	*Demand side* influences (i.e., role of poor employer HR practices or "lousy jobs")[a] in perpetuating inequality
Individual labor market activities (e.g., bootstrapping) to increase relational wealth	*Employer/organizational labor market investments* to increase relational wealth
Short-run economic dilemma: individual employer actions to reduce labor costs are the preferred way to increase competitiveness over the short run	*The fact that *collective employer action may yield the highest rewards to society* and to firms over the long run.
Homogeneity of working poor: one-size-fits-all employability practices	*Diversity in labor force* and variation in motivations and support needs
Management social constructions of key concepts: intellectual capital, high-performance work force, and relational wealth do not implicitly or explicitly refer to working poor (working poor missing persons effect)	*The failure of employing organizations to invest in the working poor through HR policies results in *work/employability seen as the problem and not the solution.*

[a]The term "lousy jobs" has been used by G. Burtless (Wash., D.C.: Brookings Institute, 1990) in *A Future of Lousy Jobs? The Changing Structure of U.S. Wages*

of the advantages and disincentives to employers of sustaining long-term employability.

The Paradoxes of Promoting Employability

A Supply Side Focus

Most research on the working poor focuses on the supply side of the labor market: how individual education and skills (also known as "human capital"), motivations, family situations, and demographics predict poverty and relate to labor market outcomes. Ironically, very little attention is given to the role of organizations that hire the working poor in perpetuating low quality human capital through the use of employment practices that do not enhance worker skills or education.[13] As several scholars—for example, Larry Hunter of the Wharton School and Gary Burtless of the Brookings Institute—have written, rather than focusing on "lousy workers," researchers and social scientists should focus on "lousy jobs."[14] They argue that economists' focus on problems in the labor supply such as the working poor's individual labor market skills and outcomes and is surprising, since research has commonly found that internal employer human resource policies such as training, compensation, benefits, job design, and career ladders contribute to earnings skill enhancement, and career progress. These well-documented relationships place the working poor at a lifelong disadvantage.[15]

If public policy were reframed to focus on demand side investments in the working poor (and, consequently, the development of relational wealth as well as and social and human capital), policy makers would suggest vastly different remedies than raising the minimum wage every few years. If entry-level jobs are not linked to upwardly mobile career ladders, do not come with employer investments in skills training, or lack access to supports such as child care, it is unlikely that welfare-to-work programs will significantly reduce poverty or improve the economic or social well-being of poor families.

The Myth of Individual Bootstrapping

Framing public policy to focus on the supply side not only overemphasizes individual labor-market activities but also encourages societal leaders to undervalue collaboration among employers, government, and nonprofit organizations. As with the current corporate focus on employment at will, welfare reform policy is based on the assumption that individual change strategies are the means to reduce policy. The prevailing lore is that an individual's work ethic and commitment to work are the main means of raising oneself out of poverty and ensuring continuous employability—the idea of "pulling oneself up by one's bootstraps."[16]

The chief inconsistency with individual bootstrapping as the predominant welfare reform strategy is that "employability" alone is not the answer. Not all jobs lead to a better life.[17] For example, many "employable" Americans continue to live in poverty because the full- or part-time jobs they hold pay low wages and lack basic benefits such as health insurance[18] In the United States, it is estimated that over 2 million individuals work full time but have incomes below the poverty level.[19] Poverty has a disparate impact on some of the most vulnerable groups in our society: women and children represent 82 percent of all persons in poor families.[20] Though at any given time, numerically there are more white welfare recipients than black recipients, longitudinal analysis shows that poor black recipients are four times more likely to have ongoing or repeat welfare spells than non-blacks.[21] This racial disparity is attributed to inadequate employment opportunities, discrimination, a higher proportion of single-parent families, and a mismatch between education and skills, and job location and demands.[22] Collaborative actions on the part of employers and other organizations, not only individual efforts, are critical to ensuring economic reform, yet these often are overlooked or deemphasized. As I discuss in relation to the third paradox, however, we must take into account the short-run economic dilemma of an employer investing more in its labor than competitors do.

Problems of Underconsumption and the Commons

The third paradox is that public policy solutions benefiting society as a whole (assuming employers act in concert over the long run) are often counter to those engendered by short-term market pressures. A short-term economic perspective typically induces individual employers to view labor costs as variable and minimize employment security as a way to increase competitiveness. Being the lower cost producer is one of the main corporate strategies taught in business schools, yet history suggests there may be clear economic benefits from limiting the growth of low wage workers, since having a large growing labor force worried about job security and adequate earnings is a constraint on the economy's growth capability. Economic growth is hindered by what classic economists refer to as underconsumption. As Joseph Schumpeter argued, even the wealthy face a profit crisis when workers lack jobs or good wages, because companies cannot reap the benefits of these workers as consumers when they cannot afford to buy products.[23]

Employers try to maximize profits by paying lower wages and minimizing employment levels, but this undercuts the ability of employees to consume the goods and services the firm must sell to increase earnings. Employers hope *someone else* will pay their workers well, offer enhanced employment prospects, and develop individual capital, but few want to be the employer that actually does it. Yet if employers do not invest in the careers and earning power of workers, even those at the lower strata, a large portion of society will be unable to afford their products. Some experts believe that the current U.S. economy is not as strong it could be because workers' real wages have not risen along with corporate profits.[24]

A historical example of this view and the employers' commons problem comes from Henry Ford's reply to the question of why he paid workers $5 a day when others were paying much less: He stated that workers could not buy his cars unless they were paid a decent wage. The problem individual employers face is that what makes sense for all firms acting together may do little to affect demand for a single firm's products. The benefit of limiting the growth of unemployed or low-paid individuals in order to increase the pool of consumers who can buy the products of a firm can be realized only under cooperative employer action.[25] Individual employers might not see why it is in their self-interest to make special efforts to hire, train, and retain lower-paid workers, despite the fact that if they did, they and society would be all better off. These practices, which make sense for the collective over the long run, do not make sense for the individual firm in the short run.

Underconsumption and a growing underclass can also impede employers' abilities to grow and achieve strategic goals in a global economy. While the United States has the highest gross national product of the fifteen most industrialized nations, its poverty rate is about 13 percent, nearly double the rates of Canada and Australia (7 percent) and much higher than France, the United Kingdom, Sweden, Germany, and the Netherlands (5 percent or less).[26] More than 14.5 percent of all Americans live in poverty, with the gap between the richest and the poorest widening to levels unprecedented since the late 1940s.

Child poverty rates are also relevant, because many of the working poor have children under the age of eighteen and child poverty has a deleterious impact on the potential of employers' future workforce. The United States ranks eighteenth in the gap between rich and poor children compared to other industrialized nations, a rate that has increased over the last ten years for all racial and ethnic groups and in both urban and rural areas.[27] Further, the United States ranks only twelfth in mathematics and seventh in science achievement of thirteen-year-olds among the fifteen most industrialized countries.[28] Thus, the negative long-term economic effects of a lack of success in welfare reform and poverty reduction can inhibit the ability of U.S. companies to grow worldwide and to hire future generations of workers.

Though collective employer action to invest in the current and future labor force is likely to yield the highest rewards to society and to firms over the long run, short-run economic pressures reduce the incentive to collaborate. Without consistent government intervention, it is unlikely that most employers will change their historical indifference to the problem of a growing underclass.

Homogeneity of the Core Workforce

The fourth paradox relates to the tendency of most employers, despite rhetoric on managing diversity and being a flexible employer, to adopt one-size-fits-all employability practices (especially for workers who are viewed as valued social assets). Typically, "promotable" employees follow traditional career paths, can work as many hours as the employer demands, need little training, and have personal lives that do not impede their abilities to fully commit to work roles.[29] Susan Jackson's writings provide a number of examples illustrating how traditional human resources management models are based on an assumption of workforce homogeneity: recruiting practices emphasize hiring from sources that have historically been reliable; training programs foster uniform ways of thinking; selection practices favor candidates who are similar to those who have been successful in the past; and policies are often designed to limit supervisor(s)' ability to address the unique needs of each employee.[30] Given these homogenous assumptions about the "ideal employee," it is unlikely that most working poor in entry-level jobs will be able to rise above the organizational cultural barriers and work themselves into the mainstream.

Social Construction of Managerial Concepts:
The Working Poor as Missing Persons Problem

The fifth paradox relates to the working poor as "missing persons" in social constructions of management concepts. An individual's ability to move from welfare client to worker to career person with long-term employability prospects may be unrealistic, given the current social constructions approach of most organizations and policy makers. For example, hot management concepts (some of which are included in this book) such as intellectual capital, high-performance work systems, relational wealth, and trustworthiness seem to exclude the working poor. Highly educated, upwardly mobile employees are worth investing in and reflect a firm's intellectual capital and long term growth potential; not low-wage workers.

The way policy makers and managers view the working poor, the way work is designed to be inflexible toward individual social needs, and the way that many workers experience jobs that are devoid of such relational wealth indicators as trust and support may be the problem and not the solution. Longitudinal research suggests that despite considerable work effort, many former welfare recipients—particularly those with families—cannot sustain low-wage jobs without earning benefits. Specifically, assistance with child care and medical care are vital benefits that are rarely offered for low-wage jobs.[31] These are basic investments that must be made before the working poor can begin to be conceived as part of a firm's intellectual capital, as contributing to a high-performance work system, or as reliable workers capable of garnering employer trust.

Moreover, the generic workplace skills learned at entry level jobs need to be valued as stepping stones up the job ladder. For example, working at McDonald's, as a crew member, as a janitor or maid, or in a day-care center can teach someone how to work under pressure, follow organizational rules, get along with others, regularly attend work, and organize and plan job activities. One study found that a significant portion of the variance among factors explaining employability was affected by these variables.[32] Employers must begin to value these skills. Some companies do this already. A majority of the managers started out at McDonald's in entry-level jobs serving customers—a fact that is valued in that company's corporate culture.

Preliminary evidence suggests that when low-wage workers are given a chance, employers are generally pleased with their performance. Findings from a 1998 Urban Institute study of five hundred employers in industries likely to have higher-than average numbers of entry-level workers found that because of the strong economy and the low unemployment rate, many employers were actively looking for workers (including welfare recipients) to fill entry-level jobs. The study, entitled *Assessing the New Federalism*, found that employers were willing and sometimes even eager to hire a worker who was or had been on welfare if the applicant showed a positive attitude and had the ability to be a reliable worker. Specific skills and education were far less important for this end of the job market.[33]

The study also found that employers generally had a positive view of welfare recipients and their performance in the workplace. Only one-fifth rated welfare recipients poorly on characteristics such as willingness to work or to be trained, motivation, and reliability. About two-fifths of employers rated welfare recipients as "extremely" or "very" reliable and positive about work, the two qualities that employers identified as being the most important when hiring someone. When the response "somewhat well" is added, the proportion of employers with positive views rises to 70 percent.

Having direct experience with the welfare recipients as employees seems to favorably influence employer attitudes. Two-thirds of employers who have hired welfare applicants have favorable views, and nearly 94 percent would hire others in the future. Three out of four employers are satisfied with welfare recipients' job performance.[34] Just imagine what would happen if employers stop viewing welfare recipients as disposable labor, as 50 percent of these hires are likely to turn over within a year.[35] More research is needed to show the economic and societal benefits that are reaped when employers view the working poor as vital to a firm's human capital, capable of being in the high-performance workforce, and worthy of investing in for the sake of long-term relational wealth.

Advantages and Disincentives to Employers: Removing Barriers to Employability

This chapter has argued that interventions focusing on employability alone are likely to be unsuccessful. To ensure the success of their employability strategies, employers must jointly strive to build relational wealth over time by investing in all workers—including low-wage entry level workers. Specifically, employers must strive to break down employment barriers such as child care, family demands, transportation, limited training in core job skills, and access to few if any medical and other benefits. Half of the welfare recipients studied report at least one of these factors as a barrier to leaving welfare and becoming economically independent. Before discussing some ways to counteract these barriers (which most likely require government intervention to remove completely), I wish to note why it is in the best interests of strategic-thinking employers to proactively change or risk future legislative mandates.

Growing Social Accountability

As argued by Greg Parston, the chief executive officer of the Office for Public Management, which advises CEOs on the formation of socially responsible strategies, the traditional ways of business organizing, most of which are related to creating shareholder value, are not sufficient to cope with the newer complexities of managing.[36] Growing public pressures for corporate accountability and social responsibility results compels firms to strike a more acceptable balance in meeting competing shareholder and societal demands. Strategic-thinking firms recognize that while shareholder values still dominate stock prices for now, organizations are being increasingly held accountable for their actions by other stakeholders such as employees, customers, and society in general. A recent example is that 28 percent of IBM shareholders voted to support mandating that all employees have the option of having a defined benefit pension as opposed to a defined contribution pension, the latter generally reducing employer economic risk over the long term. The pension design issue will reappear on the IBM proxy in 2001, much to its dismay, as IBM had assumed a unilateral employer right to manage future labor cost exposures as it saw fit. Employers who seek to increase social capital may not only be in greater harmony with their communities but also have a competitive advantage by reaping higher productivity and loyalty from their workers via progressive human resources practices. As Frederick Reichheld, a managing director of the leading strategy firm Bain and Company, argues, loyalty-based management that minimizes the need to replace employees on average every four years is a highly profitable alternative to the economics of perpetual churn.[37]

Socially accountable firms are also better positioned to countervail the growing backlash against corporations that post record profits. For example, *Time* magazine recently reported on the costs of "corporate welfare," with a 1998 cover picture of a corporate executive in the shape of a piggy bank. According to the investigative article, during one of the most robust economic times in U.S. history the federal government has paid out over $125 billion in corporate welfare, equivalent to the income tax paid by 60 million individuals and families. On average, the economic supports provided to businesses cost every working American the approximate equivalent of two weeks' pay. Suggesting that government and politicians are partly to blame, the article concludes: "[c]ompanies are manipulative. It's the nature of business to go after every dollar that's legally available; place the blame on government. This is the government's folly."[38] Thus, strategic-thinking employers may take action before public outcry demands eventual (and perhaps inevitable) government intervention.

Employer Investments in Work Family Supports

Obtaining quality child care is an obstacle for many employed parents, but it is particularly challenging for those who lack financial resources. Quality child care is expensive, leaving those who are economically disadvantaged in the worst possible situation: choose to work and leave one's child in poor care, or remain unemployed and continue to live in poverty. The average child-care arrangement for children from families with little resources will be substandard, and low-quality child care has been found to have long-lasting damaging effects on children.[39]

When employers strengthen the labor market capabilities of the heads of families living in poverty, they indirectly invest in the workers of tomorrow. It is unlikely that weak schools and poor day care will help children develop into highly capable employees. Data from the study of the Michigan Social Contract families showed that the children of welfare recipients were relatively resilient in terms of psychological well-being, family functioning, and career aspirations. Longitudinal studies show that one cannot necessarily assume the crossgenerational transmission of poverty; historically, about half of children born into poverty have remained poor as adults.[40] By abandoning negative views on the futility of business involvement in family and child-related policies, employers will be more likely to heighten investment in work/family supports and to develop linkages with local schools that are geared to benefit not only employees but also their communities.

Research indicates that employer-sponsored child care has a significant positive impact on the recruitment and retention of employees, and the lack of such benefits can be a critical barrier to labor market success.[41] Such continued investment could enhance access to productive work for parents (especially mothers) of all socioeconomic levels. Increasing access to day care for low-wage workers, as some fast-food companies such as Burger King have done, can also pay off economically. During the first year that one outlet offered a child-care voucher, more than 90 percent of applicants said they applied because of this benefit. Though the program sometimes cost up to ten thousand dollars a month, having a stable workforce was viewed as far preferable to the alternative of constant recruitment, understaffing, low morale, and continuous training.

Employer investment in child care may also benefit society as a whole by having positive psychological effects on low-income children.[42] Studies consistently show that children with the poorest educational and psychological outcomes are those whose mothers wanted to work but were unemployed. Even for teen parents, their children's achievement is more likely to depend on the household's economic level than the parent's age.[43] An extensive longitudinal study following poor American children into adulthood over two decades identifies the generally positive influences of maternal employment and investment in parents' education as a predictor of later success, despite the fact that working parents are able to spend less time with their children.[44]

Besides investing in child care, providing assistance with other family demands may also be necessary. At Marriott, for example, social workers are available to help not only with child care but also housing, language training, transportation, and even domestic violence. Marriott feels that it is cost-effective to provide these services, which contribute to a stable, motivated workforce.[45] Transportation should not be underestimated as a problem, as 36 percent of employers in a national sample stated that their entry-level jobs are not accessible via public transportation.[46] Similarly, one economist argues that the continual movement of jobs from the inner city to the suburbs essentially creates a geographic barrier to economic equality because many inner city residents find it impossible to become employed at suburban locations.[47]

The Ineffectiveness of Government Tax
Incentives Alone

Currently, state and federal governments fund a number of employer incentive programs designed to encourage the employment of entry-level workers (particularly welfare recipients). These programs include state income tax credits for hiring low-wage workers, the federal Work Opportunity Tax Credit, job training and work-readiness programs, and government job screening of candidates. Surprisingly, the 1998 Urban Institute study of employers in twelve states found that these incentive programs had little or no influence on employer's hiring decisions. Nearly 90 percent of employers were not even aware that these programs existed. The least effective were the tax credit policies alone, as some employers interviewed stated they "could not be paid enough" to hire "problem" employees, regardless of an individual's welfare status or access to government supports. Notwithstanding these statements, some incentives did generate employer interest, particularly government job training, job readiness, and screening programs that could enable employers to identify potentially successful candidates.[48]

Human Resource Systems That
Provide "Good Jobs"

Given the relatively limited employer investments in low-wage workers to date, it may be surprising that some of the former working poor have been able to achieve economic self-sufficiency under the status quo. The 1998 Urban Institute found that two-thirds of employers studied paid welfare workers six dollars an hour or less. Although nearly half provided health benefits to entry-level workers, immediate coverage began in only 6 percent of the workplaces sampled; over a quarter of the workplaces surveyed required employees to wait twelve months or longer before eligibility. Only 17 percent paid sick leave to entry-level workers, and few provided transportation (5 percent) or child-care subsidies (1 percent).[49]

What can be done to make entry-level jobs "more attractive"? Larry Hunter has created a dichotomous index of good jobs and poor jobs. Using a sample of Massachusetts nursing homes, Hunter found that good jobs offered child care, employer-sponsored training, education tuition reimbursement, employer contributions to a deferred compensation plan, wages at or above the median for the local area, a chance for significant wage growth, and a health plan. He found that when employers have customers who prefer good service, these investments are likely to pay off economically because they contribute to higher worker morale and better-trained employees.[50]

Implementing human resources strategies that improve the employment and career prospects of the working poor may also help reverse what some critics bemoan as a disturbing attitude among employers about the role of employees: instead of being human resources, workers have become just another labor cost. Although it behooves the employer to manage its labor costs, over the long run employers will lose if a growing cadre of workers have low wages and little or no job security. Renewing employer strategies that invest in workers' education, knowledge and skills, and family well-being and that provide greater employment protection and opportunity to develop skills on the job are not merely socially responsible actions. These strategies enhance relational wealth, enabling all employees to contribute more effectively—which ultimately benefits a business's bottom line.[51]

Given that the new American workforce in the dejobbed career environment has human resource policy needs that increasingly mirror those of the working poor, adapting organizations to increase the success of entry-level employees in low-wage jobs may also help employers generally transform their organizations to fit with the turbulent career context of shortened ladders and tenuous jobs. Many employees—not just the lowest paid—are likely to seek career counseling, training and retraining, flexible hours, adequate wages, work/family supports, and employment stability. Determining how to redesign organizations to make human resources systems more adaptive to individual career needs and more effective in fostering social capital and career resilience should enable firms to better tap the potential of their workforce. The problems faced by the working poor are increasingly relevant to the general development of human resource strategies in turbulent career environments.

Notes

1. Kossek, E. E. Roberts, K., Fisher, S., and DeMarr, B., "Career Self-management: A Quasi-experimental Assessment of the Effects of a Training Intervention." *Personnel Psychology* 51: 1998: 935–62.

2. Ibid.

3. Brockner, J. and Lee, R. J., "Career Development in Downsizing Organizations: A Self-affirmation Analysis. In London M. (Ed.), *Employees, Careers, and Job Creation: Developing Growth-Oriented Human Resource Strategies and Programs* (pp. 49–70). (San Francisco: Jossey Bass, 1995)

4. Harris K. M. "Life After Welfare: Women Work and Repeat Dependency." *American Sociological Journal*, 61 (1996): 407–26.

5. O'Neill D. M. and O'Neill, J. E. *Lessons for Welfare Reform: An Analysis of AFDC Caseload and Past Welfare-to-Work Programs* (Kalamazoo, Michigan: W. E. UpJohn Institute for Employment Research, 1997).

6. Ibid.

7. Harwood, J. Hype and Glory: Rush to Claim Success for Welfare Overhaul Stumbles over facts. *The Wall Street Journal* (Oct. 17, 1997), A1, A5.

8. O'Neill and O'Neill (1997).

9. See P. Cappelli, "The New Deal at Work: Managing the Market-Driven Workforce" (Boston: Harvard Business School Press, 1999).

10. Ellen Ernst Kossek, M. Huber-Yoder, D. Castellino, and J. Lerner, "The Working Poor: Locked Out of Careers and the Organizational Main-

stream?" *Academy of Management Executive*, issue on Careers in the Twenty-First Century (winter 1997): 76–92.

11. D. Leigh, "Can a Voluntary Workfare Program Change the Behavior of Welfare Recipients? New Evidence from Washington State's Family Independence Program," *Journal of Policy Analysis and Management* 14 (1995): 567–89.

12. Kossek et al. (1997), Leigh (1995).

13. L. W. Hunter, "Lousy Jobs: Why Do Organizations Choose Human Resource Practices that Reinforce the Position of the Working Poor?" paper presented at the annual meeting of the National Academy of Management, Cincinnati, Ohio, August 1996.

14. G. Burtless, ed., *A Future of Lousy Jobs? The Changing Structure of U.S. Wages* (Washington, D.C.: Brookings Institute, 1990); L. W. Hunter, "Customer Differentiation, Institutional Fields, and the Quality of Entry Level Service Jobs," working paper, Management Department, Wharton School, 1998.

15. Hunter, 1996.

16. Hunter, 1996.

17. Kossek et al. (1997).

18. S. Levitan, F. Gallo, and I. Shaprio, *Working but Poor* (Baltimore: Johns Hopkins University Press, 1993).

19. O'Neill and O'Neill (1997).

20. U.S. Bureau of the Census, *Poverty in the United States: 1990*, Current Population Reports, Ser P-60, no. 16, Washington, D.C., 1990.

21. P. Gottschalk, S. McLanahan, and G. D. Sandefur, "The Dynamics and Intergenerational Transmission of Poverty and Welfare Participation," in *Confronting Poverty: Prescriptions for Change*, editors. S. H. Danzinger, G. D. Dandefeur, and D. H. Weinberg (Cambridge: Harvard University Press, 1994), pp. 85–108.

22. H. Holzer, *What Employers Want: Job Prospects for Less-Educated Workers* (New York: Russell Sage, 1996).

23. J. A. Schumpeter, *Capitalism, Socialism, and Democracy*, 3rd ed. (New York: Harper, 1950).

24. J. C. Cooper and K. Madigan, "Growth Is Down, but Not Out." *Business Week*, September 12, 1994, pp. 27–8.

25. Kossek et al. (1997).

26. S. H. Danzinger and D. H. Weinberg, "The Historical Record: Trends in Family Income, Inequality and Poverty," in Danzinger, G. Sandefur, and Weinberg (1994), pp. 18–50.

27. L. Jensen, "Rural–Urban Differences in the Utilization and Ameliorative Effects of Welfare Programs," *Policy Studies Review* 7 (1988): 782–94.

28. Children's Defense Fund, *Stand for Children*, March 1996 mailing, Washington, D.C.

29. G. R. Ferris, D. D. Fink, and M. C. Galang, "Diversity in the Workplace: The Human Resource Management Challenges," *Human Resource Planning* 16 (1994): 41–51.

30. S. E. Jackson, "Stepping into the Future: Guidelines for Action," in *Diversity in the Workplace: Human Resource Initiatives*, editors Jackson et al. (New York: Guilford Press, 1992).

31. K. Harris (1996).

32. W. Mehrens, *Michigan Employability Skills Technical Report* (State of Michigan Department of Education and Training, Lansing, Michigan, 1989).

33. M. Regenstein, J. Meyer, and J. Hicks, *Job Prospects for Welfare Recipients: Employers Speak Out* (Washington, D.C.: Urban Institute, 1998).

34. Ibid.

35. Ibid.

36. G. Parston, "Producing Social Results," in *The Organization of the Future*, edited by F. Hesselbein, M. Goldsmith, and R. Beckhard (New York: Peter Ducker Foundation for Nonprofit Management, 1997), pp. 341–8.

37. F. Reichheld, "The Loyalty-Effect: The Hidden Force behind Growth, Profits, and Lasting Value" (Boston: Harvard Business School Press, 1996).

38. "Corporate Welfare, a System Exposed," *Time*, November 9, 1998, special Report, p. 54.

39. Kossek et al. (1997).

40. P. Gottschalk, S. McLanahan, and G. D. Sandefur, "The Dynamics and Intergenerational Transmission of Poverty and Welfare Participation," in Danzinger, Dandefeur, and Weinberg (1994), pp. 85–108.

41. E. Kossek and V. Nichol, "The Effects of Employer-Sponsored Child Care on Employee Attitudes and Performance," *Personnel Psychology* 45 (1992): 485–589.

42. J. Thoms, "Vouchers at Burger King," in *Child Care Challenges for Employers*, edited by E. E. Kossek (Horsesham, Pa.: LRP Press, 1991), pp. 287–91.

43. J. V. Lerner, *Working Women and Their Families* (Thousand Oaks, Calif.: Sage, 1994).

44. R. Haverman and B. Wolfe, *Succeeding Generations: On the Effects of Investment in Children* (New York: Russell Sage, 1995); J. Lerner and A. Abrams, "Developmental Correlates of Maternal Employment Influences on Children," in *Applied Developmental Psychology*, edited by C. B. Fisher and R. Lerner (New York: McGraw Hill, 1994).

45. B. McCarty, *Personal Communication* (Chicago, Ill.: Partnership Group, 1995).

46. Regenstein, Meyer, and Hicks (1998).

47. H. Holzer (1996).

48. Regenstein, Meyer, and Hicks (1998).

49. Ibid.

50. Hunter (1996).

51. Kossek et al. (1997).

11

Manage Your Own Employability

Meritocracy and the Legitimation of Inequality in
Internal Labor Markets and Beyond

MAUREEN A. SCULLY

The idea of meritocracy—that there is equal opportunity for individuals to
get ahead on their own merits or human capital—has long been celebrated
in the politics, culture, and institutions of the United States. Meritocracy
was made concrete and operational in the language and practices of the
internal labor market (ILM), such as promotion ladders for advancement
from within, governed by rules for measuring and rewarding merit. Meritocracy explains that inequality in ILMs is the legitimate outcome of a fair
process. As a broad legitimating ideal, meritocracy has received wide popular endorsement; in everyday practice, employees have been somewhat
skeptical. Now that the business press signals the dismantling of ILMs,[1]
there are questions as to whether there will be a crisis of legitimacy—a loss
of faith in institutions, an unwillingness to contribute effort, and/or the
mobilization of dissent aimed at creating alternative institutions.

Will there be a crisis of legitimacy? This question has two focal points:
looking back at meritocracy as enacted in the traditional employment relationship of ILMs and looking forward at meritocracy as it might be transferred to the newly emerging employment relationship. This new relationship is based on more tenuous employee connections to the firm and
shifting assignments that are continuously renegotiated.

This chapter argues that there will not be a crisis of legitimacy, for two
reasons. First, employees were sufficiently skeptical about meritocracy in
ILMs that the dismantling of ILMs does not symbolize the spoiling of a
temple of fairness. Indeed, those predicting a crisis of legitimacy may have
overestimated the actual and perceived legitimacy of meritocracy and inequality in ILMs. Second, and somewhat ironically, even though meritocracy did a relatively poor job as a legitimating ideology in ILMs—inviting
some measure of disbelief from employees who inhabited the meritocratic

contests and saw their flaws—it nonetheless has a certain cultural staying power in the United States. It is a broad, elastic ideal that can accommodate new definitions of merit, and it appeals to tendencies (both cognitive and political) to individualize people's circumstances and ignore structural issues.

The first volleys from popular writing about the new employment relationship urge individuals to "manage your own employability." A *Fortune* article exhorts: "[t]he new paradigm requires that every worker—whether just getting started or nearing retirement—continuously reassess where he stands occupationally and financially and be prepared to change direction as need or opportunity beckons."[2] The discourse emphasizes the responsibility of individuals to manage their own portfolios of connections and opportunities, rather than the responsibility of corporations to safeguard livelihoods, honor the long-standing social contract, make adjustments accountably, or appreciate and keep intact the relational wealth that their employees collectively generate. The ready language of individualism is a bulwark against critiques of the new employment relationship and forestalls a crisis of legitimacy, a crisis that might be welcome, rather than feared, for the fresh perspectives it could offer to policy debates.

This chapter has a subsidiary project in addition to assessing the portability of meritocracy and the likelihood of a crisis of legitimacy. The rising popularity of the concept of social capital triggers some concerns when one's project is problematizing meritocracy. While ILM employment arrangements pointed the attention of social scientists toward returns on individuals' human capital in organizational contexts,[3] the emerging employment relationship redirects attention to social capital. As Bourdieu notes, social capital may best be defined in its vernacular sense as "connections."[4] Social capital is separately theorized as a resource accruing to individuals and a beneficial property of communities, sometimes with authors moving fuzzily between the two (as Harris and DeRenzio observe in their critical review).[5] Whether attained through family ties, dense community links, or networking, social capital is defined by its function: the returns that structural relations bring to individuals in the form of human capital and ultimately economic capital. Social capital can get a person a job—increasingly important as ILMs are dismantled and job contests return to the open market.[6]

In this book, relational wealth—essentially "organizational social capital" as Leana and Van Buren describe it in chapter 13—is the combinatorial effect of individuals' social capital; individuals access the private benefits of social capital in a relational context. As a policy prescription from concerned "public scholars," firms should pay attention to the social capital of individuals and how it can be collectively realized as relational wealth—a particularly valuable asset for firms operating in a world of networks and trust-based contracts. In turn, individuals may realize steadier and more rewarding employment in a firm that appreciates relational wealth. Retaining the collective aspect of relational wealth emphasized in this book is an important counterweight to the tendency to individualize social capital and the individual's responsibility to amass, use, and replenish it.

In this chapter, the focus on the individualistic ideas behind meritocracy reminds us how difficult it is to keep sustained attention on a collective good. The meritocratic ideal shifts discourse and practice toward the social capital of individuals and, moreover, their responsibility for replenishing their own stock of social capital, neglecting its structural aspect. Thus, social capital may have the same problems identified with individual-level human capital in a stratified social order: some people's social capital is regarded as more valuable others'; there are differences in initial endowments of social capital that reproduce inequality; and even when those in the lowest social strata possess significant social capital, they may realize a lower rate of return on it. Thus, a firm's evaluation of its stock of relational wealth might be misguided or refracted by the class biases that influence any form of capital. This chapter examines the role that social capital may come to play in the operations and ideological justifications of the next meritocracy.

The chapter proceeds in three parts. First, meritocracy is defined and its enactment in the core procedures of ILMs is discussed. Second, employees' beliefs about whether their firm is legitimately a meritocracy are assessed, drawing on survey data from 425 employees in two nonunion firms that espouse meritocratic advancement procedures. Third, the tenacity of meritocratic language for the new employment relationship is assessed, particularly with respect to social capital as a new kind of "merit" that individuals are responsible for maintaining and that explains and legitimates unequal individual outcomes.

Meritocracy and Legitimation in Internal Labor Markets

An ideal meritocracy is based on three principles: (1) merit is a well-defined and measurable basis for selecting individuals for positions; (2) individuals have equal opportunity to develop and display their merits and to advance; and (3) the positions into which individuals are sorted map onto stratified levels of rewards, such as income or status.[7] Meritocracy has been appealing as a signal that the United States has moved beyond aristocratic inheritance to a social system based on equal opportunity. From the perspective of functionalist sociologists, meritocratic stratification insures that the most talented people will do the most difficult and rewarding jobs in a way that is beneficial to society.[8] From a critical perspective, meritocracy is a "dominant ideology" inasmuch as it reflects the experience of the elites and reproduces their privileges. It obscures the structural factors that generate disconnections between merit and social rank. The principles of meritocracy hold together like a logical syllogism: that is, one can reason backward that a person in a low position in a meritocracy has insufficient merit or has failed to take advantage of opportunities.[9]

While ILMs are rarely linked explicitly to meritocratic ideology, descriptions of ILMs are imbued with the language and logic of meritocracy. The bureaucratic governance structures of ILMs are basically systems for measuring merit and advancing individuals among stratified positions with associated reward levels. The term "internal labor market" simply highlights the fact that "the pricing and allocational functions of the market take place within rather than outside of the establishment."[10] But more than this has been at stake in ILMs, and as the employment relationship becomes externalized, there is more that changes than the locus of employee hiring and remuneration. The deep assumptions undergirding the reward system are also disrupted. Indeed, the reward system may be the most difficult element to change in the move toward "postbureaucratic" employment alternatives.[11]

ILMs have not been just a constellation of rules, procedures, and ladders with neutral meanings for employees. ILMs have made ready sense to employees inasmuch as they evoke a societal ideal and discourse about meritocracy. Stories of ascent from the lower to upper echelons, a typical part of the canon of organizational stories, are not just one more kind of story; they deeply exemplify and celebrate an American ideal.[12] For example, one of the best-selling business books, Lee Iacocca's autobiography, opens with reference to his immigrant parents and his gradual ascent up the company ladder of an automobile company to become CEO.[13] The subtext is that anyone who works hard can follow this path to success as well. The ascent from the mailroom to the boardroom is the romanticized extreme of this genre of stories, but it is a cultural resource that stands behind the practices that ILMs enact in a daily way.

In some depictions, ILMs appear implicitly to rely on employees' faith in meritocracy in order to function and to achieve for the firm the promised aims of motivation, productivity, and retention; critical accounts emphasize that ILMs are more fundamentally designed to reduce dissent.[14] ILM's rationalized advancement procedures are used as "the primary incentive device in most organizations."[15] Promotions are ideally supposed to allow firms to match individuals with jobs for which they are well suited, although this matching may involve occasional or even systematic errors. Organizational researchers have explored how rewards get attached to positions, how individuals move among positions to garner relative rewards, and how the returns on human capital can be refracted by political processes.[16]

Organizations espouse variants of merit as the basis for promotions. Lawler documents "many companies' very frequent claims that their pay systems are based on merit," despite, he continues, evidence from several studies of a low correlation between pay and performance.[17] Murphy and Cleveland report that some 90 percent of private organizations use formal performance evaluations of various types, with different dimensions of merit.[18]

In diverse theoretical accounts of the long-term employment relationship—from institutional economics to critical theories of the firm—the promise of future promotions based on predictable, fair, and rational criteria is a crucial mechanism. In institutional economic accounts, employees with firm-specific training and skills are more likely to remain with the firm and work hard if upward advancement for the meritorious is promised.[19] ILMs can offer on-the-job training without longer tenured employees' hoarding their knowledge in the fear that newer employees will replace them; that promotion rules should appear rational, reliable, and fair to employees becomes a crucial part of the functioning of an ILM. Radical critiques of ILMs point out that upward advancement is only realized by a few employees and often only in the form of small, local advances. The promise of upward advancement coopts employees and sets them in competition against one another, thus buying political stability for the firm.[20]

A Crisis of Legitimacy?

Faith in meritocracy is one of several reasons that it is difficult to contest inequality or point to its structural origins in the United States. The idea of meritocracy individualizes inequality. It is a bulwark against redistribution and the search for structural causes and solutions.

A time of transition to a new employment relationship, and the concomitant changes in life chances and rewards, might open a window for dissent, particularly to the extent that expectations are violated.[21] The taken-for-granted assumptions of the old system are suddenly exposed, and the features of the emerging system lack their own legitimating logic. For example, "broken ladders" might spur a crisis of legitimacy, especially where employees made long-term decisions about training and commitment in the expectation that the ladders were steady.[22] The rise of teamwork in the new employment relationship exposes the problems of competitive individualism and raises questions about meritocracy's assumptions.[23] Even if the transition in employment relationships is posed as a rational adaptation to prevailing conditions, the result appears to be not a neutral equilibrium but rather a situation favoring firms over employees, which, if widely recognized, might trigger a crisis of legitimacy.[24]

A crisis of legitimacy could be evidenced in many forms, from withheld effort to cynical discourse to outright dissent, compromising the productivity, retention, and industrial peace that were offered as reasons for the proliferation and usefulness to firms of ILMs. Because this legitimating ideal emphasizes individual over structural sources of inequality, a crisis of legitimacy is about galvanizing collective attention to structural issues. At certain historical moments, structural factors may become particularly evident, allowing a legitimating idea like meritocracy to be questioned. Piven and Cloward show how the widespread layoffs in the Great Depression resulted in a "poor people's movement."[25] When "good people"—like white, middle-class, white-collar employees—began to suffer economically in large numbers, not just the "lazy poor," it became easier to blame the structure instead of just blaming individuals.

In the wake of layoffs in the 1980s and 1990s, when many white, middle-class professionals were affected, we might similarly have seen such a "crisis of legitimacy" and a search for structural rather than individualistic causes and solutions. Dissent might take the form not just of individual anger, despair, or tragic tales but of collective sense-making and action. On the one hand, individuals who have the credentials that allow them to deflect blame for their economic misfortune and who have the power and cultural capital to speak out about their situation might have shaped some challenges to corporate changes. As relatively more privileged employees pushed back on punishing changes and sought alternatives, their models might also have served less advantaged employees.[26] On the other hand, it is ironic that those best poised to make such challenges are also those who may most strongly embrace the individualistic ideal. Managers who experienced downward social mobility after layoffs had more difficulty accepting and coping with their situation, more often blaming themselves, than lower level employees who collectively endured plant closings and understood the structural inequities.[27]

Despite the potential in the current historical moment, there seems to be little outcry. Indeed, as organizational theorists increasingly tune their ear to the concerns of "public scholars," they detect with some surprise the deafening silence that reverberates from disruptive changes to the traditional employment relationship. The silence about social justice concerns, rather than the lively discourse accompanying a crisis of legitimacy, is the puzzle.

Employee Skepticism about Meritocracy in ILMs: Limited Legitimacy to Lose

Why has there not been a crisis of legitimacy? My research on employees' beliefs about meritocracy in their workplaces shows that employees in ILMs have been ambivalent about whether advancement in their firms is meritocratic.[28] As a legitimating ideology, meritocracy garnered only modest support, but perhaps just enough to keep people engaged in the rituals of meritocracy (gaming their performance appraisals, plotting their next promotions, etc.). Giddens rightly notes that a legitimating ideology does not require that everyone believe, but just enough people in "crucial locations" in society. Managers might occupy one of these unspecified crucial locations.[29] However, I found that it was not simply the case that managers believed in meritocracy and those in lower positions doubted meritocratic claims. Position in the firm did not correlate to different levels of belief in meritocracy. Instead, advancement was the critical factor. Those who had

advanced more rapidly believed more strongly that the firm was meritocratic, irrespective of whether their advancement happened at high or low
rungs of the ladder. At every organizational level, the believers and disbelievers in meritocracy were mingled with those who were ambivalent.

The study to which I refer involved a survey of 425 employees across
twenty hierarchical levels of two high-technology firms that had formal
ILMs, including performance evaluation procedures, a structure of hierarchical job titles with associated pay ranges, and promises of advancement
from within.[30] Employees were asked to rate their beliefs about how aspects
of merit, or departures from merit, operated in the advancement system in
their firm. They rated ability and effort, dimensions of the classic meritocracy that have been assessed in national-level studies of Americans' beliefs
about inequality.[31] They also rated the "nonmerit" dimensions of privileged
background and luck. Interviews with employees helped in deriving more
workplace-specific dimensions of merit (performance and being a team
player) as well as what they flagged as nonmerit dimensions (getting oneself
noticed and getting good assignments, which operationalized aspects of
managerial favoritism seen as unfair). These dimensions are summarized in
table 11.1. Employees rated each one on a seven-point scale, where 7 indicated that these dimensions counted "very much" for advancement. Table
11.2 shows their ratings of how much each dimension does (and ought to)
count.

It is particularly interesting that employees appear ambivalent about
meritocracy when the merit and nonmerit dimensions are taken together.
Beliefs that merit matters can be consistent with beliefs that "nonmerit"
factors play a role. The treatment of merit and nonmerit as endpoints on a
singular scale has been updated as more recent work finds that they are
separate dimensions.[32]

It was quite possible and plausible to employees to believe that merit
governed advancement and that unfair departures from merit played a role:
the people who believe that luck counts may also believe that hard work
counts. When people narrate stories about their own experiences, this balanced view sounds like quite a sensible one. I call these people "ambivalent" but do not mean this term pejoratively, as in some treatments of ambivalence as "internally inconsistent" or "incoherent." Gamson argues for
a more appreciative view of the internal complexity of beliefs, particularly
those of members of the working class.[33]

While hard work and luck may reasonably go together, the belief that
both ability and privilege count is a more difficult one to reconcile without
obvious ideological tensions. Ability and coming from a privileged family
background are two elements that have traditionally been pitted against
each other in national-level status attainment studies.[34] I crosstabulated people's answers to the questions about ability and privilege to see if there were
people in all four cells, representing four approaches to meritocracy.

Table 11.3 shows that each of these conceptually possible groups is empirically represented in this sample. Only one-third of these employees are
"true believers" that the meritocratic ideal is realized; of those who are not,

Table 11.1 Societal and Organizational Dimensions of
Meritocracy Assessed by Employees

Dimensions of Merit	"Nonmerit" Dimensions
From the societal level:	
Ability	Coming from a privileged background
Hard work	Luck
At the organizational level:	
Performance	Getting oneself noticed
Being a team player	Getting good assignments

Table 11.2 Descriptive Results from Survey of Employees' Beliefs about
Merit

	Descriptive beliefs Mean (s.d.)	How much it counts		Normative beliefs Mean (s.d.)
		Not very much (1-4)	Very much (5-7)	
MERIT				
Ability	5.01 (1.33)	32.2%	67.8%	6.15 (0.90)
Hard work	5.15 (1.23)	29.6	70.4	6.16 (0.96)
Performance	5.30 (1.16)	22.6	77.4	6.34 (0.75)
Team player	4.97 (1.38)	34.2	65.8	5.67 (1.17)
NONMERIT				
Privilege	3.08 (1.99)	68.0	32.0	1.51 (1.03)
Luck	4.05 (1.63)	60.3	39.7	2.00 (1.18)
Getting noticed	5.36 (1.40)	34.2	65.8	3.46 (1.56)
Getting assigned	5.26 (1.26)	23.5	76.5	3.92 (1.53)

Table 11.3. Combinations of Beliefs About Merit and Non-merit
Dimensions Reveal Belief, Disbelief, and Ambivalence

	Ability Counts:	
Privilege Counts:	*Lower Belief* (1–4)	*Higher Belief* (5–7)[b]
Lower belief (1–3)	Cynics (n = 32) 8.9%	True Believers (n = 124) 34.3%
Higher belief (4–7)[b]	True Disbelievers (n = 87) 24.1%	Ambivalent (n = 118) 32.7%
		N = 361[a]

a. 64 cases (out of 425) have pairwise missing data and are not classifiable (47 people left the challenging privilege question blank).

b. The different splits (5–7 versus 4–7) detect beliefs that go against the dominant ideology, asymmetric for merit versus nonmerit.

more are ambivalent than are outright disbelievers. It appears that people have complex views of opportunity and outcomes, including "ambivalent" views about the role of merit and nonmerit factors. In this study, ambivalence is shown not just across domains, such as the work sphere and the political sphere, but even within the work domain.[35] Indeed, ambivalence may be crucial for understanding why the dissensus sprinkled throughout the system does not seem to result in dissent. The "pragmatic acceptance" of meritocracy and its prevention of a crisis of legitimacy may appear in workplace settings in the form of ambivalence.[36]

Having not been true believers in meritocracy all along, it is not surprising that employees do not have a "crisis of faith" when meritocratic promises are violated. Meritocracy may be robust despite—or rather, precisely because of—ambivalence. "Imperfect legitimation" may not be a paler shade of legitimation but actually a more enduring form. In short, this is one answer to the puzzle of silence as ILMs are taken apart.

The Persistence of the Meritocratic Idea and the Role of Social Capital

The business press reveals a similar ambivalence about meritocracy during a time of disruptive changes in the employment relationship. In a single issue of *Business Week* or *Fortune* or the newly popular *Fast Company*, one can read articles comforting employees, to the effect that "it's the economy, it's not your fault, there's nothing you can do about impending layoffs" and articles exhorting employees to "manage your employability, polish your resume, find flexible new career pathways, gauge whether you're next for a layoff and stave it off, put away your own retirement savings."[37] This ambivalence about whether workers should be collectively angry and mobilized or individualistically stoic and resilient makes it less likely that there will be a crisis of legitimacy and a search for structural solutions. A closer look reveals that the encouragement to manage one's employability, especially through networks, is essentially advice to manage one's social capital. This section considers how social capital might be popularized as a new dimension of merit, allowing an elastic idea of meritocracy to evolve and persist.

Despite the ambivalence it generates, the idea of meritocracy is unlikely to be jettisoned in the shift to new employment models. As the preceding examples of popular rhetoric suggest, it is more likely that its language and ideas will be invoked in the emerging employability model. Individuals will be alternately blamed and praised for the employment deals they work out. A refurbished version of meritocracy can be used for whatever employment system replaces ILMs, retaining the same broad, sweeping elements and aphorisms that are so familiar (such as "every person for himself," "may the best succeed," and "the cream rises to the top"). The definition of what constitutes "merit" may be what is elastic, shifting from the once-valued loyalty and commitment of employees to their flexibility and willingness to change.

Current academic work on social capital considers how much of it exists—whether at the level of individuals, firms, or communities. At these different levels, the returns on social capital come in different forms, from lower high school dropout rates for individuals to relational contracting opportunities for firms with solid reputations to lively civic life and prosperous economic development for communities. Endowments of social capital are taken to be the product of structural and cultural forces that have long been at work.

This sober treatment of social capital may not ward off its misuse. Social capital might be shifted in the vernacular from a resource that people possess to varying degrees to one that they are responsible for creating, even though this notion would be counter to the very social character of social capital; it is not amenable to individuals' manipulation of it. However, whenever some trait or resource is shown to have a return in the labor market, the language and logic of meritocracy enable a swift leap to the idea that people ought to develop or obtain more of it.

Social capital falls into a middle range of attributes that are ambiguous as to whether they constitute relevant merits or not and as such, are fair as a basis for evaluation, advancement, and rewards. That ability, effort, and performance should count are basic tenets of a meritocracy. That privilege, gender, or race should not count (in a way that reproduces inequality) is accepted as a general principle, even if its implementation is on contested terrain. Less systematic attention is given to naming and fixing class biases—making class-based social capital, discussed hereafter, slippery to detect and analyze.

Social capital can be a measure of merit or it can be a "fudge factor" in the status attainment process. When taken as a measure of merit, social capital is construed as essential to doing the job. For example, managing contacts, mingling at conferences, and having good people skills might arguably be defined as "merits" that are relevant for salespeople and consultants.

Few performance appraisal forms ask directly or only about ability, effort, and performance. Aspects of social capital appear in job descriptions, objectives, and performance ratings. Examples include intraorganizational social capital, such as being a team player, managing critical links to other departments, working well with others, or building effective networks, as well as extraorganizational social capital, such as bringing in major clients, working well with joint venture partners, or brokering deals. Possessing, displaying, and realizing social capital can depend on positional advantages, class-based linguistic style, or other factors.

Instead of a type of merit, social capital can be seen as the place in the advancement system where managerial favoritism creeps in. Employees jokingly refer to subjective factors on performance evaluation forms as "plays well with others." In a study of pay-for-skills systems, employees were quite confident that their managers would certify them for a raise for taking the relevant skills courses and plying the skills on the job.[38] When an additional measure—displaying a team attitude—was added to the pay-for-skills plan, employees had much lower probability estimates that they would rise in the pay-for-skills system. A few speculated that this relational "fudge factor" was added precisely to reduce the number of employees climbing the skills ladder.

In my study of beliefs about merit, discussed earlier, "being a team player" emerged from interviews as an accepted dimension of merit in the organization (although not as strongly normatively endorsed as ability, hard work, or performance), but "getting oneself noticed" and "getting good assignments" were offered frequently as departures from merit (see table 11.1). These phrases, when heard by employees, ring of politics and favoritism. However, they might be reasonable renderings of social capital—what one does with positional advantages and networking skills that signal one's trustworthiness is to "get oneself noticed" and "get good assignments" in order to shine and succeed in a system where employability marks success more than advancement.

As an elastic element of merit, social capital may provide some slack in an otherwise tough and unyielding meritocracy. In its simplest form, and in the original coinage of "meritocracy" by Young,[39] merit has been understood as ability. A strict meritocracy where everyone is rank-ordered by ability would be a harsh place, as Young describes in his tale of an imaginary meritocracy based on innate ability that ultimately is delegitimated and stirs rebellion. A little ambiguity about merit might add some grace, dignity, and sense of possibility to a tense scramble for advancement. This sense of possibility may be why Americans are more comfortable with the idea of "effortocracy,"[40] which allows everyone a chance to excel if they work hard and emphasizes the cherished American value of having a strong work ethic.

Whether social capital is a job necessity, a real merit, a tool for managerial manipulation, or a gentle social fiction, its definition and use can be the subject of social struggle. Inequality appears in the communicative aspect of social relations. When Coleman considers "what it is about social relations that can constitute useful capital for individuals," he highlights:

> (i) the significance of insurance, related to the obligations and expectations which arise in social relationships (so that rational individuals create obligations amongst others, which function like "credit slips"); (ii) the information which is communicated through "social relations"; and (iii) the ways in which the existence of norms and effective sanctions facilitates action (reducing transactions costs in a variety of ways).[41]

The first and third elements have been given significant attention in discussions of trust and norms. The second reminds us that a connection is empty until some communication flows through it. This communication, in style and content, might confer systematic privilege on those coming from higher class backgrounds. Studies of communication styles show that class-based socialization produces different ways of describing an event and conveying the universal versus particular features of a situation.[42] "Sounding smart"—essential to turning social capital into a job or opportunity—is a function of accent and ways of marshaling information. The particularities that characterize working-class speech, while conveying important information, may be seen as less valuable than the universalisms of elite speech, in part because elites can define their own traits as more meritorious. Members of the working class are not naive to class differences but are not always able to resist them and assert the importance of their special talents. As Sabel points out,

> [t]he craftsmen easily saw the differences [between themselves and university graduates]. They regarded their own strengths as practical experience, skill, and inventiveness in the execution of tasks and the ability to accommodate themselves to new situations and to cooperate with others. The advantages of the university graduates were good general education, careerism, polished manners, and the ability to lead.[43]

The open market for "employability" might be class-biased in terms of whose social capital has value. Someone may *know* "who knows how," but will he or she be heard and rewarded? The cultural capital of elites may be what brings out the shine on their social capital, enabling them better to signal that they are players, will fit the role, can be counted on, and are worthy members of a reputational network.

Conclusion

In closing, the notion that social capital matters increasingly for employment might be greeted in two ways. First, it is a critique of meritocracy, showing that connections rather than merit place people into valued positions. The idea that "it's not what you know but who you know" has always been a cynical retort to meritocratic claims of fairness. This critical voice can get lost in the enthusiasm for showing the renewed explanatory power of social capital. Second, social capital can potentially be interpreted as "softening" the harsh competitiveness of meritocracy, by making room for a different kind of capital that is less zero sum and more available to more people. Some of the enthusiasm about social capital—and appreciation of its aggregation into firm-level relational wealth—may come from this possibility. However, differential endowments of and returns on social capital should be scrutinized much more critically to understand how social capital can continue to produce a kind of stratification that is rationalized by meritocratic logic.

The new employability model is raising concerns, in part because it appears to be lacking in institutional safeguards. It will generate a few winners—the emerging cultural image appears in ads where a contemplative individual reclines on his beach chair using his laptop to network with people in five countries. It will probably generate many more losers, who will struggle to make ends meet in a series of tenuous and downgraded jobs. There should be greater concern that vastly unequal employment fates will emerge. At the root of an understanding of social justice for the new employment relationship is the issue of how readily meritocratic language can be redeployed to legitimate differences in individual outcomes and keep people wondering if they have no one to blame but themselves for their own employability. The search for structural solutions may be impeded by the robustness of the meritocratic idea.

Notes

1. Research on the externalization of the employment relationship and on the violation of psychological and social contracts portends and assesses a transition in the employment relationship. While ILMs may still reign as the predominant employment model, the discourse salient to employees is one of ruptured employment contracts and widespread uncertainty. To understand legitimation, employees' beliefs about the nature and fairness of employment relationships are relevant. See A. Davis-Blake and B. Uzzi, "Determinants of Employment Externalization: A Study of Temporary Workers and Independent Contractors," *Administrative Science Quarterly* 39 (1993): 195–223; C. Heckscher, "The Changing Social Contract for White-Collar Workers," *Perspectives on Work* 1 (1997): 5–8; D. M. Rousseau, "Psychological and Implied Contracts in Organizations," *Employee Responsibilities and Rights Journal* 2 (1989): 121–39.

2. L. S. Richman, "Getting Past Economic Insecurity," *Fortune*, April 17, 1995, pp. 161–68.

3. J. N. Baron, "Organizational Perspectives on Stratification," *Annual Review of Sociology* 10 (1984): 37–69; T. A. DiPrete and W. T. Soule, "Gender and Promotions in Segmented Job Ladder Systems," *American Sociological Review* 53 (1988): 26–40.

4. P. Bourdieu, "Cultural Reproduction and Social Reproduction," in *Power and Ideology in Education*, edited by J. Karabel and A. H. Halsey (Cambridge, England: Cambridge University Press, 1977).

5. J. S. Coleman, "Social Capital in the Creation of Human Capital," *American Journal of Sociology* 94 (1988): s95–s120; R. Putnam with R. Leonardi and R. Y. Nanetti, *Making Democracy Work: Civic Traditions in Modern Italy* (Princeton: Princeton University Press, 1993); H. Harris and P. DeRenzio, " 'Missing Link' or Analytically Missing? The Concept of Social Capital," *Journal of International Development* 9 (1997): 919–37.

6. R. M. Fernandez and N. Weinberg, "Sifting and Sorting: Personal Contacts and Hiring in a Retail Bank," *American Sociological Review* 62 (1997): 883–902; R. M. Fernandez, E. J. Castillo, and P. Moore, "Social Capital at Work: Networks and Employment at a Phone Center," working paper, Dept. of Sociology Stanford University, 1998.

7. N. Daniels, "Merit and Meritocracy," *Philosophy and Public Affairs* 3 (1978): 206–23.

8. K. Davis and W. Moore, "Some Principles of Stratification," in *Class, Status, and Power*, edited by R. Bendix and S. M. Lipset (New York: Free Press, 1966).

9. J. Huber and W. Form, *Income and Ideology* (New York: Free Press, 1973).

10. P. Osterman, "The Nature and Importance of Internal Labor Markets," editor's introduction to *Internal Labor Markets* (Cambridge, Mass.: MIT Press, 1984).

11. A. Donnellon and M. Scully, "Teams, Merit, and Rewards: Will the Post-bureaucratic Organization be a Post-meritocratic Organization?" in *The Post-Bureaucratic Organization*, edited by C. Heckscher and A. Donnellon (Newbury Park, Calif.: Sage, 1994), pp. 63–90.

12. J. Martin, M. Feldman, M. J. Hatch, and S. B. Sitkin, "The Uniqueness Paradox in Organizational Stories," *Administrative Science Quarterly* 28 (1983): 438–53.

13. L. Iacocca, *Iacocca: An Autobiography* (New York: Bantam, 1984).

14. R. Edwards, *Contested Terrain* (New York: Basic Books, 1979).

15. G. P. Baker, M. C. Jensen, and K. J. Murphy, "Compensation and Incentives: Practice vs. Theory," *Journal of Finance* 43 (1988): 593–616; see p. 600.

16. For example, see Baron (1984); DiPrete and Soule, (1988); C. Halaby, "Bureaucratic Promotion Criteria," *Administrative Science Quarterly* 23 (1978): 466–84; C. Halaby, "Worker Attachment and Workplace Authority," *American Sociological Review* 51 (1986): 634–49; R. Jackall, *Moral Mazes: The World of Corporate Managers* (New York: Oxford University Press, 1988).

17. E. E. Lawler, *Pay and Organizational Effectiveness: A Psychological View* (New York: McGraw-Hill, 1971), see p. 158.

18. Two exceptions to the use of merit rules are family-owned firms, which rely on loyalty or need-based distribution, and unionized firms, in which unions push for seniority systems rather than the managerial favoritism they see in merit systems. Firms with ILMs, which can be unionized or nonunionized, may use seniority systems, merit-based systems, or a hybrid of the two. A seniority-based system can be regarded as a kind of merit system, inasmuch as seniority is a proxy for merits like experience and expertise. There are also hybrids: seniority-based systems may use some additional measures of merit to break ties among employees of equal tenure, and merit-based systems may in practice resort to seniority for selecting candidates for promotion.

19. B. R. Holmstrom and J. Tirole, "The Theory of the Firm," in *Handbook of Industrial Organization,* vol. 1, edited by R. Schmalensee and R. Willig (Amsterdam: North-Holland Press, 1989); Osterman (1984); O. Williamson, *Markets and Hierarchies* (New York: Free Press, 1975).

20. Edwards (1979); D. M. Gordon, R. Edwards, and M. Reich, *Segmented Work, Divided Workers* (London: Cambridge University Press, 1982).

21. Rousseau, (1989).

22. P. Osterman, *Broken Ladders: Managerial Careers in the New Economy* (New York: Oxford University Press, 1996).

23. Donnellon and Scully (1994); M. Scully and G. Preuss, "Two Faces of Trust: How Calculative and Relational Trust Relate to Employee Commitment to Pay-for-Skills," working paper no. 3923–96, Sloan School of Management, Massachusetts Institute of Technology, 1996.

24. P. Capelli, "Rethinking Employment," *British Journal of Industrial Relations* (1995).

25. F. F. Piven and R. A. Cloward, *Poor People's Movements: Why They Succeed, How They Fail* (New York: Pantheon Books, 1977).

26. A. Hyde, "Employee Identity Caucuses in Silicon Valley: Can They Transcend the Boundaries of the Firm?" paper presented to the spring meeting of the Industrial Relations Research Association, New York, NY, April 1997.

27. K. S. Newman, *Falling from Grace: The Experience of Downward Mobility in the American Middle Class* (New York: Vintage, 1988).

28. M. Scully, "The Irony of Meritocracy: How a Legitimating Ideology Generates and Redirects Disbelief," working paper, Sloan School of Management, Massachusetts Institute of Technology, 1996.

29. A. Giddens, *Communication and the Evolution of Society* (New York: Cambridge University Press, 1979); see pp. 101–3.

30. Scully (1996).

31. Huber and Form (1973); J. R. Kluegel and E. R. Smith, *Beliefs about Inequality: Americans' Views of What Is and What Ought to Be* (New York: de Gruyter, 1986); K. Schlozman and S. Verba, *Unemployment, Class, and Political Response* (Cambridge: Harvard University Press, 1978).

32. Kluegel and Smith (1986).

33. W. A. Gamson, *Talking Politics* (Cambridge, Eng.: Cambridge University Press, 1992).

34. C. Jencks, M. Smith, H. Acland, M. J. Bane, D. Cohen, H. Gintis, B. Heyns, and S. Michelson, *Inequality: A Reassessment of the Effect of Family and Schooling in America* (New York: Harper, 1972).

34. C. Jencks, S. Bartlett, M. Corcoran, J. Crouse, D. Eaglesfield, G. Jackson, K. McClelland, P. Mueser, M. Olneck, J. Schwartz, S. Ward, and J. Williams, *Who Gets Ahead? The Determinants of Economic Success in America* (New York: Basic Books, 1979).

35. J. L. Hochschild, *What's Fair? American Beliefs about Distributive Justice* (Cambridge: Harvard University Press, 1981).

36. M. Mann, "The Social Cohesion of Liberal Democracy," *American Sociological Review* 35 (1970): 423–39.

37. "Free Agent Nation," *Fast Company* (December/January 1998):131–63.

38. Scully and Preuss (1996).

39. M. Young, *The Rise of the Meritocracy* (New York: Penguin Books, 1958).

40. R. P. Coleman and L. Rainwater, *Social Standing in America* (New York: Basic Books, 1978).

41. Summarized in Harris and DeRenzio (1997): 922, op. cit.

42. Bourdieu (1977); P. Bourdieu and J. C. Passeron, *Reproduction in Education, Society, and Culture* (London: Sage 1977).

43. C. Sabel, *Work and Politics: The Division of Labor in Industry* Cambridge, England: Cambridge University Press, 1982); see p. 88.

IV.

THE FOUNDATIONS OF RELATIONAL WEALTH
The Roles of Community, Government, Firm, and Financial Capital

What devices can firms use to develop and realize the competitive advantage of relational wealth? Flexibility with stability means that a diverse set of resources are tied to a stable whole and accessed in the context of intrinsic connections among people, technology, places, and knowledge. Our authors explore in this section the often uncharted territory of embedded relationships and economic value, and the mechanisms for enhancing both.

Judith Blau takes a broad look at the many forms economic exchange can take. In the age of the global economy, she reminds us that as workers, managers, family members, consumers, and owners of capital, we are rooted in localities whose economic arrangements exist in a "moral economy." This moral economy constitutes a form of wealth Blau labels spatial capital. Interactions tied to location downplay divisive status and roles as communal connections form the basis for relationships. Human beings, even in a global economy, will never have the fungibility that money does and will realize broad resources and economic value from the communities to which they are tied.

One location in which nonfungible resources reside is the organization itself. Harry Van Buren and Carrie Leana make a case for the distinctive qualities of organizational social capital. Its key components include those factors shaping the willingness and capacity of members to work toward collective goals, based on shared knowledge, mutual familiarity, and governance that rests on reputation and community ties. In many ways, Van Buren and Leana offer an antidote to the anomie that is characteristic of people disassociated from community ties. Organizational social capital offers a basis for renewed communal attachment, shared purpose, and enhanced fulfillment of mutual self-interest.

Jeffrey Pfeffer discusses the necessary role of government in ensuring that firms nurture relational wealth, or at least don't destroy it. He convincingly argues against the market-focused approach to employment, marshaling evidence that supports, at a minimum, a government-mandated floor on wages and job security. He notes that despite the free-market rhetoric, business welcomes government intervention when it is to its advantage. He further notes the lack of evidence supporting the market-focused approach to employment and points to the success of countries like Singapore and Germany, where government intervention in employment policies and practices is quite strong. Thus, government support in the form of laws, incentives, and policy that promotes relational wealth is a necessary component to motivate firms to create and sustain it.

The structure of financial markets has created many of the incentives modern firms face and no small number of disincentives for accumulating relational wealth. Melvin Smith, Jeffrey Pfeffer, and Denise Rousseau argue that incentive structures associated with financial capital have misled firms and their agents regarding the sustainable advantage of relational wealth. Financial capital has become less patient, to the point of day trading and ongoing investment churn as evidenced by stock turnover, shareholder impatience, and CEO turnover. The short time frame adopted by many investors erodes relational wealth and can undermine the long-term competitive advantage of a firm. Smith and colleagues argue that financial capital that is patient constitutes a necessary condition for the pursuit of strategies and practices that encourage relational wealth. Institutional changes and shareholder reorientation are suggested as means for shifting to a more patient form of capital investment in firms.

12

Relational Wealth in the Commons

Local Spaces of Work and Residence in a Global Economy

JUDITH R. BLAU

Karl Polanyi stressed that economic action and practice shape and, in turn, are shaped by the social relations that comprise social institutions.[1] Although economic practices vary widely, we still can distinguish among the forms of feudalism, socialism, colonialism, communism, capitalism, and an emerging global postcapitalism. Yet even in the contemporary global economy, many societies cling to older economic forms, such as agrarian subsistence, socialism, and communism—economies that function according to their own distinctive logic even though global markets swirl around them and threaten their existence.[2]

It was Polanyi's view that a distinctive set of social institutions helps to define, protect, and regulate the exchange relations that exist in each economic form, as well as the people who participate in them. These social institutions legitimize and are legitimated by a "moral economy," a cultural scaffolding that defines what is appropriate, fair, and just. The moral economy, from Polanyi's perspective, is essentially about relationships, and how people maintain relationships in order to promote their own well-being. In that sense, Polanyi's abstract conceptualization addresses the issues raised in this book about relational wealth. In this chapter, I will use the concept of relational wealth to give fresh meaning to the phrase "think globally, act locally." I further argue that in the contemporary global economy, proximity will engender more exchange relations that will, in turn, strengthen the local level as a site in which a moral economy will take shape. From this local moral economy emerges spatial capital, resources created through local institutions supporting the creation and maintenance of a commons. My perspective goes against prevailing assumptions based on the high levels of residential segregation in American communities, glaring disparities between white and nonwhite neighborhoods, and the decline of downtown neighborhoods, as suburbanization continues. Yet I believe that seeds are being sown that might define countervailing forces to offset these trends. My purpose is to speculate about the forms that relationships might take in American communities, which are in flux and, some might believe, are even imperiled. Further, I develop the concept of spatial capital to extend our understanding of the functioning of local institutions.

Any moral economy provides guidelines for deciding who incurs risks, determining what risks are appropriate and inappropriate, and setting norms about distribution, justice, and fairness. Obligations and rights are defined in terms of the moral economy. Central to any moral economy is the concept of economic actors—individuals, groups, households, communes, corporations, and other collectives. In addition, a wide range of conceptualizations exist regarding what can be exchanged. In some societies women are traded for land, and in others sons for dowries. The nature of the economic actor also varies. In peasant societies the household is both the production and the consumption unit; in typical capitalist societies the individual is the producer while the household is the site of consumption; and in contemporary societies, the individual may very well be replacing the household as both the production and consumption unit.[3]

Economic forms are not mutually exclusive. Even in America, which is fundamentally based on a market economy and private ownership, some firms are owned exclusively by workers. Similarly, in spite of the strong individualistic bias in American society, there are localized arrangements in which a collectivity is defined as the unit of exchange and sometimes as the unit of production as well as consumption. Ethnic enclaves, Native American reservations, rural communities, and communes are examples of places in which members generate at least some resources for the good of the larger collective. It is in the terms of a moral economy that Jankowksi describes the easy-going exchange relations between urban gangs and their communities, in which communities protect gang members from police in exchange for protection against outside gangs.[4] It is also in these terms that Stack describes kin relations among people of color, many of whom contend with a grim and possibly hostile environment.[5] Such examples suggest that the market metaphor takes too much for granted about the individual actor and is nonsensical in many forms of social life. Outside of the West, metaphors about expressive and instrumental action are very often, if not mostly, framed in terms of collective life.[6]

Polanyi's assumption is that whatever the form, every economic arrangement needs to be legitimized and embedded in daily practice. Yet this assumption encounters problems in the face of contemporary trends. First, capital markets have penetrated every region of the world, destabilizing local economies and social institutions. In the United States, this has been accompanied by the dismantling of welfare programs and the transfer of authority to the local level. In addition, internal labor markets and organizational hierarchies are being reduced if not eliminated, while occupational distinctions are eroded by technological advances. Finally, downsizing, mergers, acquisitions, and subcontracting have made many economic entities unstable.[7] In sum, there is rapid expansion of a single economic system (market capitalism), the dismantling of hierarchies (the downsizing of government and economic entities), and the weakening of safety nets. These trends pose problems for Polanyi's assumption that economic arrangements are rooted in and legitimized through practice, if legitimacy can be so readily eroded.

Understandably, concern focuses mainly on global instabilities. It appears that a universal, global economy is inevitable, along with the consequent instabilities caused by low regulation and a high degree of interdependence among settings. Yet there is also a growing fear that both traditional and modern institutions will be pulled apart by the globalizing economy. In the United States, for example, traditional routines of child rearing have been altered by increasing numbers of women in the workforce, high separation and divorce rates, and a lack of effective child-care programs. The one mother–one father family has been replaced in many households by a single parent, two parents of the same sex, a grandmother, or siblings.[8] None of these arrangements is inherently superior, but it is certain that ad hoc parenting schemes are not working well, as evidenced by soaring child poverty rates and frantic attempts to fix education and child care.[9] Another critical institution in flux is the workplace itself. Like households, jobs are no longer defined with clarity or certainty. Credentials, benefits, wages, and working hours are no longer standard, leading to a rapid growth of undesirable, even "bad" jobs.[10]

The two most important social institutions in any society are, arguably, child rearing and work. Yet in the United States, both have given way to economic forces at an alarming rate. It is inevitable that a new moral economy will emerge in which there are "standard" ways of child rearing and of finding and keeping jobs—methods that are numerically or statistically standard, involving routines, agencies, and provisions for dealing with the "nonstandard." One of the primary functions of a moral economy is to identify and prevent the conditions that cause economic and, thereby, social casualties. Typically, institutions evolve to care for the casualties that do occur. These institutions can evolve as long as there are standard forms that allow for the development of norms about equity, fairness, and justice as well as the ability to seek redress if these norms fail. Standard forms in modern, capitalist societies have included welfare, unemployment insurance, social security programs, affirmative action, public schools, and health care. Yet in the postcapitalist United States, privatization and deregulation threaten these programs. Some, like welfare, are in the midst of being abolished altogether.

If present trends continue to erode national institutions—social security, public schools, health insurance, and so forth—local communities will have to be innovative. Those that are innovative will see the emergence of many experimental solutions that are shaped in terms of local issues. After all, the most pressing daily problems are local ones. People are not "virtual" but real—they work, make love, shop, eat, play, study, and live in particular places. Although there are convincing arguments that Americans are becoming increasingly private and isolated,[11] I argue that the locale (i.e., public spaces) could emerge that deal with the practices and relationships of residents as a collectivity, albeit a weak one.

Although it is widely believed that *global* capitalism is the "only game in town," it can be argued, following Polyani's line of reasoning, that every society or group needs a locally rooted moral economy, with accompanying socioeconomic institutions that are legitimated in daily practices. Although it is evident that global institutions are rapidly evolving and international cooperation is expanding, a case can be made that there are countervailing forces that will redefine and strengthen communities. Without the hierarchical institutions that arose following World War II—the internal labor markets, bureaucracies, and corporations—and without much federalism, it is reasonable to suppose that locales will experiment and devise their own solutions to local problems.

My assumptions are the following: (1) people want more routines, rather than fewer; (2) people adopt standards when their interests are defined as collective or joint; (3) people flexibly define their memberships in various collectivities and groups; and (4) in these collectivities and groups, people are mindful of fairness. The assumptions are tied to the ways moral economies deploy their common pool of resources.

Common Pool Resources

"The tragedy of the commons" is known in economics as an example of the virtual inability of people to cooperate and the metaphor is often used in arguments to support centralized regulation. This argument states that people tend to use common resources without regard to their continuing replenishment. However, this view is counter to historical patterns in which the "commons" was cooperatively regulated for the good of the many.[12]

The assumptions made by Elinor Ostrom regarding the emergence of local institutions around routine practices are consistent with those developed in this chapter.[13] Ostrom reviews the empirical cases in which residents develop cooperative strategies to protect common pool resources (CPRs), which are resource systems that are sufficiently large as to make it costly to exclude potential beneficiaries from their use. Specifically, she emphasizes that in the midst of complex contingencies, community members supply and use CPRs in a rational manner, overcoming free-riding and other opportunistic behavior through institutionalization. This line of thinking draws on the interdependencies that invariably exist in communities and casts new light on the issue of trust. That is, trust is not naturally occurring in communities or the workplace but is generated by the recognition that some resources are not divisible and can only benefit individuals when they are held in common. Moreover, joint use promotes trust, which is, in turn, institutionalized.

The extension of these arguments is that the commons is a public good in its own right. Each individual's job contributes to the commons, which then becomes a sum of public goods in the sense that the community is more than just the sum of individual workers and their jobs. It is for these reasons that generalized trust can emerge. Workers and jobs become the basis of a community's consumption patterns, its means of maintaining infrastructures, and a way of providing the services that workers enjoy.[14]

The Capital of the Commons

The term "commons" refers to somewhat spatially defined public realms where entrepreneurial, political, community, civic, religious, educational, and recreational activities take place. This conceptualization draws attention to the many types of practices and relations in reference to a locale, and spatiality of action is stressed as being increasingly fundamental for peoples' practices and relationships. One reason for this is that residents have a shared stake in the local economy, in contrast to mobile economic actors who have few local attachments. True enough, large firms can threaten to exit, with consequent loss of jobs. This is a grave threat, but residents can unite with local leaders to diversify their economy, creating coalitions that attract a broad mix of employers to their community. Job creation is increasingly a task taken over by local governments, chambers of commerce, and planning committees. A second reason that spatiality of action is becoming important is the declining role that households play in child rearing and socialization. The current flurry of activity around charter schools, school voucher plans, day care centers, and an extended school year are reflections of community improvisation and experimentation with respect to the dilemmas of child rearing.

Just as we use the term "commons" to focus attention on locales, we should also recognize that the commons is one resource that creates other resources though the opportunities it provides for social relations. Thus, the commons is the site of what I call spatial capital. One of the reasons that commons sites produce spatial capital is that such sites are multipurpose, generating new uses and new users. In addition, because they are based on diverse contacts and relationships, they expand the opportunities for new encounters, contacts, and relationships. This enhanced social interaction, as one might expect, helps to downplay conventional social distinctions. As social relations multiply around common resours, each individual's stake in the community increases, along with his or her knowledge and familiarity with the many niches in the commons. This development in turn is expected to produce generalized trust and create a forum for a wide range of social exchanges.[15] I am not arguing that this will increase the commonality of beliefs and lifestyles. In fact, I argue the opposite—namely, that the enlightened self-interest of the commoners is derived from their differences and diversities.[16]

If the social fabric of the commons is diverse, its economy must also be diverse in order to reduce its vulnerabilities to plant closings or the exit of a corporate headquarters. Therefore, communities must court a variety of economic establishments and draw on their diverse populations to do so.[17] This means valuing the hot dog vendor, the former homeless person who works in a recycling plant, the teens who work in day care centers, the seniors who help with the literacy program for immigrants, and the farmers who sell their vegetables at the Saturday market.

For important reasons, this argument about the emerging role of the commons is counterintuitive. Just as markets are global, they also penetrate every community with little or no accountability. Plants close unexpectedly and destabilize labor just as small businesses do, and expansion into an area can be followed by a severe contraction. Financial planners and corporate executives in distant headquarters may have little regard for what happens in the communities in which their funds are vested. However, some important countervailing forces may help to create viable commons, including:

- The aforementioned devolution of federal authority, at least in Western nations. While this has accompanied the dismantling of the welfare state, it can bolster the perception that local governments, businesses, and residents must take greater responsibility for their communities.[18]
- Immigration, which in many parts of the world has increased the social, cultural, and economic diversity of communities, making them more complex and providing incentives for cooperative efforts.
- A dramatic increase in the activity of local organizations. This includes nonprofit organizations and churches that focus on local issues and also increase the level of involvement of residents.
- A decline in the influence of the local elite, occurring in concert with a decline in the number of large, family-owned businesses.
- The erosion of social status differences. In spite of great economic inequalities at the local level, communities help overcome class differences through expansion of the service sector and narrowing educational gaps.
- An increasing need for local services as traditional firms exit the business of educating workers and providing benefits.

In short, communities are fairly active places these days, with greater reliance on diverse services and more common contact among social groups.

Historically, local economic actors—from plantation owners and colonists to the owners of large factories—maliciously exploited local labor and local resources. They could do so, in part, by virtue of their control over the commons. Workers and their families, as well as local businesses and politicians, depended on these large economic actors and their establishments. However, in the contemporary economy, distant owners cannot so easily exert control over the commons even though they have an economic interest to do so. "Distant owners" are, in fact, shareholders. Some shareholders are very rich, some are managers, some own more shares than others, and many do not even know they own shares. But none has as large a stake in the community as hot dog vendors, office workers, the dentists, and every parent. It is no longer rare for residents in a community to mobilize against a particular factory or corporation over employment conditions, safety standards, or environmental practices. While it is still true that residents and workers have much to lose because the factory or corporation can choose to go elsewhere, distant owners have less pervasive control when they have no stake in the commons. They have no spatial capital and, in principle, will cede to the demands of those who do if the costs of ceding are less than the costs of moving.

The Commons as a Site for Social Action

Common activities are important because virtually all adults work and, therefore, depend on local services. Through these services, they expand their social networks and the diversity of their contacts. Thus, networks in the commons are extensive and far-reaching, involve numerous people, and for the most part are likely to center on fairly mundane activities. Sites in the commons include schools, churches, parks, buses, auditoriums, cafes, bars, athletic facilities, and community centers. In part, these sites are usually important because they are often multipurpose, a characteristic that enhances intergroup relations through the common use of these sites by a group of people who might not otherwise interact. The overlapping users of sites are not segregated by age, race, ethnicity, gender, occupation, and residence. In the commons, their worlds collide. Though the relationships people develop in the commons are for the most part civil and casual, it is worth noting that the participants' common stakes are of some significance in the aggregate, if not individually.

When successful, commons activities and programs create the need and opportunity for further interaction. Local organizations and programs expand to meet more demand than was originally anticipated. For example, the public library may become the center for bilingual classes, a provider of online services, and the instigator of a program for senior citizens. Colleges and firms cooperate to establish recreation centers for seniors and playgrounds for children and give their workers time off to volunteer at these facilities. In this way, activities in the commons provide fertile ground for new relationships and networks, and inevitably they create even more diverse relationships. They also undermine the conventional distinctions people make: a physician and a sales clerk may find themselves at the same child-care center or downtown cafe and may discover a mutual interest in jazz or stockcar racing. A Latino professor and an African American construction worker may strike up a conversation at the bus stop about baseball.

Fairly high educational achievement, a shared mass culture, and historical experiences with diversity and geographic mobility have given Americans an unusual but often untapped capacity for authenticity and empathy in their daily contacts. And during recent decades, social status differences have become increasingly slippery, owing to the growing informality of dress codes (few men wear ties and many people wear jeans), the easy familiarity that governs rituals of communication (first name, please), and the proliferation of democratizing sites (ethnic restaurants, sports bars, mall cafes, bowling alleys, and cinemas). At least it can be said that the seeds of the commons have been sown.

Arguably, the institutionalization of the commons accompanies the erosion of social boundaries. As men and women participate equally in the labor market, they also participate equally in commons activities—in health clubs, shops, and daily household routines. They go to the same hair salons and hardware stores. The commons offers high culture and popular culture, but for a variety of reasons, the line between "high" and "popular" is now blurred, and the more public both become the more blurred they will be. Group, ethnic, racial, and gender identities are affirmed, uncloseted, and celebrated in the commons. The answer to the most perplexing question of all—"Where to put the children?"—is, of course, "In the commons." A cursory comparison of any community's phone directories for, say, 1989 and 1999 will confirm that public facilities for children—day care, after-school care, swimming pools, horse-riding camps, academic camps, computer camps—have increased dramatically.

Although rich suburbanites and poor urbanites have different ecological niches, their shared needs for services often bring them together in alliances that cross boundaries. The very agency or individual initiative that matters increasingly in solving individual problems of home-work-children can be expected to help solve the collective problems involving home-work-children. These problems are neutral and cross the lines of race, class, and gender, so solutions for some will be solutions for many. As communities address these problems, they will ideally involve all who have stakes in the solutions. Thus, social action involves exchanges that cross lines of social difference—notably race, class, and gender. These exchanges help to undo the cultural casualties of modernism: namely, racism, class pretensions, and sexism.

The concept of the commons and people's attachment to local sites is at odds with the distinction between "locals" and "cosmopolitans"[19] because, arguably, people now fit into both categories. Their education and travel experiences are considerably equal, and their work and social roles are more complex. People no longer frame themselves in terms of given roles and statuses. Similarly, contrary to historical contrasts between cities and rural areas,[20] I am suggesting that there are not dramatic differences between large and small communities. A somewhat more controversial argument, given the global economy and global consumption, is that local sites are particularized in terms of local action and particularize that local action as well. Although others have suggested the competition among local sites will intensify as each courts investors,[21] my argument is that even if this is true, the local site will energize itself in the process. Investors will make location decisions that respect workers' preferences, and workers will prefer places that have amenities, safety nets, flexible labor markets, and community investments in child-care programs and schools.

The Plural Self

We participate in many worlds and have dispersed selves and multiple identities, as Charles Taylor, Rose Coser, Michael Walzer, Ernest Gelner, and Georg Simmel point out.[22] Agency is a matter of negotiating among a repertoire of roles and situations. We can term this phenomenon the plural self, which grows from the fact that people establish their identity as they participate in multiple, fragmented worlds and no group, community, organization, or occupation claims their undivided loyalty. Agency, in other words, involves negotiation. Yet, arguably, this conception must assume that people intermingle considerably more than might be expected on the basis of our segregated communities. Plural selves could not emerge without encounters with "the other," without contact with people who are different from ourselves, and without opportunities to see the world from different points of view. In other words, the nature of contemporary places and households helps to bring people together even if in fleeting and fragmentary ways. While it is true that the wealthy and the poor are not typically neighbors, reliance on a pool of common resources has become increasingly important.

An alternative concept of agency is that there is only a singular self, a rational actor, that calculates advantages at every turn.[23] But this idea ignores the fact that bundles of problems are collectively generated and can only be collectively negotiated. Besides, the singular self has negative externalities, such as the consequences of personal ambition and self-interest, that cannot be tolerated in diverse communities. Thus, the investments people have in the commons—in schools, day care centers, entrepreneurial services, political parties—give them an incentive to build and maintain relations within the commons. The free rider is an anathema to local collective routines and is an anomaly in a community of people whose well-being depends on joint participation in endeavors and at common sites.

Spatial groundedness of plural selves restores individuality, but it is not the neoliberal conception of individuality either but rather an individuality that expresses the plural commitments of multiple roles into which contemporaries are divided. The plural self is the individual who is reconstituted in daily practices and can therefore be considered materially and pragmatically grounded. The spatial groundedness of plural selves is a hedge against extremist identity movements and also offsets the competitive intensities associated with neoliberalism.

Trust

Although some have emphasized that trust is only possible under conditions of perfect information,[24] it is more commonly argued today that trust is a function of imperfect information and uncertainty. As Misztal states, "trust always involves an element of risk resulting from our inability to monitor others' behavior, from our inability to have complete knowledge about other people's motivations."[25] Trust becomes more important when social reality is uncertain, and to reduce contingencies and uncertainties people take risks by building trust. This form of trust is no longer fostered by tradition and shared values as it was in premodern societies, nor is it a byproduct of routinized interdependencies, as has been the case in modern societies. Our highly nontraditional ties and nonroutinized interdependencies, combined with our sunk costs in locale, generate incentives for agents, in their plural selves, to cooperate in local spaces. The commons matters for trustworthiness because people are not virtual in their communities, as they are in telecommunications and in the stock market, and reality creates a basis for people to be at least somewhat reliable and trustworthy.

Under modern conditions, the best sources of trustworthiness were the private nuclear family and the organization. The nuclear family ensured stability and conventionality for a group made up of three, four, five, or maybe more, but the normative emphasis was always on loyalty and mutual regard. The statuses, rules, hierarchies, and structured labor markets of organizations promoted accountability and predictability. However, as the nuclear family unravels and organizations become contingent and highly improvisational, plural selves become increasingly dependent on local resources. The short-term and long-term contingencies with which plural selves must contend are inconsistent with the shared values of families and also with relations that are highly structured. My concept of trust highlights that it is institutionalized around diverse local practices, even when it is provisional and contingent. Plural selves create a generalized dependence on a common pool of resources, and, in turn, bonds of generalized trust.

Paradoxically, the plural self is merely potentially constructed. There is an uneasy intersection of roles in the commons (citizens, parents, residents, homemakers, voters, shoppers, diners) with specialized work roles (CEOs, managers, workers, professionals, clerks, storeowners). For this reason, generalized trust, not highly focused trust, is what emerges and establishes the norms for participation in the commons and the workplace. Trustworthy citizens in the commons do not use their work roles to gain special perks or advantages. The bank manager gets no better treatment on the basketball court than anyone else, and a low-salary city employee may serve on the board of a large nonprofit organization. The good citizen, like the good sport, enters and leaves arenas in which local action occurs and returns again to participate.

Such interactions institutionalize generalized exchange and trust. There is a collective understanding that promotes an easygoing equality that is reinforced by practice but also by language and communications and through symbolic classifications. All homemakers are considered to be equal, but homemakers may also be construction workers and CEOs. Likewise, homemakers, construction workers, and CEOs are equal (ambiguous though it seems) because they are members of the commons. The plural self makes this possible and thereby constructs a generalized and institutionalized trust around assumptions of equality. Given the ambiguity of roles in the commons, it would be rude to challenge any reliable citizen's right to participate. This institutionalized trust protects the plural self from its own internal contradictions and also protects relationships from their contradictions. The feminist, for example, can be a homemaker, a gay activist, and a loving parent; the CEO pumps gas just like anyone else; union members and company managers can coach Little League together; and Pentecostal preachers work with Presbyterian ministers in building houses for the needy. Trust within the commons is based on a conspiracy of silence about the daily contradictions of plural selves. Identities, ideologies, and different relations to capital are disguised and masked.

Role Washes

The plural self is not particularly coherent, predictable, or reliable during the course of a day, week, or month. The self moves, as Goffman[26] suggests, across stages in a temporal progression and in interaction with different others in various settings. It is in the commons where the generalized plural self is, in a sense, reconstituted, by civil and human routines.

People finesse transitions and role changes in the commons. A "stroll" through the commons allows people to "wash out their roles." At Little League games, preachers, CEOs, clerks, and mechanics all wear jeans. At the shopping mall, everyone gets the same treatment. The commons is status-neutral, democratic, and egalitarian, and the commons erodes differences in status and prestige. Even if much of the commons is about mass culture, this culture seeps into local practice and is particularized as people make it concrete and relate it to their own lives. Mass culture talk—about the Yankees, Oprah, Bill Clinton, and Bart Simpson—radically trivializes differences in status, occupations, gender, race, and ethnicity. Status, hegemonic culture, high religion, high art, high culture, and highbrow do not easily play out in the commons.[27] Much activity in the commons is not serious but is instead ironic, amused, and amusing. As escape from the multiple demands exerted on components of plural selves, the commons asks for little except authenticity, civility, and nonpretentiousness. For the most part, the serious commitments and problems associated with one's private life lie elsewhere.

Such conditions, in other words, are not conducive to high rates of sustained participation or to high value consensus. Communities cannot provide a basis for shared communitarian experiences.[28] The commons supports pluralism around life, work, death, and children. To be sure, it is also the grounding for identity movements—for solidarities built on gender, race, and ethnic identities. The commons is cluttered with political, cultural, and social movements. There are campaigns for saving squirrels, renaming streets, supporting local schools, banning public smoking, feeding the homeless, expanding support for reproductive rights, and closing abortion clinics.

Yet the very forces that give rise to social, political, cultural, and identity movements also counteract their corrosive effects on the commons. People have many roles that are at stake in the community, and playing out any one identity violates shared understandings of the ways in which the commons must function. People also have too many diverse roles that make up their plural selves to risk a full skirmish over a single one. As this suggests, however, there is a difference between generalized trust, which conceals the contradictions of practices in people's temporally dynamic roles, and trust in particular individuals in their particular roles. Generalized trust involves a shared conception of communality and some threshold level above which participation is expected, but participation is mostly casual and members' involvement in common matters is intermittent.

Public life is neither mostly intense nor particularly greedy.[29] However, public places are ones in which people can "wash out their roles" and relocate themselves with respect to other commitments. Successful public places have contrivances that encourage people to linger in their public roles. These devices include penny exchange cups, tip jars, newspapers in cafes, toys in retail stores, street musicians, and parades. Good planning produces friction in public places by stopping or slowing traffic and thereby increasing the probabilities of random interaction and civility.

It bears restating that public places, where people go to wash out their identities, place a premium on vagueness. Relationships that develop in public places rest on civility. They are not so "deep" that people disclose their motivations, identities, or desires, but they are "deep" to the extent that they compensate for the demands made in specialized spheres. The commons is, more generally, for public selves, providing opportunities for intergroup contact and crosscutting role relations[30] and eliciting "authentic" communications among people who drop their specialized roles.

I have argued that interpersonal relations in public sites are based on the tacit consensus that "role wash" occurs as people transit in and out of their identities. The collective stake in the commons is that it is where humanity is affirmed, although I have suggested that this may actually be a collective conspiracy that none must confess about their complicities in other realms.

Social, ethnic, racial, and economic diversities are valued not merely for their cosmetic value; the commons thrives on such diversities because they affirm the complexities and contradictions of the plural self.

Implications for Workers

Economic geographers, such as David Harvey,[31] have analyzed the spatial processes underlying economic exchange and their consequences for communities, workers, and labor markets. This work is highly pessimistic, stressing the destructive effects of highly mobile capital. Under conditions of high capital circulation, investment, and reproduction at the global level, Harvey indicates that wealth accumulation requires continuous circulation of capital, expansion of the cost of commodities, unrelentingly high rates of reallocation of labor power, and rapid redeployment of capital. Central in Harvey's analysis is that there is no socially fair and just "spatial fix" in the post-capitalist economy. As he describes, "capitalism perpetually strives, therefore, to create a social and physical landscape in its own image and requisite to its own needs at a particular point in time, only just as certainly to undermine, disrupt, and even destroy that landscape at a later point in time."[32]

The "spatial fix," according to Harvey, is inevitably based on local pro-growth, pro-capital, and anti-labor coalitions, which, in turn, up the ante of ruthless, competitive inter-place, inter-regional, and inter-class competition. This is consistent with the views of other geographers, including Jamie Peck and Doreen Massey.[33] Their general diagnosis is particularly grim, but it may not sufficiently take into account the nature of social organization in locales. My argument has to hinge on the premise that locales will resist the relentless forces of the market by various means. These could include: high taxes on investors, corporate investments in the local economy, and requiring investors to cooperate with local planning committees, labor unions, governments, existing companies, and nonprofits. Other methods of community solidarity include provisions for work in exchange for services, community representation on the boards of enterprises, and commoners' participation in companies' decisions.

All workers—whether they are wage-earners, salary-earners, or contract employees—have stakes in their communities. In terms of the themes developed by Leana and Rousseau and other authors of this book, all have relational wealth through their spatial relations. Space is endogenous to action through cognitive and subjective processes, but it is also exogenous, as people objectify their own interests in terms of the interests of others. Although predictions that the rate at which capitalist expansion will intensify may be correct, it is important not to underestimate agency in locales in which people have stakes, not only in their jobs but also in their house-holding activities, which, in turn, presuppose a broad range of social institutions.

In sum, I have focused on reasons to believe that local communities are potentially robust to the extent that they are based on broad social institutions and diverse populations, and I have also suggested that local labor decisions affect everyone who works. For these reasons, all workers and their dependents have stakes in the commons. Space, I have argued, is not merely defined by its market value but is also endowed with collective, community value, in which residents have vested spatial capital that expands with increments of collective effort. Multiple roles, complex work, and child-care responsibilities enrich the lives of plural selves and also create incentives to participate in local affairs, thus creating the possibility of more, not less, democracy, and of a moral economy that is negotiated in terms of diverse and overlapping interests.

Notes

1. Karl Polanyi, *The Great Transformation* (Boston: Beacon Press, [1944] 1957).

2. James C. Scott, *The Moral Economy of the Peasant* (New Haven: Yale University Press, 1976).

3. For an early analysis, see Thornstein Veblen, *The Vested Interests and the Common Man* (New York: Augustus M. Kelley, [1919] 1964); Charles E. Lindblom, *Politics and Markets* (New York: Basic Books, 1977).

4. Martín Sánchez-Jankowski, *Islands in the Streets* (Berkeley: University of California Press, 1991).

5. Carol B. Stack, *All Our Kin: Strategies for Survival in a Black Community* (New York: Harper and Row, 1974).

6. Recent theoretical and empirical work on Chinese guanxi is especially useful. See Lisa A. Keister, "Social Ties and the Formation of Chinese Business Groups," *Sociological Analysis* 2 (1998): 99–118; Nan Lin and Yanjie Bian, "Getting Ahead in Urban China," *American Journal of Sociology* 97 (1991): 657–88.

7. Chris Tilly and Charles Tilly, *Work under Capitalism* (Boulder, Colo.: Westview Press, 1998); Judith R. Blau, *Social Contracts and Economic Markets* (New York: Plenum, 1993); Richard B. Freeman, ed., *Working under Different Rules* (New York: Russell Sage Foundation, 1994).

8. The percentage of single-parent families increased from 13 percent in 1970 to 31 percent in 1995 and is projected to continue increasing, U.S. Bureau of the Census, *Statistical Abstracts of the United States*, Washington, D.C. 1997.

9. Greg J. Duncan and Jeanne Brooks-Gunn, eds., *Consequences of Growing up Poor* (New York: Russell Sage Foundation, 1997).

10. Arne L. Kalleberg, Barbara F. Reskin, and Ken Hudson, "Bad Jobs in America: Standard and Nonstandard Work Arrangements and Job Quality in the United States," *American Sociological Review* 65 (2000): in press.

11. Robert Putnam. *Making Democracy Work* (Princeton: Princeton University Press, 1993).

12. This term was misleadingly introduced into economics by Garrett Hardin, who advocated strong restrictions on individual rights. See Matt

Ridley, *The Origins of Virtue* (Harmondsworth, England: Penguin, 1997). Historical research summarized in Ridley (pp. 231–3) indicates that to the contrary, medieval commoners always had rules to preserve the collective good; see also Scott (1976).

13. Elinor Ostrom, *Governing the Commons* (Cambridge, England: Cambridge University Press, 1990).

14. John Urry, *Consuming Places* (London: Routledge, 1995).

15. It is in the latter sense that one might draw parallels between the commons and conceptualizations of the "public sphere," as considered by Jürgen Habermas, *The Structural Transformation of the Public Sphere* (Cambridge, Mass.: MIT Press, 1989).

16. Such a spatially informed conception of social action is considered by Benno Werlen, *Society, Action and Space* (London: Routledge, 1988).

17. Amartya Sen (*On Ethics and Economics* [Cambridge, Eng. Blackwell, 1987]) distinguishes well-being—the enactment and fulfillment of material needs—from agency, the enactment and fulfillment of social needs. I borrow from this conception.

18. Tony Spybey, *Globalization and World Society* (Cambridge, England: Blackwell, 1996); Peter Eisinger, "City Politics in an Era of Federal Devolution," *Urban Affairs Quarterly* 33 (1988): 308–25.

19. Robert K. Merton, "Patterns of Influence," in *Communications in Research*, edited by Paul F. Lazarsfeld and Frank Stanton (New York: Harper, 1948/49), pp. 226–57.

20. For example, see Arthur J. Vidich and Joseph Bensman, *Small Town in Mass Society* (New York: Doubleday, 1958).

21. See Roland Robertson, *Globalization* (London: Sage, 1992).

22. Charles Taylor, *Sources of the Self* (Cambridge: Harvard University Press, 1989). Rose L. Coser, *In Defense of Modernity* (Stanford: Stanford University Press, 1991). Michael Walzer, *On Toleration* (New Haven: Yale University Press, 1997). Ernest Gellner, *Plough, Sword, and Book* (London: Collins Harvil, 1988). Georg Simmel is the early notable theorist in this tradition; see *Conflict and the Web of Group Affiliations* (New York: Free Press, 1955).

23. Jon Elster, *The Cement of Society* (Cambridge, England: Cambridge University Press, 1989).

24. Ronald S. Burt, *Structural Holes* (Cambridge: Harvard University Press, 1992).

25. Barbara A. Misztal, *Trust in Modern Societies* (Cambridge, England: Polity, 1996), p. 18.

26. Erving Goffman, *The Presentation of Self in Everyday Life* (New York: Doubleday, 1959).

27. Pierre Bourdieu, *Distinction* (Cambridge: Harvard University Press, 1984).

28. One feature of communitarian thought is that local autonomous units promote shared values. See Raymond Plant, *Community and Ideology* (London: Routledge and Kegan Paul, 1974).

29. See Lewis A. Coser, *Greedy Institutions* (New York: Free Press, 1974).

30. Peter M. Blau, *Inequality and Heterogeneity* (New York: Free Press, 1977).

31. David Harvey, "The Geopolitics of Capitalism," in *Social Relations*

and Spatial Structures, editors Derek Gregory and John Urry (London: Macmillan, 1985), pp. 122–63.

32. Ibid., p. 150.

33. Jamie Peck, *Work-Place* (New York: Guilford Press, 1996); Doreen Massey, "New Directions in Space," in Gregory and Urry (1985), pp. 9–20.

13

Building Relational Wealth through Employment Practices

The Role of Organizational Social Capital

HARRY J. VAN BUREN III AND CARRIE R. LEANA

Over the past decade, changing employment practices—especially down-sizing, outsourcing, and the use of contingent workers—have been the sub-ject of considerable public discussion. The term "downsizing," for example, was coined in the 1970s to refer to the shrinking size of cars; not until 1982 was the term applied to humans who were losing their jobs.[1] When organ-izations began to fire large numbers of employees, questions about the hu-man costs associated with such events became part of the public discourse and attracted the attention of individuals, employers, and public policy makers.[2]

Less apparent, however, are the organizational costs of particular em-ployment practices and their effect on the collective actions that are the basis of existence for any organization. Many observers have noted that practices such as downsizing, outsourcing, and the use of contingent work-ers treat employees as costs rather than assets. When this philosophy toward the workforce is enacted through various employment practices, it places organizations at risk of losing the "organizational social capital" they have built up. Organizational social capital is a resource reflecting the character of social relations within the firm. It is realized through members' collective goal orientation and trust and, we will argue, is a major source of relational wealth for a firm.

Earlier in this volume, Leana and Rousseau defined relational wealth as the surplus value of an organization beyond its fixed assets and human capital. Organizational social capital helps explain why relational wealth exists and how it can be fostered or destroyed. In this chapter, we sum-marize the organizational social capital model, describe ways that organizational social capital can enhance relational wealth, discuss the concept in the context of contemporary employment practices, and conclude with an analysis of how employment practices can build or destroy relational wealth in organizations.

Models of Social Capital

Social capital has become a popular topic in recent years among academics and practitioners, in part because of its emphasis on voluntary relationships among people. For example, social capital can be used to explain low drop-out rates among students in Catholic schools and has also been put forth as the solution to a number of social ills.[3] A robust literature has grown on the general topic of social capital, in which more of this intangible asset based on the value of social relationships is generally seen as better than less.

Despite the growing literature on social capital, the term remains difficult to define. What constitutes social capital depends on the level of analysis: are we focusing on an individual, a region, or society as a whole? Many social capital theorists locate the concept at the individual level, describing it in terms of "brokerage opportunities" that an individual possesses based on his or her location within a social structure, particularly on the basis of numerous and strategically based weak ties with others.[4] Others view social capital as a societal or regional phenomenon and value such capital according to the societal norms that facilitate the formation of voluntary enterprises of mutual benefit.[5] Such enterprises may not exist in societies where individualism is rampant.[6]

There are essentially two social capital literatures. The first focuses on a private-goods model that defines social capital as an asset of an individual person or organization, which is based on one's position within a social network[7] or on accrued social assets such as prestige or educational credentials. In the private-goods model, the individual person or organization possessing social capital benefits directly from its existence and use [8] and so has an incentive to build and to maintain it. The individual who spans structural holes of disconnected others is able to act as a "broker," transferring information from one group to another.[9] When individuals maintain many fragile ties that do not overlap across social groups, they maximize their personal networks and enhance their ability to gather information.[10] The focus of this literature is on the ways in which individuals shape their social arrangements and strategies for private benefit.

The second group of social capital literature concerns a public-goods model, in which the social unit or collective benefits directly from the presence of social capital and individuals benefit only indirectly.[11] The norms and collectivist values that engender successful collective action are not "owned" by any one individual; rather, they function at the societal or regional level to make collective action possible. The concept of organizational social capital follows this approach, treating the organization as a society in which social relations inhere.

The Organizational Social Capital Model

In earlier work we developed a model of social capital that is sited at the organizational level and jointly owned by the collective and each of its members. Because of this joint ownership, a model that explains how relational wealth is created through organizational social capital must include the perspectives and interests of the organization as a whole as well as each of its members, incorporating public- and private-goods aspects of social capital. Rational individuals will probably not "invest" in actions that increase organizational social capital without some assurance that they will benefit, even if the benefits are gained indirectly and over the long run. As a byproduct of other organizational activities, we propose that organizational social capital is integral to the success of current and future action.

Organizational social capital has two primary components: associability and trust. *Associability* is defined as the willingness and ability of participants in an organization to enact organizational goals rather than focussing only on their individual goals.[12] If wealth is created relationally, then some means of assessing how individuals relate to each other in the service of some common good is needed. But mere sociability is not enough, because not all socialization leads to sustained collective action. Associability requires not only sociability but focused sociability held by members of a collective who strive to achieve a common objective. The members must not only agree on their goals but also be able to effect them through collective action. Only after a collective goal is agreed on can the work necessary to achieve it be divided and coordinated among members in ways that ensure its completion. Associable organizations therefore exhibit collectivist tendencies in that they are characterized by cooperation among members and an emphasis on group welfare.[13] In such organizations, individuals achieve their personal goals through participation in a collective that is doing work they believe to be desires and consistent with their values.

Collective goals provide a basis of evaluation for each member of the organization and also serve as a set of implicit, self-imposed norms that guide individuals to behave in ways that benefit the collective. However, individuals also want to benefit personally from their actions—in short, they don't want to be "suckers" whose actions on behalf of the collective benefit everyone but themselves.[14] For the organizational social capital model to work, individuals must believe that their participation in a collective will be personally rewarding. We take up this issue with a discussion of trust, the second component of organizational social capital.

Trust is a concept that has been much discussed in the management literature. In general, trust is seen as good and necessary for organizations in which people must work together; without it, the costs of monitoring others would be likely to outweigh any benefit derived from collective action. But trust also has a historical dimension: people are more likely to work with one another when they have already had successful interactions, and groups that have had a history of successful collaboration are likely to exhibit higher trust than those without such a history.

Trust has been discussed in a variety of ways, two of which are relevant to this discussion. The first of these is the differentiation between fragile and resilient trust.[15] Fragile trust is based on individual perceptions of immediate rewards; individuals will be willing to extend fragile trust if they think doing so is in their best interest. In order to exist, fragile trust requires that the results of a collaborative venture be perceived as both sufficient and predictable. Such agreements are often governed by formal, contractual means; because the relationships among the parties are based on the generation and distribution of benefits, considerable attention needs to be given to ensuring that each party lives up to its end of the bargain. In contrast, resilient trust is based on stronger and more numerous links between the organization and its members; it is based on one's experience with the other parties and/or beliefs about their moral integrity. Most important, while fragile trust does not survive occasional transactions in which benefits and costs are not equal, resilient trust can survive such transactions. The ways in which fragile and resilient trust are developed are instructive; fragile trust depends on developing a strategy of reciprocity while resilient trust is built through ongoing reciprocity norms.

Thus far, our discussion of trust has focused on dyadic trust—that is, trust between two parties who are known to each other in direct relationship. But another kind of trust is relevant to the study of organizations; this kind of trust rests on affiliation and reputation. It is possible to trust someone, of course, without that person being known to you. If you believe that an unknown party shares norms and behaviors with you—because, for example, you both belong to the same organization—then you might be more likely to extend trust than if such shared affiliation was absent. Putnam describes a "generalized" trust that relies not on knowledge of individuals but on norms and behaviors generally held by those within the social unit.[16] This trust characterizes organizations and other systems with strong social capital. Instead of relying on formal contractual means of ensuring compliance with a specific party, generalized trust allows for agreements to be made without face-to-face knowledge and the "safety net" provided by formal arrangements.

Granovetter has noted that ties need not be strong to be both resilient and good bases for collective action.[17] Weak ties can strengthen a system's social capital because they strengthen interaction across subunits, connecting the system itself. Organizations that rely too heavily on strong ties (such as those based on familial relationships) may actually find themselves limited in size and scope.[18] In order to facilitate successful collective action, organizations need to encourage both weak and strong ties that are resilient.

We have suggested that a firm needs both associability and trust in order to have some level of organizational social capital. Without trust, it is unlikely that associability will exist. Trust alone does not provide the basis for successful collective action but must be combined with agreed-on goals that focus individuals' activities toward fulfillment of a common objective.

How Does Organizational Social Capital Build Relational Wealth?

As noted in the introduction to this book, relational wealth can be defined as the difference between the market value of a firm and the combined value of its fixed assets and individual human capital. This surplus value is inherent in the social relationships within the organization. The relationship between organizational social capital and relational wealth is therefore twofold: first, in practical terms, part of the value denoted as relational wealth can be thought of as organizational social capital (enabling the latter to be at least partially quantified). Second, the existence of organizational social capital is necessary for the creation and sustenance of relational wealth.

We propose that organizational social capital can generate relational wealth by: (1) justifying individual commitment to the collective good; (2) facilitating flexible yet stable work organization; (3) serving as a mechanism for managing collective action; and (4) facilitating the development of intellectual capital in the firm.

First, the existence of organizational social capital justifies individual commitment to a collective good. Olson notes that in the absence of compulsion, individuals must have incentives to join in collective action.[19] Organizational social capital provides individuals with a rationale for deferring the immediate achievement of individual goals in favor of longer term group and organizational goals. If individuals are to act as "good agents"— that is, act in ways that benefit their principals directly and themselves indirectly, they must have some assurance that (1) their work will be consistent with their values and (2) the organization will treat them fairly.[20] When organizational social capital is lacking, individuals will find self-serving behavior to be more personally rewarding than behavior on behalf of others. To structure effective collective action, organizations can pair agents and principals who share the same values—and ensure that the former are treated fairly by the latter.

Second, organizational social capital provides a base from which work can be flexibly organized and carried out.[21] Much recent research has focused on the adoption and diffusion of high-performance work practices across a variety of industries and occupational groups.[22] Organizational social capital allows for flexible stability in work organization. There is ample empirical evidence for the proposition that high-performance employment practices (i.e., employee-involvement teams, job rotation, contingent compensation) are positively correlated with desired organizational outcomes such as quality and efficiency, and make employees more amenable to change. These, in turn, require cooperation and trust—the hallmarks of organizational social capital. By emphasizing collective identity and action and relying on generalized trust rather than formal monitoring and economic incentives, organizational social capital should facilitate the adoption of flexible high-performance work practices that can enhance a firm's relational wealth.

Third, organizational social capital can build relational wealth by reducing transaction costs.[23] Economists have long recognized that organizations can be efficient solutions to the hazards of engaging in economic transactions. Recent work on psychological contracts has also emphasized the potential benefits of relational rather than transactional arrangements between employers and employees. Both of these approaches suggest ways in which relations and norms can present organizations with opportunities for collective action. Organizational social capital can make collective action more efficient because it becomes a substitute for the formal contracts, incentives, and monitoring mechanisms that are necessary in systems with little or no social capital among organizational members. One rationale for building and sustaining organizational social capital is that doing so reduces transactions costs because it negates the need to negotiate and renegotiate shared understandings of purpose and practice.

Finally, social capital can contribute to an organization's stock of relational wealth by facilitating the development of human capital. Organizations with strong social capital can produce and combine knowledge and transfer information among members quickly and efficiently.[24] Nahapiet and Ghoshal (1993) note that social relations, shared languages and metaphors, and relational trust all facilitate exchanges among parties while also encouraging flexibility and risk-taking. In contrast, members of organizations with low social capital are unlikely to engage in much sharing; such organizations can be thought of as collections of individual contractors trying to pursue maximum direct advantage. The existence of organizational social capital makes it rational for individuals to contribute to collective goals and share information—a valuable asset, especially if competitors do not possess it—with other members.

Thus far we have described some aspects of our model of organizational social capital model and explained how organizational social capital can build relational wealth. Next we explain how employment practices contribute to the creation of organizational social capital and, in turn, relational wealth.

Organizational Social Capital and Employment Practices

An organization's employment practices shape the relationships among its members, as well as their ability to generate organizational social capital. Workplace relationships also require maintenance beyond the push to attain immediate goals, necessitating intentional efforts on the part of the firm to maintain organizational social capital. Practices such as downsizing and contingent employment—which are typically detrimental to relationships in the workplace and, in turn, to the creation of relational wealth—can be analyzed from the perspective of organizational social capital.[25] Workplace relationships, however, also require maintenance that is separate from immediate goal attainment—necessitating both slack resources and intentional efforts at maintaining organizational social capital.

As discussed earlier, stable yet flexible relationships among organizational members contribute to the creation and maintenance of organizational social capital. Thus, one way that organizations can enhance their social capital is by adopting employment practices that promote stability among members as well as flexibility in how employees are deployed within these stable relationships. This strategy suggests that practices like downsizing should be undertaken only rarely, if at all, and that employers should instead pursue a high-performance work model that entails investments in training, job security, collaborative work, and joint learning. Although organizational social capital is built over time, it can be destroyed quickly, requiring a long-term rather than short-term orientation in employment relationships. At the same time, compensation practices that reward only individual achievement may undermine organizational social capital.

A second way to build organizational social capital is through the use of organizational reciprocity norms that focus on a common organizational philosophy and the corresponding behaviors that exemplify and promote that philosophy. An overarching organizational philosophy supported by specific employment practices can substitute for stable employment relationships in building organizational social capital. When an organization selects and promotes individuals who share goals, it builds organizational social capital by sending signals to other members of the organization that reinforce organizational values.

Particular attention must be given to reciprocity as an organizational norm. It is well established that fairness in the employment relationship can have positive effects on organization-level outcomes.[26] We suggest that reciprocity is a norm with similar organizational benefits. We have already noted that organizations rely on the willingness of individuals to subordinate their short-term individual objectives to long-term organizational objectives. Organizations with an existing norm of reciprocity are better able to keep all of their members together in service to the collective good; conversely, organizations that do not have widespread adherence to this norm are likely to have members who put their interests ahead of the organization's. Thus, the norms can serve as a stabilizing factor, even if the individual players change. In this way, organizational social capital and relational wealth can be built through a strategy of stable flexibility.

Another way in which the strategy of stable flexibility can build organizational social capital is through bureaucracy and specified roles. The classic model of bureaucracy as described by Max Weber in his *The Theory of Social and Economic Organization* is that of an organization in which positions are depersonalized and specified, making qualified individuals interchangeable. Specialized roles and procedures for monitoring individual compliance with those roles can generate a system with high organizational social capital. There are some functions and organizations in which this model of employment relations works well. The military is one example, because the purpose of military training is to create individuals who work within a system that contains associatibility and trust yet is designed to make personnel interchangeable. Organizations within less predictable environments are likely to find a highly bureaucratic structure, bureaucratic structure to be less effective.

Relational Wealth and Employment Practices

Organizational social capital, we propose, helps create relational wealth. There are a number of different kinds of capital, including human, physical, and financial. Physical and financial capital are easily replicable, human capital somewhat less so. But organizational social capital cannot be created for its own sake or purchased on an open market. Rather, it is a byproduct of successful collective action that makes future collective action possible.

The concept of relational wealth provides a useful corrective to employment practices that emphasize hiring and promoting individuals with high levels of human capital while reducing the level and the wages of employees who are not considered critical to the organization (because of their relatively low human capital). The winner-take-all phenomenon reported by Frank and Cook poses problems for successful collective action (since organizations that reward a few stars are likely to engender mistrust and resentment in the remainder of their workforce).[28] Individuals with seemingly rare skills are needed by most organizations,[29] but collective action still requires the active cooperation of all of an organization's participants, not just those few whose skills are highly valued in the external labor market. In this way, the organizational social capital model helps organizations consider social processes, not just human capital, in the creation of relational wealth.

Matusik and Hill, for example, note that the use of contingent workers in certain situations (such as dynamic, turbulent environments) can reduce cost structures and increase flexibility while creating new knowledge.[30] Left unanswered, however, is the question of whether the skills of contingent employees will be focused in ways that benefit the entire organization.[31] This is not to say that human capital is unimportant to organizations but rather to suggest that knowledge of the organization, agreement with its goals, and perceptions of dyadic and generalized trust all allow individuals to use their human capital in ways that benefit the collective. As suggested in the introduction to this book, there must be a balance between flexibility and stability that serves the needs of employees and employers alike.

Finally, the subject of organizational justice as it influences perceptions of trustworthiness has not received the attention it deserves from organizational scholars. Many contemporary employment practices affect perceptions of trustworthiness. (We have alluded to the winner-take-all phenomenon as one source of mistrust within organizations. There is growing evidence that employment practices that emphasize individual achievement are inappropriate in settings where team production occurs.) Organizational action is a process in which individual contributions are socially embedded. When organizations lower their worker's paychecks or downsize their workforces, they often downsize their organizational social capital as well—with deleterious effects on the creation of relational wealth.

There is a complex relationship between relational wealth and human capital. In the best possible environment, human capital enhances relational wealth at the same time that relational wealth allows the full value of human capital to be realized. If relational wealth is measured as the surplus above the value of individual human capital and fixed assets, this implies that the ways that human capital is deployed by the organization and used by individuals for the benefit of the collective are themselves influenced socially. It is not enough to simply stockpile human capital without regard to the shared norms and values that make sustained collective action possible. Neither are most organizations likely to focus exclusively on attracting and compensating people with skills deemed to be rare without considering the organization-level effects on associability, trust, and shared norms and values. The full value of human capital cannot be realized in organizations with low levels of social capital.

Further research is needed on how organizational contexts affect the need for and formation of organizational social capital. The connections among human resources strategies, organizational social capital, and human capital also need further exploration. It is possible for organizational identification to occur quickly in environments where members do not know each other well or do not share particular norms and values.[32] In other environments, lengthy histories of working together are needed to accomplish collective action successfully. We note here, however, that organizational social capital—however created and sustained—is common to organizations that utilize human, physical, and financial capital in ways that create relational wealth.

We conclude our discussion of relational wealth, employment practices, and organizational social capital by proposing that the organizational social capital model provides a good explanation for why some organizations create relational wealth and others do not. Over the long run, employment practices that enhance an organization's stock of social capital will often lead to an enhanced ability to generate relational wealth. In contrast, employment models that focus on costs may be ineffective because they ignore the social nature of collective action. In short, an organization that has social capital provides a good forum for individual contributions to a collectively defined goal. In the next section we offer an explanation for why managers might choose not to adopt employment practices that enhance organizational social capital.

Avoiding the Commons Problem: The Fragility of Relational Wealth

Any discussion of contemporary employment practices would be incomplete without a consideration of ethical issues. While the United States does not have a tradition of job property rights, many view practices like downsizing and the use of contingent workforces as violations of implicit social and psychological contracts.[33] We have discussed how employment practices affect the creation of relational wealth by encouraging or discouraging organizational social capital. But if our analysis is correct, then another question must be asked: why do organizations act in ways that reduce organizational social capital, if doing so often harms the organization in the long run? To answer this question, we turn our attention to an analysis of the commons problem as it affects organizational decision making.

We have noted that employment practices that promote the creation and maintenance of organizational social capital can be linked to the creation of relational wealth. But organizational social capital, as already noted, is a public good. Like all public goods, it is therefore subject to the tragedy of the commons suggested by Hardin.[34] When individuals encounter a commonly held asset such as a grazing field, they have an incentive to withdraw as much value from it as possible, even if this will exhaust the asset entirely. The tragedy is that everyone with access to the commons has this incentive; if every person acts on it, the commonly held resource will ultimately be destroyed. What is rational for each individual leads to a result bad for the collective. The commons problem can only be solved by some sort of cooperative or coercive scheme.

Burton and Dunn apply this model to employment relations, proposing that labor collectively is a commons that can be exploited and used by employers. Employers have incentives to use resources such as employees and their skills but do not always have significant incentives to replenish the commons by providing training to improve the stock of labor skills.[35] In the same way we can view organizational social capital as a commons from which managers have incentives to withdraw resources without replenishment, to the long-run detriment of the organization. When organizations engage in downsizing to increase profitability (as opposed to downsizing that comes out of strategic realignment), outsource work or use contingency arrangements, or reduce compensation and benefits to reduce labor costs (which imposes the hidden cost of worker resentment on the organization), they are in effect transforming organizational social capital into short-term profit. In addition, because organizational social capital is jointly owned by the organization and its members, managers may have incentives to appropriate its value for their own use. Corporations that base the compensation of senior managers on short- or medium-term profitability may promote short-term rather than long-term thinking.

Jackall notes that the tension between short-term profitability and longer term competitive advantage is often resolved in favor of the former. In one vignette, he describes how a manufacturing organization "milked" a plant by depriving it of needed resources for physical plant maintenance.[36] As one manager said,

> I don't think there's anything wrong with milking a plant. As long as you know that you're milking it. As long as you know you're going to run it down for three or four years and then sell it to some unsuspecting fool. And you show him the papers on the plant and you don't tell him what money you haven't put back into the operation.

Just as plants can be milked by deferring maintenance, so can organizations be milked by reducing the costs associated with maintaining strong social capital.

When management compensation is based on short-term performance, incentives to appropriate the true source of the organization's value for themselves—the organizational social capital that makes relational wealth possible—are strong.

We have noted in this chapter that relational wealth is created by combining organizational social capital with human, physical, and financial capital. The latter forms of capital are all fungible to varying degrees and can generally be procured in the market. But organizational social capital cannot be sought out for its own sake or purchased on the external market; rather, it is built up over time by individuals working together successfully. Organizational social capital, like trust, takes a long time to create but can be destroyed quickly. The organizational social capital model suggests the need for a longer term view of employment policies and practices. In the short run, organizations can "cash in" some of their social capital stock by reducing workforces and cutting compensation. But in the long run, organizations are generally better off by nurturing and building organizational social capital, an asset owned by everyone in the organization.

But how can the organization commons be preserved—that is, how can organizational social capital be preserved? Certainly there is a need for enlightened managers who understand the tension between the short and the long run and act to preserve and build social capital to ensure that their organizations continue to create relational wealth. Beyond this recommendation, the general doctrine of employment-at-will can be modified to put public policy at the service of employment practices that engender stable relationships in which trust is present. In the long run, more research into the effects of employment practices is needed to demonstrate how they can improve both organizations and their members.

Conclusion

While cost-effectiveness is certainly important, the primary rationale for using one employment practice as opposed to another should be its effect on an organization's ability to accomplish its mission. The concept of relational wealth helps focus the debate about which kinds of employment practices enhance an organization's ability to engage in collective action. In part, employment practices matter because they affect an organization's stock of social capital, which is necessary for the creation of relational wealth.

Notes

1. L. Uchitelle and N. R. Kleinfield, "The Price of Jobs Lost," in *The Downsizing of America* (New York: Times Books, 1996), pp. 3–36.

2. C. Leana and D. Feldman, *Coping with Job Loss: How Individuals, Organizations and Communities Respond to Layoffs* (New York: Lexington Books, 1992).

3. J. Coleman, "Social Capital in the Creation of Human Capital," *American Journal of Sociology* 94 (1988): s95–s120.

4. M. Granovetter, "The Strength of Weak Ties," *American Journal of Sociology* 78 (1973): 1360–80.

5. F. Fukuyama, *Trust: The Social Virtues and the Creation of Prosperity* (New York: Free Press, 1995).

6. E. Banfield, *The Moral Basis of a Backward Society* (New York: Free Press, 1958).

7. R. S. Burt, *Structural Holes* (Cambridge: Harvard University Press, 1992a); R. S. Burt, "The Social Network of Competition," in *Networks and Organizations: Structure, Form, and Action*, edited by N. Nohria and R. Eccles (Boston: Harvard Business School Press, 1992b), pp. 57–91; R. S. Burt, "The Contingent Value of Social Capital," *Administrative Science Quarterly* 42 (1997): 339–65.

8. M. Belliveau, C. O'Reilly, and J. Wade, "Social Capital at the Top: Effects of Social Similarity and Status on CEO Compensation," *Academy of Management Journal* 39, 6 (1996): 1568–93.

9. Burt (1992a).

10. Granovetter (1973).

11. S. Asefa and W. Huang, *Human Capital and Economic Development* (Kalamazoo, Mich.: Upjohn Institute, 1994); R. Putnam, *Making Democracy Work: Civic Traditions in Modern Italy* (Princeton: Princeton University Press, 1993b); F. Fukuyama (1995).

12. C. R. Leana and H. J. Van Buren III, "Organizational Social Capital and Employment Practices," working paper no. 775, University of Pittsburgh, 1998.

13. C. Early, "Social Loafing and Collectivism: A Comparison of the United States and the People's Republic of China,"*Administrative Science Quarterly* 34 (1989): 565–81.

14. N. L. Kerr, "Motivation Losses in Small Groups: A Social Dilemma Analysis," *Journal of Personality and Social Psychology* 45 (1993): 819–28.

15. P. Ring, "Fragile and Resilient Trust and Their Roles in Economic Change," *Business & Society* 35: (1996) 148–175; P. Ring and A. Van de Ven, "Structuring Cooperative Relationships between Organizations," *Strategic Management Journal* 13 (1992): 483–98.

16. Putnam (1993b).

17. M. Granovetter, "Economic Action and Social Structure: The Problem of Embeddedness." *American Journal of Sociology* 91 (1985): 481–510; M. Granovetter, *Getting a Job: A Study of Contacts and Careers* (Chicago: University of Chicago Press, 1985); J. Coleman, "Social Capital in the Creation of Human Capital," *American Journal of Sociology* 94 (1988): s95-s120; R. Putnam, *Making Democracy Work: Civic Traditions in Modern Italy* (Princeton: Princeton University Press, 1993).

18. E. Banfield, The Moral Basis of a Backward Society (New York: Free Press, 1958); F. Fukuyama, *Trust: The Social Virtues and the Creation of Prosperity* (New York: Free Press, 1995).

19. M. Olson, *The Logic of Collective Action: Public Goods and the Theory of Groups* (Cambridge, MA: Harvard University Press, 1965).

20. K. Eisenhardt, "Agency Theory: An Assessment and Review," *Academy of Management Review* 14 (1989): 57–74; B. M. Mitnick, "The Theory of Agency and Organizational Analysis," in *Ethics and Agency Theory*, edited by N. Bowie and R. Freeman (New York: Oxford University Press, 1992), pp. 75–96.

21. Ichniowski et al., 1996.

22. C. Ichniowski and K. Shaw, "Old Dogs and New Tricks: Determinants of the Adoption of Productivity-enhancing Work Practices," in *Brookings Papers on Economic Activity*, edited by M. Baily, P. Reiss, and C. Winston (Washington, D.C.: Brookings, 1995), pp. 1–65; M. Scully and G. Preuss, "Two Faces of Trust: The Role of Calculative and Relational Trust in Work Transformation," working paper no. 3923–96, Massachusetts Institute of Technology, 1996.

23. R. Coase, "The Nature of the Firm," *Economica*, n. s. (1937): 386–405; O. Williamson, *Markets and Hierarchies* (Cambridge, Mass.: Free Press, 1975).

24. J. Nahapiet and S. Ghoshal, "Social Capital, Intellectual Capital, and the Organizational Advantage," *Academy of Management Review* 23 (1998): 242–66.

25. C. R. Leana, Downsizing's Downside. *The Chicago Tribune Magazine* (April 14, 1996): 14–16, 18.

26. R. Folger and R. Cropanzano, *Organizational Justice and Human Resource Management* (Thousand Oaks, Calif.: Sage, 1998).

27. M. Weber, *The Theory of Social and Economic Organization* (New York: Oxford University Press, 1947).

28. R. Frank and P. Cook, *The Winner-Take-All Society* (New York: Free Press, 1995).

29. D. C. Bok, *The Cost of Talent* (New York: Free Press, 1995).

30. S. F. Matusik and C. W. L. Hill, "The Utilization of Contingent Work: Knowledge Creation, and Competitive Advantage," *Academy of Management Review* 23 (1998): 680–97.

31. S. D. Nollen and H. Axel, "Benefits and Costs to Employers," in *Contingent Work: American Employment Relations in Transition*, editors K. Barker and K. Christensen (Ithaca, N.Y.: ILR Press, 1998), pp. 126–43.

32. D. M. Rousseau, "Why Workers Still Identify with Organizations," *Journal of Organizational Behavior* 19 (1998): 217–33.

33. H. J. Van Buren III, "Layoff Lingo: Corporations Sugarcoat Mass Firings," *Business and Society Review* 96 (1996): 51–2.

34. G. Hardin, "The Tragedy of the Commons," *Science* 162 (1968): 1243–8.

35. B. K. Burton and C. P. Dunn, "Collaborative Control and the Commons: Safeguarding Employee Rights," *Business Ethics Quarterly* 6 (1996): 277–88.

36. R. Jackall, *Moral Mazes: The World of Corporate Managers* (New York: Oxford University Press, 1988).

14

Governance of the Employment Relationship

From Rhetoric to Public Policy

JEFFREY PFEFFER

Conventional American-style wisdom about the government intervening in employment relationships asserts that the best policy is no intervention at all. One frequently hears the argument that the fall of Communism and the difficulties of many socialist economies show the folly of central intervention in markets, including labor markets. The recent economic problems of Japan, Indonesia, Thailand, Korea, and other so-called crony capitalist economies are taken as additional evidence that settles the debate about whether government intervention in the economy is ill-advised. *The Economist*, among other observers, has declared the triumph of essentially unfettered market capitalism over a "stakeholder" model which would consider interests other than those of owners, such as employees.[1] The overarching claim is that markets work best when they are unencumbered by government intervention. Government cannot be trusted to promote economic efficiency, and government intervention in labor markets is inevitably beset with parochial and partisan politics that create outcomes that are unpredictable and of dubious value:

> Institutional wage-setting systems, social security provisions, rigid working-time regimes, and legal layoff and dismissal restraints imposed in many European countries came to be widely regarded as essential in causing . . . employment inertia in adjusting to the more volatile economic environment of the later 1970s and 1980s.[2]

Certainly in the United States, this positive view of virtually unregulated labor markets has carried the day—regardless of its empirical or philosophical merits. As Wever has noted, "Americans . . . believe that political intervention in markets . . . should be extremely limited and should not involve active labor or industrial policies."[3] The Dunlop Commission's attempts to reform U.S. labor laws, undertaken to reflect the new realities of collective bargaining in contrast to its decades-old legal framework, foundered on opposition from both business and labor.[4] Attempts to reform the tort-based wrongful discharge system, which some consider to be enormously inefficient,[5] as well as a failure in providing adequate or cost-efficient redress to those fired,[6] have similarly failed in virtually every state where such reforms have even been proposed.

The United States has moved to further deregulate, both by law and through diminished resources for enforcement, a labor market that was already one of the most market-based in the world. For example, a smaller proportion of the economy's resources is devoted to ensuring workplace safety, administering wage and hour regulations, and enforcing the antidiscrimination laws than was the case in past decades.[7] At the same time, the argument for the advantage of unfettered labor markets and the superiority of the U.S. model appears to be persuading governments around the world. Various other countries, beginning with the United Kingdom in the early 1980s under Margaret Thatcher and spreading elsewhere to include Australia, New Zealand, Canada, and parts of continental Europe, are altering their labor policy regimes to more closely resemble the U.S. model.[8]

Nonetheless, as we will show, research on the effects of government intervention in labor markets is much more equivocal than the prevailing rhetoric would suggest. Moreover, considerations other than economic efficiency require at least some form of public policy intervention. Finally, successful public policies have been designed to remedy problems that emerge in strictly market-based employment relations. These three sets of findings taken together suggest the benefits of a much more proactive role for public policy in employment than we currently see in the United States.

Some Want It Both Ways

Many interest groups, particularly the U.S. business community, have inconsistent preferences and views regarding government involvement in production and labor markets. At the same time that business leaders espouse a free-market ideology, manufacturers in industries ranging from automobiles to apparel have sought and have frequently received protection from foreign imports. Companies fight vigorously against minimum wage increases, Occupational Safety and Health Administration efforts to develop and enforce workplace safety regulations, and budget increases for the Equal Employment Opportunity Commission that could help reduce the agency's substantial case backlog. Yet at the same time these companies look to the government to solve labor market problems that are largely of their own making. Two examples of this come quickly to mind.

In the collective bargaining domain, companies have opposed labor law changes that might enhance employees' ability to form unions. Groups such as the National Labor Policy Association have stopped efforts to increase the penalties for engaging in unfair labor practices or to restrict firms' ability to hire replacement workers during labor disputes. The apparent position is that strikes and union relations are better conducted free of government interference. Note, however, that when there are strikes, firms are quick to ask for government support. For instance, during the 1983 copper miners' strike against Phelps Dodge, the state of Arizona provided highway patrol and National Guard protection for replacement workers. The state also arrested numerous striking miners and their spouses, although none of those arrested was ever successfully prosecuted.[9] More than a decade later, when American Airlines pilots went on strike just before Thanksgiving 1996, the company asked President Clinton to force the pilots back to work, citing the possible disruption of airline service as a national emergency. Although the United Parcel Service sought intervention when it faced a strike about a year later, the government in this case declined to intervene. It is clear that firms involved in labor disputes do want government at all levels to intervene on the companies' side in their interactions with collective bargaining representatives, rather allowing the market to work itself out.

A similar ambivalence about the role of governmental intervention in the labor market is evident in the Silicon Valley. This home of entrepreneurship and free-market capitalism generally eschews government intervention and particularly fights regulation of the labor market. High-technology companies mostly pursue nonunion strategies and are known for using "contract" employees who are actually regular employees, in violation of Internal Revenue Service regulations as well as state unemployment agency rules. The companies also commonly use temporary help and resist efforts to regulate the use of such help, including the amount that can be used and the benefits such workers must receive. High-technology companies have imported foreign workers and have pushed for expansion of visas that permit such workers to immigrate, at times running afoul of U.S. immigration laws. The companies consistently argue for more open labor markets and fewer restrictions on immigration, in general advocating governmental nonintervention in the employment relationship.

Nonetheless, this position of governmental nonintervention is not consistently held throughout the high-technology sector. In early 1998, such employers claimed to be experiencing a skills shortage. However, instead of Silicon Valley employers training their own workers, most companies looked to publicly funded courses offered in local schools and community colleges to prepare and educate their labor force. Employers wanted these schools to be more attuned to the demands of particular firms for workers with certain skills. This situation suggests that firms want public policy–makers to ensure a supply of educated talent, just as long as the government doesn't regulate the employment conditions of those workers.

We would expect interest groups to advocate public policies that favor their interests, and it is hardly surprising that the most powerful interest groups—most often business—prevail in these political contests. It does seem more than a little contradictory, however, for interest groups to argue against government intervention in certain matters but actively seek it when the groups' purposes would be served, such as the case of the airline pilot strikes described earlier. The obvious inconsistency in this position makes it hard to sympathize with the pleas for unfettered labor markets that are put forth by some media, employers, and their associations.

The Effects of Government Intervention

The neoclassical economic position regarding government intervention is straightforward: virtually all forms of government regulation raise labor costs, including establishing minimum wages, mandating overtime pay for people who work more than a certain number of hours, imposing safety and health regulations, and making it more difficult and costly to fire people or lay people off. All things being equal, then, firms will use less of anything that costs them more, so higher labor costs should cause them to substitute capital for labor and reduce their employment base. Thus, the basic assumption is that government intervention results in higher unemployment, lower levels of total employment, and a situation in which those who work benefit at the expense of those who don't have jobs at all, through higher wages and better working conditions.

Before considering some evidence on these issues, a few preliminary observations are in order. First, as Wilensky has shown, there is virtually no correlation between an economy's rate of job creation and unemployment rate. He found that many of the economies that created the most jobs had relatively high rates of unemployment and also noted relatively small and sometimes negative relationships among measures of economic performance, such as the rates of inflation, economic growth, and unemployment. He has further shown that the rate of job creation depends mostly on migration and the divorce rate, two factors that tend to bring more people into the labor force but are not typically considered to be part of government labor-market policy.[10] Wilensky's findings suggest there may be more complex relationships among various indicators of employment and, for that matter, among employment and other economic variables, as well as a limited effect of government policies in fostering or retarding growth in employment.

Second is the issue of whether creating lots of low-paying jobs that are unsafe and unstable is desirable from a social welfare perspective. Hamermesh noted that a reduction in employment need not be harmful to overall social goals. Rather, "it may be desirable to reduce variations in employment among those fewer workers who have jobs."[11] As indicated by the ongoing debate about income inequality and wage levels in the United States, the question is not just whether or not people have jobs but what kinds of jobs they have. In that sense, evaluating public policies solely on the basis of whether or not they have detrimental effects on either unemployment or job creation is almost certainly too narrow a set of criteria to use.

Third, evaluating the effects of labor market interventions on various labor market outcomes is a difficult activity characterized by incredibly sloppy use of language. One particularly troublesome example is the use of the terms "labor rates" and "labor costs." Labor rates—the hourly wage people earn—are not the same as overall labor costs, which reflect the rate of pay as well as the productivity of workers. To say that the average German worker makes about thirty dollars per hour says little about German labor costs. Although it isn't clear from recent discussions in the media, Germany, with its apprenticeship system and high level of skills and training, has very productive workers and is one of the major exporting nations. The same can be said of Japan, another country with comparatively high labor rates. After Ford Motor Company raised its wage on January 1, 1914, from $0.80 to $5.00 per day, an increase of more than 600 percent, the firm's profits doubled that year.[12] Turnover decreased dramatically at the higher wage rate, as did the *costs* of turnover, which included disruptions in production and quality problems that came from having inexperienced workers on the assembly line. Without considering productivity and quality differences, the rate of pay tells us little about a country's or a company's competitiveness.

Finally, labor costs are not the only factor affecting the operation of labor markets. Rates of unemployment, job creation, and economic growth depend on myriad factors, including national fiscal and monetary policies as well as the technological, social, and educational infrastructure of a country's economy. To say that western Europe has high unemployment because of some government policy toward employment, without considering monetary policy and other macroeconomic factors, may overlook the whole picture.

Even with these provisos, research on the effects of public policy intervention on the labor market shows surprisingly small consequences that are often positive, rather than negative. Hamermesh investigated the effect of the 50 percent premium for overtime work mandated by the 1938 Fair Labor Standards Act in the United States and concluded that there is only a negligible effect of this overtime policy on total employment using the best guesses about labor elasticities of supply and demand.[13] His data also suggest that the American unemployment insurance system, in which unemployment insurance rates reflect firms' layoff practices, protects employment. This employment protection effect is pronounced, particularly when compared to a system with the same rules, eligibility, and benefit levels but financed from general rather than firm-specific payroll taxes.

Many studies of the effects that labor-market regimes have on employment focus on the effects of various employment protection policies and examine the relationship between changes in the level of economic output (gross domestic product) and employment levels. The assumption is that a lower elasticity of employment in response to changes in output reflects differences in employment protection regimes across the various countries. Empirically, Abraham and Houseman found less adjustment of employment levels to changes in economic output in Japan compared to the United States, and a subsequent study also observed more employment stability in Germany as well.[14] Hart reviewed a number of studies demonstrating different responses across countries and across industries in response to more or less permanent shifts in product demand.[15] Hamermesh critiqued some of the assumptions of these studies, noting that the studies provide empirical facts without giving convincing interpretations of these facts.[16] The adjustment of employment to changes in economic demand could occur for reasons other than differences in employment protection policies. Moreover, the studies do not permit researchers to ascertain which employment protection policy, of the many typically in place in any given country, has the most effect.

Although the studies don't show what policies affect employment, their findings do help us determine which policies do not. Countries vary little in their responses to shifts in aggregate demand, raising "doubts about whether legal employment security regulations account for a significant share of cross-country variations in overall employment and job creation performance."[17] In fact, the available evidence strongly suggests that law and policy follow, rather than lead or direct, how employers tend to respond. Summarizing a great deal of empirical evidence, Buechtemann commented:

> Where legislators have imposed legal rules and procedures . . . these were frequently congruent with rather than in opposition to firms' own work force adjustment preferences, as manifested in the prevalence of similar endogenously evolved practices, rules, and procedures before the introduction or tightening of employment security laws.[18]

Differences in labor-market behavior between the United States and Europe are frequently less pronounced than is imagined and belie the assumption that European employment protection policies profoundly affect employers. There is, for example, very little difference in employee dismissal rates between the United States and major European countries.[19] Bertola ranked countries in terms of their restrictiveness and severity of employment security regimes and correlated those rankings with various indicators of labor-market performance. He generally observed very low correlations, which caused him to conclude that "by themselves, job security provisions . . . neither bias the firm's labor demand towards lower average employment at given wages, nor bias wage determination towards higher wages and lower employment."[20] Other studies using aggregate data have generally reached the same conclusion: employment security policies do not have strong negative effects on employment.[21]

In addition to analyses of the data on the effects of public policy, the reactions of management serve as another indicator of whether public intervention in the employment relationship is having adverse effects. If it was, one would expect to see managers advocating the repeal of various public laws. However, this is not what one observes in Germany, which has some of the most restrictive regulations governing the employment relationship. Wever's study of the German industrial relations system found that German employers preferred their system of works councils and codetermination. German employers did not take the opportunity, when a relatively conservative Social Democratic party controlled the government, to press for reforms to make German labor law more like that of the United States.[22] Throughout western Europe as well as in Singapore and other far eastern countries, employers accept the fact that labor is not just another commodity, legitimating state intervention in the labor market. Even in the United States, one observes relatively little concerted effort on the part of employers to eliminate minimum wage laws, occupational safety and health regulations, child labor regulations, or even the more recently passed law requiring sixty-day notice of plant closing or significant layoffs. This employer tacit acceptance—or at least the absence of concerted resistance to government intervention—indicates that these interventions do not have the harmful effects on firm competitiveness that is often asserted.

Other Rationales for Public Policy

We have shown that there is little empirical evidence that various forms of government labor-market interventions have deleterious effects on economic efficiency, if they have any effect at all. Even if there were effects on various measures of economic efficiency at either the societal or firm level, there are other rationales besides efficiency that warrant public policy intervention, including jobs and job creation, building human capital through training, helping to ensure macroeconomic stability by encouraging stable employment and addressing concerns over income inequality, social justice, and fundamental human rights. This is not an exhaustive list, but it illustrates the point.

Two examples of public policy interventions that realize their goals are found in Singapore and Germany. Although Singapore is noted for its free-market economy, its government plays an active role in facilitating the creation of jobs and the building of the nation's human capital.[23] Singapore is one of many industrialized countries that has a training levy, a tax on payrolls that is partially returned to firms to compensate them for training activities. Obviously, if firms do not invest as much in training as they pay toward the levy, they lose the money. Singapore is also a country that has encouraged a tripartite union, company, and government approach to industrial development. The government of Singapore has encouraged education and skill-building to move the economy from one based solely on low labor costs to one founded on industries that have a higher value-added component and rely on knowledge and skill. The result of these policies is truly remarkable. In 1960, Singapore was a struggling Third World economy with a per capita income of $1,300; by 1995, the country had a per capita income of $25,000.[24] An analysis of the development of Singapore's strong presence in the semiconductor industry concluded:

> The services provided . . . [including] good training services and human resource support, add up to a favorable environment for conducting high technology business. This environment is the result of highly focused policy implementation . . . rather than the outcome of the operation of "market forces."[25]

Germany is a country with mandated codetermination, a strong union movement, and active employment protection policies. When the automobile company Volkswagen was faced with excess capacity, it undertook a number of actions to avoid laying off more people than was necessary. It instituted a shorter work week, a program of limited-duration unemployment for younger workers (during which they received training), and a flexible work program entailing a gradual increase and then decrease in working hours over an individual's life.[26] The company, which operated in a public policy environment that encouraged responsible behavior, viewed its actions as being "the right thing to do"—to maintain employment and the economic benefits, such as wages and taxes, that accrue from employment:

> Throughout the world, mass unemployment has become one of the most pressing problems of modern times. The automotive industry has been hit by a crisis of restructuring and excess capacity. It would have been easy enough . . . to follow the example of many other companies and simply shed jobs. But, as "Every Job Has a Face," the company . . . decided . . . to break out of the vicious circle of mass unemployment. It is all very well for market trends, technological progress, or productivity to define personnel requirements—but these factors alone should not be allowed to dictate the nature of the solution to the problem.[27]

Understanding the role of public policy in the employment relationship requires us to address the fundamental purpose of the business corporation. Public policy is either sound or counterproductive to the extent that it helps companies achieve their purposes, so purpose and goals are inevitably intertwined with discussions of what firms are supposed to do and how government intervention helps or hinders them. In the United States, the almost unquestioned assumption is that firms should simply maximize shareholder value; however, there are a number of challenges to that position. Aoki used game theory models of decision making to show that firms that take the interests of their employees seriously, in addition to those of their shareholders, are likely to make better decisions even from an efficiency point of view.[28] Arguing less from economics and more from philosophy, Dennis Bakke, the CEO of AES Corporation, writes that a corporation "is 'a person' with similar rights and responsibilities as other persons in society. I would argue that high on the list of responsibilities of a person—or citizen—is to act in a way to meet his or her own needs and the needs of fellow citizens."[29] Although Bakke notes that shareholders should be important because they provide capital, he also argues that companies could not exist without customers, employees, banks, and suppliers of other resources. In a world where intellectual capital and knowledge are increasingly important factors of production and are in many respects more scarce than financial capital, the primacy of financial capital may not make sense. After all, those who supply the scarcest and most critical resources typically exert the most control over organizations.[30]

Public policy governing employment relations must also address fundamental human rights and moral values. Although not widely known, particularly in North America, the United Nations (UN) has developed a Universal Declaration of Human Rights that was later elaborated in its covenants on political and civil rights and on economic, social, and cultural rights. These policy statements and pronouncements were developed in an attempt to try and prevent a recurrence of the terrible events of the 1940s and to promote freedom and well-being worldwide. The code condemns racism, sexism, discrimination, the exploitation of child labor, slavery, and forced labor, and affirms that freedom of association is a fundamental human right.[31] The UN declaration was ratified 273–0, with forty three abstentions, and implemented in covenants of the International Labor Organization, the Organization for Economic Cooperation and Development, and the World Trade Organization, among others. The declaration means that all people have fundamental rights and freedoms that are their birthrights. "All governments, institutions, and individuals have a moral responsibility to respect and honor human rights," even in the workplace.[32] Some would maintain that it is not enough to leave things to the market or to chance—rather, governments are morally obligated to intervene in the labor market to protect these fundamental human rights. This includes enforcing anti-discrimination laws, child labor laws, and other laws that protect people's rights of association and freedom. As moral obligations, these rights supersede considerations of economic efficiency and growth.

Social welfare and morality provide rationales for government intervention in labor-market arrangements. Although out of fashion in a world in which laissez-faire capitalism reigns supreme, it is important to recognize the variations in the degree of government intervention in other economically developed countries, as well as the connection between public policy and human rights and morality.

Can Public Policy Work?

Even if we admit that markets may fail to supply training and employment security[33] as a result of collective action problems, and even if we recognize the role of public policy in enhancing employment outcomes, we still must ask whether there is evidence that public policy can be effective. The answer is obviously yes. The transformation of Singapore's economy is at least partly the result of government policies encouraging training, cooperation with unions, and implementation of more effective employment practices.[34] Kuruvilla's analysis demonstrates the tremendous difference in the development trajectories of the Philippines and Singapore. In 1960, the Philippines was richer than Singapore and also had the advantage of a closer relationship with the United States. Over the ensuing three decades since, Singapore has far surpassed the Philippines on every indicator of economic progress and labor-market performance. Although there a number of explanations for this difference, one important account turns on Singapore's activist intervention in the labor market in ways that built human capital and permitted the development of value-added, high-technology industry.

Numerous comparisons of the U.S. system with both the German and Japanese economies conclude that the U.S. model stimulates innovation in individual firms but does not do as well at diffusing these innovations in a way that benefits the broader society. As Wever wrote,

> The Japanese and German political economies make it easy for labor and management to disseminate improvements in work systems, methods of production organization, labor–management relations, and so on throughout companies, industries, and the economy. In both countries, these improvements hinge on extensive and intensive education and training of the workforce as well as highly effective mechanisms for helping those who have finished school to make the transition to the private sector workforce.[35]

Buechtemann showed that public policy often merely reflects what many progressive employers are already doing. If that is the case, does the codification of such practices actually produce any gains? He argues that it does, for a number of reasons.

> First . . . it provides a supporting structure and incentive for sunk investments and the overall efficiency gains inherent therein. Second, "by adopting the rule that the majority of the labor-market bargainers would reach if they bargained over the issue, [it] will save those . . . bargainers the cost of crafting a tailor-made rule" (Leslie, 1989: 230). Third, by legally codifying implicit or explicit terms . . . it largely avoids the efficiency losses incurred from a redefinition and reassignment of existing property rights. Fourth, by merely universalizing what the majority of firms practice . . . it produces little additional costs. Fifth, by drawing immediately on the efficient practices in the

advanced sectors of the economy, it avoids the problems and risks of regulatory failure. The legal codification of common practices . . . may result in substantial gains in overall socioeconomic welfare.[36]

Thus far, we have relied on comparisons of public policy interventions across countries. Is there evidence that such interventions can be useful in the United States? Once again, the answer is yes. For example, the mayor of Louisville, Kentucky, gathered representatives from the labor unions, local businesses, and government to overcome a labor relations climate that had earned the city a reputation as "Strike City" and resulted in the loss of thirty-five thousand to forty thousand jobs in the early 1980s.[37] The tripartite group successfully developed joint training requirements and helped companies such as Phillip Morris and Louisville Gas and Electric forge less adversarial relations with their unions. In another example, the Wisconsin Regional Training Partnership began in 1992 to cope with the fact that "advanced skills and mutual trust are collective goods which individual firms . . . are unwilling or unable to supply in adequate quantities."[38] The organization was based on a mutual compact.

Firms support the regional economy by investing in worker training, paying good wages and reorganizing production so as to take advantage of greater workforce capabilities; workers and unions develop the skills and accept the responsibility and authority which high performance production systems demand of them; and public agencies support the . . . bargain by coordinating training and manufacturing extension efforts and by assisting in the creation of a regional infrastructure to broaden and institutionalize the effort.[39]

A preliminary evaluation of this effort showed an increase in training expenditures as well as increased use of flexible manufacturing techniques and high-performance management practices. These and other, similar examples make the case that even in the United States, public policy can contribute to the evolution of the employment relation in ways that benefit all participants in the labor market.

Conclusion

Discussions of the role that public policy should play in building systems of more effective and more humane management practices have contained more rhetoric and emotion than fact and analysis. The presumption has been that labor markets work efficiently without policy interference, public policy invariably fails, and government intervention is more likely to make things worse than better. There is actually little evidence consistent with these ideological beliefs. Numerous quantitative studies suggest that many managers do not fear—and may even welcome—government assistance in setting the conditions of employment. Although there is pervasive evidence of market failures in the provision of training and employment security, there are also examples of public policy interventions that help to build human capital and establish high-performance work arrangements. The facts are inconsistent with the dominant rhetoric and assumptions about how things are, can be, and should be.

In the end, beyond the concerns over economic efficiency, we face an important fact: people spend a good portion of their lives at work. They depend on employment for income, retirement resources, health care, and other benefits. People form friendships at work; their jobs are important for their social identities; and their work experiences affect their mental and physical well-being. Acknowledging these well-accepted facts implies that there needs to be active consideration and debate about how public policy should seek to affect employment relations and how it can best accomplish these goals. The presumption of nonintervention is fiction; the government is already involved. Considerations of fundamental human rights and well-being dictate that governments should work for the common good. In doing so, public policy can help build and use social capital to the benefit of companies and the people who work for them.

Notes

1. "Stakeholder Capitalism," *Economist* February 10, 1996, pp. 23–5.

2. Christoph F. Buechtemann. "Employment Security and Labor Markets," editor's introduction to *Employment Security and Labor Market Behavior Interdisciplinary Approaches and International Evidence* (Ithaca, N.Y.: ILR Press, 1993), pp. 3–66.

3. Kirsten S. Wever, *Negotiating Competitiveness* (Boston: Harvard Business School Press, 1995). See also Susan Tolchin and Martin Tolchin, *Dismantling America: The Rush to Deregulate* (Boston: Houghton Mifflin, 1983).

4. John T. Dunlop et al., *Report and Recommendations of the Commission on the Future of Worker-Management Relations*, U.S. Department of Labor, Washington, D.C.: 1994.

5. James N. Dertouzos and Lynne A. Karoly, *Labor-Market Responses to Employer Liability* (Santa Monica, Calif.: Institute of Civil Justice, 1992).

6. James N. Dertouzos, Elaine Holland, and Patricia Ebener, *The Legal and Economic Consequences of Wrongful Termination* (Santa Monica, Calif.: RAND, 1988).

7. U.S. Department of Labor, *Report and Recommendations: Commission on the Future of Worker-Management Relations*, Washington, D.C., 1994.

8. Jeffrey Pfeffer, *The Human Equation: Building Profits by Putting People First* (Boston: Harvard Business School Press, 1998).

9. Barbara Kingsolver, *Holding the Line* (Ithaca, N.Y.: ILR Press, 1989).

10. Harold L. Wilensky, "The Great American Job Creation Machine in Comparative Perspective," *Industrial Relations* 31 (1992): 473–88.

11. Daniel S. Hamermesh, "Employment Protection: Theoretical Implications and Some U.S. Evidence," in Buechtemann (1993), pp. 126–47.

12. Peter F. Drucker, "Knowledge–Worker Productivity: The Biggest Challenge," *California Management Review* 41 (winter 1999): 79–94.

13. Hammermesh (1993).

14. Katherine G. Abraham and Susan N. Houseman, "Job Security and Work Force Adjustment: How Different Are U.S. and Japanese Practices?" *Journal of the Japanese and International Economies* 3 (1989a): 500–21; Katherine G. Abraham and Susan N. Houseman, "Employment Security and Labor Adjustment: A U.S.–German Comparison," unpublished manuscript, University of Maryland, 1989b.

15. R. Hart, *Working Time and Employment* (Boston: Allen and Unwin, 1987).

16. Daniel S. Hamermesh, "Labor Demand and the Structure of Adjustment Costs," *American Economic Review* 79 (1989): 674–89.

17. Buechtemann (1993), p. 16.

18. Ibid., p. 44.

19. Ibid., p. 21.

20. B. Bertola, "Job Security, Employment, and Wages," *European Economic Review* 34 (1990): 851–86.

21. S. M. Burgess, "Employment Adjustment in U.K. Manufacturing," *Economic Journal* 98 (1988): 81–103; S. M. Burgess and S. Nickell, "Labour Turnover in U.K. Manufacturing," *Economica* 57 (1990): 295–317; S. J. Nickell, "The Determinants of Equilibrium Unemployment in Britain," *Economic Journal* 92 (1982); 555–75.

22. Wever (1995).

23. Sarosh Kuruvilla, "Linkages between Industrialization Strategies and Industrial Relations/Human Resource Policies: Singapore, Malaysia, The Philippines, and India," *Industrial and Labor Relations Review* 49 (1996): 635–57.

24. A. Mathews, "A Silicon Island of the East: Creating a Semiconductor Industry in Singapore," *California Management Review* 41 (1999): 55–78.

25. Ibid., p. 72.

26. Peter Hartz, *The Company That Breathes* (Berlin: Springer-Verlag, 1996).

26. Ibid., p. 96.

28. Masahiko Aoki, *Information, Incentives, and Bargaining in the Japanese Economy* (Cambridge, Mass.: Cambridge University Press, 1988).

29. Dennis Bakke, "An Alternative View of Corporate Governance," *Director's Monthly* 22 (September 1998): 1–5.

30. Jeffrey Pfeffer and Gerald R. Salancik, *The External Control of Organizations: A Resource Dependence Perspective* (New York: Harper and Row, 1978).

31. Roy J. Adams, "Labour Rights as Human Rights: Implications of the International Consensus," paper prepared for the annual meeting of the Industrial Relations Research Association, New York, N.Y., January 1999.

32. Ibid., p. 1.

33. David J. Levine and Laura D'Andrea Tyson, "Participation, Productivity, and the Firm's Environment," in *Paying for Productivity: A Look at*

the Evidence, edited by Alan S. Blinder (Washington, D.C.: Brookings, 1990), pp. 183–243.

34. Kuruvilla (1996).

35. Wever (1995) p. 11.

36. Buechtemann (1993), pp. 62–3. See also D. L. Leslie, "Economic Analyses of Labor Law," in *Proceedings of the 41st Annual Meeting of the Industrial Relations Research Association*, edited by B. D. Dennis (Madison, Wis.: Industrial Relations Research Association, 1989), pp. 227–35.

37. Richard N. Block, John Beck, and Daniel H. Kruger, *Labor Law, Industrial Relations, and Employee Choice* (Kalamazoo, Mich.: Upjohn Institute, 1992).

38. Joel Rogers and Eric Parker, "The Wisconsin Regional Training Partnership: Lessons for National Policy," Working Paper #3, Berkeley, CA: National Center for the Workplace, University of California, October, 1996.

39. Ibid.

15

Patient Capital

How Investors Contribute to (or Undermine)
Relational Wealth

MELVIN L. SMITH, JEFFREY PFEFFER, AND
DENISE M. ROUSSEAU

The recent victory of a dart-throwing chimpanzee over a financial analyst
in choosing a successful portfolio highlights our limited success in predicting firm performance. Comparing the accuracy of stock pickers to those
meteorologists who predict the weather, we find few striking differences
over the last fifty years. Except one—meteorologists are getting better. Why
can't we predict firm performance better? We can, but if we depend on only
a small set of short-term financial indicators (such as quarterly earnings) to
predict financial performance, we are likely to do no better than chimpan-
zees (and meteorologists will keep improving).[1]

The focus on short-term indicators, particularly in the United States, is
due to the impatience of much of the capital market. This means that investors, the business press, and many executives are preoccupied with a
limited set of short-term indicators (note that as this chapter is being written, today's article in the *Wall Street Journal* gives yesterday's Dow Jones
Industrial Average in five-minute intervals).[1] This economic short-termism
leads to an overreliance on a few widely used measures of firm performance, with dysfunctional consequences for sustained firm competitiveness
and long-term investments in the firm and its workers. This chapter addresses the importance of *patient capital* for sustained economic competitiveness, social stability, and worker well-being. Patient capital refers to
long-term investments focused on creating economic value by levering the
complex of resources that requires time to build. We address symptoms and
consequences of impatient capital and what can be done to shift the focus
of firms and investors toward building long-term wealth.

Symptoms of Impatient Capital

Investment used to mean contributing something today in the hope of greater return in the future. Impatient capital's score card focuses more on today's tallies than tomorrow's cumulative results. Signs of short-term economic thinking and investment decisions are everywhere.

Day Trading

Investors now trade stocks so frequently and hold such diversified portfolios that they have become detached from the underlying business activities of the companies that they own.[2] Many investors don't even know the full names of the companies whose shares they are buying and selling, only their symbols. As a result, Wall Street has become increasingly short term–focused over the past several decades. The number of shares changing hands on a typical day in 1990 was equal to three months' worth of trading in 1960.[3] And the volume of trading has continued to grow throughout the 1990s. This growth in trading activity has been fueled in part by a dramatic increase in the amount of day trading taking place. Day traders are individuals who trade in and out of stocks all day but generally sell out by the close to avoid the risk that the price of the stocks they are holding will fall at the next day's opening.[4] Day trading has been called the "ultimate in instant financial gratification."[5]

As evidence of the growth of the day-trading phenomenon, the number of day traders—over 275,000, per current estimates—is up from an estimated five thousand in 1997 and only a few hundred several years before that.[6] These day traders generate about 12 to 15 percent of the NASDAQ stock market's daily volume. In addition, there are now approximately seventy day-trading firms across the country, many offering day-trading schools to teach their clients a host of moneymaking strategies.[7] Day-trading web sites offer online trading, computerized stock picking systems, daily newsletters, investor chat rooms, and online and/or e-mail delivered training courses.[8] Its excitement and the allure of instant riches have even led some down a path of day-trading addiction. Mental health professionals from all across the country have begun to report cases of individuals seeking treatment for their compulsive Internet-based stock trading.[9]

Mutual Fund Portfolio Turnover

Mutual funds and pension funds in combination own 47 percent of all publicly traded stocks and 57 percent of the largest one thousand U. S. corporations.[10] Given this level of investment, the portfolio turnover ratios of these funds can have a significant impact on the level of (im)patience of capital in the market. Looking at mutual fund turnover, in 1996 the portfolios of the ten largest mutual funds (excluding the Vanguard Index 500) averaged 76.5 percent. Turnover of the largest mutual fund (Fidelity Magellan) was 155 percent.[11] The fact is, many mutual funds today average annual portfolio turnover of greater than 100 percent, whereas twenty years ago the average was only 30 percent.[12] A study of the stock trading activity of 64,715 individual investors from 1991 to 1996 showed similar results. The average annual common stock portfolio turnover of those investors was over 80 percent, indicating that the investors held the typical stock for only fifteen months. Among active traders the turnover rate was nearly 25 percent each month, or 300 percent annually.[13] These portfolio turnover rates provide further evidence that capital is growing increasingly impatient. In contrast, note a recent headline, "Impatient Price Seeks Patience with His Funds,"[14] describing how mutual fund guru Michael Price defended the underperformance of his funds as a temporary downturn in these otherwise valuable investments. Price argued that people shouldn't get distracted by the gains day traders are making. Yet the question is, will he or his investors resist the day-trading allure?

CEO Turnover

The rate of CEO turnover in U.S. organizations is also increasing. A study of one hundred large corporations showed that the number of leadership changes from 1980 to 1983 was three times greater than the number of changes from 1960 to 1964.[15] More recently, a 1998 survey of Fortune 100 companies performed by the national outplacement firm Drake Beam Morin showed that 31 percent of these companies had replaced CEOs since 1995 and 20 percent had done so since 1997.[16] According to Drake Beam Morin, "[d]uring the prolonged economic boom, such high turnover indicates that CEO's face unrelenting pressure from Wall Street, boards of directors, analysts and shareholders to meet short-term business goals." Increase in performance-based CEO turnover can be construed as yet another sign of the impatience of the U.S. capital market. It is difficult to argue with making CEO retention decisions on the basis of performance, but what indicators are actually being applied in arriving at these decisions? If investments made in training or new technology are docked against the score card of a CEO in the same ways that the company's electric bill is, there is less incentive for CEOs to expend resources that will enhance the firm's performance in the future, especially under another executive's tenure. In consequence there is less incentive to make investments in technology and people that while costly in the short-run can provide a basis for longer term value creation.

Shorter Vesting Periods for "Long-Term" Incentives

Many firms offer executive-level managers so-called long-term incentives, such as stock options and deferred compensation. Long-term incentives are intended to reward planning, strategic thinking, and personal commitment to the firm's sustained success. However, the vesting period after which such incentives can be accessed is often relatively short and getting shorter. Options now vest in four years instead of five, and deferred compensation is often available after three years with the firm. Disney paid Michael Ovitz, who had been hired as president ten months earlier, $38.8 million in severance pay and let him keep $3 million in options after terminating him for nonperformance. Perhaps learning from the dangers of short-termism, the compensation committee creating his successor's agreement provided a base salary more than 20 percent below competitive practice but granted him $8 million in options vesting seven to ten years later.[17] Nonetheless, shorter vesting periods are the norm. Moreover, some firms grant as much as 30 percent of their stock options and short vesting periods to CEOs and other named officers rather than sharing the wealth with employees. In such cases, neither the long-term interests of the firm nor the workers are served as well as would be the case if a broader base of the firm's stakeholders were rewarded for enhanced firm performance.[18]

Instability in Business Strategy

The combination of high CEO turnover and focus on short-term results creates a disincentive for the pursuit of a sustained business strategy over time. New CEOs seeking to make their mark on a firm often make aggressive changes in the firm's structure, manpower, and market presence. Initiatives begun under an earlier regime often lose steam even if not formally disbanded, as lower level managers reorient themselves with what they believe are the new top management's expectations. Successful internal organizational change can be difficult to implement in the face of short-term focus and frequent CEO changes. Change efforts can take several years to produce visible business results, especially in the case of complex organizational changes such as investments in information technology or fundamental restructurings of corporate culture and work practices.[19] Moreover, successful change efforts necessitate trust in the top management team, a condition that can be difficult to sustain in the face of frequent executive-level shake-ups.[20] Under such conditions, frequent CEO turnover can seriously undercut a firm's ability to implement and sustain complex change.

Sustaining a business strategy where value creation and competitive advantage are increased over time can be especially difficult where CEOs frequently come and go in the face of heavy penalties for top management in response to short-term downturns.

Why Has Capital Become Impatient?

Impatient capital originates not in the inherent structure of financial markets but in the ways in which American society has structured its financial markets. As Robert Reich points out, financial markets are human made.

In a capitalist economy, firms are owned by individual investors. And it is the owners who reap the reward or pay the costs for the firm's behavior. (Corporations as a particular ownership form can last longer than the lifetimes of any of their owners, and have a particular legal standing as such.)[21] In an earlier chapter Ritter and Taylor tied the emphasis on owner rights, and the simultaneous deemphasis on worker protections, to American agency laws.

The origins of impatient capital lie in the legal structure of publicly traded firms and in the psychology of investors. Corporations issue stock certificates to represent ownership of shares in the corporation. At certain times, the corporation issues dividends on these shares, which represent a share of the profits of the firm. The shares of ownership in the corporation are bought and sold in the stock market. The price of a share represents the present value of the stream of dividends that people expect to receive from the corporation and the total stock market value of a firm represents the value of the stream of profits that the firm is expected to generate. Thus the objective of the firm, maximizing the present value of the stream of profits, is sometimes equated with the goal of maximizing stock market value—assuming that the flow of future profits is publicly known. This is another way of saying that we assume there is certainty regarding the future. Of course there is not, and the present value of the firm reflects how much someone is willing to pay to purchase the firm, regardless of what its actual future value might be. In effect, there can be sizeable subjectivity in the value of a firm depending on investors' tolerance for risk and how they interpret the firm's actions and current performance combined with anticipated future events. Markets are as much a psychological and social phenomenon as they are an economic one. In effect, the proverbial "invisible hand" has a human face.

Since stock price can be viewed as the value of the firm, increases in stock price are often attributed to the success of its management. Moreover, these managers, while often distinct from owners, are widely rewarded, particularly in the United States, with stock options to align their interests with those of shareholders. In theory, managers are rewarded for adding value to the firm since increased stock price is taken as a reflection of value added. However, a strong overall market can increase stock price even where managers underperform. Thus, rewarding managers for absolute increases in stock price, as opposed to relative gains in relation to the market, can overreward poor performers. Nonetheless, absolute returns are the basis for most stock options and in some cases actually trigger the vesting of options as well as other forms of "long-term" managerial compensation.[22] The dynamics of impatient capital derive from the co-occurrence of several factors, as follows.

Prominence of Institutional Capital

Other things being equal, the fewer the number of owners, the more influence they are likely to have on the way an organization is run. For this reason, family-owned businesses often have distinct and idiosyncratic cultures, in many cases treating workers as extensions of the family. Without outside shareholders to answer to, such businesses can adopt short- or long-term perspectives regarding key business decisions, depending on the values of the owning family members. In the case of a corporation's stockholders, there are often many individual owners. Diffuse ownership is often linked to greater short-term focus since investors have little attachment to the firm itself.

The past few decades have seen the rise of institutional investors, firms that represent the interests of many individuals (e.g., mutual funds of investment houses, such as Fidelity, or pension funds such as CALPERS or TIAA-CREF). Although institutional investors seek to manage risk by distributing their investments across a variety of corporations and financial instruments, they often are among the largest segment of shareholders of a particular corporation. Because institutional investors move their funds around to manage risk, many churn their holdings frequently. Indeed, the flood of mutual fund investment in and out of developing countries, notably in Latin America, has collapsed markets, battered currencies, and threatened governments.[23] Typically, a given institutional investor will have only 1 to 2 percent of a company's stock, and the average institutional investor holds stock for less than two years (down from seven years in 1970).[24] Publicly traded firms, therefore, increasingly rely on a transient ownership base.

More Information More Quickly

In the United States our sense of time has changed; time seems more compressed. Work once completed in a week might now be completed in less than a day, through the availability of faxes, e-mail, the Internet, and their offshoots. Faster cycle times for work have occurred, with an expansion of data made available by technological monitoring, giving us word counts for documents, call durations for telemarketing, and whole varieties of itemized costs. The availability of a lot of data, quickly, and often in real time, makes short-term monitoring of outcomes convenient and difficult to resist in an increasingly competitive environment. Robert Frank and Philip Cook have written compellingly in their book *Winner Take All*[25] about the escalation of competitive pressures and an increase in the number of losers relative to winners in a marketplace that reacts quickly to changes in quantitative indicators. The question remains whether more data equals more information.

Higher CEO Salaries Pressuring for Performance

Higher compensation packages are one means of attracting executive stars. Hypercompetition in the marketplace creates high demand for managers with good track records. Bigger stock options packages and a robust economy have escalated CEO pay since the late 1980s. According to Robert Frank, "the scale for what's at stake is enlarging." This means that with more rivals for market share and risks from losses increasing, firms engage in bidding wars, offering bulked-up compensation packages to recruit a top-notch decision maker.[26] Spiraling CEO pay and greater public (worker and stockholder) scrutiny (the AFL-CIO maintains a web site posting CEO pay in unionized firms) has created tremendous pressure to visibly justify the high CEO price tag.

Measurements That Don't Distinguish Long-Term Incentives from Organizational Slack

Ritter and Taylor in their chapter make a cogent case for how investors can appropriate the long-term incentives earned by workers by slicing those with medium to high seniority from the payroll. Having highly paid senior workers can be a sign that the firm is "fat" or that it is fulfilling its obligations to compensate those people who have contributed to the firm in the past at levels higher than what they were once paid. Accounting systems fail to account for the variety of forms that "deferred" compensation actually can take.

Other expenses are actually investments but may not be construed as such. Is spending money training people or developing them through successive assignments an investment in the future or an unnecessary perk? Current accounting practices cannot effectively evaluate developmental activities and the value they contribute to the firm through enhanced workforce capabilities. The result of the flawed measurement systems firms use is confusion regarding a firm's truth wealth and exploitation of one set of organizational stakeholders (workers) for the short-term benefit of stockholders.

Changes in Government Policies and Laws

Regulatory and other changes have occurred in corporate ownership, stock valuation, and capital budgeting practices that have rigged the entire U.S. economic system to favor and reward short-term investments and management over patient capital.[27] According to the Council on Competitiveness, American firms out-invest foreign competitors in such industries as telecommunications and pharmaceutics and are more active in funding startup ventures and emerging industries. However, relative to Japanese and

German firms, the United States underinvests in such critical areas as research and development and human resources. The Council notes that 47 percent of R & D investments in Japanese firms are classified as long term, in contrast to 21 percent in the United States.

Capital gains laws and tax depreciation schedules fail to reward investors and managers for their patience. Long-term capital gains is defined by the U.S. Internal Revenue Service as based on an investment held for a year! Michael Porter has suggested that long-term investing would be more attractive if current capital gains rates required assets be held for five years before qualifying for the lower rate and indexed these gains for inflation. A powerful tool for changing investor behavior is to create incentives for buying and holding larger blocks of equity securities in individual companies.[28] Similarly, a permanent R & D tax credit plus a credit for the cost of employee training programs could substantially support a more long-term view.[29] Absent concerted efforts to reform the regulatory system in favor of rewards for patient capital, short-term business myopia is not likely to change.

Market-based Ideology

Although market-based factors are pertinent to a myriad of decisions in everyday life, there are varied belief systems regarding how the market factors should enter into our thinking, as individuals, workers, managers, and investors. In American business two fundamental and seemingly different forces are operating: shifts toward contingent capitalism, which put short-term market factors and interests of owners ahead of workers, and movements toward cooperative capitalism, which builds a community of interests, blurring the boundaries between workers and owners.[30] Lean production firms reflect the former and team production systems the latter. This dichotomy may ring true, but it is not clear cut in practice. Even high-performance firms committed to teamwork downsize their core labor forces and tighten investments in training and development to manage earnings reported to stockholders. But improved shareholder returns in the short run are only meaningful as an indicator of long-term firm value when the firm's potential to create future value is not diminished in the process.

Consequences of an Impatient Capital Market

The consequences of impatient capital are felt at all levels of American society. We have mentioned the reluctance on the part of many U. S. firms to invest in long-term initiatives that would negatively impact short-term operating results. Instead, corporate strategies over the past decade have been dominated by dramatic cost-cutting initiatives in the form of downsizing or restructuring.

Downsizing

Surveys have shown that one-third to one-half of all medium and large U.S. firms have downsized annually since 1988, and over half of all Fortune 1000 firms experienced a major restructuring in 1987 alone.[31] Although downsizing has become such a widespread practice among U.S. firms, several recent reports have questioned its efficacy as a cost-cutting strategy. Research has shown that firms that have downsized generally have no better bottom-line results than organizations that have not. Further, when considering the long-term implications, it is likely that many downsized firms are actually worse off than their counterparts that have chosen not to engage in downsizing for purposes of cutting costs.[32]

Downsizing in an effort to cut or control costs can be viewed as a direct consequence of an impatient capital market. In itself, downsizing can result in several additional effects, which are indirect consequences of capital's impatience. Among those indirect consequences are a reduction in research and development expenditures, negatively impacted employee attitudes and behaviors, and difficulty in attracting and retaining intellectual capital. Perhaps the most significant effect of downsizing is the erosion of relational wealth by the impairing of value-adding mechanisms as described by Coff and Rousseau in their chapter. Capabilities embedded in stable relationships among workers and between workers and the firm are readily eroded when a critical mass of workers is laid off.

Declining Investments in Research and Development

In determining how much to invest in research and development, a firm's managers must weight the short-term uses that money might be put to versus the advantages it might create in the long run.[33] Impatient shareholders pressure managers in organizations to opt for the best short-term decision, which often means allocating fewer funds to research and development. In support of this argument, researchers have shown that downsizing negatively impacts the research and development capacities of organizations.[34] Not surprisingly, long-term investment is positively associated with innovation while short-term investment and innovation are negatively related.[35] Broad-based declines in research and development investments can serve as an impediment to economic development. Recognizing this fact, several states have begun to adopt R & D incentives in the form of tax credits or capital investment deductions. The Oregon Department of Economic Development, for instance, recently evaluated the state's R & D incentives and concluded that they had helped to encourage existing companies to increase R & D efforts and that they had helped to attract new companies to the state. Similarly, a recent study conducted by Coopers and Lybrand concluded that the federal R & D tax credit is such a powerful incentive that it will ultimately pay for itself due to its impact on productivity and economic growth.

Increasing Negative Employee Attitudes and Behaviors

Downsizing to cut short-term costs can negatively affect surviving employees' performance, retention, and attitudes.[36] Survivors are likely to experience feelings of guilt, stemming from the fact that they have maintained their jobs while others have lost theirs. They are also likely to experience increased stress, due to both the increased workload associated with picking up the slack for those who have lost their jobs and the fear that they themselves may fall victim to a future downsizing. Other attitude changes include reduced levels of trust, satisfaction, and organizational commitment.

Attitude changes downsizing's survivors experience are often accompanied by changes in behavior as well: increased tardiness, absenteeism, and turnover, as well as decreased productivity. Survivors are often more cynical and opportunistic and more likely to engage in retaliatory behaviors such as theft and providing poor customer service.[37] Thus, it appears that while downsizing may enable an organization to cut costs in the short term, there may be potentially severe long-term ramifications.[38]

Difficulties in Attracting and Retaining Intellectual Capital

Another indirect consequence of an impatient capital market is the difficulty that employers can have attracting and retaining talent after downsizing. As noted, downsizing survivors are likely to experience stress due to the increased workload that often accompanies the departure of coworkers. As this stress gives way to intention to leave and ultimately to turnover, firms can lose many of their better employees. Indeed, research suggests that it is the highly motivated individual with a strong commitment who is most susceptible to burnout.[39] In addition, it is the more competent employees who will have the greatest appeal to competitors seeking talented individuals, thus making them more likely to leave for alternative opportunities. Supporting these points, a recent study of 406 restructured companies found that one out of every five reported that they lost valuable contributors with critical skills or needed talents after a downsizing.[40] As Coff and Rousseau argue, these firms are unlikely to even realize what they have lost by way of collective knowledge and capabilities when large proportions of people from the same work groups have left.

The loss of intellectual capital takes on even more importance since companies are finding it difficult to fill key positions at all levels.[41] This is especially true at the executive level, where the elimination of middle management through downsizing has left many organizations without qualified individuals in internal succession pipelines to replace departing executives. The problem is further exacerbated by the fact that executive loyalty is at an all-time low. Development Dimensions International (DDI), a global human resources consulting firm, estimates that 75 percent of executives are currently marketing themselves in some way or another.[42] In addition, McKinsey and Company, after surveying six thousand executives at seventy-seven major corporations, concluded that executives don't know some of the most important facts about their companies' talent and that managers really don't know why their good people leave.[43]

Managed Earnings

Impatient capital has also led to a fudging of the numbers in many firms. Recognizing the psychology of their investors who want stable growth, where gains are unpredictable, CEOs sometimes manage their quarterly earning reports. Where managers believe growth occurs faster than can be sustained, many companies have tweaked their earnings reports to protect the stock from wild bounces over mild events.[44] The result of managed earnings is inaccurate feedback to the firm's constituents, even regarding the short-term health of the firm. As we have described, impatient capital gives firms less reason to invest in any form that is not immediately evident in short-term indicators. In effect, firms then "teach to the test," like elementary school teachers trying to avoid community wrath over low standardized test scores. But unlike teachers, executives are actually in the position to manipulate some of the scores.

Where Do We Go from Here?

At the heart of the patient capital debacle are two related questions: how are the interests of the firm's stockholders and other stakeholders best served? How can we forecast more accurately the future value of the firm so as to promote long-term value creation and sustained competitive advantage?

We suggest that these questions share a common answer. This book argues that creating sustained value added by deploying relational wealth serves both the interests of a firm's owners as well as its employees and the communities in which they live. Owners want to grow their investments, and workers and communities value both increased wealth and stability. The benefits of patient capital accrue when investors can justify taking the long-term view, permitting the emergence of advantages embedded in relations between people, attachments between workers and firm, and the development of shared knowledge that resides in flexible stability. Taking the long-term view is made possible both by better appreciation of factors that create value in a firm and by creating an agreed-on set of value-adding indicators.

Patient capital exists where a firm's managers and workers act as stewards of the shareholder's investments and are committed to long-term shareholder value. The success of family businesses and many other closely held startups depends on access to capital that they do not have to pay back too soon, gaining time to flourish.[45] This orientation looks to long-term value creation as a basis for growth and profitability and a sustained relationship with all a firm's stakeholders. Many family businesses turn reliable, trusting relationships into a strategic advantage. One dimension of that advantage is the power of patient capital in making investment decisions:

> When our products' costs are high, we can work to aggressively build market share despite tighter margins . . . our nonfamily business rivals worry about showing consistent profits, so they pull in their horns when costs are high. But when what we buy is in the low-cost stage of its cycle, we can really make up the profits.[46]

Though smaller privately held businesses have the competitive disadvantage of limited capital, they can allocate what funds they have in ways that offer longer term value. Organizational and institutional supports for patient capital can offer corporations many of the advantages that closely held businesses have, without their limitations on accessing investors.

Shifting our focus to long-term value creation entails a capability to forecast the future better than what many investors and firms exhibit today. Improved forecasting requires us to look at the actions that create that future and make assessments accordingly. Financial indicators are obviously not actions. They are outcomes that depend on actions. The management of planning, innovation, human resources, technological improvement, and customer relations are good places to begin.

Patient capital is reflected by mutual fund managers and investors who study firms in depth—to understand how they function internally rather than just focusing on how they score in the financial short run. Evidence that a firm is a "high-performing work organization" is high on the list. High-performing work organizations have superior internal management practices combined with a focus on customer satisfaction. These firms innovate simultaneously in technology, human resource practices, and strategic planning. Technology is used to pursue and implement strategic plans not because it looks like the thing to do; human resources are highly involved in planning too, as partners in success. Effective internal management produces internationally competitive outcomes—and improved financial performance, too. Motorola, for example, estimates that it saves over $2 billion annually from its quality programs, which emphasize technology combined with teamwork.

The current American focus on short-term results has undercut the development of metrics for long-term value added. At present, the details of measuring high performance work organizations are not agreed on, and indicators of actions firms take to build long-term competitiveness, such as building relational wealth, have little uniformity. To improve investor decisions and support long-term investment, new ways are needed to index firm performance.

Since we do not have common, established metrics to assess long-term investments across industries and market segments, does this mean there is no such a thing as good practice? Not on your life. We know what the issues are; we are just now beginning to understand how to make comparisons across industries and market segments. Indicators such as investments in training, rates of turnover, and the like can be referenced to industry and market segment averages. Nonetheless, we need more research to understand how best to interpret indicators of relational wealth. How much training is a good amount of training? How much personnel stability is needed for enhanced learning and managed interdependence? At Motorola, the answers may take one form; at Disney, it may be another.

Common indicators are possible. But they require investors to pay a little more attention to the nature of the business and its internal workings. Indeed, high-performance firms cultivating relational wealth are more likely themselves to be gathering performance data on their innovation rates (e.g., sales from new products relative to total) or competency rates (e.g., current skills assessed relative to strategic demands). These firms are more likely to have lower rates of absence (a powerful measure of worker satisfaction and commitment and an indicator of health status issues such as substance abuse) and on-the-job accidents. Many of these measures are *nonfinancial*. However, that fact does not detract from their usefulness. We already know that nonfinancial measures can be extremely valuable in gauging economic strength. Commonly used nonfinancial indicators such as the Consumer Confidence Index (based on the public's perception of the economy) have provided valuable information for decades.

We advocate that investors survey nonfinancial as well as financial indicators in evaluating companies. We suggest that corporate annual reports move toward standardized reporting of nonfinancial indicators with measurement practices consistent with those standards employed today in auditing financial indicators. Consensus is needed regarding what set of nonfinancial indicators best capture organizational health and firm growth potential. Organizational researchers, investors, and workers, including managers, must enter into a dialogue, focusing attention on core activities and processes that yield long-term success. The next step is creation of consensus and development of a standardized measurement system that provides investors and managers with information on the internal workings of firms to improve predictions of future success. Our point is not to replace financial indicators with nonfinancial ones. The point is that nonfinancial indicators can provide predictive information not available from short-term financial ones.

Conclusion

In evaluating and forecasting firm success, investors and managers must pay attention to a broader set of nonfinancial as well as financial indicators. Annual reports, management information systems, and financial analysts should focus attention on employee development, customer relations, and innovation and report data accordingly. Companies cannot manage what they do not measure. If we don't measure critical drivers of long-term firm performance, we cannot correct, encourage, or make investment decisions regarding it. To turn investment toward patient capital and reap its benefits, we need a shift in the way firms and investors keep score.

Notes

1. Thanks are due to Dan Ilgen and Ben Schnieder for inspiring this opening. Greg Ip, "After Milestone, Blue Chips Fall 128.58 Points," *Wall Street Journal*, May 5, 1999, pp. C1, C19.

2. M. T. Jacobs, *Short-Term America: The Causes and Cures of Our Business Myopia* (Boston: Harvard Business School Press, 1991), p. 10.

3. Ibid., p. 17.

4. C. Vinzant, "The World of the Hard-Core Day Traders," *Fortune*, February 15, 1999, 196–7.

5. M. Preddy, "Day Traders Ride Risky Market," *Detroit News*, February 16, 1999, p. B1.

6. K. Weisul, "Day Traders Take to the Internet, Creating a New Cottage Industry," *Investment Dealers' Digest*, November 3, 1997, pp. 16–7.

7. I. J. Dugan, "States Sue Day Trading Firms, Online Investors Often Skirt Rules," *Times-Picayune* (New Orleans edition), February 3, 1999, p. C1.

8. K. Yakal, "The Electronic Investor: Sites for Day Trippers," *Barron's*, February 16, 1998, p. 50.

9. R. Buckman, "The Internet-Stock Frenzy: These Days, Online Trading Can Become an Addiction," *Wall Street Journal*, February 1, 1999, p. C1.

10. T. A. Stewart, "CEO Pay: Mom Wouldn't Approve," *Fortune*, March 31, 1997, pp. 119–20.

11. Ibid.

12. J. Walsh, "Bigger Mutual Fund Isn't Always Better," *Times-Picayune* (New Orleans) November 23, 1997, pp. F1–2.

13. J. Glassman, "Researchers Think It's Better to Hold'em Than to Fold'em: Study Indicates Many Shuffle Portfolio Too Much," *Houston Chronicle*, June 1, 1998, p. 4.

14. *Wall Street Journal*, April 26, 1999, p. C1.

15. S. Worchel, S. Jenner, and M. Hebl, "Changing the Guard: How the Origin of New Leader and Disposition of Ex-leader Affect Group Performance and Perceptions," *Small Group Research* (August 1998): 436–51.

16. D. Hogsett, "Survey: CEO's under Pressure," *Home Textiles Today*, September 21, 1998, p. 24.

17. Jack L. Lederer and Carl R. Weinberg, "Largesse Oblige," *Chief Executive* (September 1999): 127, 38–55.

18. Ibid.

19. P. S. Goodman, *Missing Organizational Linkages* (Newbury Park, Calif.: Sage, 2000).

20. D. M. Rousseau and S. A. Tijoriwala, "What's a Good Reason to Change? Social Accounts and Motivated Reasoning in Organizational Change," *Journal of Applied Psychology*, 84 (1999) 514–528. Interestingly, Worchel and his colleagues found that new leaders were more likely to

behave in a humanistic fashion to members where the former leader remained and when that new leader was internal to the group (in contrast to the behavior of outside leaders); Worchel, Jenner, and Hebl (1998).

21. H. R. Varian, *Intermediate Microeconomics: A Modern Approach*, 4th ed. (New York: Norton, 1996).

22. A. Johnson, "Should Options Reward Absolute or Relative Shareholder Returns," *Compensation and Benefits Review* (January/February 1999): 31, 38–43. L. C. Bickford, "Mergers and Acquisitions: How Executive Compensation May Affect a Deal," *Compensation and Benefits Review* (September/October 1997):29, 53–9.

23. J. F. Peltz, "U.S. Investors Flock to Risky Foreign Funds: Despite Recent Losses in Mexico More Dollars Chase Profits around the Globe and Leave Smaller Markets Reeling," *Los Angeles Times*, November 19, 1995, p. 1.

24. L. Reynolds, "Changing Mind-sets: Taking the Long View of Investment Planning," *Management Review* December 1992, 31–3. Quoting Michael Useem.

25. R. Frank and P. Cook, *The Winner-Take-All Society* (New York: Free Press, 1995).

26. T. Hausman, "Predicting Pay," *Wall Street Journal*, April 8, 1999, p. R9.

27. Reynolds (1992)

28. According to the American Society for Competitiveness, Harvey Kahalas, Chairman.

29. Reynolds (1992).

30. M. Carnoy, M. Castells, and C. Benner, "What Is Happening to the U.S. Labor Market?" part 1, "A Review of the Evidence," unpublished manuscript, University of California at Berkeley, 1996.

31. B. C. Luthans and S. M. Sommer, "The Impact of Downsizing on Workplace Attitudes," *Group and Organization Management* (March 1999): 49.

32. For more in-depth discussions of the downsides of downsizing, see C. R. Leana, "Corporate Anorexia May Wind up Being Fatal," *Los Angeles Times*, November 8, 1995, p. B11; C. R. Leana, "Downsizing Won't Work," *Chicago Tribune Magazine*, April 14, 1996, pp. 15–6; and M. A. Mone, "How We Got Along after Downsizing: Post-Downsizing Trust as a Double-Edged Sword," *Public Administration Quarterly* (Fall 1997):309–36.

33. Kevin J. Laverty, "Economic 'Short-termism': The Debate, the Unresolved Issues, and the Implications for Management Practice and Research," *Academy of Management Review* 21,3 (1996): 825–60.

34. D. Dougherty and E. H. Bowman, "The Effects of Organizational Downsizing on Product Innovation," *California Management Review* 37, (1994) 4: 28–44.

35. Shaker A. Zahra, "Governance, Ownership, and Corporate Entrepreneurship: The Moderating Impact of Industry Technological Opportunities," *Academy of Management Journal* 39, (1996) 6: 1713–35.

36. For a listing of research publications on this topic, see M. A. Mone (1997), p. 316.

37. Ibid., pp. 316–7.

38. Luthans and Sommer (1999).

39. J. E. Moore, "Are You Burning Out Valuable Resources?" *HR* (January 1999): 93–7.

40. A. G. Bedeian and A. A. Armenakis, "The Cesspool Syndrome: How Dreck Floats to the Top of Declining Organizations," *Academy of Management Executive* (February 1998): 58.

41. S. Cliffe, "Human Resources: Winning the War for Talent," *Harvard Business Review* (September/October 1998):18–9.

42. R. J. Grossman, "Heirs Unapparent," *HR* (February 1999):36–44.

43. Cliffe (1998).

44. R. McGough, "Executive Critical of 'Managed' Earnings Doesn't Mind If the Street Criticizes Him," *Wall Street Journal*, April 16, 1999, pp. C1–C2.

45. C. Solomon, "Maine's Loan Fund Helps Small Firms in a Crunch," *Wall Street Journal*, March 4, 1998, p. NE1.

46. J. Ward and C. E. Aronoff, "The Power of Patient Capital," *Nation's Business* (September 1991): 48, 50.

Building and Sustaining Relational Wealth

Concluding Thoughts

CARRIE R. LEANA AND DENISE M. ROUSSEAU

This book has drawn on scholarship in the field of organizational behavior to challenge prevailing assumptions about how economic advantage occurs. The authors' collective efforts call attention to the economic advantages associated with building and maintaining relationships within and between firms. Much research into labor productivity and capital investment has focused on the economic value generated by tangible firm assets. We suggest that additional economic value can reside in the connections among a firm's less tangible assets and their connections to the whole. Although frequently downplayed in the pursuit of short-term gains in capital markets, economic advantages embodied in ongoing relationships, ties of people with their work settings, coworkers, customers, and the firm itself, generate firm wealth and its potential to add value in the future. Just as the stock market is but one dimension of an economy, financial and human capital are but two of several forms of wealth. Relational wealth is economic value where the whole is greater than the sum of its parts.

Together the authors demonstrate that the relationships comprising modern firms provide a means of accessing resources that would otherwise be squandered in making both day-to-day as well as strategic business decisions. The advantages of strong relationships are realized when organizational practices encourage learning and the development and maintenance of organizational memory. Such practices promote problem solving and flexible deployment of workforce capabilities in response to competitive challenges. Our focus has been on the ways in which firms achieve strategic advantages by at once maintaining flexible yet stable relationships within the firm and with external customers and suppliers.

Foundations of Relational Wealth

We have defined relational wealth as the value created by and for a firm through its internal relations among and with employees, as well as its external alliances and reputation. The authors not only argue for the advantages of relational wealth but identify the mechanisms by which relational wealth may be generated, sustained, or undermined. This perspective regarding relational wealth rests on the following facts.

Trust is the essential foundation for collective action. Trust is the willingness of a person to be vulnerable to the intentions of another. Intentions of others are best predicted through a history of interactions and reputation developed over the course of time and proximity. This shared history, and the trust it can yield, can be used to effectively predict future courses of action. The past does matter in all social relations, and in the case of firm-to-worker relations (or firm-to customer/supplier relations), whether a firm has been trustworthy in the past has a profound impact on the firm's ability to get others to join their interests with its interests in the future. As Pearce points out in chapter 4, all firms want trustworthy workers. Whether trustworthy workers will in turn want the firm will depend on its track record and future credibility. The same can be said for suppliers, customers, regulators, and other parties with which the firm interacts.

Relationships are substitutes for more costly means of coordinating and motivating work. A committed workforce is less likely to leave in the face of short-term difficulties. It is more likely to behave in the organization's interests under circumstances that are otherwise difficult to monitor. Such a workforce is also more likely to deploy investments made in training on behalf of the firm that trained them. Comparable benefits can be seen for relationships growing out of ongoing encounters in local communities and stable relations between customers and suppliers. Realizing these benefits depends fundamentally on the existence of trust.

Knowledge is embedded in stable relationships and it is most effectively accessed in the context of those relationships. Over the last forty years, organizational researchers have operated from a different set of assumptions than have economists, focusing on the psychological and social rather than just the economic aspects of organizational life. In the process they have identified frequently overlooked advantages offered from ongoing relationships, many of which are detailed in Coff and Rousseau's discussion of how relational wealth mechanisms account for the combined value of skills, equipment, and capital that exceed the market value of discrete assets.

Employee contributions to the firm can be divided into two types of work: (1) task performance, where specified job demands—particularly those of a technical nature—are accomplished; and (2) contextual performance: behaviors that improve the coordination of work, contribute to effective management of interdependence, and provide support for the work performed by others.[1] Although technical job demands tend to be more explicitly recognized by the firm and embodied in its human resource practices, contextual performance contributes more to the firm's capacity to respond to uncertainty and unanticipated problems. Contextual performance is particularly valuable when work is interdependently carried out, enhancing the performance of not only the individual contributor but also his or her coworkers. To use a sports analogy: if workers were basketball players, task performance would be measured by the total number of points scored by an individual player, while contextual performance would be realized through the number of player "assists."

Strong contextual performance is characteristic of more stable social settings where people are familiar with their coworkers, where managers know the people who work for them and are able to recognize and appreciate how critical interdependencies affect the overall performance of their work unit. Unfortunately, such tacit resources are easily overlooked and often undervalued by a firm's management. The two groups best positioned to recognize the value of tacit resources are the workers attempting to get things done day-to-day and the customers whose demands challenge the firm's capacity to look and act responsive. Even firms that acquire workers through employment agencies, as Davis-Blake and Brouschak describe in their chapter, often seek to reap the benefits of a stable workforce familiar with the work setting, each other, and the firm's clientele. Escalating competitive economic conditions make the "extra" benefits associated with contextual performance a competitive advantage in attracting and keeping customers—one that will be difficult for competitors to recognize, let alone copy.

Wealth has its greatest worth in context. Relational wealth is tied to settings such as firms, communities, or regions, which themselves can be wealth creating. Wealth, in the form of knowledge, skills, relationships, and so on is almost always contextualized. It has its greatest worth in particular contexts; removed from these, it may no longer have much value. Recall the scene in the film *Titanic* where the villain attempts to get into a lifeboat by bribing the deckhand with wads of cash. The deckhand, knowing he himself will go down with the ship, replies "What good will that do me now!" Wealth of any form loses much of its value when separated from the social settings that created it. Firms that poach the talent of a competitor might realize only limited gains if that special competence is derived from the knowledge, skills, and capabilities we have described here as relational assets: resources embedded in the relations between people and between the firm and its constituencies.

Markets are not forces of nature but rather are human-made, created by societal institutions, in particular laws governing securities and taxation. The fables Ritter and Taylor relate in chapter 2 call attention to the assumptions that laws have built into our markets. Markets can be restructured to improve long-term efficiency. People can redesign aspects of markets to create greater economic benefits over time. As Pfeffer points out in chapter 14, markets can also be redesigned to balance the interests of their many stakeholders. We are only now coming to understand the complex linkages that exist between firm and worker investments in one another and their resultant impact on productivity and sustained economic value. Linkages between investments at one level and benefits at another are lagged and take time to manifest themselves. Thus, training workers and promoting cooperation across work groups may not translate quickly into performance gains for the individual firm. Such investments tend to pay off over time as the changes they induce become increasingly intermingled and aligned into more effective collection action. Patient capital, whether arising because of the discipline of investors or the requirements of the law, promotes investment in pursuit of lagged but powerful gains in wealth.

In sum, the preceding facts bolster the case for relational wealth. They also raise questions about the prevailing assumptions held by managers and scholars regarding the effects that market structures have on firms.

Challenging Prevailing Market Assumptions

Markets are governed by laws that reflect assumptions about how wealth is best created and sustained. Some of these assumptions are at odds with the relational wealth view of the firm described in this book. We explore several of these assumptions here and offer arguments that counter the prevailing economic wisdom underlying these assumptions.

Workers now have highly mobile, "boundaryless careers" that are at odds with a relational wealth view of the firm. A boundaryless career is the opposite of an organizational career. Boundaryless careers mean interfirm mobility for workers based on their ability to leverage their knowledge, skills, and relationships built over time through varied employment experiences. Whereas traditional careers were viewed as tied only to a single employment setting, the last decade has seen the rise of greater mobility for all segments of the population.

The promise of a boundaryless career is employability that is not dependent on whether the firm one currently works for continues to need one's services or to exist at all. However, the boundaryless career's implicit goal is to provide more satisfying and sustained employment, not mere mobility. Employability means the capacity to obtain meaningful and economically advantageous work, whether with another firm or with one's current employer. It is not the opposite of job security but rather a new facet of it— employment that factors in the quality of employment, both economically and psychologically, from the perspective of the worker.

Employability in the public's mind appears to have a variety of meanings. For some it *is* the opposite of job security, synonymous perhaps with "only you are responsible for managing your career because there is no job security." In effect, the worker is a free agent and the firm is merely a setting in which the worker exercises choices in his or her interest with little employer input or contribution. For others, employability means that firms will do what they can to help displaced workers find new employment, a promise made in the attempt to effectively manage a downsizing or restructuring.

Still others may view employability as the implicit guarantee of a job for life.

Our view of employability is more the middle road, capitalizing on relational wealth, wherein firms and workers invest in the development of skills and relationships that bring value to one another over time. This mutual investment recognizes that continuing to build skills, knowledge, and understandings pertinent to the external market serves both their interests. The key overlap between both boundaryless careers and relational wealth is the accessing of knowledge, skills, and capabilities, through diverse ties to work settings and the people in them. Lester Thurow has argued that the biggest unknown for individuals in the modern economy is how to have a career in a system where there is no career.[2] Our answer is that careers are made by accumulating knowledge and skills that add value, particularly through ties to work groups, networks, and firms that deepen and further enhance that learning. Ties to firms still matter, although they take more forms than traditional "company man" models of employment.

At the heart of relational wealth are social relations and linkages among people who are embedded in a context of aligned goals and social relations. Boundaryless careers, characterized by interfirm mobility, are themselves largely tied to particular locations, both geographic and industrial. In particular, what Blau calls a locale's spatial capital is deployed in the maintenance and development of interfirm mobility via connections to regions and industry clusters, such as Silicon Valley, that support social networks, reputations, and the basis of trust between people. In effect, many forms of boundaryless career are special cases of accumulated relational wealth, transferred by networks of individuals to broader collectives such as Silicon Valley, Inc, or to the extended networks of such firms as Arthur Anderson and McKinsey, which have current employees and alumni tied together through a variety of roles and relations over the course of their careers.[3] Thus, relational wealth need not reside only within the physical boundaries of a firm and can extend to a broad network of past, present, and potential employees.

A relational wealth model will not work in the United States. There are several variations on this argument but the gist is that relational wealth is incompatible with U.S. values. According to this reasoning, relational wealth is fine in collectivist societies like Japan or for the socially democratic Europeans, but Americans are too individualistic and too mobile to benefit from relational wealth.

The facts are otherwise. Despite its reputation for high turnover and job "churning," the U.S. labor market has historically provided stable, near-lifetime employment to nearly a third of the labor force. These individuals—largely white males—would hold a job for an average of more than twenty years, compared to the modal worker who holds a job for about eight years. The U.S. labor market has always been marked by high turnover and many job changes for some segment of its workforce (women and minorities) while another (white males) has had highly stable employment for decades. This pattern has remained largely unchanged since the 1960s.[4] To the extent that white males have traditionally had more options in jobs and career paths than have women and minorities, their job stability can be assumed to be a choice. Thus, that segment of the American workforce that historically has had the most choices appears to have a preference for stable and longer term employment.

American individualism is itself no barrier to building strong relationships within and across firms. As observed by Alexis deTocqueville in his visit to the United States in the nineteenth century, American society is noteworthy for its capacity to form associations for a common purpose. This American "associability" is, like its individualism, strongly task centered, where sharing, mutual support, and concern for the broader community reflect the value of cooperating to achieve goals individuals cannot readily accomplish on their own. As defined by Van Buren and Leana in chapter 13, associability is the willingness and the ability of participants to subordinate individual goals to collective ones in order to achieve purposes that can only be accomplished collectively. American associability emphasizes active participation, cooperation, attachment, and the creation of associations to address personal needs and shared social problems. Thus, Americans may be less individualistic than they are commonly portrayed when they are given choices about managing their careers. At the same time, the American value of associability can operate to the firm's advantage in its efforts to motivate and strengthen collective action. In this way American firms, particularly those with high-performance strategies, can compete by levering their accumulated relational wealth.

Since relational wealth is tacit and not readily observable, it cannot be measured. The corollary is that if it cannot be measured, then it cannot be rewarded, encouraged, or accounted for. And if it cannot be rewarded, encouraged, or accounted for, it cannot be managed and thus it cannot create value for the firm.

Of course, lots of important organizational phenomena are tacit or intangible, such as job satisfaction, organizational culture, group cohesion, or consumer confidence. The fact that these phenomena are difficult to see directly doesn't diminish their importance. One advantage of viewing firms through an organizational lens rather than just an economic one is that organizational researchers focus on documenting the more abstract aspects of organizational life and in doing so foster the widespread recognition of their occurrence, significance, and manageability.

Much of the "glue" that constructs organizational life out of human behavior and perception is not clearly visible but rather is manifested indirectly through bundles or patterns of values, behaviors, and practices. Relational wealth is no exception. Possible indicators of relational wealth exist at a variety of organizational levels, including (but not limited to):

• The length of time supervisors/managers have known and/or supervised their workers

- The array of coworkers individual employees have available from whom they can seek advice, information, and support
- Employee turnover relative to an industry or occupational average
- Internal career ladders for employees
- Employee promotion rates
- Time in setting for individual workers
- Work group familiarity with individual members
- Incentive pay based on group and firm performance rather than just individual contribution
- Investments in worker training and development
- Investments in retraining
- Proportion of internal firm work units/departments members have contacts with
- Proportion of equipment within the unit that all members are competent operating
- Proportion of workers in the firm or unit with customer contact
- Affective commitment reported by employees
- Collective trust between employer and employee and among employees
- Positive labor relations benefiting both workers and the firm
- Investments in intellectual capital that do not reside in one or a limited number of individuals
- Firm-level goals connected to rewards for groups, managers, and workers
- Existence of various organizational commons shared by all organization members (e.g., cafeteria, training sites, communal gathering places, electronic communities)

This is just a partial list of the potential indicators of relational wealth. Some of these may be assessed by examining archival records or company procedures. Others may be measured through employee attitude surveys. Relatively new research techniques such as network analysis also provide a mechanism for capturing and assessing the relational wealth of firms.

How to Turn Relational Wealth to Your *Competitor's* Advantage

It's not difficult to identify firms that erode whatever relational wealth they have potentially accumulated: firms that repeatedly downsize, don't train, or undercut their managers' abilities to behave in a trustworthy fashion toward their workers. Such firms may be easy targets for competitors as these competitors realize that whatever relative advantages these firms have are of the kind that are easily duplicated (by acquiring technology) or poached (by hiring away the people who used that technology). Competitors may be more likely to prey on firms that squander relational wealth. A firm low in relational wealth can be recognized by its competitors, customers, and current and potential employees through the following indicators.

A firm's key actors behave as if they don't know that relational wealth exists. Relational wealth squanderers view turnover as a replacement problem rather than an indicator of knowledge lost or disruption incurred. One symptom of a replacement view of turnover is that managers start interviewing to recruit new workers rather than doing exit interviews first (or at all). Managers are also moved in and out of work units without attention to the impact on the workforce. Whatever development systems are available are thus undermined, since managers cannot know their workers well enough to put such systems to use. Feedback systems are weak, and compensation places little emphasis on contributions people make to the overall performance of the unit. Failing to recognize advantages available to them via accumulations of relational wealth, many firms fail to do even the minimum to enhance its capture and deployment.

Employability is treated as the worker's problem. Employers using the concept of employability as a euphemism for "no job security" typically make little or no investment in training. Firms that view labor as a commodity have a short-term and arm's-length relationship with the workforce. Their human resources function typically adopts an *agency* approach, focused on acquiring people, monitoring and compensating them, and complying with labor law. It plays little role in dealing with fluctuations in demand for labor except to recruit when more workers are needed and to lay people off when deemed necessary. This agency view separates the firm's interests from those of labor.

An agency approach by itself may remain viable for firms that operate in extremely unstable markets or where there is no sustainable competitive advantage except the ability to react fast (as we would expect to find in the entertainment industry or in professional sports). More typically, however, market demands and competitive pressures are not so simple. For these firms, escalating interdependence and complexity in the employment relationship introduce an additional set of critical activities that in turn increase the complexity of the human resources function.

Where human resources incorporates activities that build *community*, it deals in resources and advantages that cannot be bought on the external market but can only be accessed through building relationships. The human resources function expands to include the creation and use of common resources for learning, innovation, stability, and risk reduction. Community resources take time to develop and nurture. An unbridled agency approach is inherently unstable. It erodes existing community resources, creating knowledge losses for firms and insecurity for workers. Unbridled agency makes new community resources impossible to develop. At the same time, an unbridled focus on community may be too inflexible. Firms often find it necessary to cannibalize existing work groups to respond to new opportunities and need to terminate workers when they do not effectively contribute. Balancing agency with community means attention is paid to the process whereby work and workers are moved to new settings so as to sustain trust, social relations, and mutual attachment between firm and workers. It means that terminations reflect due process and perpetuate a sense of justice. Joining agency and community in the human resources function creates flexible stability for workers and the firm.[5]

Inequity in risk and gain between workers and financial investors. Free agency in employment without job security or easy access by workers to financial markets creates unequal risks and gains between workers and firms. Although firms can hedge their bets by investing in other companies or capital markets, an engineer in New Jersey cannot trade a 15 percent stake in himself for a comparable claim on an architect in Los Angeles. Essentially, portfolio theory is a useful guide for making prudent financial investments, but it is not a practical course of action for workers deciding how to invest their labor. Equitable risks and gains for workers relative to their employers derive from their relations with those employers and their ability to build personal wealth through employment.

The conflicts of interest that have characterized owners and labor since the start of the Industrial Revolution have been transformed in many countries by a shift toward employment relations that are based on trust and partnership.[6] Partnership interjects collective interests into the world of agency marked by worker–employer transactions. Using trust as a basis for cooperation, partnership often entails greater sharing of financial information with workers, as is evident in such practices as "open book" management. Partnership and shared information reinforce the message that labor, management, and owners have interests in common. Convergence in the interests of a firm's various constituencies has contributed to economic growth for high-involvement firms.[7] Greater risk sharing between workers and owners is evident in the addition to fixed pay (salary) of variable pay (incentives) based on firm performance.[8] Firms that would have workers share the risk of a volatile marketplace, greater job insecurity, or fluctuations in pay must also be prepared to share the reward. As a result, entrants to the American labor market, as workers or as managers, are more likely to expect information regarding the firm's financial condition and an equity stake in the firm or profit-sharing.[9] Relational wealth is more likely to be built where equitable sharing of risks and information exists.

Institutionalized dysfunctional conflict between labor and management. Contrary to popular belief, many unionized work settings are strong in relational wealth. Kelley notes that unionized firms have been far more effective at implementing new technology than their nonunion counterparts, when union workers, who are typically more highly skilled, participate in the process of technology implementation.[10] However, firms such as General Motors and Firestone have continually undermined the potential accumulation of relational wealth via a stable workforce through decades of high-conflict union-management relations. Whereas partnership promotes access to accumulated knowledge and an array of contributions enhancing collective interests, adversarial labor–management relations are difficult to overcome without a major overhaul of industrial relations within a firm. While the interests of owner-managers might not overlap entirely with those of workers, the two parties can share a common concern with the welfare and long-term viability of both the workforce and the firm. This is possible when relational wealth is present and all but impossible in its absence.

Poorly managed change. It is a truism that firms that have lost relational wealth by eroding trust will have more difficulty getting either of them back than they did creating them in the first place. The most common reason for the erosion of relational wealth is poorly managed organizational change. Effectively managed change involves workers, suppliers, customers, and other affected groups in the process. Involvement means shared information, a voice in decision making, and attention to the costs that changes generate for participants (from skill deficits to the stress of uncertainty to job loss).

The courses of actions available to firms to overcome the difficulties and liabilities just described are consistent with human resource strategies designed to create a socially complex organization where constituencies are highly attached to the firm and embedded in distinctive ways of organizing—ways that give it inimitable competitive advantage.[11] First, such firms operate with some level of employment stability. Second, in such firms there is sufficient employee attachment to the firm that many valued rewards will be nonfinancial in nature and workers are willing to invest in firm-specific skills. Third, there are clear and well-adhered-to psychological contracts: promise-based beliefs about what the parties owe each other, involving managers, workers, customers, and suppliers. Attention to promises and commitments creates trust and can make a firm resilient in the face of change, when losses of trust are most likely to surface. Finally, relational wealth is best sustained when the firm and its employees make investments in a strong culture and shared language to reinforce attachment, trust, and stability.

Why Is Relational Wealth a Particular Problem in United States–based Firms?

Readers will note that the managerial and market assumptions that this book takes to task are overwhelmingly American ones. This is not to say that relational wealth is not a concern outside the United States. However, U.S. laws regarding corporate governance and employment have promoted a short-term orientation in business planning and wealth assessment that is distinct. In effect, U.S. firms are in a particularly disadvantaged position regarding the development and deployment of relational wealth.

Other American societal trends have compounded the problem. Over the past fifteen years in the United States, there has been a marked decline in voters' support for government influence upon markets.[12] This phenomenon, coupled with the decline in unionization and the "small government" trend beginning with the Reagan administration in the 1980s, has made the market a more salient factor than collectively negotiated contracts or wage norms in employment. The growth of pension funds and the aging of the population mean that more Americans may focus on the value of their asset holdings, may worry about the inflationary consequences of higher wages, and thus may be more likely to side with the financial sector in its drive for higher profit margins.

Market thinking is evident at all levels of American society. Weak job property rights mean that employment conditions may be continually re-negotiated on the basis of real or perceived market forces. We incur many benefits from this flexibility, yet we seem to increasingly underestimate the costs to relational wealth and stability engendered by such a market-based focus.

Relational wealth also may be a greater concern in the United States than other countries because of the relatively weaker society-level mechanisms fostering security. In the United States, safety nets exist at the level of the person but seldom at the level of the social unit or the institutions that support it. Thus, we may have cushions for some individuals who fall through the webbing, but we pay little attention to the circumstances that erode the value of the commons, on which all depend (e.g., schools, neighborhoods). This problem is exacerbated by firm mobility. The country is large enough so that geographic location can be a strategic choice for firms; thus, these economic institutions can bypass the problems experienced by regions that are underserved by broader social institutions.

This is not to say that the United States is the only society in danger of squandering relational wealth. Countries can also have tremendous difficulties creating it in the first place. The absence of relational wealth, and the high costs to be paid by neglecting to create or sustain it, are evident in the former Soviet Union. When society itself is unstable, markets cannot function effectively. The result is a palpable loss of hope or sense of options with regard to the quality of life or employment. With weak infrastructure, firms are too overwhelmed with the day-to-day challenges of remaining in operation to invest in people, and have little credibility as sources of non-monetary reward (e.g., accomplishment, self-esteem).

The value of the society itself is undermined. The predicament of the former Soviet Union challenges an implicit assumption in modern culture, one that says that structure and formality are negative, leading inevitably to eroded flexibility and therefore decreased effectiveness (i.e., bureaucracy equals red tape). The infrastructure provided by procedures, rules, and en-forceable contracts is taken for granted and therefore discounted. So too are the resources provided by existing structures such as the community college system, professional associations, and independent unions. Yet all of these would be sorely missed in their absence. Because in its benign form, bu-reaucracy promotes procedural justice and consistency, it can serve to re-move the appearance of politicking from organizational decision making.[13] Infrastructure, like bureaucracy, is not an end in itself but a means to an end.

With its focus on the individual rather than the collective, the wide sep-aration between economic and social institutions, the erosion of citizen con-fidence in government, and the previously noted rise in individual investment in financial markets, the United States is not particularly fertile ground for planting or growing relational wealth. As has been shown throughout this book, this places United States firms and American workers at a disadvantage relative to many of their competitors throughout the world. We believe that this can change.

Building and Sustaining Relational Wealth

Relational wealth is a complex phenomenon, one that is not simply created or maintained by any one person, firm, or social institution. Government institutions, business firms, people acting individually and collectively, and the observers and researchers of organizational life all have distinct roles to play.

The Role of Government

A world-class economy needs a world-class education system for its labor force and consumers, stable communities in which its participants live, work, and consume, and a secure pension system for those who have built that economy. These are difficult to achieve in the absence of concerted and coherent national efforts. Government can act to ensure that a stable infra-structure is in place—one that is consistent in quality across geographic regions. Thus, one central role of government is to build and sustain the commons.

In an economy increasingly dependent on knowledge and intellectual capital rather than physical labor and tangible assets, government invest-ment in education makes economic as well as social sense. There are several ways to do this. Most prominently, the federal government can play a greater role in setting standards for K-through-12 education and, more im-portant, providing resources to assist schools and geographic regions in meeting those standards. State and local government also play a prominent role in ensuring that educational benefits are not disproportionately enjoyed by economically advantaged regions and populations. Here, government in-volvement can range from enforcing laws restricting the concentration of educational benefits to certain populations, to making greater investments in community colleges and other public education systems.

Another way government can help build the infrastructure that encour-ages relational wealth is through strengthening communities and the spatial capital discussed by Blau in chapter 12. She suggests measures that strengthen and stabilize communities, such as state incentives for corpo-rations to invest in the local economy and exit barriers for disinvestment. She also suggests more involvement by workers and community members in company decisions. Requiring investors to cooperate with local planning committees in exchange for state investment is one example of government measures to develop and maintain spatial capital.

A second role of government is in setting the legal context in which labor is utilized. In this regard, government regulates employment most often by setting a "floor" on practices such as pay, health and safety, and hours and other conditions of employment. Thus, we have legislation in the United States establishing a minimum wage, mandating sixty days' notice before employment termination, and banning the use of child labor. Overtime requirements and the regulations enacted by the Occupational Safety and Health Administration are other examples of this "setting the floor" approach to government involvement in private sector employment practices.

In chapter 14 Pfeffer makes a compelling case for going beyond these minimums. Pointing to successes in countries like Singapore and Germany where labor practices are often closely regulated and firms' freedom to employ at will is constrained, Pfeffer argues for a more activist public policy approach. An obvious area where government can help to strengthen relational wealth within firms is through labor law reform. The ability of workers to exercise their rights to organize and strike without fear of dismissal, meaningful penalties to induce firms to comply with existing labor laws, and the easing of restrictions on systems of informal cooperation between employers and employees in unionized settings are all productive areas of reform for encouraging relational wealth.

A third critical role for government is in encouraging patient capital. As Smith, Pfeffer, and Rousseau note in chapter 15, firm managers are discouraged from long-term investment by American capital gains laws and tax depreciation schedules. These authors suggest several ways that government can act to encourage patient capital: for example, changing the time frame for Internal Revenue Service classification of long-term capital investments to five years rather than the current one year; offering tax incentives for investments in research and development; and setting incentives for firms to invest more in training and retraining their workforces.

Finally, government sets the stage for how fundamental values like fairness, equity, and justice will be enacted in economic institutions. Social welfare policies, investments in education and community infrastructure, and government unemployment and retraining benefits all affect both the creation and the distribution of relational wealth within society. Employment discrimination laws, laws ensuring the fundamental rights of workers to organize and withhold their labor, antitrust laws, and laws safeguarding job security for employees during their work years and safe pensions after their retirement all affect not only the level of relational wealth generated by a society and within individual firms but also how the benefits of relational wealth will be distributed. Without trust, relational wealth cannot be created or sustained. Without fairness, trust is not possible. A fundamental role of government in creating and sustaining relational wealth, then, is not just to encourage the creation of relational wealth, but to ensure fairness in the distribution of its benefits.

The Role of Firms

As Van Buren and Leana point out in chapter 13, firms can have the greatest impact on relational wealth through their employment practices. These authors argue in favor of employment practices that enhance organizational social capital by building associability and trust within the firm. Such practices focus on flexible stability in the workforce and include a range of employment practices that have been associated with high-performance work. These include employment security, incentive compensation, employee involvement in decision making, and selective recruitment of personnel.

Practices such as downsizing and certain uses of contingent labor, conversely, diminish organizational social capital and thus the relational wealth of the firm. Van Buren and Leana note that firms that engage in these sorts of practices without a strategic rationale are essentially trading long-term social capital for short-term cost savings. This creates problems in terms of employee commitment to the organization and essentially creates a self-fulfilling destructive cycle. When firms regularly engage in downsizing to reduce employment costs, employees in turn become more vigilant about other opportunities and thus are more likely to be poached by competitors. Because employees don't stay with the same employer, the company in turn has no incentive to invest in employee training and development. This lack of development in turn fuels more employee turnover. Thus, neither employee nor employer over time will see it in their interest to invest in building relational wealth. The effect of this over the long term, as we have argued, is that organizations' abilities to create inimitable advantages over competitors are eroded.

High-performance firms and those with large stores of relational wealth can realize benefits in the form of enhanced performance and commitment from their current workforce. At the same time, they benefit from their external reputations as good employers. Workforce stability is required by high-performance work systems to sustain the knowledge and organizational capabilities that make them competitive. American firms competing for labor have particular reasons to maintain a reputation as "an employer of choice" in order to attract competent workers. Employer reputation acts to some extent as a compensating factor for the country's otherwise weak labor laws. Thus, newspapers and magazines frequently headline the "Ten Best Companies to Work For," and television news specials showcase firms that are "family friendly" or "great workplaces for women and minorities." The value Americans place on a firm's loyalty to its workers is evident in the public reaction to the massive layoffs at AT&T and other large firms in the mid-1990s. Despite high stock prices and generous CEO compensation packages, firms were cutting large segments of their workforces, using downsizing as an ongoing business strategy rather than a last resort.[14] In the case of AT&T, public outrage led to a backlash as customers shifted their phone service to competitors.

The Role of Workers

Employees themselves are clearly central to the creation and maintenance of relational wealth. In many ways, they take their cues from their employers. As we have noted, employees with choices in the labor market have historically elected to remain with an employer rather than move from job to job. At the same time, employability in the form of having skills valued in the market is increasingly important for workers. But real employability derives from both workers and firms making decisions about job assignments and skill development that are informed by market-related concerns. This means that each promotes the development of those skills valued by the external labor market as well as within the firm to directly enhance worker employability.

Just as employers have responsibilities to employees if relational wealth is to be maintained, employees and their representatives must have commitments to the firm. Relational wealth can only be built and sustained when both parties are trusted and are contributing members of the partnership. As noted earlier, labor cooperation rather than adversarial conflict is an important condition for relational wealth.

The Role of Organizational Research:
The Rise of the Public Scholar

We close this book with an admonition to our colleagues in the academy. Providing the language and tools to describe, measure, and assess the value of relational wealth are the role of the organizational researcher—one who assumes a more public presence in the debate on the value of agency and community in organizational life.

The 1990s have brought a reemergence of the "public scholar"—the academic who attempts to address rather than merely observe critical problems in society.[15] Public scholarship can take many forms but includes participation in public policy formation and enactment; influencing public opinion through writing for a broader audience than the traditional academic press; or working with community groups and other such organizations for positive social change. Public scholarship is not just individuals engaging in community service or evincing interest in public affairs. It requires that, but it also entails applying what we know as organizational researchers—our unique perspectives, theories, and research traditions and findings—to issues of concern to the broader society.

The study of relational wealth provides an opportunity for organizational researchers to be public scholars.[16] The issues involved are of critical importance to people, firms, and the entire society. Will free agency or community be the dominant philosophy governing employment practices? Will stability or mobility be the goal? Will labor and management work in partnership to their joint benefit, or must they have inherently competing interests that override common concerns?

For too long business in the United States has been based on a narrow and, in itself, unrealistic set of assumptions regarding how businesses operate within markets and how they ought to operate. As Pfeffer points out in chapter 14, much of this perspective has been based on ideology rather than research and fact. Agency and markets are assumed to always trump community, regardless of the facts and the actual experience of organizational life. Organizational researchers can contribute as public scholars by providing rigorous studies of the specification, role, and effects of relational wealth.

First, we must focus on better specifying the relational wealth construct. In this book, we have offered some suggestions regarding various indicators of relational wealth, but more systematic work needs to be done. Relational wealth offers a new view of organizational linkages, structures, and relationships, by examining the *inter*unit mechanisms that exist in firms (between persons and between groups and organizations). The study of relational wealth will cross several levels of analysis, involving studies of individual attitudes and behavior, work unit processes, and organizational outcomes. Second, we need empirical work rigorously examining the economic consequences that relational wealth and its diverse mechanisms create for firms over time. At its core, relational wealth is concerned with the meaningful association of individuals within organizations and with external constituencies. Our studies of relational wealth will need to marshal evidence on how the costs of instability and lack of trust in these associations might become apparent to firms, work groups, persons, and society. What are the costs of our current course aimed at enhancing free agency and mobility? Who are the beneficiaries of our current course? In addition, market conditions no doubt affect both the motivation and the ability of firms and individuals to engage in relational wealth-enhancing behavior. Thus, it will be important to understand the value of relational wealth in periods of both economic growth and retrenchment. Finally, if relational wealth is to be a useful construct for managers and employees, we need to better specify how it is created and destroyed. For firms and individuals who want to enhance relational wealth, our research must provide the necessary information to develop meaningful strategies, behaviors, and practices to do so.

The question of how firms best operate in and for a society is answered to an uncomfortable degree by mantra and myth. The mantra is the market, evidenced by an almost unquestioning acceptance of its apparent wisdom.[17] The myths are rooted to a great extent in the tendency to discount the assets associated with stability while overvaluing the presumed benefits from unmitigated free agency. The myths are based on the assumption that people should work for the benefit of the economy rather than the economy working for the benefit of people. The myths are based on snapshot analyses of the short-term consequences of worker–firm investments and challenged by the facts afforded by time-lapse photography's longer term view.

These myths are ripe for overturning.

Notes

1. Stephan J. Motowidlo and James R. Van Scotter, "Evidence That Task Performance Should be Distinguished from Contextual Performance," *Journal of Applied Psychology* 79 (1994): 475–81.

2. Lester Thurow, "Building Wealth," *Atlantic Monthly* (June 1999): 57–71.

3. Career opportunities based on knowledge and experience embedded in relationships are described by several scholars of boundaryless or, in this case, interorganizational careers, including: Annalee Saxenian, "Beyond Boundaries: Open Labor Markets and Learning in Silicon Valley," pp. 23–39; Michael Best and Robert Forrant, "Community-based Careers and Economic Virtue: Arming, Disarming, and Rearming the Springfield, Western Massachusetts Region," pp. 314–30; Candace Jones, "Careers in Project Networks: The Case of the Film Industry," pp. 58–75; Cherilyn S. Granrose and Bee Leng Chua, "Global Boundaryless Careers: Lessons from Chinese Family Businesses," pp. 201–17, all in *The Boundaryless Career: A New Employment Principle for a New Organizational Era*, editors, Michael B. Arthur and Denise M. Rousseau (New York: Oxford, 1996).

4. Martin Carnoy, Manuel Castells, and Chris Benner, "What's Happening to the U.S. Labor Market?" part 1, "A Review of the Evidence," unpublished manuscript, University of California, Berkeley, 1997.

5. Denise M. Rousseau and Michael B. Arthur, "The Boundaryless Human Resource Function: Building Agency and Community in the New Economic Era," *Organizational Dynamics*, 1999, Spring, 7–18.

6. For the most part, employee-owned firms have not been economically more successful than those where owners and labor are distinct, a fact attributable at least in part to the fact that most employee-owned firms became so by buying out the owners of less profitable firms. On the other hand, law partnerships and medical practices traditionally are owned by at least some of their members.

7. Jeffrey Pfeffer, *The Human Equation* (Boston: Harvard Business School Press, 1998).

8. S. Rynes and B. Gephart, *Compensation*, Frontiers in Industrial/Organizational Psychology Series (San Francisco: Jossey-Bass, 2000).

9. D. M. Rousseau and Z. Shperling (2000). Pieces of the action: Ownership, power and the psychological contract. Paper presented at the Academy of Management meetings, August, Toronto. Stock ownership by employees is another relevant trend (see B. Parus, "Stock Become Prevalent as a Compensation Tool," *American Compensation Association News* (September 1998): 12–5.

10. M. R. Kelley, "Participative Bureaucracy and Productivity in the Machine Products Sector," *Industrial Relations* 35 (1996): 374–99.

11. J. Natphiet and S. Goshal, "Social Capital, Intellectual Capital, and

Organizational Advantage," *Academy of Management Review* 23 (1998): 242–66.

12. Carnoy, Castells, and Berner (1997).

13. J. Pearce, G. Bigley, and I. Branyicki, "Bureaucracy and Procedural Justice," *Organizational Science*, in press.

14. J. J. Keller, "Expected AT&T Cuts Put Chief on Spot—Big Workforce Reducations Could Draw Same Fire That Hit Predecessor," *Wall Street Journal*, January 23 1998, A3.

15. This discussion is based on remarks by Carrie Leana, Tom Kochan, Bill Ouchi, Jeffrey Pfeffer, and Peter Cappelli at a symposium titled "Organizational Researchers as Public Scholars" at the annual meeting of the National Academy of Management, San Diego, August 1998.

16. Academics from many social science disciplines such as political science, sociology, and especially economics have traditionally been comfortable in the role of the public scholar, assuming influential positions in the policy arena and as popular purveyors of academic ideas and insights. Some easy examples from economics include Laura Tyson in the public policy domain and Paul Krugman and Lester Thurow as academic writers well known to the informed public. In contrast, organizational researchers, along with their theoretical perspectives and research traditions, remain largely invisible in these domains.

17. For an interesting discussion of how the business press has begun to deify the market, see H. Cox, "The Market as God," *Atlantic Monthly* (March 1999): 18–23.

Index